Foundations of Sport Management

— THIRD EDITION —

Andy Gillentine, PhD
University of South Carolina

R. Brian Crow, EdD
Slippery Rock University

FiT Publishing

A Division of the International Center
for Performance Excellence
West Virginia University
375 Birch Street, WVU-CPASS
PO Box 6116
Morgantown, WV 26506-6116

Library of Congress Card Catalog Number: 2014944267

ISBN: 978-1-935412-57-1

Cover Design: Bellerophon Productions

Front Cover Photos: Flag pic: drial7m1 © courtesy of istockphoto.com; Money/contract: max_carpenter © courtesy of istockphoto.com; Man with notepad: © courtesy Celso Pupo rodrigues | Dreamstime.com; Calculator: © Sergey Gavrilichev | Dreamstime .com; Interview: Chad_Henne © courtesy of bigstockphoto.com

Back cover photos: Soccer men: Jakkrit Orrasri © courtesy of bigstockphoto.com; Citi field: cpenler © courtesy of bigstockphoto.com; Crowd: Paco Ayala © courtesy of 123rf.com

Production Editor: Nita Shippy

Copyeditors: Rachel Tibbs and Alex Kirk

Typesetter: Bellerophon Productions

Proofreader: Maria denBoer

Indexer: David denBoer

Printed by: Data Reproduction Corp.

10 9 8 7 6 5 4 3 2 1

FiT Publishing
A Division of the International Center for Performance Excellence
West Virginia University
375 Birch Street, WVU-CPASS
PO Box 6116
Morgantown, WV 26506-6116
800.477.4348 (toll free)
304.293.6888 (phone)
304.293.6658 (fax)
Email: fitcustomerservice@mail.wvu.edu
Website: www.fitpublishing.com

Dedication

This book is dedicated to my father, Frank Gillentine, who embodied the meaning of hard work, ethical behavior, love of family, and an understanding of all that sport has to offer. I appreciate and miss you every day.

—AG

The third edition is dedicated to my two children, Sam and Hannah—who give life purpose and meaning, and to the memory of my father, Robert, whose tireless work ethic continues to inspire me.

—RBC

Contents

Acknowledgments

I wish to acknowledge my wife, Glenna, for her continued patience and support for the duration of this revision. Thanks for always being a great sounding board for good ideas and bad ones and loving me enough to tell which ones were which and when to quit talking and get back to work.

I would like to recognize the chapter authors for their work and contributions to this second edition and the many students without whom this book would not exist. I should also recognize all of the sporting events and venues that allowed me to take countless photographs in order to shoot the select few used in this edition of the text.

Thanks to the publisher and editors at FiT for their continued support of this text.

Finally, I wish to acknowledge my friend and co-editor Brian Crow, Thanks B., it has been fun as always.

—AG

The success of this textbook is due to the contributions of each chapter author—your initial work and subsequent updates have made this project fun and inspiring. Andy Gillentine—it's always a pleasure to be your colleague and writing partner. From our brief time together at USM to now, it's been a great ride. Andy Ostrow—thanks for the encouragement to put this book together.

—RBC

Preface

FOR THE EDUCATOR

The continued dramatic growth of the sport industry over the last 35 years has given many individuals the initiative to pursue careers in this dynamic industry. In order to prepare these future sport administrators, it is important that educators continue to monitor and adjust educational programs and professional preparation needs. The third edition of *Foundations of Sport Management* is designed to provide an initial introduction to the sport industry to those students interested in a career in sport. In order to have an opportunity to succeed in this industry, it is important for the future administrator to move beyond water cooler or ESPN SportsCenter discussions and recognize the multiple and often complex components of the sport industry.

This text is written in a contemporary manner to enhance comprehension and to minimize the shock factor for those examining the sport industry for the first time. The contents of the text were designed to address the core competencies initially identified by the North American Society of Sport Management (NASSM) and the National Association of Sport and Physical Education (NASPE) and now supported by the Commission on Sport Management Accreditation (COSMA). It is the goal of the editors to briefly introduce each of the core competencies and instill a sense of excitement in the student regarding each subject. We hope that the reader will leave each chapter with a feeling of "Wow! That's cool! I'd like to know more about this!"

Each chapter is designed to both inform and entertain the student. Cartoons from the popular comic strip "In the Bleachers" by Steve Moore have been used to make the text more enjoyable for students than the ordinary type-filled pages they might have come to expect from regular college textbooks, and to perhaps match, if only in some small way, some of the passion and excitement they might feel for the subjects of sport and sport management. Additionally, supportive quotes from a variety of sources are used to introduce areas of importance. Key words are highlighted in each chapter to help emphasize main points and important terminology. Review questions are supplied at the conclusion of each chapter to help the student master the material provided.

It is our hope that instructors will appreciate the availability of PowerPoint presentation for each chapter. The slides are designed to allow for simple modification by individual instructors. A comprehensive test bank has also been made available for instructors and consists of a wide variety of objective questions.

Too often textbooks fail to identify their targeted audience and consequently try to be everything for everyone, from the casual reader to the PhD student. The authors of this text have chosen to target undergraduate students, and this book is written to address that specific audience. The intent of this text is not to teach individual subjects in their entirety, but simply to introduce them and generate interest and understanding in continued study of the sport industry. Each of the chapter authors was selected as a recognized expert in his or her area and represents the next generation of sport industry authorities.

FOR THE STUDENT

You are about to embark on the study of one of the most dynamic, exciting, and visible industries in the world today. Throughout your academic career, you will be exposed to a variety of topics, career options, and issues to research; embrace them, and become passionate about your study of sport management. Oftentimes in sport, there are hundreds of applicants for a single job—what will make your résumé stand out? As you read this, think of the classmates in your Introduction to Sport Management class. What makes you different? You can distinguish yourself by understanding and applying the principles found in this text, along with gaining practical experience in a variety of sport settings. Best wishes as you embark on your academic study of the sport industry.

1

Introduction to the Sport Industry

Andy Gillentine, R. Brian Crow, and Josh Harris

> "SPORT IS NOT SIMPLY ANOTHER BIG BUSINESS. IT IS ONE OF THE FASTEST GROWING INDUSTRIES IN THE US, AND IT IS INTERTWINED WITH VIRTUALLY EVERY ASPECT OF THE ECONOMY—FROM THE MEDIA AND APPAREL TO FOOD AND ADVERTISING . . . SPORTS IS EVERYWHERE, ACCOMPANIED BY THE SOUND OF A CASH REGISTER RINGING INCESSANTLY."
>
> —*Michael Ozanian*

INTRODUCTION

The sport industry continues to be one of the largest and fastest-growing industries in the United States and the world (Plunkett, 2013). This accelerated growth has fueled the continued desire of many people to pursue a career in the sport industry. Countless students each year, in the US and abroad, enter academic programs specializing in the study of sport management to prepare for a future in sport.

In addition to the rapid growth of the sport industry, the nature of sport business has changed as well. Sport is now a major component of the entertainment industry, competing for the discretionary income of fans worldwide. Gone are the days of collecting gate receipts in "cigar boxes" (Gillentine, 2012). Sport is now a multibillion-dollar industry and growing. This increases the need for sound administrative and business practices, as well as for individuals specifically educated for the unique nature of the sport industry.

Learning Objectives
Upon completion of this chapter, the reader should be able to: • Understand the growth of the sport industry • Describe the growth of the academic study of sport management • Identify the myths surrounding the sport industry • Discuss the unique features of the sport industry • Elaborate on the challenges of selecting a career in the sport industry

© 2002 Universal Press Syndicate   www.ucomics.com

"… There! Smell that? I *love* the aroma of a major league ballpark. Smells just like money!"

WHY A CAREER IN SPORT?

Before launching into a college degree program and professional career in sport, individuals should fully understand the commitment and dedication required for success in this field. In order to evaluate their current status, it is important to answer the most basic of Socratic questions: *Why?*

Probably the most common answer to this question is "I love sports!" While it is important to have a passion for your work, a love of sports is probably not enough to ensure a happy and productive career in the sport industry. Upon entering the sport profession, this "love of sport" becomes a job and, like all jobs, will have its good moments and bad. If your motivation also includes "getting to watch lots of games," your time and money may be better spent purchasing a 65-inch Ultra HD television. When you choose sport as a career, you will be preparing for the upcoming event while others are tailgating in the parking lot; most likely you will be working during game time, in addition to several hours before and after the event. Your passion has now become your occupation. Helping others enjoy watching the event while you earn your paycheck is the reality.

Another common answer is "I hope to rub elbows with the rich and famous." While you may have greater access to well-known athletes, coaches and celebrities, don't be misled in thinking they will be your new lunch buddies. Frequently, entry-level sport managers find themselves disappointed after meeting the "star player" of their new

Welcome to the Sport Industry!	
Cost of an typical college degree in sport management:	**$80,000**
Number of weeks you will work nights and weekends in this industry:	**52**
Percentage of friends who will ask for free tickets:	**100%**
Seeing your stadium full of cheering fans despite a poor record:	***Priceless***

Photo courtesy © Andy Gillentine

employer. According to David Samson, President of the Miami Marlins, "Quite often you will find these guys are immature, overpaid, and over indulged, just because they can throw hard" (David Samson, personal communication, January 17, 2004).

Others enter the sport industry with dollar signs in their eyes. The sport media is full of stories chronicling the astronomical salaries and monies generated in the sport industry. While it is true that a lucrative living can be made in the sport business, the reality is that few in the management of sport receive those salaries. The vast fortunes of the owners of today's professional sport franchises were typically made outside of the sport industry. Don't be disappointed though; a comfortable living can be made in sport management . . . but individuals must be prepared and patient to work toward that level of compensation.

Opportunities in Sport: Myth and Reality

The sport industry is subject to a high level of public scrutiny. Daily, and even hourly, fans evaluate every move made not only by the players on the field, but also by the executives directing the organization. This constant evaluation, however, does not ensure the credibility of those making the evaluation. Therefore, many "myths" regarding the sport industry continue to flourish and proliferate (additional myths are also discussed in various chapters). Many of these myths focus on the potential for a career in the sport industry. Most of these myths are based upon antiquated ideas and/or outdated information, while others merit closer analysis because they include accurate information but are presented in a questionable context. Listed below are some of the most frequently cited myths, compiled from a variety of sources, about seeking a career in the sport industry.

1) **Opportunities are limited and the field is saturated with applicants.**
   It seems almost paradoxical to state that sport is one of the fastest growing industries worldwide and in the next breath state that opportunities are limited. While obviously there are not an unlimited number of jobs available in the sport industry, there are, in fact, jobs available. In order to be successful in the sport industry, individuals must be mobile. Opportunities in sport are found in locations ranging from New York City to Stillwater, Oklahoma, to

Portland, Oregon, and all points in between. Individuals wishing to enter the sport industry must be willing to "go where the jobs are." Often people are too myopic in their vision of where they are willing to work, and therefore limit their access to jobs. With regard to oversaturation of the job market, most administrators will agree there are never enough qualified applicants for positions, while there are always too many unqualified ones. It is important for individuals to appropriately prepare and position themselves to become attractive to potential employers.

2) Short-term opportunities are not worthwhile.

One of the quickest and most effective ways to enter the sport industry is through internships (see Chapter 15). Quite often these positions are designed to be seasonal or short term. They do, however, provide the individual with the experience necessary to apply for better full-time opportunities as they arise. Often, individuals will fill multiple short-term internships in order to gain valuable experience and to begin networking in the sport industry. During events such as the Sony Open tennis tournament, which attracts more than 300,000 guests annually to Key Biscayne, Florida, numerous volunteer and intern opportunities exist. Over 2,000 volunteers and staff work together to produce an event that has become one of the most popular tennis tournaments among fans and players alike. Opportunities such as this are not only good résumé builders, but also provide you with an avenue to showcase your skills for today's sport industry executives. Furthermore, do not be discouraged from accepting positions that initially indicate a specific beginning and ending date. View each of these opportunities as a chance to gain new skills and to showcase your abilities.

3) Opportunities for minorities are limited.

While the number of minorities holding high-ranking sport industry positions is verifiably low, these numbers are improving (Lapchick, 2008). As more and more minorities decide to pursue a managerial career in the sport industry and prepare themselves for that career, we will see a continued change in the demographic make-up of sport managers. The process is, and will be, slower than any of us desire, but the sport industry has always been willing to allow individuals the opportunity to pursue this career option and is often more willing than the rest of society to judge a person on their successes rather than on their race, ethnicity, or gender. The formation of several organizations such as the National Association of Black Sports Professionals (NABSP), the Black Entertainment and Sports Lawyers Association (BESLA), the Black Sports Agents Association (BSAA) and The Association for Women in Sports Media (AWSM) are representative of organizations whose mission is to increase opportunities for minorities by enhancing their presence, awareness, and industry exposure (Lapchick, 2007). As a result of these (and other) efforts, it hoped that the number of minorities in administrative positions will continue to increase.

Becoming successful in a management position in the sport industry requires the same skills athletes must have to succeed: dedication, commitment, and a willingness to work harder than your competitors.

Photo courtesy © Andy Gillentine

4) **Opportunities for females are limited.**

As you will learn in Chapter 2, there are laws protecting the rights of women in the workplace. But beyond that, the sport industry is witness to an unprecedented growth in the number of females entering and advancing in the workplace. Events such as the *SportBusiness Journal's* (SBJ's) *Game Changers: Women in Sports Business* and Venues Today's *Women of Influence* are excellent showcases for the contributions of women in the sport and entertainment industry. There certainly is, however, much room for improvement. One only needs to look in the "Careers" section and the "People" section in a recent issue of the *SportsBusiness Journal* to see that while women are represented, all things are not equal. In fact, look at the *SBJ* Top Forty Under Forty, or the listing of Top Sport Executives, and notice the number of women.

Despite the continued existence of these myths, the sport industry does offer many exciting, challenging, and rewarding positions for those deciding to pursue this career path. Managerial challenges in the sport industry may be compared to completing a crossword puzzle. You can clearly see the problem that needs to be solved; there is at least one clue to help identify the best possible answer; the answer's position in relationship to the entire situation is evident; and once the answer is found, immediate gratification is mentally and visually present.

THE EVOLUTION OF SPORT MANAGEMENT EDUCATION

The growth of the sport industry far exceeded the expectations of scholars and researchers in the late 20th century, who projected that the GNP for the industry would consume more than $121 billion (Meek, 1997; Pitts, 2001; Rosner, 1989). However, actual estimates after the turn of the century show these numbers to be far too conservative, with various researchers putting the number somewhere between $200 billion and $425 billion (Pitts & Stotlar, 2003; Plunkett, 2013; "The Sport Industry," 2007). These estimates have varied widely due to the unimaginable explosion of opportunities within this industry, which is good news for those who want to pursue a sport-related career.

As employment opportunities in the sports industry have grown, the need for training of sport professionals has received much attention. Universities have quickly tried to
develop sport management curricula at the graduate and undergraduate levels to fill the
need for professionals trained specifically in sport management (Stier, 1993). In fact, as
of July 2013, the North American Society for Sport Management (NASSM) website
places the number of universities offering a sport management curriculum at approximately 350, a substantial increase from the first established program in 1966. In addition, membership in NASSM, including that of sport management faculty members
and students, has reached over 1,000 for the first time in its history.

As the interest and participation in sport have grown to all-time highs, so has the
need for professional preparation of sport managers. Large numbers of undergraduates
and sport professionals are rapidly returning to the campus to take discipline-specific
courses to improve the current or potential employment opportunities (Parkhouse,
2005; Parkhouse & Pitts, 2005). The impetus for the development of a sport administration academic program developed when Walter O'Malley (of the Brooklyn Dodgers)
urged University of Miami (FL) educator James Mason to imagine the effectiveness of
individuals specifically trained to deal with the business of the growing sport industry
(Mason, Higgins, & Owens, 1981):

> I ask the question, where would one go to find a person who by virtue of educa-
> tion had been trained to administer a marina, race track, ski resort, auditorium,
> stadium, theatre, convention or exhibit hall, a public camp complex, or a person
> to fill an executive position at a team or league level in junior athletics such as a
> Little League baseball, football, scouting, CYO, and youth activities, etc. . . . . A
> course that would enable a graduate to read architectural and engineering plans;
> or having to do with specifications and contract letting, the functions of a pur-
> chasing agent in plant operations. There would be problems of ticket selling and
> accounting, concessions, sale of advertising in programs, and publications, out-
> door and indoor displays and related items. (Mason et al., 1981, p. 44)

From this modest and carefully orchestrated beginning, sport management and sport
administration programs have grown rapidly throughout the United States and the
world. The curriculum proposed by Mason in 1957 was considered "ahead of its time"
and was not implemented by the Coral Gables institution (Sawyer, 1993). Mason started
the first graduate program in Sport Administration at Ohio University in 1966. Ironi-
cally, Biscayne College, now known as St. Thomas University, located only 15 miles
from the University of Miami campus, became the first university to establish an undergraduate program in sport administration (Masterlexis, Barr, & Hums, 2012). These
formative years of the Sport Management Academic discipline (1967–1987) are identified as the Era of Maturation (Gillentine, 2013). The era is characterized by the growth
of academic programs and the emergence of academic leaders in sport management.
Dr. Guy Lewis is recognized as one of the leaders during this era for his role in the development of sport management programs at the University of Massachusetts and the
University of South Carolina (Appenzeller & Appenzeller, 2008; Roach, 2010). In 1971

Table 1.1. Eras of Sport Management	
The Era of Incubation	(1957–1966)
The Era of Maturation	(1967–1987)
The Era of Unbridled Growth	(1988–2000)
The Era of Dualism	(2001–2007)
The Era of Reflection, Assessment & Refinement	(2008–present)
Source: Gillentine (2012)	

at the University of Massachusetts, Lewis developed one of the first degree-granting sport administration programs (Parkhouse & Pitts, 2001). Dr. Lewis later collaborated with other progressively minded sport management professionals to establish the Department of Sports Administration (now the Department of Sport & Entertainment Management) at the University of South Carolina (Gillentine, 2012; Roach, 2010). The South Carolina program is significant, as it was created as an independent sport management department not affiliated with an education, recreation or physical education department or college (Baugus, 2008).

The expansion of academic programs was not confined to undergraduate and master's degree programs. Results of a study completed in 1996, and reconfirmed as recently as 2013 from the NASSM website, showed that no fewer than 27 universities offered doctoral programs with at least an emphasis area in sport management (Gillentine & Crow, 1996). Despite this finding, sport administration/management academic programs struggle to find enough discipline-specific trained professionals to fill their faculty needs (Mahony, Mondello, Hums, & Judd, 2004).

The rapid development of sport management graduate programs occurred through the independent efforts of various universities throughout the country. The lack of coordination between schools caused a fragmentation in the development of programs. Each university or department was free to establish its own priorities and areas of emphasis (NASPE/NASSM, 1993). The sport management/administration programs were established and housed in different departments (general business, physical education, management, etc.) according to university preference (Bridges & Roquemore, 1992).

The Sport Management Arts and Science Society (SMARTS), a group organized at the University of Massachusetts, Amherst, first examined this curricular fragmentation (Masteralexis et al., 2012). From the initial explorations of the SMARTS organizations, greater emphasis was placed on the academic credibility of graduate sport management programs. The recognized need for a standardized review of sport management curricula and programs prompted the formation of the North American Society for Sport Management (Parkhouse, 2005).

The National Association for Sport and Physical Education (NASPE) organized a Sport Management Task Force in 1986 to begin the development of standardized core competencies. The NASPE task force formed a partnership with the North American Society for Sport Management to further explore and develop the standardized core requirements for sport management programs. The recommended standards established by the joint task force identify minimum competencies that should exist in undergraduate and graduate sport management programs. Standards were also established identifying the minimum number of course offerings and faculty needed to offer a program. The Sport Management Program Review Council (SMPRC) was created through the NASPE/NASSM task force to help universities "attain and maintain excellence in undergraduate and graduate education for sport management" (NASPE/NASSM, 1993). *Formed partnership* For 15 years the SMPRC reviewed programs, volunteering for the approval process through use of the identified criteria, and evaluated the program curriculum by area and as a whole.

The development of minimum program requirements and the move toward standardization were the first steps to establish credible sport administration and sport management curricula. In 2005, representatives from NASSM and NASPE reconvened to discuss organizing a body for the *accreditation* of sport management programs. Two committees were developed to explore the accreditation process and the identification of appropriate standards for accreditation. Nine months from their inception, the committees provided their preliminary reports to representatives of NASSM and NASPE. The leadership from both organizations solicited and collected feedback from all constituencies regarding the movement toward program accreditation. From the subsequent discussions, a proposal for the formation of a Sport Management Accreditation body was developed ("Sport Management Accreditation," 2007).

Through the joint efforts of NASSM and NASPE, the Commission on Sport Management Accreditation (COSMA) has been created to provide accreditation and related services for sport management programs (see Table 1.2). As required by accepted academic accreditation policies and procedures, COSMA will exist as an independent accrediting body, with a Board of Commissioners formed from its membership. NASSM and NASPE identified a timeline to officially launch the COSMA organization in July 2008 (COSMA History, 2008). The failure to properly train and prepare managers and administrators is the number one cause of management failure today. Over ninety-eight percent of managers are placed in positions for which they have not been properly trained (Bridges et al., 1992). To help ensure that sports professionals do not follow the same pattern of failure, it is imperative to continue developing quality sport management programs. In order for the sport industry to maintain consistent educational and preparation standards, it is important that universities recognize and implement the recommended standards, ultimately leading to program accreditation.

Purpose of the COSMA

The purpose of the COSMA is to promote and recognize excellence in sport management education in colleges and universities—at both the undergraduate and graduate levels—through specialized accreditation. Institutions, students, employers, and the general public all benefit from the external verification of quality provided through the COSMA's accreditation process. They also benefit from the process of continuous quality improvement that is encouraged by the COSMA's developmental approach to promoting excellence in sport management education.

Table 1.2. Characteristics of Excellence in Sport Management Education

Excellence in sport management education has many different components that must be considered during the evaluation process.

Excellence in sport management education normally displays the following characteristics:

- The sport management program has a clearly defined and relevant mission and broad-based goals that are consistent with those of the institution.

- The sport management program has a strategic plan that is in touch with the realities of sport management education and the marketplace, and that is consistent with the strategic plan of the institution. This strategic plan is driven by the approved mission and broad-based goals of the sport management program.

- The sport management program has developed and implemented an outcomes assessment process that promotes continuous improvement in the sport management programs and operations, and that is linked to the strategic plan of the sport management program.

- Students in the sport management program develop, both personally and professionally, into well-educated, ethical, competent sport management professionals.

- The sport management program operates in an environment that encourages and promulgates innovation and creativity in sport management education.

- The sport management program has meaningful and effective linkages between the classroom and practitioners in the sport management community, thereby providing assurance of relevancy and currency in the academic programs.

- The sport management program encourages cooperative relationships with other educational units, both external and internal, which are consistent with its mission and broad-based goals.

- Faculty in the sport management program model ethical character and integrate ethical viewpoints and principles in their teaching.

- Faculty in the sport management program are effective teachers who are current in their fields and active in their professional contributions to their institution and discipline. Further, the faculty are positively engaged within their sport management program and contribute to its mission and broad-based goals through appropriate faculty development and faculty evaluation processes.

- The mix of academic and professional credentials of the sport management faculty is worthy of the respect of the academic and sport marketplace communities.

- The mission of the institution and its sport management program is effectively communicated to current and prospective students.

- The institution provides adequate resources to the sport management program to accomplish its mission and broad-based goals.

- The curricula in the sport management programs reflect the mission of the institution and its academic unit, and are consistent with current, acceptable practices and principles of professionals in the academic and sport marketplace communities.

- The curricula in the sport management programs ensure that students understand and are prepared to deal effectively with critical issues in a changing global environment.

- The content of sport management courses is delivered in a manner that is appropriate, effective, and stimulates learning.

- The sport management program recognizes the role of practical and experiential learning as a relevant component of sport management curricula.

- The institutional organizational structure supports excellence in sport management education.

Source: Commission on Sport Management Accreditation

WHAT'S THE DEAL WITH THE NAME?

The rapid development of sport management academic programs also created another point of confusion within the industry: the name. Individuals examining sport management academic programs will find them listed under a variety of different titles. The most common names for academic programs are either sport(s) management or sport(s) administration. While most professionals agree that the particular name of the program is much less important than program course content, it is important to understand why there are differences in *sport* and *sports*, *management* and *administration*. The early academic programs in sport were frequently housed in departments of physical education.

Therefore, the programs were referred to as *sports* management or *sports* administration. The term *sports* typically refers to separate sports activities such as football, baseball, etc. The implication, then, is that *sports* management would therefore encompass only the management of these sports activities. *Sport*, on the other hand, offers a more universal description of the variety of activities and occurrences in the sport industry as a whole. These

activities may include planning, organizing, and controlling sport programs (discussed in Chapter 4). Parks and Quarterman (2002) offered a clarifying analogy by surmising that the difference between *sport* and *sports* is similar to the difference between *religion* and *religions*. While *religions* refers to the different beliefs and denominations (i.e., Catholicism, Baptism, Judaism, Islam, etc.), *religion* is a broader term that encompasses leadership, belief, operation, and function.

The variance between the use of *administration* or *management* also traces its origins to its original home department. The term *administration* was typically associated with those programs and individuals working in the public sector, such as high school or university athletic directors. Since many early programs were housed in physical education departments, the use of this term seemed most logical. The term *management* was typically associated with those organizations and individuals working in the private sector. As graduates of those early programs often saw a larger job market available in educational settings, many programs adopted the term *administration* in their name. Regardless of the name, the true test of an academic degree lies in the program content.

UNIQUE ASPECTS OF THE SPORT INDUSTRY

The need for discipline-specific academic preparation for the sport industry is magnified by the uniqueness of several primary features included in the discipline. While at an elementary level these features are similar to skills needed in other business ventures, closer analysis clearly identifies how this industry differs from others. Mullin (1980) first identified three unique features of sport management: marketing, finance, and career paths. Parks et al. (2002) suggest that the social influence of sport is an additional unique feature of this industry. Gillentine and Crow (2005) further expanded the identification of features unique to sport management by identifying the customer base (fans) and venues as components that separate the sport industry from other business enterprises.

Marketing

The marketing aspects of sport offer a great many challenges to the sport professional. Not only does the sport marketer have to clearly identify who the customer is, it is also necessary to recognize where the customer will consume the product. Unlike many products, the same sport product may be consumed in multiple ways simultaneously. Additionally, the sport product is commonly produced and consumed at the same time, offering the marketer little room for adjustment. The specifics of the unique features of sport marketing are covered in Chapter 7.

Finance

A brief overview of sport finance will quickly indicate the unique components of this industry. Few industries generate the multiple sources of revenue than the sport product does. In many instances, more revenue is generated from these alternate revenue streams than from the core product itself. The sport product also differs from other industries in that multiple forms of business enterprise (corporations, partnerships, sole proprietorships, and non-profits) exist within the same environment. Additional detailed explanations of these varied financial and economic differences will be offered in Chapter 6.

Career Paths

As the sport industry continues to mature and evolve, new positions and job descriptions will emerge. There are few areas of career emphasis that are not currently available through the various branches of the sport industry. In addition to the emergence of new positions in the sport industry, the current trend toward diversification of the sport industry workforce will continue. The move toward diversification will generate additional positions for underrepresented groups throughout the sport industry. Future changes in technology will only serve to launch new positions within the industry.

Social Influence of Sport

In order to view the social impact of sport, one only needs to attend a sporting event and observe the myriad emotions and actions of the crowd. Not only will they support their chosen team, they will suffer with them if they are not successful. Fans demonstrate their emotional and psychological attachment to the event; they will also show their involvement through the purchase of ancillary items from the sport product. From the playing fields to the water cooler, sport is pervasive throughout our country. In the summer of 2008, it is estimated that just over 2 billion people—almost one third of the world's population—watched the Beijing Summer Olympics Opening Ceremony ("Opening Ceremony," 2008). These social implications of sport will be discussed in greater detail in Chapters 2 and 13.

Customer Base (Fans)

Fans (customers) are yet another consideration that adds to the unique aspects of the sport industry. Rarely is such an intense sense of loyalty found in other industries. Sport fans also often exhibit intense levels of identification with the sport product through which they feel psychologically connected to a team (Wann, Merrill, Russell, & Pease, 2001). This connection is not deterred by poor seasons or regional location, which allows for expansion of the sport product, and it is further strengthened with the proliferation of social media combined with the ability to consume the sport product in ways that were not available even ten years ago. Fans also add to the uniqueness of the sport product in that they can influence potential revenue streams of the sport organization in a variety of ways outside of consumption of the core product. Team names and logos are present on almost any product imaginable and are purchased by fans. While loyal customers may have strong feelings regarding a particular consumer good, rarely do you find them painted in corporate colors cheering for their favorite detergent!

Sport Venues

Lastly, the venues in which sport events take place further separate this industry from most others. Most often an industry operates in a single setting, which typically offers a

Photo courtesy © istockphoto.com

quite controlled environment. The sport industry however, produces and displays its product in a variety of settings that are subject to a variety of external influences. The sport product may also be consumed in a variety of venues at the same time. This consumption can take place at the stadium or arena, the consumer's home, a sports bar or restaurant, on a radio, via the Internet, or most recently, mobile devices. While the sport manager may not be able to control these environments, he/she must recognize the impact they may have on the sport product. The sport manager must recognize the potential impact that the venue has on customer satisfaction with the sport product.

SUMMARY

The sport industry is a dynamic, exciting, and visible field for career opportunities and academic study. Ultimately, your mastery of the field will provide you with the opportunity to advance beyond entry-level work to a rewarding career. As you look back at the information in this chapter regarding the growth of sport and the study of sport management, think of ways you can improve upon the body of knowledge contained herein. You represent the future of the sport industry, and therefore are responsible for knowing the history and fundamentals of the field, as well as building upon it for the future.

Learning Activities

1. What are some of the myths surrounding employment in the sport industry? Why do they continue to exist?
2. Identify and discuss the unique aspects of the sport industry.
3. What professional opportunities are available in the sport industry?
4. Explain the differences between *sport* and *sports*, and between *management* and *administration*.

Suggested Reading

Brassie, P. S. (1989, November/December). A student buyer's guide to sport management programs. *Journal of Physical Education, Recreation, & Dance, 60*(9), 25–28, 404–498.

Boucher, R. L. (1998). Toward achieving a focal point for sport management: A binocular view. *Journal of Sport Management, 12*, 76–85.

Cuneen, J., & Sidwell, J. (1998, Winter). Evaluating and selecting sport management undergraduate programs. *The Journal of College Admissions, 158*, 6–13.

Danylchuk, K. L., & Judd, M. (1996). Journal of sport management: Readership survey. *Journal of Sport Management, 10*, 188–196.

Hardy, S. (1987). Graduate curriculums in sport management: The need for a business orientation. *Quest, 39*, 207–216.

Olafson, G. A. (1995). Sport management research: Ordered change. *Journal of Sport Management, 9*, 338–345.

Pitts, B. G., Fielding, L. W., & Miller. L. K. (1994). Industry segmentation theory and the sport industry. *Sport Marketing Quarterly, 3*(1), 15–24.

Slack, T. (1996). From the locker room to the boardroom: Changing the domain of sport management. *Journal of Sport Management, 10*, 97–105.

Weese, W. J. (1995). If we're not serving practitioners, then we're not serving sport management. *Journal of Sport Management, 9*, 237–243.

Ziegler, E. F. (1987). Sport management: Past, present, future. *Journal of Sport Management, 1*(1), 4–24.

Weese, W. S. (2002). Opportunities and headaches: Dichotomous perspectives on the current and future hiring realities in the sport management academy. *Journal of Sport Management, 16*, 1–17.

Zakrajsek, D. B. (1993). Sport management: Random thoughts of one administrator. *Journal of Sport Management, 7*, 1–6.

References

Appenzeller, H., & Appenzeller, T. (2008). *Successful sport management*. Durham, NC: Carolina Academic Press.

Baugus, R. V. (2008, June/July). The pro's prof. *Facility Manager*, 43–48.

Bridges, J. B., & Roquemore, L. L. (1992). *Management for athletic/sport administration*. Decatur, GA: EMS.

COSMA history. (2008). Retrieved from: http://www.cosmaweb.org/history

Gillentine, A. (2000). The evolution of sport administration/management graduate programs. *MAHPERD Journal, 4*(1), 7–10.

Gillentine, A. (2012). Moving mountains: The need for shifting paradigms in sport management. In A. Gillentine, B. Baker, & J. Cuneen (Eds.), *Critical essays in sport management: Exploring and achieving a paradigm shift*. Phoenix, AZ: Holcomb Hathaway Publishing.

Gillentine, A., & Crow, B. (1996, February 13). *Sport management doctoral programs*. Paper presented at the Annual Convention of the Southern District Alliance of Health, Physical Education, Recreation, & Dance. Biloxi, MS.

Gillentine, A., Crow, B., & Harris, J. (2005). Introduction to the sport industry. In A. Gillentine & B. Crow (Eds.), *Foundations of sport management* (1st ed.; pp. 7–8). Morgantown, WV: Fitness Information Technology.

Lapchick, R. (2007). Group's growth a positive step for diversity in sports business. *SportsBusiness Journal*. Retrieved from http://sportsbusinessjournal.com/article/57402

Lapchick, R. (2008). *2007 racial & gender report card*. Orlando, FL: The Institute for Diversity and Ethics in Sport.

Mahony, D., Mondello, M., Hums, M., & Judd, M. (2004). Are sport management doctoral programs meeting the needs of the faculty job market? Observations for today and the future (perspectives). *Journal of Sport Management, 18*, 91–110.

Mason, J. G., Higgins, C., & Owen, J. (1981). Sport administration education 15 years later. *Athletic Purchasing and Facilities*, 44–45.

Masterlexis, L. P., Barr, C. A., & Hums, M. A. (2005). *Principles and practice of sport management* (2nd ed.). Sadbury, MA: Jones & Bartlett.

Meek, A. (1997). An estimate of the size and supported economic activity of the sports industry in the United States. *Sport Marketing Quarterly, 6*(4), 15–21.

Mullin, B. J. (1980). Sport management: The nature and utility of the concept. *Arena Review, 4*(3), 1–11.

NASPE-NASSM Joint Task Force. (1993). Standards for curriculum and voluntary accreditation of sport management education programs. *Journal of Sport Management, 7*, 159–170.

Opening ceremony draws 2 billion viewers. (2009). Retrieved from http://blog.nielsen.com/nielsenwire/media_entertainment/beijing-opening-ceremonys-global-tv-audience-hit-2-billion/

Parkhouse, B. L. (2005). *The management of sport: Its foundation and application* (4th ed.). New York, NY: McGraw-Hill.

Parkhouse, B. L., & Pitts, B. G. (2005). Definition, evolution, and curriculum. In B. L. Parkhouse (Ed.), *The management of sport: Its foundation and application* (4th ed.; pp. 2–14). Boston, MA: McGraw Hill.

Parks, J., & Quarterman, J. (2002). *Contemporary sport management*. Champaign, IL: Human Kinetics.

Pitts, B. (2001). Sport management at the millennium: A defining moment. *Journal of Sport Management, 15*(1), 1–9.

Pitts, B. G., & Stotlar, D. K. (2002). *Fundamentals of sport marketing* (2nd ed.). Morgantown, WV: Fitness Information Technology.

Plunkett Research. (2013). Introduction to the sport industry. Retrieved from http://www.plunkettresearch.com/sports-recreation-leisure-market-research/industry-and-business-data

Roach, F. (2010, August/September). Reality vs. Jerry Maguire. *Facility Manager*, 30–35.

Rosner, W. (1989). The world plays catch-up: Sport in the 90s. *Sports Inc., 2*, 6–9.

Sawyer, T. H. (1993). Sport management: Where should it be housed? *Journal of Physical Education, Recreations, & Dance, 64*(9), 4–5.

Sport management accreditation. (2007). Retrieved from http://www.nassm.com/InfoAbout/NASSM/ProgramAccreditation

Stier, W. (1993). *Alternate career paths in physical education: Sport management*. Washington, DC: ERIC Clearinghouse on Teaching and Teacher Education.

The sport industry. (2007). *SportsBusiness Journal*. Retrieved from http://www.sportsbusinessjournal.com/index.cfm?fuseaction=page.feature&featureId=43

Wann, D., Merrill, J., Russell, G., & Pease, D. (2001). *Sport fans*. New York, NY: Routledge.

2

Why Sport Management Matters

Catriona Higgs

"SOME PEOPLE THINK FOOTBALL IS A MATTER OF LIFE AND
DEATH. I ASSURE YOU, IT'S MORE SERIOUS THAN THAT."

—Bill Shankley

INTRODUCTION

Sport is one of the largest businesses in the United States, eclipsing real estate, retail trade, health care, banking, and transportation and generating somewhere in excess of $441.1 billion dollars (Plunkett Research, 2008). The phenomenal global impact of sport has resulted in the academic study of this area from a variety of different perspectives. Sports are popular and public activities that offer exciting opportunities for understanding their close relationship to any society. As Humphreys and Ruseski (2008) state, individuals can participate in sport in a variety of different ways—for example, by attending, watching, or listening to an event. It is this accessibility that contributes to making sport such a successful industry. The rules of sport transcend national boundaries and mitigate social differences. Because of the status of sport in American culture and social life, there is a need to analyze the political and cultural importance of sport from both a national and global perspective and to ascertain how new media distribution channels will affect the continued popularity of this activity. Sport sociologists focus

---

Learning Objectives

By the end of this chapter the student should be able to:
- Describe the reasons why sport managers should study sport
- Identify current myths in sport
- Understand what we can learn from studying sport from a social perspective
- Understand the relationship between society and sport
- Understand why diversity is such an important topic for sport managers
- Outline the major laws that prohibit discrimination in the workplace
- Describe the major methods utilized in socio-cultural studies to understand sport behavior

In the Bleachers © 2014 Steve Moore. Dist. by Universal Uclick
www.gocomics.com/inthebleachers

**"I was a star athlete in kindergarten,
but I peaked too soon."**

on all of these issues, including an analysis of sport as an industry; the political and cultural implications of sport; sport and globalization; the relationship between gender, class and economics; deviance in sport; the nature of competition; the impact of the media on sport; and the social organization of sport. Carefully examining the sociological analysis of sport competition and participation enables us to learn more about human social organization in the sport setting (Coakley, 2010).

In many sport management classes, the primary focus of learning for students is on managing, communications, public relations, and marketing in the sports industry. While many students are interested in sport and have a passion for and a good working knowledge of trivia, statistics, fantasy sport and teams, few students understand the complexities of sport as a social institution and phenomenon. We all think we know a great deal about this activity, but we often readily buy into the myths that are perpetuated by those involved in playing, coaching, or producing and managing sport. It is important to separate the truth from the falsehoods so that we can gain a clear idea of the role of sport in our lives. Students will gain a great deal from an analysis of sport from a sociocultural perspective that is applicable to their future roles as sport managers and to their own knowledge base in sport.

Why should we study this subject and why is it important that we dispel the myths surrounding this activity? Understanding the answers to those questions will enable you to become a better consumer of sport, a more knowledgeable fan, and ultimately a better sport manager.

WHY SHOULD WE STUDY SPORT?

"The saddest day of the year is the day baseball season ends."

—Tommy Lasorda

Undoubtedly, why we should study sport is an important question for any student and appears to be easily answered by the following examples:

- **Sport is omnipresent.** It is all around us and affects our lives in many different ways. It is an important part of our lives and thus merits our attention. We all know of people whose lives revolve around their favorite team or athlete, and there have certainly been many iconic moments in sport over the past decade that have wowed us and kept us enthralled. Sport fans often know more about sport trivia than what is happening economically or politically in the US or the world. According to the Fantasy Sports Trade Association (2012), 35 million people over the age of 12 spend countless hours building teams to compete against other fantasy owners. Why are so many people interested in what appears to be a relatively trivial and unimportant part of society? The answer is fairly simple: Sport is a fascinating and multidimensional activity, full of daring, drama and spectacle, amazing victories and heartbreaking defeats. It is a way that, for a few hours, we can forget about the rest of our lives, problems, and concerns and focus on something that is far more exciting. We love sport and most of us want to know, learn about, and engage in it.

- **Sport coverage has increased dramatically over the past decade.** It is impossible to access the Internet, pick up a newspaper or switch on the radio or television and not see some form of sports coverage or sports sponsorship. Television, in particular, has been responsible for bringing sport to the masses, although watching sport through Internet live streaming and on mobile devices has increased exponentially over the past five years. For example, over 3600 hours from the 2012 London Olympics were streamed live by NBC, an indication of the growing importance of this form of media. Network and cable stations utilize sport to attract viewers and advertise other television programs. The Super Bowl, the Olympic Games and other major sporting events attract millions of viewers each year (they are often among the most watched TV programs annually) and thus are able to command millions of dollars in advertising revenues and sponsorship.

- **Many of the role models/heroes adopted by our children are athletes.** Players such as Tim Tebow, LeBron James, Dwayne Wade, Sidney Crosby, and Tom Brady are instantly recognizable and have an impact on the way our children act, dress,

Photo courtesy © istockphoto.com

and think. These athletes are viewed as role models and heroes and often combine skill with a devotion to charity, family, and community projects (Parry, 2009). The media coverage afforded to these sport stars (both on and off the field/court) is phenomenal and can often be damaging if the athlete/coach falls from grace, as witnessed by the extensive and mostly negative coverage of the Tiger Woods scandal in 2009 and the intense furor over the Ray Rice domestic abuse video in 2014. Similarly, the 2012 Penn State scandal and the revelations by the Freeh report (2012) were not only covered by dedicated sport channels, but were front-page news stories on all major networks. There is no doubt that our sport-obsessed culture can even pardon athletes like Michael Vick, whose heinous crimes are now largely forgiven with his success on the football field.

MYTHS IN AMERICAN SPORT

"Football is like life: it requires perseverance, self-denial, hard work, sacrifice, dedication, and respect for authority."

—Vince Lombardi

Myths are stories based on traditions or legends that often become reality. Beneath the visible, known, highly explicit surface of sport, there lies a whole other world composed of hidden beliefs and motives. We are constantly assailed by a number of myths or misperceptions that appear to be real and help to explain sport, making it more manageable for us as fans, consumers, and sport managers. Our feelings and attitudes about sport are largely affected by the media, which has a tremendous influence on shaping our cultural beliefs and perpetuating the myths that surround this activity. An overwhelming number of people get their information from accessing the Internet, watching television, and socializing with others, rather than reading a textbook. As such, we often fall victim to the ways in which the media delivers and shapes our perceptions of sport. The information presented to us is often highly subjective, usually sensationalized, and sometimes very biased. The packaging of athletes and their sport stories is a vital part of the coverage of the event, and an analysis of the sociocultural aspects of sport reveals the following myths/misconceptions:

- College sports programs generate millions of dollars, making huge profits for their universities.
- Title IX has resulted in complete equality for men's and women's education-based athletic programs.
- Gambling in sport poses no risk to the sport or its participants.
- Sport is a wonderful way for children (regardless of skill level) to help build self-esteem and develop good character and leadership traits.
- Politics does not affect sport.
- Most communities benefit economically and psychologically from supporting a professional sport franchise, and therefore the community should pay for or approve massive tax breaks for expensive renovations or building new stadiums.

- Drug abuse is not that big a problem in most professional sports.
- The physical demands and training regimes associated with sport benefits the athlete.
- Sport is one of the few places in society where minority participants get equitable treatment.

WHAT CAN WE LEARN FROM STUDYING SPORT?

"Sports do not build character . . . they reveal it."

—John Wooden

Sport is an important element of American life that is so pervasive we are all affected by it. Studying sport from a social perspective helps us understand the culture of our society and help dispel some of the previously discussed myths (Donnelly, 2004). Imagine that a Martian spaceship landed in America on the day that a major sports event was being covered. What could those visitors learn about our society from watching that sports event and our reactions to it? If the event was the Super Bowl, perhaps the Martians could conclude that we as Americans loved activities that were fast-paced, competitive, exciting, and aggressive. In addition, the signage around the stadium may help the alien conclude that there are major connections between sports and the business world. In watching the advertisements shown during the breaks in competition, they may also understand how economics play an important part in defining what sport is in this country. In short, we study sport from a social perspective to learn more about our culture.

Culture represents the norms and values of individuals and groups within society. Sport in America mirrors what is occurring in the rest of our society. Politics, economics, inequities, social relationships, and deviance in society can all be viewed through an analysis of sport. Sport, in essence, is a microcosm of American culture. Thus, the more we understand about sport, the more we can reflect on what is happening in the rest of society.

FRAMEWORKS FOR UNDERSTANDING THE RELATIONSHIP BETWEEN SPORT AND SOCIETY

"Individual commitment to a group effort—that is what makes a team work, a company work, a society work, a civilization work."

—Vince Lombardi

Not all researchers agree about what is important in studying sport and society. The method of analyzing sport from a cultural perspective has resulted in the development of a sub-discipline called *sport sociology*. Sport sociology as a discipline is comparatively new and has only gained credibility as an area of study since the 1970s. Sports sociologists are interested in how humans relate to each other in the sport context, how values affect these relationships, and how humans organize and value sport activities (Coakley, 2010). Sport sociology is a social science and derives most of its methods and theories from its parent subject, sociology. Sport sociology is often a difficult and complex area to analyze because social phenomena in the sports world are complex, subtle, and elusive. Sport is a *dynamic* activity that is constantly evolving and changing. Sport sociologists conduct research into the development of sport, patterns of culture, social perspectives, values, and sports organizations. Sport sociologists have many questions about what is important and what is not. Key sociological theories and research methods examine how sport has developed and what contemporary issues impact this activity. Understanding and applying these perspectives to a study of sport in the social context can be a valuable tool for students who wish to further their understanding of this area.

WHAT AREAS DO SPORT SOCIOLOGISTS INVESTIGATE?

Sociologists study sport in a variety of different ways. The focus of analysis is not confined solely to elite athletic experiences (such as professional, Olympic, or intercollegiate participation); rather, sociologists are interested in all facets of involvement in sport and physical activity (including youth sport). Areas of consideration include, but are not limited to, the following:

"Sport Sociology"

- Sport and social values
- Socialization into sport
- Youth sport
- Sport and education (interscholastic and intercollegiate)
- Sport and the economy (sport as a business entity)
- Sport and the political system (sport policy)
- Violence in sport
- Use of performance-enhancing substances
- Gambling and sport
- Sport and religion (brought into focus by the actions of athletes like Tim Tebow)
- Sport and the mass media
- Social stratification
- Diversity issues in sport
- Future of sport

Analyzing these areas permits us to look beyond statistics, teams, and trivia into a more meaningful exploration of the impact that sport has on our everyday lives. The analysis of sport from a longitudinal perspective (e.g., youth sport through interscholastic, intercollegiate, and professional participation) gives us an opportunity to review the major influences in our decision to engage in this practice and to explore the reasons for our continuance/non-continuance in this activity. The following questions can be answered by reviewing our own experiences:

- Why did we play the sports we played?
- How did we become interested in those particular activities as opposed to others?
- How were those early experiences related to social class, race, gender and community?
- How was our morality and character shaped and altered by these competitive sport experiences?
- What was the role of our parents/guardians/coaches in developing our love of sports?
- How has participating in sport affected our lives (positively and negatively)?

An investigation of the close relationship between the economy and sport reveals the multi-dimensional nature of this activity. To say that sport is "big business" is truly an understatement in the 21st century. Similarly, those who purport that politics have no impact on sport need to understand and appreciate how local, national, and international governments affect sport participation and sport consumption.

A brief review of the political events that have surrounded the last 100 years of Olympic competition is enough to convince anyone that political interventions, particularly boycotts, are a fundamental part of international sport competition. Major problems in society (e.g., drugs, violence, gambling) can also be analyzed in the sports context. Understanding why these social problems exist in sport helps to explain the motivations of athletes, coaches, and owners who engage in these practices and the pressures that lead to these abuses. Why do athletes commit violent acts on and off the field? Why do athletes take performance-enhancing substances? Why do fans riot? Why do male athletes abuse women? Why did the most influential figures at Penn State choose to cover up the child abuse committed by Jerry Sandusky? All these questions can be answered from a sociological perspective and will enable sport managers to increase their understanding of how these cultural issues operate in a sport business context.

DEVIANCE IN SPORT

A quick review of any local/national newspaper, sports channel, or specific sports event quickly reveals that some athletes (like some non-athletes) are engaged in deviant activities. Michael Vick, Aaron Hernandez, Adrian Peterson, and Greg Hardy are examples of athletes who have been accused/ convicted of committing deviant acts on and off the field. Are athletes more deviant than non-athletes, or are they just more visible in the media and their deviant acts therefore more noticeable? *Deviance* is any act that violates the norms of an activity (Coakley, 2010); it is prominent in both the sport and the business worlds. However, what is considered normal in sport (e.g., aggressive plays, violent actions on the court/field)

Photo courtesy © Andy Gillentine

would be considered deviant in other areas of society. Sport requires a measure of competitiveness and aggression that would be frowned upon in any other social sphere. However, even in sport there are normative (acceptable behaviors) for athletes. Athletes are expected to pursue victory as zealously as possible, but we do not expect them to apply a "win at all costs" mentality to this quest (at least not if this involves cheating to win). Unfortunately, the focus on achievements and victory often leads athletes to make choices between what is morally right and what may give them a "competitive" edge (Woods, 2007). Taking performance-enhancing substances, for example, has become one of the most important areas for discussion and policy among sport organizations and sport sociologists. The use of drugs in sport is a not a new phenomenon. Although steroid use has been the focus of much of this attention, athletes in a variety of sports use drugs to improve their performance. Wrestlers and jockeys have used diuretics for many years to make weight; cyclists in the Tour De France have been accused of taking stimulants and blood doping to remain competitive (in fact, Lance Armstrong was recently stripped of his seven Tour de France titles and banned from the sport of cycling for this kind of substance abuse); Olympic archers and biathletes have taken "downers" (such as alcohol and beta blockers) to steady nerves and dampen arousal levels; and World Class skiers such as Bode Miller have endorsed the use of erythropoietin (EPO— a drug used to stimulate the growth of red blood cells) to increase endurance. Most sport organizations have responded to the rampant use of drugs in sport by devising drug testing policies and procedures to try to combat this problem. However, their efforts have been hampered by the increasing sophistication of drug compounds that cannot be detected, the scientific use of masking agents and stacking (cycling on and off drugs) regimes used by athletes, in addition to the resistance of players unions to negotiate stricter penalties for the violation of drug testing in Collective Bargaining Agreements (CBAs). In fact, this issue was a major sticking point in the 2005 NHL CBA. Drug abuse will likely remain at the forefront of modern sports well into this century and is likely to be an issue for many sport managers who work directly with athletes and are often confronted with ethical dilemmas in the workplace.

Another concern of many sport sociologists is the incidence of on- and off-field violence in sports. Football is the most popular sport in the US primarily because it appeals to us as Americans on many levels. It is a tough, aggressive, competitive activity that reflects Americans' cultural values. We watch this sport and revel in the aggressive nature of the plays. The media often highlights the most violent of acts (tackles, sacks) and replays these events numerous times. A measure of risk is assumed by all athletes on the field; however, the concern of many is when athletes have problems in turning off this aggression off the field. The number of violent incidents that athletes have been involved with over the past decade suggests that there is some cause for concern, especially when we look at the rise in violence against women by male athletes. Albert Haynesworth is just one example of an NFL player (there are dozens more and not just in this league) who has been arrested a number of times for simple assault, but there is no definitive research that proves that athletes are more likely to commit offences against women than non-athletes.

DIVERSITY AND SPORT

"Prejudice is a burden which confuses the past, threatens the future, and renders the present inaccessible."

—Maya Angelou

Perhaps the most important area for sport managers to appreciate and understand is that of diversity (Cunningham, 2010). Sports sociologists study the effects of social stratification, social class mobility, and status. An in-depth analysis of these factors is critical to understanding the diversity of the modern workplace and the resultant challenges of establishing employee and customer relations. Thus, in the 21st century, a focus on all discriminatory practices related to diversity in the workplace is critical. Functioning as an effective and efficient sport manager requires an understanding, true appreciation, and constant application of non-discriminatory practices. Diversity is more than just an analysis of racism and sexism. According to the U.S. Equal Employment Opportunity Commission (U.S. EEOC), federal laws including Title VII of the Civil Rights Act of 1964, the Americans with Disabilities Act (ADA) and the Age Discrimination in Employment Act (ADEA) specifically address the illegality of any employment-based discrimination with regard to race, color, religion, gender, national origin, disability, or age (Carr-Rufino, 2007). Sexual harassment, sexual orientation, and gender identification are also addressed in Title VII.

Race/Color Discrimination

Although African Americans represent a large percentage of those who play professional sports, the opportunities for advancement to the administrative, front office, and coaching ranks are sadly limited for this minority group (Lapchick, 2012). Additionally, the contributions of Mexican Americans, Native Americans, and Asian Americans to sport have largely been ignored. Focusing on these issues is critical to our understanding of sport and to enhancing our role as sport managers in a diverse, global, and complex society.

Title VII of the Civil Rights Act of 1964 covers federal, state, and local governments, employment agencies, labor organizations, and private employers of 15 or more people. The law states that it is unlawful to discriminate against any employee or applicant for a position based on his or her race or color (U.S. EEOC, 2012). The law prohibits discrimination in all phases of the hiring, employment, promotion, work compensation, and termination spectrum. Further, it is illegal to discriminate based on personally held or social stereotypes and assumptions about the competence, characteristics, or performance of any racial group. For example, the sport manager would be creating a hostile work environment by telling jokes that portray an individual or group in a negative light (either to the individual or behind his or her back). Such actions are illegal. Examples of stereotyping that may lead to a negative work environment also include the use of disparaging remarks and criticisms or negative statements made in relation to a person's race or color (Landry, 2005). Such actions are termed "verbal harassment." Race/color discrimination violations also include isolating one group from interaction with others in the workplace (segregation) and requesting pre-employment information regarding race that may be used in excluding a job candidate from selection for employment.

Sex Discrimination

While sport is largely considered to be a meritocratic organization that does not discriminate according to sex, an analysis of stratification and diversity issues in sport can quickly reveal the realities (National Women's Law Center, 2012). Sport has long been a male preserve, and females have been excluded from participating in sport-related activities (Acosta & Carpenter, 2006). Federal laws prohibit such discrimination. In reference to the school and university setting, Title IX was passed 40 years ago in 1972 as part of the Educational Amendments Act and prohibits sex discrimination in education agencies that receive federal funding. Title IX has been effective in improving participation levels of females in sport associated with educational settings (Carpenter & Acosta, 2006). The law, however, has not erased deep-rooted personal prejudice and discrimination against women athletes and administrators.

Title VII of the Civil Rights Act of 1964 prohibits sex discrimination in areas outside the education setting, such as in fitness centers, sport arenas, and other venues. Because sport is still organized and controlled primarily by white men, the "glass ceiling" that exists in the business world is certainly restrictive to women who wish to advance to upper management and front office positions in the sports world (see the Racial and Gender Report Card from the Devos Sport Management Program). As a sport manager, it is imperative that management positions are equally representative of all facets of the public sector, and do not reflect bias in hiring based on the sex of the applicant.

Sexual Harassment

Sexual harassment can be found in many forms in the workplace. The Pregnancy Discrimination Act, an amendment to Title VII of the Civil Rights Act of 1964, provides protection for pregnancy-based discrimination including pregnancy, childbirth, and pregnancy-related medical conditions. Further, pregnancy cannot be used as a reason to refuse to hire a woman. It is within the bounds of the law for an employer to request a doctor's statement regarding any work-related limitations due to pregnancy; however, an employer must hold open a position that was temporarily vacated due to a pregnancy leave.

Title VII also protects men and women against workplace sexual harassment, including requests for sexual favors from those in a position of power (i.e., supervisors) or those serving as co-workers, workplace conditions that create a hostile or unwelcome environment for either gender, and same-sex harassment.

EEOC statistics for 2011 show 28,534 charges of sex-based discrimination representing 28.5% of all charges (99,947 charges total). In 2011, 11,364 sexual harassment charges were brought (83.7% from women) yielding $52.3 million in monetary compensation alone. Obviously, it is imperative that the sport manager understands and implements workplace practices that are free of all forms of sexual discrimination (Landry, 2005). Programs focusing on the prevention of sexual harassment should be mandatory and include sensitivity training for all managers and employees, the establishment of a procedure for filing complaints, and quick resolution/action regarding every sexual harassment issue filed (Marshall, 2005).

Religious Discrimination

The EEOC has been taking a very tough stance against unreasonable employer positions when it comes to religious discrimination in the workplace. It is illegal for employers or employees to discriminate based on religious beliefs in the workplace (U.S. Commission on Civil Rights). This includes during the hiring process, during the creation of work schedules, during the promotion process, or in establishing workplace rules. In fact, a manager is required to make reasonable efforts (accommodations) to provide workplace flexibility regarding various religious convictions of workers, as long as those accommodations do not infringe on the beliefs or work environment of other employees (this is called undue hardship). The manager must also take care to prohibit workplace religious harassment among employees and ensure that one person's religious beliefs do not result in negative workplace business interests for others in the facility. For example, the manager must take care to assure that additional business costs are not incurred as a result of their decisions regarding workers' religious convictions, and that one group of employees does not receive special considerations regarding salary, work schedule, or work materials to the detriment of other groups or individuals.

Disability Discrimination

The Americans with Disabilities Act (ADA) of 1990 and ADA Amendments Act (2008) protects individuals with disabilities from being discriminated against in the workplace. The ADA Amendments Act delineates a person with disabilities in a very broad manner, retaining the original intent of the 1990 law that stated a person with a disability is an individual who "has a physical or mental impairment that limits one or more major life activities, has a record of such an impairment, or is regarded as having such an impairment" (EEOC, 2011). As in previous areas of discrimination, the manager has the responsi-

Photo courtesy © Ancy Gillertine

bility of accommodating schedules, modifying facilities, and adjusting policies and operating procedures for individuals with disabilities. Again, there is an undue hardship consideration wherein the accommodations enacted by the manager must not involve additional expense or hardship for the business owner, and the work or product produced by the facility must be of the same quality as expected from all employees (Sharp, Moorman & Claussen, 2010).

Age Discrimination

Because many organizations have fewer than 20 employees, thus generally negating the position of a Human Resource officer for the company, it is critical for the sport manager to be aware of and implement non-discrimination in all areas of the workplace.

This is true when working with individuals who are given less than satisfactory entry opportunities, job placement, work scheduling, and promotion/retention opportunities. The Age Discrimination in Employment Act (ADEA) of 1967 was initially passed to protect workers age 40 and older from age discrimination in the above-mentioned areas. The ADEA was amended by the Older Workers Benefit Protection Act of 1990 (OWBPA) to include a focus on age discrimination and loss of workplace benefits. The OWBPA also provided for older worker protection in the area of protocol establishment that must be followed when employers are asked to waive their rights when filing settlement claims regarding age discrimination. This legislation is particularly critical to workers who have been affected by company mergers, acquisitions, and job displacement due to downsizing.

METHODS USED IN SOCIOCULTURAL STUDIES TO UNDERSTAND SPORT BEHAVIOR

Sport sociologists largely rely on the methods of the parent discipline (sociology) to research areas in sport. Sport sociology is a social science, and as such the concentration of research in the area is geared toward the collection of accurate and verifiable evidence. Surveys (questionnaires) are valuable, quantifiable methods of learning about group and individual preferences and opinions. Sometimes the facts we need are not recorded by anyone and we have to ask people questions. For example, asking a fan what motivated them to attend a particular sports event can provide us with very valuable information regarding consumer (fan) behavior. A questionnaire can be completed by an individual in a fairly short period of time and may produce a large volume of data that can be analyzed quickly and efficiently. Interviews with fans, participants, and sport consumers are also widely used to explain various aspects of sports participation and consumption. Interviews can be more revealing than surveys, especially when open-ended responses are used to gather information. A closed-ended (yes/no) response tells the researcher very little about the actual reasoning behind a decision. Asking questions such as "why" can be far more revealing; some of the most interesting studies are ones that use this approach singularly (e.g., ethnographic studies). Observational studies also produce data that can help a sport sociologist understand aspects of sports participation and can help managers be more effective in areas relating to customer service (e.g., mystery shopping). For example, subjects who are unaware that they are being watched and their behavior recorded are acting naturally in their environment and are not being asked to recall past information or misrepresenting their experiences (as in an interview). There are many other methods of collecting data; however, the main responsibility of the researcher in this area is to accurately collect, record, analyze, and interpret the facts. In our search for the truth, we rely on scientific methods of data collection to accurately describe what really exists as precisely and objectively as possible. The use of cross-disciplinary and multi-disciplinary approaches to data collection has resulted in a much broader and more focused interpretation of human interaction in the sport context.

CONCLUSION

"In our lives we will encounter many challenges, and tomorrow we face one together. How we accept the challenge and attack the challenge head on is only about us—no one can touch that. If we win or lose this weekend, it will not make a difference in our lives. But why we play and how we play will make a difference in our lives forever."

—Beth Anders

Examining sport from a socio-cultural perspective is obviously critical for those entering the sport management profession. Concepts related to sport and other social institutions are important for the sport manager to understand. The development of modern sport has been influenced by many factors that have affected our perceptions about this topic. In addition, the concepts of diversity discussed in this chapter are critical from many perspectives. The workplace is changing and evolving and the kinds of people that we now see and service in sport are from diverse backgrounds. An examination of the demographic shifts likely to occur in this century (indicated by the results from Census 2010) reaffirms the need to be well versed in multiculturalism and inclusion. A good sport manager is one who affirms diversity in the workplace and promotes the concepts of multiculturalism and inclusion. Differences should be embraced and not feared, and individuals should be judged on their merit, not on the color of their skin, what they choose to believe, or how they live their lives. Confronting prejudice and discrimination in the workplace is a difficult thing to do, but as a manager it is important to realize that part of your responsibility lies in challenging the barriers to employment diversity, thereby providing a safe and secure workplace for all employees. Strategies for managing diversity are important for achieving workplace equity; however, the first step in the process must be a review of one's own prejudices and an examination of why these prejudices exist. Only when we confront our own fears and discriminatory behaviors can we begin to effect change in others.

LEARNING ACTIVITIES

Discussion Questions

1. Describe any personal experiences that you have had with discrimination. How did these situations affect you, and what did you learn from these experiences?
2. Does sport bring people together or tear them apart—what specific instances can you think of to support your view?
3. What does the recent Penn State scandal and subsequent cover up reflect about college sport in the US?
4. What impact does legislation have on managing a sport organization? Provide specific examples from this chapter to support your answer.
5. How can the rampant use of drugs in sport be curbed? Do current drug testing policies work?

6. Should Lance Armstrong have been stripped of his seven Tour de France titles? Justify your decision.

7. Has sport been a positive force in your life and those of your friends?

8. What was the primary reason you got involved in sport? Do you still play sport at a competitive level?

9. Who were your heroes growing up? If they were sport stars why did you choose them? What makes a great/bad role model?

10. How do you access information on sport? How often do you access information on sport?

Projects to Be Completed Outside of Class

1. Go to the website of a professional franchise or college athletic department and access the page that introduces their management team. Record the following:
   a) Number of male vs. female managers
   b) Types of managers by gender (e.g., is the athletic director a man or woman? Is the assistant director of marketing a man or a woman?)
   c) If pictures are provided, how many minority managers are there in this organization?

   Once you have collected this data, answer the following questions:
   a) Is there a disparity in gender of those associated with the franchise or sport organization?
   b) Are the administrative positions staffed by only men, only women, or a percentage of both?
   c) Are the administrative positions staffed only by Caucasian personnel, or are underrepresented groups evident in top management?
   d) Is the wording used by the franchise or sport organization inclusive or exclusive according to gender, race, or ability? Provide specific documentation of your findings.

2. Choose two of the myths outlined in this chapter. Using the web or other resources, provide two examples of specific information that helps to refute each myth.

3. Attend a sports event at your college or university. Observe how the sports event is presented to the audience. Report on the relationships and connections you witness between the event and the concepts discussed in this chapter (i.e., signage, ages of spectators, promotions for spectators, reactions of fans to calls by officials, reactions of fans to opposing fans).

4. Analyze the content of a sports section of a local or national newspaper. Record the following information:
   a) The number of articles featuring male athletes
   b) The number of articles featuring female athletes
   c) The number of photographs featuring female athletes
   d) The number of photographs featuring male athletes

e) The number of articles featuring minority athletes

f) The number of photographs featuring minority athletes

g) Answer the following questions: Who does the media choose to focus on with regard to sport? Which gender/races are most included? Which gender/races are most excluded?

5. Review the drug testing policies of the NFL, NBA, MLB and the NHL. Compare and contrast the efficacy of each.

In-Class Learning Experiences

1. **Hitting a Triple:** In groups of three, determine three reasons why sports coverage has increased dramatically over the past decade. You have three minutes to complete this activity. Be prepared to share your reasons with the rest of the class!

2. **Once Upon a Time.** Many athletes are viewed as role models by children and youth. With a partner, write a fairy tale ("Once upon a time, there was a child who . . .), in which the child in the story emulates undesirable attributes of professional athletes (i.e., greed, drug abuse, gambling, poor sportsmanship, bullying). The negative attributes should not contribute positively to the growth or social interaction of the child in any way. Share your story with another pair in the class. Then, correct the two stories so that "all lived happily ever after!"

3. **The Three R's.** A female employee is being sexually harassed and is told by her boss that it is not a good time to "make waves." With a partner, analyze this scenario using the following three steps: 1. REFLECTION: "How did the events in the scenario relate to one another?" 2. RESEARCH: "What concepts or principles in the field of sport management will help us to understand what happened?" 3. RESPOND: Ask the students to list specific actions that should have been added, omitted, or applied differently to "fix" the scenario. An extension of this activity is to have students create different scenarios, using chapter material.

4. **Shared Feelings.** Create a list of words that describe you and your experiences. Include reference to gender, race, marital status, year in school, favorite food, hobby, religion, political affiliation, club membership, athletic team membership, sports you like to watch, sports you like to play, favorite dessert, pet ownership, favorite vehicle, socioeconomic status, favorite chain restaurant, favorite sports teams. Share this list with two other people, and compare your similarities and differences. What does this exercise tell you about yourself and those in your class, as related to this chapter?

5. **Ready, Set, Go.** Get ready, because this active learning strategy adds the element of *time* in decision making. Each student in class has been given a scenario relating to a diversity problem or issue. Seated face to face in two concentric circles, each pair of students has 60 seconds to share their scenarios and to elicit a solution to each. At the end of a minute, the outer circle of students is cued to move one seat to the left. The sixty-second timer is restarted, and the process begins again. Remember to take notes on each collaboration, for discussion at the end of

the activity. Stop this activity after 8 or 9 rotations. You will each take turns sharing your solutions to your scenario. Was thirty seconds enough time to "solve" each scenario? In real world settings, time is always a critical factor during decision making. Therefore, care must always be taken to arrive at solutions in both an appropriate and timely fashion.

References

Acosta, V., & Carpenter, L. (2006). *Women in intercollegiate sport: A longitudinal study—29 year update—1977–2006.* Unpublished manuscript, Brooklyn College, NY.

Americans with Disabilities Amendments Act (2008) (Public Law 110–325 ADAAA).

Carr-Ruffino, N. (2007). *Managing diversity.* Boston, MA: Pearson.

Coakley, J. (2010). *Sport in society: Issues and controversies* (10th edition). Boston, MA: McGraw Hill.

Cunnigham, G. B. (2010). *Diversity in sport organizations* (2nd edition). Scottsdale, AZ: Holcomb Hathaway.

Davis, R. (2002). *Inclusion through sports.* Champaign, IL: Human Kinetics.

Equal Employment Opportunity Commission (2011). *Sex based charges.* Retrieved from http://www.eeoc.gov/stats/sex.html

Humphreys, B. R. & Rusescki, J. E. (2008). The size and scope of the sport industry. Retrieved from http://college.holycross.edu/RePe/spe/Humphreys

Landry, F. J. (Ed) (2005). *Employment discrimination litigation: Behavioral, quantitative and legal perspectives.* San Francisco, CA: Jossey Bass.

Lapchick, R. (2012). *Race and gender report card.* Retrieved on November 30, 2007, from www.bus.ucf/sport

Marshall, A. M. (2005). *Confronting sexual harassment: The law and politics of everyday life.* Burlington, VT: Ashgate.

National Women's Law Center (2012). 40 years of *Title IX.* Retrieved from http://www.nwlc.org

Parry, K (2009). Search for the hero: An investigation into the sports heroes of British sports fans. *Sport in society, 72*(4), 212–226.

Sharp, L. A, Moorman, A. M., & Claussen, C. L. (2010). *Sport law: A managerial approach.* Scottsdale, AZ: Holcomb Hathaway.

U.S. Commission on Civil Rights (2005). Clearinghouse Publication, 70.

Woods, R. B. (2007). *Social issues in sport.* Champaign, IL: Human Kinetics.

3

Communication and Media Relations in Sport

Andy Gillentine, R. Brian Crow, and Galen Clavio

INTRODUCTION

Sport organizations, like all other enterprises, strive to send a unique message to their many stakeholders. For example, consider the San Francisco 49ers of National Football. The 49ers have successfully orchestrated the construction of the new $1.3 billion Levi's Stadium in Santa Clara that the team believes will help them to compete financially and on the field with other teams in the league (Rosenberg, 2013; Robinson, 2013). The owner of the team (as well as other team officials) and the city of Santa Clara are in constant communication with fans, sponsors, researchers, broadcasters, fantasy league players, schools, community groups, city officials, employees, volunteers, suppliers, vendors, licensees, and dozens of other individuals and organizations on a daily basis (Table 3.1). This information exchange occurs in a variety of ways: via phone calls, email, personal meetings, text messages, visits to a web page, written correspondence, visits to schools or hospitals, and other various methods of communication. If the 49ers and/or the city had failed to maintain open lines of communication with each of these groups, it is doubtful that they would be able to generate the approval needed for the new stadium. It is clear that sport organizations rely on communication to survive in today's media-savvy environment. A clear and consistent message is more likely to be understood by the recipient and responded to in a positive manner.

Learning Objectives

Upon completion of this chapter, the reader should be able to
- Understand the important role of communication in the sport industry;
- Identify the various components of effective communication;
- Recognize the barriers to effective communication;
- Discuss the importance on nonverbal communication; and
- Appreciate the role of media relations in the sport organization.

In the Bleachers © 2012 Steve Moore. Dist. by Universal Uclick

www.gocomics.com/inthebleachers

"Hockey was more fun to watch when they duked it out for real and not on Twitter."

Effective communication in sport is one of the most important and pervasive qualities and competencies a sport manager can possess. Communication can run the gamut from interpersonal and small group communication to public mass communication networks. The importance of developing communication skills necessary for success in the sport industry is heightened by the tremendous growth of electronic media. The expansion of media coverage of the sport industry will only continue to grow as innovative technologies offer sport managers new avenues through which to communicate. Therefore, it is essential that sport managers have a strong appreciation of the power of contemporary communication mediums, both as a means of connecting with key constituents and as an advantage that requires increasingly greater management skill and coordination.

INTERPERSONAL AND SMALL GROUP COMMUNICATION

Table 3.1. Sport Managers Communication Demands	
• Team Owners/Administration	• City Officials
• Coaches	• Vendors
• Competing Sport Organizations	• Sponsors
• Staff members	• Researchers
• The media	• Game Officials
• Boosters	• Players
• Fans	• Parents
• Faculty	
Modified from Anshel (1997)	

Sport mangers must constantly refine their communication skills in order to effectively deliver information to the diverse groups with which they may interact. From casual conversation with colleagues to formal meetings with financial sponsorship partners, the sport manager must be prepared to maximize the effectiveness of communication. The development of effective communication skills requires the sport manager to (1) acknowledge the importance of effective communication, (2) commit to an honest and frequent appraisal of their communication strengths and weaknesses, and (3) demonstrate a willingness to invest time and effort to improve upon those weaknesses.

Keys to Effective Communication

In order to become an effective communicator, the sport manager must understand that communication is a multifaceted skill. The sport manager must recognize the multiple techniques for effective communication, evaluate the various methods through which communication can occur, and select the most appropriate action or actions. **Effective planning** is often overlooked during the communication process, which compromises the usefulness of the information. After determining the most effective method(s) to utilize, the sport manager must effectively plan the content of the message and the timing for release of the information as well as estimate the content, speed, and consequences of the recipient's feedback.

Once the plan is in place, the sport manager must ensure the integrity of the information to be distributed. It is important that the **content** of the message is accurate and free from bias or inflammatory language. It is also important for the sport manager to establish his or her **credibility** with the intended audience. The credibility of the sender directly affects the perception of the receiver regarding the content of the message. Credibility is enhanced through an established reputation, a long history of truthful and accurate communication, and legitimacy. **Personal credibility** goes hand-in-hand with **message credibility**. Honest communication from the organization results in trust from the audience. Failure to be honest—for example, repeatedly denying trade rumors that ultimately prove to be true—will often damage the organization and administrator's credibility. Never distribute information before it has been checked for accuracy. It is better to have a short delay in sending a message than to send one with inaccurate information.

Table 3.2. Guidelines for Effective Communication	
• Plan for communication	• Be honest
• Establish consistent daily communication	• Encourage upward, downward, and lateral communication
• Respect other viewpoints	• Praise (in public) and criticize (in private) behavior, not the person
• Utilize humor	• Do not use sarcasm or embarrass others
• Never use stereotypes or prejudicial statements	• Avoid negative humor and obscene language

Additionally, the sport manager must consider the *type of information* being transferred. **Complex information** may be potentially confusing and must be carefully presented in order to avoid creating additional communication problems. Also, the *emotional content* of the message has to be considered. Often the information transmitted from the sport organization—for example, the trading of a star player or firing of a coach—contains emotionally charged content for recipients (i.e., fans, boosters, players). These messages must be delivered in the most positive manner possible. Also, specific words can be laden with emotion. Words related to sex, religion, and politics may evoke a response from recipients that may affect the delivery of the message.

Barriers to Effective Communication

Sport managers must also recognize that there are inherent barriers to effective communication. These barriers may be typically categorized into three distinct categories: (1) Linguistic barriers, (2) Psychological barriers, and (3) Environmental barriers. While it may be impossible for the sport manager to completely eliminate these barriers, methods to minimize the potential impact of each should be considered during the communication planning process.

The classic Abbot and Costello comedy routine *Who's on First?* depicts a conversation between two friends regarding the players of a baseball team. The ensuing miscommunica-

Table 3.3. Barriers to Effective Communication
• Linguistic barriers
• Psychological barriers
• Environmental barriers

tion is a perfect example of a **linguistic** barrier to effective communication. Students should visit YouTube and search for this classic video clip.

Linguistics is defined as "the study of the nature, structure, and variation of language, including phonetics, phonology, morphology, syntax, semantics, sociolinguistics, and pragmatics" (The American Heritage Dictionary, 2000).

While each of the above areas identifies an important component in the study of linguistics, perhaps the most important components are *semantics* and *sociolinguistics*. Semantics is defined as the meaning or the interpretation of a word and/or sentence. Individuals often define terms differently, which could impact the content of the message. The sport administrator must be cautious in the selection of terminology to ensure the proper interpretation of the message. This difference can lead to miscommunication or disagreement over a topic that both groups may actually agree upon.

Closely related to semantics and an area of great importance is sociolinguistics. Sociolinguistics refers to the impact that differing social and/or cultural groups have on the meaning and interpretation of language. Words or phrases often have a very different meaning from group to group. Social variables that could impact communication may include ethnicity, religion, economic status, and level of education. Given the diverse audience the sport manager interacts with on a regular basis, it is critical these differences be noted. For example, certain language used by college students during a college

Table 3.4. Components of Linguistics
Phonetics: different sounds that are employed across all human languages
Phonology: patterns of a language's basic sounds
Morphology: the internal structure of words
Syntax: how words combine to form grammatical sentences
Semantics: the meaning or interpretation of words
Sociolinguistics: the effect of all aspects of society, including cultural norms, expectations, and context, on language

Photo courtesy © Andy Gillentine

athletic event might be interpreted differently by a 51-year-old man and his 18-year-old daughter (Cramer & Schietzer, 2004).

The **environment** may also pose barriers to effective communication. The designated audience may not effectively receive verbal messages delivered in a crowded, noisy, or uncomfortable room. Distractions may impede a person's ability to hear and accurately interpret the message. The temperature and other weather conditions, such as high winds, rain, and snow, can promote levels of discomfort that may impede communication. While it is impossible for sport managers to control all of these environmental barriers, it is important to recognize them and to minimize their impact.

Additional environmental concerns can involve the physical structure of the facility. Aside from noise issues, inadequately furnished facilities may also create a level of discomfort, which might in turn impede effective communication. In an attempt to offset this problem, many administrators have turned to feng shui experts to help them design meeting spaces that incorporate comfortable seating and facilitate an effective communication environment (Broadhead, 2001; McCullough, 2013).

Additional potential barriers to effective communication in the sport industry are **psychological** barriers. Psychological barriers are outside the scope of linguistic and environmental barriers, manifesting instead in the mind of the intended audience. While these barriers are among the most difficult to identify, the sport manager must recognize these potential barriers and take actions to offset or change them. Foremost among the psychological barriers is the **perception** of the information or sender of the message. Perception is defined as the "recognition and interpretation of sensory stimuli based chiefly on memory" (The American Heritage Dictionary of the English Language, Fourth Edition, 2000). Individuals often rely on past experiences to positively or negatively interpret newly received information. While positive perceptions will most likely help the sport administrator, negative perceptions regarding the administrator, organization, or situation can damage the effectiveness of the message. Public perception and attitudes toward the organization must be continually monitored. If negative perceptions are ignored, innuendo, rumors, and other misinformation can be perceived as factual if immediate action is not taken to correct them.

The Communication Network

Peterson, Miloch and Laucella (2007) stated that "the sport organization is created, developed, and maintained through the communicative actions of the stakeholders" (p. 124). In order for these actions to be effective, the sport manager must recognize the importance of the **flow of communication** amongst all stakeholders. The sport organization must develop an information flow that moves downward, upward, and laterally.

Downward communication refers to information that is transmitted from the upper levels of management to the middle and lower levels of the organization. Frequently sport managers maintain communication systems that only allow for downward communication, eliminating the opportunity to receive valuable information and feedback from others in the organization.

The **upward** flow of information allows for upper management to receive information from subordinates, customers, suppliers, etc., that may be useful in correcting current operations and/or determining the future direction of the organization. Failure to develop an effective system to gather **feedback** from within the organization and its customers results in upper level management that is out-of-touch with its constituents.

Lateral communication refers to communication that flows between the various individuals or groups at the same or equivalent levels of management. This exchange of information is important to ensure that duplication of materials and information is not occurring within the organization. This type of communication can also be useful to help foster employee involvement and empowerment within the organization.

The communication network also includes identifying the medium through which the communication will be transmitted. These communication networks include *verbal communication, nonverbal communication,* and *mass media communication*. Each of these communication mediums requires specific levels of understanding by the sport manager in order to maximize its effectiveness.

The most commonly used method of communication is verbal communication. Estimates indicate that 70% of a person's day is spent in at least one form of verbal communication (Sarthe, Olson, & Whitney, 1973). Verbal communication consists of speaking, listening, reading, and writing. In order to improve verbal communication, it is important for sport managers to

Table 3.5. Verbal Communication	
We hear half of what is said	50%
We listen to half of that	25%
We understand half of that	12.5%
We believe half of that	6.25%
And we remember half of that	3.125%
Martens, 1987	

consider multiple components of spoken communication. Aside from the credibility of content addressed earlier, sport managers need to consider articulation, tempo, and volume. These components are referred to as paralanguage, the features which accompany verbal communication but are not considered part of the language system.

Articulation refers to the ability to clearly enunciate words. Speakers may need to overcome national or regional accents that may impact the listener's understanding of the message. Speakers should also be aware of the correct pronunciations of words and terms used in delivery. Mumbling is another aspect of articulation that can impact the message. Speakers should strive to speak as clearly as possible and to carefully enunciate each word during a presentation. Although the speaker may initially feel awkward in this careful manner of speech, the reward is an audience that properly decodes the message.

Tempo refers to the speed at which we speak. Novice speakers often have a tendency to speak too rapidly in an important situation. This can be due to increases in adrenaline or general nervousness. Regardless of the reason, effective communication requires speakers to speak slower than normal when addressing a group. Another aspect of tempo that should be avoided is a sing-song manner of speech, in which the pitch and timing of words follow a pattern that can be distracting to the listener.

Speakers should also be aware of the volume of their voice. In addition to always speaking slower than normal, speakers should also speak louder. A general rule of thumb is to speak in a manner such that someone in the back of the room can easily hear you. This should be a consideration when addressing a large group. Often it is better to err on the side of caution and utilize a microphone than to not be heard.

Another important aspect of verbal communication is listening. Research indicates that individuals spend roughly half of their daily verbal communication listening. The late Mark McCormack, founder of International Management Group (IMG), stated that the most important skill an administrator can have is effective listening. McCormick advocated active listening, a method through which the listener actively and physically participates with the speaker.

Table 3.6. Steps to Improve Listening
• Be prepared to listen
• Listen openly
• Concentrate on message
• Do not judge speaker
• Observe mannerisms and gestures of speaker
• Identify main concepts and points
• Eliminate distractions
• Be committed
Adapted from Martens, 1987

Nonverbal Communication

Powerful nonverbal messages are transmitted through the mannerisms and physical actions of the sport manager. The way the speaker utilizes the space in which he/she is delivering the message, and the presentation of their physical attributes and appearance, sends additional information to the recipient, which may or may not reinforce their verbal message. Sport mangers must be aware of the importance of these nonverbal communication cues and take the appropriate actions to manage them effectively.

The study of how an individual communicates through their use of space is referred to as **proxemics**. This form of communication includes not only the amount of space between the receiver and the sender, but also how the speaker utilizes the environment. The appropriate use of space can have a dramatic impact on the effectiveness of communication. Often individuals are able to disengage from the speaker if specific personal space or physical barriers are present. It is important for a sport manager to effectively use the space available to deliver his/her message. Space may also provide the speaker with a "buffer zone" to increase his or her own level of comfort (Table 3.7).

The appearance and physical mannerisms of a speaker are referred to as **kinesics**. This may include the speaker's posture, gestures, facial expressions, and eye movement.

Table 3.7. Hall's Proxemic (Distance) Model	
Public Distance	10" or more
Social/consultive Distance	4'–10'
Personal/casual Distance	1½'– 4'
Intimate Distance	0"–18"
Hall, 1959	

It is important for a speaker to demonstrate good posture when speaking to an audience. Good posture—standing erect, shoulders back, head up—gives the image of a confident speaker, which may help with credibility issues mentioned earlier. The sport administrator may increase the effectiveness of the message through the use of effective eye and facial movements. Occasionally, speakers unintentionally send messages to listeners through inappropriate facial or eye movements. NFL quarterback Jay Cutler was publicly criticized for his facial and eye movements as well as his overall body language during his career (Gallo, 2012; Gantt, 2013). Dallas Mavericks owner Mark Cuban is often lampooned for his animated facial expressions from his actions at NBA games as well as from his appearance on the television show *Shark Tank*. Speakers must carefully study their own appearance in order to make appropriate changes or modifications in both of these areas.

The use of physical gestures, including touching, can help the speaker in emphasizing important points of information and also in conveying the sincerity of the message. Simple gestures can send a variety of messages to the audience, and it is important for speakers to review the gestures they commonly use or to identify ways to increase their use. In today's litigious society, sport managers need to exercise caution, though, when touching individuals. It should be recommended that the speaker know the recipient well before initiating any physical contact. Casual touching can increase the level of perceived familiarity with the speaker through appropriate use of space as mentioned earlier.

MASS MEDIA COMMUNICATION

"The Medium is the Message"

First penned by Marshall McLuhan, it has long been regarded that "the medium is the message." This indicates that, in fact, the means of interaction and communication often serve as the most pivotal means of the message in communication. This is true also of sport. There has been a longstanding relationship between sport and the medium of communication, and the synergy of sport and communication methods has grown even greater with the advent of new and social media at the beginning of the 21st century.

Sport Media

Sport media is a broad term encompassing many aspects of how sport consumers receive information. This information can be delivered directly by a team, league, or sport

organization (via Internet and related technologies) or through mass media (traditional and new media). The growth of sport in the United States, both in participation and spectatorship, can be attributed in part to the increasingly complex role media plays in our lives. All the issues to be considered when dealing with sport and media are too numerous for one textbook chapter. However, several important topics will lead you to a greater understanding of the role media plays in our participation and consumption of sport.

Historical Perspectives

Print media

Organized sport in the United States has evolved tremendously in the past 150 years. Along with that evolution has come an increased thirst for information regarding those sports. Initially, the limited coverage of sport events, and even more limited advertising and promotion of those events, was through *newspapers*. These papers had narrow circulation and quite often not even one writer solely responsible for sport. Compare that to the late 20th century, during which most metropolitan newspapers employed several dozen sportswriters. Sports writing improved dramatically after World War I, as the US population became increasingly literate.

Sport, however, continued to grow in popularity, and many professional sport organizations, as well as the precursor to the NCAA, were formed around the turn of the twentieth century. Media coverage of sport continued to evolve as well, with *radio* becoming a major influence beginning in the 1920s. The first radio broadcast of a professional baseball game was in 1921 on KDKA radio in Pittsburgh. This new competition forced sportswriters to change their style of writing; since the game itself was on the radio, they had to provide in-depth, comprehensive information not available on the radio broadcast.

When television became a permanent fixture in the 1950s, sports writers had to change again, becoming investigative reporters and explaining how and why things happened instead of what happened. As of 2001, newspapers devoted 20–25% of their space to sports news (Nichols, Moynahan, Hall, & Taylor, 2002).

Newspapers and the companies that published them reached a crossroads at the dawn of the social media era in the early 2000s. The traditional "news cycle," which saw reporting of stories focused on the release of the morning's newspaper, became threatened by the growing popularity of the social medium Twitter, sports blogs, and the 24-hour cable news channel. Many news organizations were forced into massive layoffs of employees (Sonderman, 2012), in most cases due to falling advertising revenues and declining readership levels. Newspaper companies have been forced to reorient their business towards online news dissemination, leaving the future of the physical paper copy of newspapers in doubt.

Radio

By the 1930s nearly 300 million radios were being used in the United States. All 16 major league baseball teams broadcasted their games live. Interestingly, play-by-play announcers did not travel with the team in those days; they would recreate the broadcast using Western Union tapes of the game (Nichols et al., 2002). Radio went from local broadcasts in its early days, to national network broadcasts in the middle of the twentieth century, and then back to broadcasts aimed at local audiences after World War II (Nichols et al., 2002). National radio broadcasts are again becoming popular, with the advent of satellite radio services such as Sirius Radio and XM Radio, and the utilization of podcasts allowing people to listen to radio shows on their phones and portable devices.

Television

The first televised sporting event was in 1939—a baseball game between Columbia and Princeton. The growth of professional sport and the growth of television as a viable medium run parallel. In the late 1940s and early 1950s, television in the US was fledgling, with only 190,000 TV sets in use in 1948. Sport—because the events already existed, and there were no sets to build and no actors to hire—became attractive programming (Baran, 2014).

Sport was popular with television executives for several reasons: (1) it attracted a regular weekend audience, (2) it created cross-promotion, (3) it was popular with viewers, and (4) ownership of sports rights adds "credibility" to a network or cable outlet. Today there are more than 500 national and regional cable networks, and over 80% of homes subscribe to cable. ESPN, established in 1979, was the first 24-hour, all-sports network. Television rights fees are a significant source of revenue for professional and intercollegiate teams.

Television specifically and media in general impact our sport consumption daily. For example, prior to 2000, it was rare to see a major college football game played on any day but Saturday or Thursday, or a professional game on any day but Sunday or Monday. But in 2004, ESPN proudly announced it would telecast live NCAA and NFL football over 19 straight days. College teams from less visible conferences such as the Sun Belt and Mid-American Conference grudgingly play on Tuesday, Wednesday, or Friday evening for two reasons; exposure and revenue.

While ESPN has been the dominant sports television property since the 1980s, other networks and services have entered the fray in recent years. The Fox television network announced in 2013 that it would be launching a national multi-sport network called Fox Sports 1 (Sandomir & Chozick, 2013), which will carry a variety of domestic and international sporting events. The NBC television network launched its own NBC Sports Network in 2012, and created a buzz by acquiring the rights to the increasingly popular English Premier League (Sandomir, 2012). The Big Ten Conference, a major collegiate sports conference, launched the Big Ten Network in 2007 in partnership with Fox, and the network's success has generated huge financial windfalls for the conference's teams (Ozanian, 2012). Other conferences have followed suit with their own networks, and one university athletic department, the University of Texas, even launched its own individual network (The Longhorn Network) in a partnership with ESPN.

Internet and Social Media

No media have changed the landscape of sport communication more than social media and the Internet. While newspapers initially popularized sport and television turned it into mass spectacle, the Internet allowed fans unprecedented access to sports news, interaction, games, and commentary. The Internet has transformed the way traditional media do their jobs, and a large number of those functions now take place on the Internet. Social media has created an effective and direct pipeline of information and interactivity between sports figures and fans, rendering traditional media coverage unnecessary in many cases. The Internet has also helped to break down international barriers, allowing sports like European football (soccer) to blossom in popularity in the United States, and leagues like the National Basketball Association (NBA) to develop huge fan bases in places as distant as China and Argentina.

The Internet did not start off as popular as it now is. From the foundation of the World Wide Web in 1992 until the advent of the social media age in 2004, the Internet was mostly seen as an addendum to traditional media. Newspapers focused their advertising and content production on the physical, paper version as opposed to the web site version. Live video streaming was rare, and most consumers watched sports programming through their cable television package. Sport team web sites tended to act as little more than repositories of information, with scant opportunities for users to interact with players and coaches. While most sport communication workers thought the Internet was an important communication venue, very few in 2004 would've considered it the most important one.

However, since 2004 the Internet and its associated modes of communication have increased exponentially in importance. The creation of Facebook in that year gave people a way to personally connect over the Internet in a way that had not been possible before. In less than a decade, Facebook's membership grew from 1 million at the end of 2004 to over 1 billion worldwide by the close of 2012 (Associated Press, 2012). Embedded within the Facebook architecture is a targeted marketing and advertising system, allowing products and companies to reach customers in more effective ways than traditional media advertising. Sports teams have created "fan" pages on Facebook, providing them an ability to write messages directly to fans, notify them of team news, and showcase photo and video content of players, coaches, and team personnel. The Los Angeles Lakers Facebook page had over 16 million fans as of 2013, while international soccer team FC Barcelona had over 42 million Facebook fans (Sports Fan Graph, n.d.).

YouTube, the first major streaming and archive video service, was launched in 2005. YouTube allows users to create accounts and post their own videos, and many sports teams and leagues have used YouTube to extend their brands and enhance outreach with fans. Popular leagues like the NBA have used YouTube to highlight specific players and provide fans with access to archived broadcasts of games. Major League Baseball, which resisted placing their content on YouTube for years, finally relented in 2013, allowing live streaming of games via YouTube to customers outside of the United States (O'Keefe, 2013), in addition to archived games and other video features. Video streaming has become hugely popular in general on the Internet, with leagues launching their own proprietary services, and media companies such as ESPN creating Internet-only video channels.

Twitter, another popular social medium, was launched in 2006 and quickly grew into a phenomenon. The Twitter architecture allows for users to create short, 140-character messages known as "tweets" and post them publicly, thereby allowing other users to view and comment on those tweets. A tweet can be text-only, or can contain a link to a picture, a video, or a piece of written content. Many sport entities, from teams to leagues to individual players and coaches, have used Twitter feeds to communicate directly with fans, and to bypass traditional media channels. Twitter has also become very popular among sport media outlets, with reporters and columnists using it to augment their traditional coverage. During games, many reporters will converse with fans and other media about the game, creating a so-called "second screen" sports experience that both enriches the sport communication landscape and threatens the financial order that currently exists (Shields, 2012).

The sports blog world also continues to play an important part in online conversation and discourse about sports. Thriving Internet-based communities of writers, commentators, and fans have come into existence around nearly every major professional and college sports team. Ideas and concepts that are supported by these communities, such as metrics in baseball and possession-free statistical analysis in basketball, have become the focus of debate regarding the coverage of sports.

Social media are increasingly used by sport fans to gather information and interact with other fans (Clavio & Walsh, 2012), while athletes utilize it to promote their brands and personalities through both direct and indirect means (Frederick, Lim, Clavio, Pedersen, & Burch, 2013). Fans and teams use social media features such as hashtags to create virtual conversations during major sporting events, unfettered by geographical distance (Blaszka, Burch, Frederick, Clavio, & Walsh, 2012). As important as social media and Internet communication technologies are to the sport world now, they are destined to grow even more in importance in future years.

SPORTS INFORMATION

The current relationship between sport and the media has come a long way from the "good old days" when beat writers were on professional sport team payrolls and traveled

Photo courtesy © iStockphoto.com

with their team, in large part to share a public relations "goodwill" account with local and very loyal fans. Today, the relationship between sport and the media has become more tenuous, juxtaposing a more critical, yet accountable forum regarding professional sport organizations and athletes, while at the same time providing a multitude of enhanced outlets to promote and discuss these same sport products.

Historically, the formalization of "media relations" departments occurred similarly to the development of the sport industry during the 1950s. In response to the rise in interest of spectator sport, media outlets—specifically, local papers and radio outlets—increased their coverage and requests for information from sport organizations at both the professional and collegiate sport levels. As these requests intensified, the need for full-time sports information directors emerged and the official office of media relations was born. Today, this department works very closely within the greater public relations umbrella of the sport organization, which includes the growing area of community relations. Not only is this unit responsible for the ongoing dissemination of sports information outputs (Table 3.8), but it is also regarded as the first point of contact within the sport organization. It is essential that this department play a very proactive role, working closely with the management and marketing units of the organization, to craft a uniform message to their community. However, challenges exist to this model of doing business, particularly as social media make it more difficult to craft and issue uniform messages across the span of the organization. Due largely to concerns about poor public relations, many leagues and sport organizations have felt compelled to censor or forbid their employees and athletes from using Twitter and other social media. However, these efforts often make the organization appear old-fashioned or out of step with the times.

Present Perspectives

Sports Journalism

Current insights with regard to sport and media point in particular to the role of sport journalists and sports journalism as having a major impact on the development of the sport industry. Specifically, these individuals, coupled with the increased scrutiny of star

Table 3.8. Sports Information Outputs	
The sports information or media relations director is responsible for delivering many outputs to their media outlets on a very regular and timely basis. These include the following pieces:	
Media Releases	Designed to positively position the sport organization and disseminate information about future developments or happenings within the organization.
Fact Sheets	Delivered in a more timely matter, these are designed to showcase future opportunities for the organization as well as highlight specific facets.
Pre-game Notes	Similar in nature to fact sheets, these are produced prior to sporting events to profile key players and match-ups, as well as interesting and informative team notes.
Hometown Features	Geographically targeted to correspond to key targets, these are developed to highlight key individuals in their hometown region, while also positioning the organization in a positive light.
Media Guides	A very detailed analysis of all facets of the organization, including in-depth profiles of team members, an organization management overview, and information related to each competition (home and away).
Game Programs	For distribution at every home game, these are intended for both consumers and the media to profile the particular match-up and current happenings of the organization.

athletes and the enhanced style of investigative reporting, have created a magnifying glass approach to the sport media relationship. As such, increased scrutiny and management of sport media is warranted by sport managers. This elevated intensity and reliance on the media is also most apparent in the television outlets, where the ratings game for sport programming has intensified. This is also similar to the impact of the Internet, where increased product extensions and sports information is communicated with sport fans and media alike.

Future Considerations

The future relationship between sport and the media will continue to provide examples of synergies and opportunities for grander levels of importance and influence for sport organizations and sport media outlets. The continued merging of sport and entertainment, including media integration, a number of leading media outlets, and national television companies, will further capitalize on utilizing sport and sport properties to enhance their program lineups. In addition, new media will continue to emerge, such as digital media technology, which will generate a whole new genre of communicating with sport fans. A number of factors will contribute to this paradigm shift with regards to sport media, but will include global media convergence of professional sport outlets, sport property ownership by media conglomerates, and global sport markets.

The continued growth and expansion of Internet and wireless services will dramatically change communication strategies employed in the sport industry. The possibilities for interactive consumption of the sport product will expand potential exposure of such goods. These possibilities will present exciting challenges to sport administrators and serve as a continuum for the importance of effective sport communication.

SUMMARY

- Effective communication in sport is one of the most important and pervasive qualities and competencies a sport manager can possess.
- Effective communication requires that sport managers (1) acknowledge the importance of effective communication and (2) demonstrate a willingness to invest the time and effort to improve them.
- The keys to effective communication include effectively planning the message; the integrity of the message, and the credibility of the content.
- Sport managers must consider the type of information being transferred in the message. Messages that contain complex information need to be carefully planned before being issued. Messages that contain information or words that may have emotional content should also be carefully reviewed before sending.
- Three major barriers to effective communication are Linguistic barriers, Psychological barriers, and Environmental barriers.
- The sport manager must appreciate and understand the flow of communication throughout the organization. In an effective communication network, information flows downward, upward, and laterally.
- The major media through which communication typically is transmitted includes Verbal mediums, Nonverbal mediums, and Mass Media mediums.
- Sport media is a broad term encompassing many aspects of how sport consumers receive information.
- Mass media communication includes newspapers, radio, television, and Internet mediums.
- Offices of sports information are important sources of information for the public and for the sport professional.
- The future relationship between sport and the media will continue to provide examples of synergies and opportunities for grander levels of importance and influence for sport organizations and sport media outlets.

Learning Activities

1. Daily, there are a number of media and sport related issues occurring in the sport industry. Using current examples, consider how the media influences sport and how sport organizations interact with the media, from both a proactive and reactive perspective.
2. It has been said that the relationship between media and sport is a necessary "synergy," meaning each needs the other to survive in today's marketplace. Discuss.

3. Interpersonal and nonverbal communication are all-important competencies central to the responsibilities and effectiveness of a sport manager and leader. Discuss how these characteristics are intertwined with the other important qualities of a contemporary sport leader.

4. From the chapter, it is noted that the developments in sport media have paralleled those of sport (as an industry and leisure activity). That being said, describe how future developments and expectations in the sport world will affect the delivery and needs of sport media to future sport consumers.

References

Anshell, M. (1997). *Sport psychology: From theory to practice* (3rd ed.). Menlo Park, CA: Benjamin/Cummings.

Associated Press. (2012, October 23). Number of active users at Facebook over the years. *Yahoo! Finance*. Retrieved from http://finance.yahoo.com/news/number-active-users-facebook-over-years-214600186--finance.html

Baran, S. (2014). Retrieved from http://www.museum.tv/eotv/sportsandte.htm

Blaszka, M., Burch, L. M., Frederick, E. L., Clavio, G., & Walsh, P. (2012). #World Series: An empirical examination of hashtag use during a major sporting event. *International Journal of Sport Communication, 5*, 435–453.

Broadhead, M. B. (2001). Feng Shui in the workplace. *Feng Shui Times*. Retrieved from http://www.FengShuiTimes.com

Clavio, G., & Walsh, P. (2013, March 4). Dimensions of social media utilization among college sport fans. *Communication and Sport*, DOI: 10.1177/2167479513480355.

Cosell, H. (1973). *Cosell*. New York, NY: Simon & Schuster.

Cosell, H., & Whitfield, S. (1991). *What's wrong with sports*. New York, NY: Simon & Schuster.

Cousens, L., Dickson, G., & O'Brien, D. (2004, June). *Beyond boundaries: A comparative investigation of change in the fields encompassing North American and Australian professional sport organizations*. Paper presented at the 2004 NASSM Conference, Atlanta, GA.

Emanuel, R., Adams, J., Baker, K., Daufin, E., Ellington, C., Fitts, E., & Okeowo, D. (2008). How college students spend their time communicating. *International Journal of Listening, 22*(1), 13–28.

Frederick, E. L., Lim, C., Clavio, G., Pedersen, P. M., & Burch, L. M. (2013). Choosing between the one-way or two-way street: An exploration of relationship promotion by professional athletes on Twitter. *Communication & Sport*, DOI: 10.1177/2167479512466387

Gallo, D. J. (2012). Jay Cutler inspires body language lesson. Retrieved from http://espn.go.com/blog/playbook/fandom/post/_/id/11380/jay-cutler-inspires-body-language-tips

Gantt, D. (2013). Cam Newton's offseason of self-awareness. Retrieved from http://profootballtalk.nbcsports.com/2013/06/29/cam-newtons-offseason-of-self-awareness/

Gorman, J., & Calhoun, K. (1994). *The Name of the Game*. New York, NY: John Wiley & Sons, Inc.

Hall, B. F. (2004, June). On measuring the power of communications. *Journal of Advertising Research, 44*, 181–187.

Hall, E. (1959). *The Silent Language*. Garden City, NY: Doubleday.

Helitzer, M. (1992). Taming the beast: Riding out a sports crisis. *Sport Marketing Quarterly, 1*(2), 33–42.

Key, M. R. (1975). *Paralanguage and Kinesics (Nonverbal Communication)*. Metuchen, NJ: The Scarecrow Press, Inc.

Koppett, L. (2003). *The Rise and Fall of the Press Box*. Toronto, ON: Sport Classic Books.

Mahony, D. F., & Moorman, A. M. (2000). The relationship between the attitudes of professional sport fans and their intentions to watch televised games. *Sport Marketing Quarterly, 9*(3), 131–139.

Martens, R. (1987). *Coaches Guide to Sport Psychology*. Champaign, IL: Human Kinetics.

Masteralexis, L. P., Barr, C. A., & Hums, M. A. (1998). *Principles and Practices of Sport Management*. Gaithersburg, MD: Aspen Publishers, Inc.

McCullough, M. (2013). Everyday Feng Shui: Success in 2013: Let your office work for you. Retrieved from: http://beniciaherald.me/2013/01/04/everyday-feng-shui-success-in-2013-let-your-office-work-for-you/

McDonough, P. (2007). Does DVR play-back

really hurt advertisers? TV ratings: the new math. Retrieved from http://www.nielsen.com/consumer_insight/issue1/ci_story1.html

Nichols, W., Moynahan, P., Hall, A., & Taylor, J. (2002). *Media Relations in Sport*. Morgantown, WV: Fitness Information Technology.

O'Keefe, C. (2013, April 30). Putting content on YouTube is a big step for MLB, but they still have a long ways to go. *SB Nation Lookout Landing*. Retrieved from http://www.lookoutlanding.com/2013/4/30/4286098/putting-content-on-youtube-is-a-big-step-for-mlb-but-they-still-have

Ozanian, M. (2012, September 27). The Big Ten Network's winning game plan. *Forbes.com*. Retrieved from http://www.forbes.com/sites/mikeozanian/2012/09/27/the-big-ten-networks-winning-game-plan/

Rabin, C. (2008). Florida Marlins stadium likely to clear final legal hurdle. Retrieved from http://www.miamiherald.com/sports/baseball/florida-marlins/story/697432.html

Robinson, R. (2013). How Santa Clara scored big in attracting the 49ers, Super Bowl L. Retrieved from http://www.sanjoseinside.com/news/entries/5_23_13_santa_clara_49ers_super_bowl_L/

Rosenberg, M. (2013). 49ers new Santa Clara stadium cost goes up again—to $1.3 billion. Retrieved from http://www.mercurynews.com/ci_23414780/49ers-new-stadium-cost-goes-up-again-1

Sandomir, R. (2012). Deal with Premier League gives NBC 380 games. *New York Times*. Retrieved from http://www.nytimes.com/2012/10/29/sports/soccer/premier-league-deal-gives-nbc-380-soccer-games.html

Sandomir, R. & Chozick, A. (2013, March 4). Seeing riches in sports TV, Fox will create new network. *New York Times*. Retrieved from http://www.nytimes.com/2013/03/05/sports/fox-planning-national-sports-network-it-hopes-can-challenge-espn.html?pagewanted=all&_r=0

Sarthe, S., Olson, R., & Whitney, C. (1973). *Let's talk*. Glenview, IL: Scott & Foreman.

Shields, M. (2012). Second-Screen sports options circumvent TV rights pacts. *AdWeek*. Retrieved from http://www.adweek.com/news/technology/second-screen-sports-options-circumventing-tv-rights-pacts-139468

Smith, G. J., & Blackman, C. (1977). *Sport in the mass media*. Ottawa, ON: Canadian Association for Health, Physical Education and Recreation, University of Calgary Press.

Sonderman, J. (2012, June 14). 600 newspaper layoffs in one day is, unfortunately, not a record. *Poynter*. Retrieved from http://www.poynter.org/latest-news/mediawire/177145/600-newspaper-layoffs-in-one-day-is-unfortunately-not-a-record/

Stoldt, C. G., Smetana, G. K., & Miller, L. (2000). Changes in the USA Today's sports coverage patterns during the National Basketball Association lockout: Implications for sport managers. *Sport Marketing Quarterly, 9*(3), 124–130.

Stotlar, D. K. (2000). Vertical integration in sport. *Journal of Sport Management, 14*(1), 1–7.

Turner, P. (1999). Television and internet convergence: Implications for sport broadcasting. *Sport Marketing Quarterly, 8*(2), 43–49.

Vasquez, D. (2008). Pondering the DVR Effect this season. Retrieved from: http://www.medialifemagazine.com/artman2/publish/Television_44/Pondering_the_DVR_effect_this_season.asp

What's a blog? (2008). Retrieved from http://www.blogger.com

4

Management and Leadership in the Sport Industry

Jeremy S. Jordan, Aubrey Kent, and Matt Walker

> "MANAGEMENT IS DOING THINGS RIGHT; LEADERSHIP IS DOING THE RIGHT THINGS."
>
> —*Peter Drucker*

INTRODUCTION

Management is defined as "a process of achieving organizational goals with and through other people within the constraints of limited resources" (Chelladurai, 2009, p. 99). Achieving goals is at the heart of why organizations are formed. Thus, management is critical to organizational success, whether through increased operational efficiency or by improving product and service quality. Leadership is likewise seen as a main driver of organizational success. Simply watching the NBC television show *The Apprentice* tells us that leadership skills are a highly attractive asset for potential employees.

In order for an organizational advantage to accrue, its resources must be valuable, rare, and difficult to imitate or substitute for (Barney, 1991). Some companies, nonetheless, conform or mimic the successful activities of others, enabling them to become strategically successful—especially in response to uncertainty (DiMaggio & Powell,

Learning Objectives

Upon completion of this chapter, the reader should be able to
- Explain the four functions of management;
- Differentiate between the three skills of management;
- Identify the different types of decisions made by managers and how they go through the process of making decisions;
- Discuss the 10 managerial roles and how they are related; and
- Compare and contrast leadership v. management.

In the Bleachers © 2013 Steve Moore. Dist. by Universal Uclick
www.gocomics.com/inthebleachers

"It's a text from our new left fielder. If you want him to hustle, he wants another two million bucks."

1983). Just as a company seeks to differentiate itself from its competition, developing leadership skills can make *you* a source of competitive advantage for an organization, since these skills can set you apart from others. Consequently, those with leadership aspirations can mimic the activities of successful leaders in order to become more proficient.

As the sport industry continues to grow, visionary leaders as well as competent managers will increasingly be in high demand. Leadership and management skills are always transferable, meaning you will be able to utilize them whether you work in marketing, event management, or any of the operational areas couched in the sport industry. In this chapter, we explore the core functions, skills, and roles of management, as well as offer a discussion of leadership from its theoretical foundations. The many facets of management are more easily understood if divided into the basic functions, skills, and roles that managers are expected to master.

FUNCTIONS OF MANAGEMENT

Managers can significantly impact the success of an organization. Research on this topic has identified (and confirmed) different management functions regardless of job context. These functions are classified as: (1) planning, (2) organizing, (3) directing, and (4) monitoring. Classification of managerial functions into these areas helps us understand what managers do and more importantly what to expect when you assume a managerial position in sport. However, because sport organizations are constantly evolving, these functions do not represent a comprehensive list of responsibilities, but rather a starting point for understanding the complexities of sport management. Furthermore, these functions are not always sequential and quite often managers must revert to a previous function to adhere to the required adjustments.

Planning

The planning function of management involves the establishment of goals for the organization and its members, as well as identifying the actions necessary to achieve those goals. Organizational goals tend to be general statements that help identify the direction of the sport organization. Because goals are broad in nature, they tend to be difficult to measure with an underlying level of subjectivity. For example, the Reading Phillies minor league baseball team might have the goal of increasing attendance at their home games. While this goal helps identify an important issue for team management, it does not identify what actions will be implemented in order to achieve the goal and what standards of measurement will be used for evaluation. Therefore, after an organization identifies selected goals, it is important to create measurable objectives that will lead to the successful achievement of established goals.

Attendance increase Objectives, by design, tend to be more specific than goals. They are also measurable so subsequent evaluation can take place. A specific objective for increasing attendance at home games could be to increase walk-up attendance (i.e., tickets sold on game day) by 10%. This objective is measurable and, if met, allows the team's management to meet, in part, the established goal of increasing attendance. However, what is not known is how the team's management will go about increasing walk-up attendance. When establishing organizational goals, it is important to work within organizational constraints. These constraints are limitations placed on the organization that influence the creation of goals and organizational activities. Constraints can come from within the organization (internal) or from the environment in which the organization operates (external). For example, a professional sport team that desires a new stadium within the next five years must consider internal and external constraints when beginning the planning process. Internal constraints could be related to the amount of funding available. If the team has not been able to generate the revenues needed to pay for the new stadium, they must seek assistance for the portion they are unable to cover. Therefore, the team could request that some of the costs associated with the new stadium be paid with public funds (i.e., property, sales, and/or hospitality taxes). The willingness of local and state government to allocate public funds for the new stadium represents an external constraint (i.e., given the difficulty of passing new tax legislation). If public funds have been used for stadiums in the past or for other sport teams in the area, there may be reluctance on the part of government officials to allocate the necessary funds for the stadium. Additionally, if the team has had limited success and by extension does not have a large local fan base, receiving public approval for the funding proposal may be difficult. Therefore, when executing the planning function, it is important to understand both the internal and external constraints placed on the organization. Failure to identify these constraints could result in the development of goals that are not likely to be achieved by the organization.

The planning function of management normally involves both long-term and short-term plans. Long-term plans (often called "strategic plans") involve goals and objectives to be achieved in the future. For example, an event management company may have a strategic plan of hosting a marathon in five years. This plan will have many components, but one major aspect will be to raise the needed funds through donations and sponsorships to pay for the event's logistics. The strategic plan may establish goals for securing permits, generating policies, identifying equipment needs, personnel needs, establishing committees, securing sponsors, securing volunteers, and general marketing and operational issues needed to plan the race. In contrast to strategic plans, short-term plans tend to involve goals that are more immediate in nature. In line with the previous example, event organizers may have a kick-off campaign to introduce the race plans with the objective of raising 5% of the estimated costs. Once the organization has established its goals, objectives, and specific action plans, the next function of management must be organizing.

Organizing

The organizing function of management involves the identification of tasks that must be completed in order to achieve the goals identified in the planning process. In addition, the delegation of these tasks to different work groups or employees is equally as important. In other words, management must decide what things need to be done and who will be responsible for them. Not only does this process involve creating individual responsibilities but it also entails grouping related tasks together for efficiency. Often this type of grouping job positions involves the creation of departments that are responsible for certain tasks and responsibilities. A professional sport organization may create a ticket department that is responsible for selling season tickets, mini-packs, and single-game tickets. Achievement of each task may require a slightly different action plan; however, linking them together in one department will allow individuals trained in ticket sales to work on each of the three assigned tasks. The manager's job is then to decide which employees are best qualified for certain tasks and who will be responsible for making sure these tasks are accomplished. This point identifies another aspect of organizing, which is the development of an organizational chart. As mentioned, part of organizing is grouping job responsibilities and assigning these tasks to individuals. This process is represented in graph form by developing a chart, which identifies different departments in the organization and how these departments are linked. An additional aspect of organizational charts is the identification of management personnel who are responsible for the different departments. For example, figure one identifies the organizational structure of intercollegiate athletic marketing department.

Organizational charts should be developed for each individual department as well as the organization as a whole. According to Bridges and Roquemore (2004, p. 201), organizational charts should demonstrate the following:

1. Positions of responsibility (who is in charge of what)
2. Lines of authority (who has the power to do what)
3. Manager-employee relationships (levels of management)
4. Formal communication channels (who reports to whom)
5. Lines of responsibility (who is accountable for specific tasks)
6. Grouping of related work activities

Directing

Once managers have completed the planning process and assigned work tasks, they must motivate and direct employees to achieve the established goals. A successful man-

Figure 4.1. (UM Organizational Chart)

UNIVERSITY OF MIAMI INTERCOLLEGIATE ATHLETICS

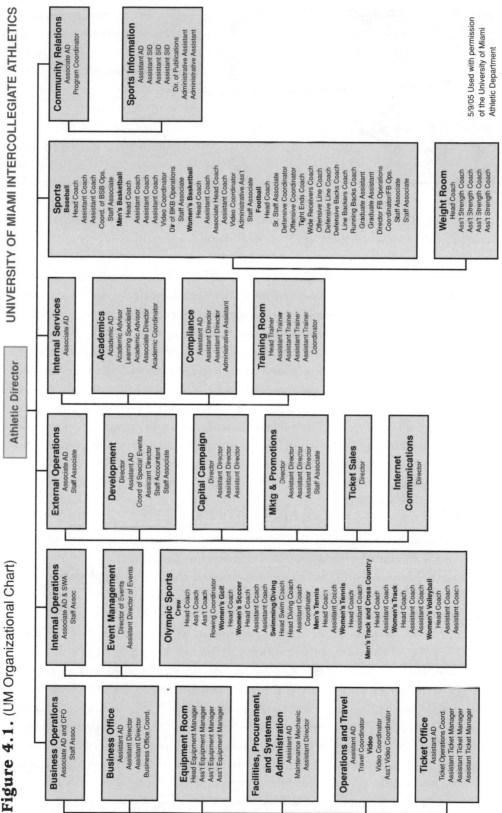

5/9/05 Used with permission of the University of Miami Athletic Department

Photo courtesy © Andy Gillentine

ager will direct employees to put forth their best efforts when implementing action plans. The directing function of management tends to be one of the most difficult to fulfill because it involves direct interaction between management and employees. Each employee is likely to respond to managerial direction and motivation efforts differently. This means that a manager cannot use a 'best-practice' approach to all situations, nor when dealing with all employees. Therefore, successful managers should be able to adapt their style to fit the requirements of a particular situation. Two main elements of the directing function are facilitating task accomplishment for employees and providing motivation for them to perform those tasks to the best of their ability.

In the majority of situations, the responsibility of management is to delegate appropriate tasks to employees and make certain the assigned tasks are completed efficiently. This means that a manager must provide assistance to accomplish a task, or evaluate the progress of an employee to make sure the task will be completed in the allotted time. Simply put, the role of management is to provide employees with the resources, skills, and assistance necessary to complete assigned tasks. When managers provide these supporting elements to employees, it leads to increased employee productivity and job satisfaction as employees are less likely to encounter "roadblocks" at work, which can lead to frustration (House, 1971). Therefore, in order for managers to successfully direct employees, they must understand the work that is needed and be able to facilitate the process by which it is completed.

MOTIVATION

The second aspect of directing involves motivating employees to put forth maximum effort in the workplace. Being an effective motivator includes the ability to identify employee needs and desires, and to provide processes that enable employees to achieve their goals. While this is sometimes a complicated process, successful managers will understand that effective motivation requires an appropriate balance of tangible, intangible, intrinsic, extrinsic, monetary, and non-monetary rewards. Essentially, different people will be motivated by different things in the workplace. For example, a group ticket sales representative for the Washington Wizards may be motivated by the possibility of receiving a $4,000 bonus if she meets her sales targets for the season. In contrast, a collegiate marketing director may be motivated by the satisfaction he receives from selling out every home basketball game of the season through various promotions. In another setting, a marketing intern for Under Armour may be motivated because she was recognized as "employee of the month" in her department. The previous examples illustrate how employees are differently motivated, underscoring the need for managers to accurately discern employee needs and match their motivational strategies.

Monitoring

The final managerial function is monitoring. This function involves the evaluation of employees, workgroups, or the organization as a whole on the progress made towards achieving established goals and objectives. The performance of employees and workgroups must be periodically monitored to determine if changes are warranted or if current performance levels are appropriate. The control outlined in this process establishes a set of "checks and balances" for the organization but should not be viewed as a replacement for sound planning and organizing. The aforementioned monitoring process involves three critical steps:

1. Developing standards that will be used to evaluate performance.
2. Conducting the evaluation by comparing actual performance to the desired performance identified by the standards.
3. Taking appropriate action to correct a situation when the desired standard of performance is not being met.

syllabus days Developing performance standards generally takes place before employees begin working on an assigned task. For example, in any Sport Management course, the instructor will likely spend part of the first day explaining how your performance in class will be evaluated. If this was to occur at the end of the semester it would be impossible for you to make the necessary adjustments to improve your grade. The standards of evaluation must be clearly identified, explained, and should be easily measured in addition to being directly related to the established objectives and goals associated with each task.

The next step in the monitoring process is evaluating the performance of the organization, workgroup, or employees against previously established standards. Important considerations here are: who will conduct the evaluation, how the evaluation process will occur, and when it will take place. Persons selected to conduct the evaluation should have knowledge of the task being performed and have the authority to make the necessary changes if performance does not match a particular standard. It is likely that the evaluation will involve both quantitative and qualitative measures, with the primary mode of evaluation being a quantitative assessment. Quantitative measures involve evaluations of performance based on some type of easily measurable component. For example, if the managers of Wilson Sporting Goods had an objective to sell more youth baseball

Table 4.1. Factors Affecting Employee Performance
• Deficiencies in employee performance due to effort or motivation to perform the tasks
• Employee not having the necessary technical skills to successfully complete the task
• The performance standard is unrealistic and must be adjusted
• The employee, workgroup, or organization does not have the resources required to complete the task
• Poor planning or organizing
• Unclear task assignment

gloves then the previous year, the evaluation process would involve comparing the previous year's sales with the current year. This evaluation involves the comparison of quantifiable outcomes (e.g., number sold). Qualitative measures of work performance involve evaluations that are more difficult to assess accurately and objectively. For instance, employees might be evaluated on their contributions to group projects, attitude at work, or other behaviors that contribute to overall work performance. Additionally, qualitative work evaluations normally involve discussions with employees to determine their feelings about the work experience and the tasks they have been assigned.

MANAGERIAL SKILLS

Just as an employee develops skills necessary to complete assigned tasks, managers must work on developing their skills in the workplace. Also, managers will have to use these skills at different times, and, in certain situations, a combination of the skills. This point reinforces that being a manager can be very difficult due to the complexities of the work environment. We explore the skills of management by dividing them into three different categories: (1) technical skills, (2) human skills, and (3) conceptual skills. Like any other activity that requires a certain level of proficiency, managers must work at becoming better at each of the skills outlined and seek opportunities to practice and refine them.

Technical skills involve knowledge of operations, activities, and processes necessary to accomplish organizational goals and objectives. You can think of technical skills as the "know how" in terms of what tasks employees are assigned. For example, an advertiser who designs logos and promotions for professional sport teams must have thorough knowledge of the graphics software used to create eye-catching stadium signage and other ancillary media items. In addition to understanding the technical aspects of a task, managers must be able to educate and supervise employees on the task and be able to handle any difficulties that prevent employees from completing assigned responsibilities.

A second skill critical to being an effective manager is the ability to work with and supervise a variety of different employees. Thus, the **human skill** of management involves aspects of leading, communicating, motivating, and generally dealing with all aspects of employee relations. The difficult element of this skill is that each employee will be unique and respond to managerial influence in varying ways. This means that a manager must understand what strategies to use when communicating, motivating, and supervising various employees in their work group.

A final skill required of managers is the ability to conceptualize how the different parts of the organization fit together so that established goals and objectives can be achieved. The managerial term "synergy" describes this **conceptual skill**, in that a manager must be able to understand how the different departments of the organization are linked. Often you will hear someone say it is important to understand the "big picture"

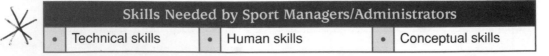

Skills Needed by Sport Managers/Administrators		
• Technical skills	• Human skills	• Conceptual skills

when establishing a plan of action or organizing employees into work groups. This big picture approach requires the manager to abstractly imagine how things would best work together so that the organization can be efficient in its use of resources and effective in achieving its goals.

One particular management skill that requires a mastery of all of the above-described categories is **decision-making**. There is the distinct possibility that as you read this chapter you have already had to make a number of decisions today. These decisions could range from very simple, such as what to eat for breakfast, to difficult decisions such as choosing a career path. When making a decision, whether simple or difficult, you must gather and evaluate necessary information so your decision can be informed and based on relevant facts.

Decision-making is a **primary skill** a manager will have to utilize when fulfilling the functions of management and executing the different skills necessary to direct employees towards the achievement of established goals and objectives. In fact, the ability to make correct decisions when confronted with organizational opportunities or challenges is one of the main factors that distinguishes good managers from bad.

When making decisions, managers will be confronted with issues that are potential problems for the organization, as well as issues that represent opportunities for growth and advancement. Chelladurai (2009, p. 157) defined a problem as "a situation that reduces or could reduce the effectiveness of the organization, or a situation that disrupts operations." For instance, an athletic director could be confronted with a problem if severe weather forces the cancellation of a home football game, creating the need to reschedule the game at a later time. Solving this problem involves not only rescheduling the game with the other school, but making sure that all groups involved (i.e., media, concessions, transportation, security, EMT's) can be present on the new date. While a problem has the potential to disrupt the operations of an organization, opportunities represent issues or situations that could benefit the organization in terms of profitability, improved production or services, and growth (Chelladurai, 2009).

Decisions managers have to make can also be simplistically classified as routine or complex. A routine decision is one that could involve clear decision criteria, be repetitive in nature, and involve the application of established rules or policies. An example of a routine decision would be purchasing the same model of baseball cleats each time they wear out. Due to your familiarity with the product, the processes of information search, evaluation, and post-purchase behavior are not likely to be engaged. In contrast, complex decisions are those that have more complicated decision criteria, can be difficult to clearly define, and often involve no set policies that can be used in the decision-making process. For example, the Indianapolis Colts were awarded the first selection in the 2012 NFL draft. The decision of which player to select first was one that did not involve a set policy and to some degree was difficult to clearly define. The choice to select Andrew Luck with the first pick was a subjective decision by the Colts, and one that will not be determined as correct until after the team is fully able to evaluate Luck's performance. There are no set rules or policies (other than the needs of the team) that dictate which player should be selected, and often teams may not use the same decision

Table 4.2. Problem Solving Methodology	
1.	Define and clarify the problem or opportunity.
2.	Identify the decision objectives.
3.	List, categorize, and analyze all relevant information related to the decision.
4.	Identify any issues that may present "roadblocks" to arriving at the correct decision.
5.	Generate possible alternatives that solve the problem or capitalize on an opportunity.
6.	Select the best two or three alternatives for consideration.
7.	Make your decision by selecting the best alternative.
8.	Implement the decision by activating policy or rule changes and necessary action steps.
9.	Evaluate the effectiveness of the final decision after it has been implemented.

criteria as the previous year because there are different players available in the draft. Whether confronted with a complex or simple decision, managers will often use a systematic decision-making approach to gather and analyze information. This process helps ensure that all relevant facts and information related to the decision will be considered, which increases the likelihood that the best decision will be made. While there are a number of different systematic decision-making models that can be utilized by managers, Railey and Tschauner (1993) suggested a basic process that can be implemented by managers in a variety of settings.

In addition to using a systematic process when making decisions, managers must also understand the ramifications of their decisions. Managers use their conceptual skills to determine the immediate and long-term effects of a decision. Furthermore, managers must consider how different groups or individuals will respond to decisions that are made. Decision-making also involves the inclusion of employees in the process. Chalip (2001) suggested that employees may provide assistance to management personnel in areas such as planning, generating ideas, problem solving, developing organizational policies/procedures, and governance. The benefits of including others in the decision-making process include the following: (a) the ability to gather and analyze a larger quantity of information relevant to the decision that must be made; (b) increased likelihood of members having more comprehensive understanding of the problem/opportunity being considered; (c) improved member support of the final decision because they have been allowed to contribute in the decision-making process; and (d) less difficulty implementing the decision due to the fact that members have increased understanding and are supportive of the decision.

Despite these benefits, there are potential difficulties that also must be considered by managers when evaluating whether to include others in the decision-making process. One difficulty is that group decision-making tends to take a longer period of time compared to the manager making the decision alone. A second challenge is that group members may possess limited job experience, which hinders their ability to assist in the decision-making process, particularly concerning complex decisions that require skills that take time to develop and refine. Finally, employees may not have access to information that is required when making a decision (e.g., employee personnel files or company financial statements). In light of these benefits and challenges, a manager must be able to determine under what circumstances it would be best to include others in the decision-making process and when it would be best to make the decision alone. In order to accomplish this task, managers can turn to the following three questions about a particular decision.

1. How important is the quality of the decision?
2. How much do others within the organization have to support and commit to the decision?
3. What is the timeframe for making a final decision? (Chalip, 2001)

As the quality required for a decision increases, so do the benefits associated with including others in the process. Remember, including employees in the decision-making process increases the amount of information that is accumulated and also increases the quality of possible solutions. If the execution of a particular decision is going to require support from employees, it may be advantageous to allow group members to provide input, thereby increasing the amount of ownership they have in the final decision. Finally, the amount of time available to make a decision will influence whether others can be included in the process or not.

A final consideration when discussing the appropriate decision style to use is the determination of which employees should be included in the decision-making process. Chalip (2001) suggested that employees should be included in this process (a) when they have information that is relevant to the issues being considered and (b) when the final decision will directly affect them or will require their support when being implemented. Also, decisions that are more complex or risky require individuals with diverse viewpoints and opinions, potentially improving the quality of the solutions and alternatives provided to the manager. This increases the possibility of analyzing a decision from different perspectives and the creation of alternatives that are unique or represent a new approach to solving problems or taking advantage of an opportunity.

MANAGERIAL ROLES

In addition to understanding the different functions of management and having the ability to implement the skills necessary to achieve organizational goals, managers must often fulfill particular roles within the organization. Mintzberg (1975, p. 54) defined a managerial role as "an organized set of behaviors identified with a position" and established that in most organizations a manager will occupy one of ten different roles at any particular time. These roles can be grouped into three different categories: (1) interpersonal, (2) informational, and (3) decisional.

Interpersonal Roles

A manager's formal position in an organization requires them to interact with employees. As such, the **figurehead** role involves the manager fulfilling certain ceremonial functions. For example, an athletic director can fulfill this role by presenting an award to a team or an individual student-athlete. In this situation, the athletic director is not only representing the athletic department but the university in recognizing the accomplishments of teams or individuals. The second role involves the manager being a **leader** to subordinates. This role may require the manager to hire, train, supervise, motivate, and evaluate employees in the workplace. When discussing the leader role, Mintzberg (1975, p. 55) stated that "the influence of managers is most clearly seen in the leader role" and that, by their position, managers have significant power in this regard. However, their ability to use this power is largely dependent upon their capability to lead. The **liaison** role refers to the manager's ability to develop and cultivate relationships with individuals and groups in other departments or from different organizations. For instance, when Jeffrey Loria, the owner of the Miami Marlins, sought funding for the franchise's new stadium, he had to work with officials representing Major League Baseball, Miami-Dade County, and the state of Florida. In this situation, the team owner is the connection (or liaison) between the sport franchise and the league, city, and state officials. The type and quality of relationships that managers develop when fulfilling this role can have an impact on departmental or organizational success.

Informational Roles

Managers have access to many different sources of information based on the position they occupy and the number of interpersonal contacts in the workplace. After gathering information, managers must then process what was learned and distribute relevant pieces of information to different groups within the organization. Therefore, the manager can be viewed as an information center who executes the roles of monitor, disseminator, and spokesperson. As **monitor**, the manager must search the internal and external environment for information that could influence the organization. While in this role, the manager seeks information from liaisons, subordinates, superiors, different media sources, and the network of contacts that a manager develops over time. As **disseminator**, the manager screens information and passes it along to employees. Furthermore, a manager acts as a bridge between employees who exchange information but are unable to access one another. Finally, as **spokesperson**, the manager communicates information to groups that are outside the organization. For example, in attempts to be the host nation for an upcoming World Cup, the national governing body for soccer, government, tourism board, and other management and legislative personnel from given cities will have to present their bid to the Fédération Internationale de Football Association (FIFA) detailing the benefits and challenges of having such a mega-event in their nation.

Decisional Roles

Decision-making is a primary skill of management that is used in many of the situations with which a manager will be confronted. Fulfillment of the aforementioned informational roles allows the manager to access the information necessary to make informed decisions. Therefore, the interpersonal and informational roles that a manager occupies combined with his or her formal position in the organization places the manager in four decisional roles: (1) entrepreneur, (2) disturbance handler, (3) resource allocator, and (4) negotiator.

Entrepreneurial managers look for ways to improve their work group, adapt to internal and external changes, and direct the organization towards opportunities that stimulate growth. This means that managers should always be cognizant of new ways to use organizational resources. For example, the concessions manager of a professional stadium who streamlines the inventory and ordering process so he will be better able to track product sales would be fulfilling the managerial role of entrepreneur.

In the role of **disturbance handler**, managers are responsible for reacting to changes affecting the organization that are unexpected and beyond immediate managerial control. These are situations that could cause significant hardships for the organization if not dealt with. In 2011, management personnel for the National Football League (NFL) and the NFL players' association had to deal with major changes due to the labor dispute between the league and its players. Managers on both sides functioned as disturbance handlers by reacting to the lockout, which could have pejoratively impacted future NFL operations.

When managers distribute organizational resources to different employees or work groups, they are acting as **resource allocators**. Most organizations have a limited number of resources available and allocating the appropriate amount of resources becomes a very important task. Some professional sport leagues have limits on how much salary money teams can pay to players. The presence of salary caps means management personnel must decide what salary will be paid to each player while making sure to stay within the guidelines of the salary cap restrictions.

The final decisional role identified by Mintzberg (1975) is **negotiator**. In this role, managers are responsible for conferring with employees and work groups located within the organization, as well as those that are on the outside. In order to accomplish organizational goals and objectives, management must often negotiate with other groups with regard to resources or other factors that influence the operations of the organization. Returning to our NFL example, representatives from the league and players' association negotiated the terms of a new collective bargaining agreement, resulting the lockout ending.

MANAGEMENT VS. LEADERSHIP

A long-standing debate is whether or not there is a difference between a manager and a leader. While there are fairly strong points to be made on both sides, the consensus of management scholars seems to be forming around the idea that yes, there is a difference. That being said, what is the difference? One way to view the difference between management and leadership is to look at their core responsibilities. Managers must have technical skills as well as some human skills. Leaders must have a command of all three skill sets and in order to be truly successful, must have a mastery of human and conceptual skills.

For some, the manager is the individual in charge of daily activities in the workplace. This person is their immediate supervisor, and the person to whom they must be most attentive. For these same individuals, the person they identify as the leader might be someone they have never met. For example, an individual working in an entry-level district sales position for Nike might never meet the company CEO Phil Knight. So the question becomes, how can Phil Knight lead someone whom he has never met? Well, that brings us to the core of the definition between managers and leaders, and also reminds us of the discussion about organization that we had earlier. Phil Knight is primarily responsible for establishing the overall vision, mission, and organizational culture at Nike. While people in management positions have much more direct contact with employees, they are functioning within the environment created and maintained by the leadership.

At this point, it is important to note that, while different, there should not be a value judgment placed on the management vs. leadership debate. While describing differences between the two, it might be easy to get the impression that leadership attributes are somehow superior and more desirable than management ones, which is simply not the case. They both have an important role to play in an organizations' success, and one cannot prosper in any business without the other. Additionally, one person can display elements of one or the other at any given time, as they are not mutually exclusive concepts. In this vein, it is more useful to view management and leadership as distinct *processes*, but *not* as different types of people.

Leadership

Leadership is a phenomenon that has been present and of interest to society for almost as long as civilization has existed. A profound curiosity with leadership has led to a vast amount of research in the social science literature. In fact, many might say that the history of the world is traced through the history of great leaders. From Moses to Mohammed, to Joan of Arc to Napoleon, to Winston Churchill to Ghandi, to Nelson Mandela to Martin Luther King, we record our history through the chronicling of great leaders. Sport management researchers have likewise been enamored with the concept of leadership, whether it concerns how coaches deal with their athletes, how athletic directors motivate their employees, or how people create successful sport companies.

As much as leadership has been studied, what it is and how it works has yet to clearly materialize. Within the academic community, a clear definition of leadership has remained elusive, and it has been noted that "there are almost as many definitions of leadership as there are persons who have attempted to define the concept" (Stogdill, 1974, p. 259). However, "most definitions of leadership reflect the assumption that it involves a process whereby intentional influence is exerted by one person over other people to guide, structure, and facilitate activities and relationships in a group or organization" (Yukl, 1998, p. 3). This general definition would be our preferred definition of leadership, because it contains the three elements we deem critical for leadership. Leadership is **complex**, **relational**, and involves **induction** (i.e., if your followers would have reached the same destination in your absence, you have not truly led).

Evolution of Leadership Theory

Research in the area of leadership has been extensive, comprised of different themes that have evolved over time. As a result, the definitions of leadership have changed to reflect these themes. Leadership literature has largely focused on theoretical issues that have developed from early trait theories, to behavioral theories, to more recent situational and contingency theories, and to the contemporary conceptualizations known as visionary, charismatic or transformational leadership (i.e., "the new leadership"). Also included in this evolution are specific applications of leadership theory appropriate for certain industrial contexts, among them the Multi-Dimensional Leadership model, designed specifically for use in the sport domain.

Some of the earliest systematic attempts to conceptualize leadership were known as the **trait theories**. This approach focused on the characteristics, or attributes, that distinguished leaders from non-leaders, which include physical characteristics (e.g., height and appearance), personality traits (e.g., arrogance and self-esteem), and general ability traits (e.g., intelligence, insight, and energy). Hundreds of trait studies were conducted in the early and mid-1900s, but it was ultimately realized that this line of research was not going to yield a consistent relationship with leadership effectiveness. It did, however, become clear that while particular traits were not predictors of leadership success, certain characteristics would (in some situations) increase the likelihood of a leader emerging. In general, effective leaders appear to be more likely to have traits such as self-confidence, high energy, stress tolerance, integrity, and maturity than will unsuccessful or non-leaders (Yukl, 1998).

As the limitations of the trait theories became evident, many researchers shifted the focus of their studies towards specific behaviors exhibited by leaders. The **behavioral approach** emphasized what leaders and managers actually did on the job, as opposed to their personal characteristics. The behavior leadership theorists focused not only on what leaders would do, but also on how often and at what intensity they would perform certain things to distinguish themselves as leaders. The perceptions of followers to this leader behavior would then, in turn, influence them to act in the manner that they saw fit.

Descriptive research into the leaders' decision-making, monitoring practices, and motivating and problem solving processes would be characteristic of the behaviorist approach (Yukl & Van Fleet, 1992). The major contribution of the behavioral line of research came from the Ohio State University in the 1950s, which classified leader behaviors into two independent categories: (1) task-oriented behaviors (i.e., initiating structure) and (2) people-oriented behaviors (i.e., consideration). From these classifications, certain leader behaviors came to be associated with prescribed follower and organizational outcomes. However, the reliability of such associations was suspect. After a point it became clear that these broadly defined categories were too abstract to provide the basis for understanding the true complexity of leadership and the role requirements of leaders. As Yukl and Van Fleet (1992, p. 160) stated, "As we found in the trait research, the behavior research suffers from a tendency to look for simple answers to complex questions." As such, the behaviorist view of leadership spurred the emergence of the consideration of time and circumstance alongside leadership traits and behaviors. The results of this development in leadership thinking came to be more commonly known as the *situational leadership theories.*

The **situational approach** attempted to build upon the foundation that was laid by the study of traits and behaviors. Situational leadership studies (also referred to as "contingency theories") resulted in an understanding that traits and behaviors would only be successful to the degree to which any particular situation allowed. Intervening, or moderating, factors were now being brought into the picture by researchers when assessing the overall impact, or appropriateness, of leader behavior. Among the theories that gained recognition in this era were Fiedler's Contingency Model (1967), House's Path-Goal Theory (1971), and Hersey and Blanchard's Situational Leadership Theory (1977).

These models and theories focused on how different moderating variables could affect the outcomes of certain leader behaviors. While these theories provided some deeper insight into the nature of leadership and its effectiveness, many of them were too generally stated and were not empirically testable (Yukl, 1998). As with the behavioral theories, the **contingency approaches** also tended to oversimplify the process of leading by focusing on the "one best way" to behave in certain situations. This lack of flexibility ultimately revealed that these theories had very little utility for improving the effectiveness of practicing managers. Despite their shortcomings, the contingency theories do make a positive contribution for improving the effectiveness of managers in a general sense.

Contemporary Theories

Over the past two decades, leadership researchers have developed a broader perspective of the leader-follower relationship because they examined changes in the followers that resulted from leader influence. This approach led to the **contemporary theories** of leadership that characterized the leader as charismatic, inspirational, visionary, and/or transformational. Bryman (1992) collectively termed these contemporary approaches "the new leadership" paradigm. Visionary leadership researchers focused on the effectiveness of leaders who were able to extrapolate future goals and successes from the mundane day-to-day activities that consume a leader's time and energy. These leaders are purported to make this a shared vision with others in the group or organization through the leader's heightened communication skills (Bennis & Nanus, 2003).

Charismatic Leadership

Charismatic leadership theorists focused on leaders from the perspective that they were perceived to have certain exceptional qualities, which allowed for greater influence over followers in particular situations. German sociologist Max Weber, often cited as the ultimate authority on charisma, saw charismatic leadership as a combination of certain magical qualities a person possesses that are inaccessible to other, non-charismatic people (Weber, 1997). It is these unique qualities and attributes that compel followers to devote themselves to the leader. House (1977) was also a major contributor in this area, suggesting that the characteristics of a leader that make up charisma consist of high-levels of self-confidence and a need to influence others, coupled with a dominant personality and a strong conviction in their beliefs. Charismatic leaders have been described as role models for their followers, who build their image so as to create an impression of success and competence.

Transformational Leadership

Charisma is an important component in transformational leadership, but is not the only important element. Bass (1985, p. 31) defined charisma as "a necessary ingredient of transformational leadership, but by itself is not sufficient to account for the transformational process." Combining charismatic and visionary qualities with the ability to persuasively communicate that vision to followers constitutes a major component of transformational leadership. Transformational leadership theory focuses on the leader-follower relationship and examines how this relationship can be beneficial to both parties—to the group and to the organization as a whole (Bass, 1990; Bass & Avolio, 1994). This theory has two parts: (1) transformational leadership and (2) transactional leadership.

Transformational leaders are those people who "seek to raise the consciousness of followers by appealing to higher ideals and moral values such as liberty, justice, equality, peace, and humanitarianism, not to baser emotions such as fear, greed, jealousy, or hatred" (Yukl, 1989, p.210). These leaders heighten follower expectations and instill in them a greater desire to put forth the effort needed to achieve. Transformational leaders are able to make the followers feel like part of the changing environment through support, which instills higher self-esteem and a willingness to change, put aside self-interest, and commit themselves to the leader's vision (Bass & Avolio, 1994).

As described by Bass and Avolio (1994), transformational leadership theory has four major components labeled "the Four I's": (1) Idealized influence; (2) Inspirational motivation; (3) Intellectual stimulation; and (4) Individualized consideration.

Idealized influence refers to the position of the role model that the transformational leader assumes in the eyes of followers. This characteristic closely mirrors the term charisma used by other leadership theorists. This leader will be highly respected, admired, and trusted as a result of demonstrating high moral standards and ethical conduct. The leader will put the followers' feelings and needs above his/her own, which will lead to a heightened sense of commitment and a desire to emulate the leader and be leaders themselves.

Inspirational motivation refers those leaders who inspire and motivate those around them. This component of transformational leadership involves the leader's ability to communicate clearly with followers and to demonstrate the commitment and ability to solve problems and achieve goals. These leaders strive to continually offer positive words of encouragement to provide self-confidence and self-esteem needed to empower, motivate, and inspire their employees.

Intellectual stimulation resides in the leader's ability to challenge followers' creativity and innovativeness. Followers are encouraged to try new ideas and to question traditional techniques, assumptions, and problem-solving methods. The intellectually stimulating leader also provides followers with the means to follow through on their initiatives. Through this process, followers are enabled to formulate their own methods of problem solving, which encourages them to take on positions of leadership in future situations.

Individualized consideration refers to the role of coach, or mentor, that the transformational leader assumes. The leader stimulates followers to achieve higher levels of potential by creating new learning opportunities, increasing responsibility, and recognizing individual differences. The individually considerate leader is an effective listener who keeps open constant and effective lines of communication, and attempts to be physically accessible to all followers.

The other element of transformational leadership theory is called *Transactional Leadership*. Transactional leaders motivate people by appealing to their self-interests, and by developing a relationship with their followers based on an exchange of effort for reward. This reciprocal relationship can exist comfortably, but the transactional leader would more aptly be classified as a manager, rather than a leader. It is important to note that transactional and transformational leadership are not mutually exclusive concepts. Leaders can display varying degrees of either behavior, depending on the situation. However, those leaders who consistently display more transformational behaviors have been shown to be considerably more effective than those leaders who are consistently transactional (Bass & Avolio, 1994).

Multidimensional Model of Leadership (MML)

Chelladurai (1978; 1993) attempted to synthesize the earlier approaches to the study of leadership by developing the Multidimensional Model of Leadership. This model of leadership incorporates the leader, follower, and situational context dimensions of leadership. According to the MML, situational characteristics (e.g., group size, structure, tasks, and goals, as well as technology, social norms and expectations), leader characteristics (e.g., personality, ability, experience), and member characteristics (e.g., demographics, attitudes, ability) are precursors of leader behavior.

Table 4.3. *Yukl's (1998) Guidelines for Transformational Leadership*
• Articulate a clear and appealing vision and explain how the vision can be attained
• Act confident and optimistic and express that confidence in followers
• Provide opportunities for early success and celebrate these successes
• Use dramatic, symbolic actions to emphasize key values
• Lead by example
• Empower people to achieve the vision

Leader behavior is further classified as being that which is required, preferred, or actual. Required leader behavior takes into account situational constraints on behavior (e.g., organizational goals, structure, technology, group task, social norms, external regulations, nature of the group). Preferred leader behavior incorporates the type of behavior that followers would like to see in their leader, while actual leadership behavior describes how a leader behaves in a given situation. It is the congruence of these three factors that, in large part, determines the levels of performance and satisfaction that are consequences of leadership in the MML. More recently, elements of transformational leadership theory have been included in the MML to reflect the assertion that these types of leaders will be able to significantly influence the environment within which they function. That is, they will be able to alter the situational and member characteristics in such a fashion that they can essentially create the facilitating conditions needed for them and their organizations to succeed (Chelladurai, 2009).

CAN YOU BE A GREAT LEADER?

Until now, we have focused a lot on *what leadership is*, but not on *what leaders do*. It is the actions of leaders that will lead followers to form an opinion of that person, for better or worse. There are three main criteria that people use when evaluating your quality as a leader. They will take note of (1) your use of power and influence, (2) how you communicate, and (3) how you make decisions. The decision-making options that a leader has at his or her disposal were detailed earlier in the "management skills" section, but now we would like to discuss the other two criteria.

Sources of Power and Influence

Simplistically stated, leadership is one's influence over followers. This influential process permeates organizations and mastering it is a key to being an effective leader. As Yukl (1998, p. 175) noted, "To understand what makes managers effective requires an analysis of the complex web of power relationships and influence processes found in all organizations." Further, it is the use of power in relationships that will contribute to the perception of a leadership style. Managerial power can be defined as a person's potential

capacity to influence the contextual elements of an organization, as well as the attitudes and behaviors of others.

French and Raven (1959) identified five primary sources of power for leaders in organizations that were labeled *reward power* (ability to reward), *coercive power* (ability to punish), *legitimate power* (authority to make requests), *expert power* (special knowledge), and *referent power* (charisma). Another source of power in organizations is derived from the political processes that are inherent within them. These political processes are, in fact, merely mechanisms by which individuals can increase their power within an organization. As outlined by Pfeffer (1981), *political power* refers to processes such as forming coalitions, keeping control over key decisions, co-optation (i.e., undermining expected opposition), and institutionalization (i.e., filtering information to artificially inflate ones importance). Leadership success "depends greatly on the manner in which power is exercised. Effective leaders use power in a subtle, careful fashion that minimizes status differentials and avoids threats to self-esteem. In contrast, leaders who exercise power in an arrogant, manipulative, or domineering manner are likely to engender resentment and resistance" (Yukl, 1998, p. 202).

Communication Styles

Most management and leadership experts and researchers assert that communication is the foundation for effectiveness (Church, 1994). Moreover, organizational communication is underscored by the importance of several other concepts such as understanding, interpersonal warmth, trust, and openness. This makes sense when you consider that the word "organization" implies a coordinated effort by a group of people, and that communication is critical for coordination. Without effective communication, people in the organization would not know what to do or what others were doing. The vast majority of a leader's time is spent communicating with others, whether it is speaking or listening to others, emailing, text messaging, writing personal notes, or reading material transmitted from others. However, to be a good leader you must understand that how you communicate sends messages equally as strong as what you communicate. It therefore stands to reason that employees must also be satisfied not only with the leader's communication but also with the more general communication lines that exist within the organization. As a leader, the established communication patterns will be important in crafting a leadership image.

SUMMARY

- As the sport industry continues to grow and become more complex, the need for effective managers and leaders has increased. Critical to the success of sport organizations are individuals that can direct employees towards the accomplishment of established goals and objectives.
- The many facets of management are more easily understood if separated into the basic functions, skills, and roles that managers are expected to master. The functions of management include: (a) planning (establishment of goals and objec-

tives); (b) organizing (delegation of tasks); (c) directing (leading and motivating); and (d) monitoring (evaluating performance).

- The skills needed to be an effective manager can be separated into three categories: (a) technical (knowledge of operations); (b) human (interpersonal skills); and (c) conceptual skills ("big picture"). A manager will often use a combination of these functions and skills when fulfilling the ten managerial roles identified by Mintzberg.

- Decision-making is a primary skill that managers will have to utilize when fulfilling the functions of management and executing the different skills necessary to direct employees towards the achievement of organizational goals and objectives.

- Decision-making is a complex activity that involves dealing with problems and opportunities; decisions that are routine or complex; and whether to include others in the decision-making process or make the decision in an autocratic manner.

- One issue that arises in most management courses is the difference between being a manager and being a leader. Managers tend to focus more on technical and human skills while leaders must have competency in all three skills. Furthermore, leaders may be required to deal with more "big picture" issues that affect the organization.

- Successful organizations must have people that are effective managers and leaders, and at times these roles are occupied by the same person. Therefore, it is helpful to consider management and leadership as distinct processes but not as different types of people.

- Study of leadership has evolved from initial examination of leader characteristics to the "new leadership paradigm" that examines the changes in follower attitudes and behaviors that result from the influence of the leader.

- Leadership theory can be separated into (a) trait approach (focus on leader characteristics/attributes); (b) behavioral approach (emphasis on leader actions/behaviors); (c) situational approach (relationship between leader, member, and the situation); and contemporary theories (charismatic, transformational, and transactional leadership).

- The multidimensional model of leadership (MML) has attempted to combine the different approaches and theories into one explanation of effective leadership. This theory explores different antecedents that influence what a leader will do and combines this with the required, actual, and preferred leader behavior.

- The three criteria most often used to evaluate whether someone is an effective leader include: (1) the leader's use of power and influence; (2) ability to communicate; and (3) how the leader makes decisions.

Learning Activities

1. Of the four functions of management, directing is often identified as one of the more challenging responsibilities of being a manager. Discuss why directing employees can be difficult and what you can do to become better at this function.

2. First discuss feedback as it relates to organizational goals and tasks. Second, explain how you would provide feedback to an employee who has not performed up to desired standards. What strategies could you use to improve performance and what could be done to make sure the employee does not become frustrated or discouraged.

3. First explain the different managerial roles described by Mintzberg. Second, use these roles to provide an illustration of how the General manager of a professional hockey team could fulfill the different managerial roles identified. For example, as a resource allocator the General manager must determine the operational budget for the team for the upcoming fiscal year.

4. Discuss the differences between management and leadership based on the chapter you have just read. Give an example from the sport industry to illustrate these differences. For example, describe someone whom you feel is a quality manager but may not be a quality leader and vice-versa.

5. Why should others be included in the decision-making process? As a manager what challenges would you have to overcome when allowing employees to contribute in decision-making? Under what circumstances do you think it would be best for a manager to make decisions using an autocratic decision-making style?

6. Briefly describe the evolution of leadership theory and trace its path to the contemporary theories of today. Within this response, detail why some of the early theories were inadequate and, further, why the newer theories are more appropriate in terms of the progression of management and leadership theory.

7. In groups of 3–5 students, identify ten individuals you think exhibit good leadership qualities in sport. Which characteristics do they have in common? Which are different?

Suggested Reading

Bennis, W., & Nanus, B. (2003). *Leaders: Strategies for Taking Charge*. New York: Harper & Row.

Summit, P., & Jenkins, S. (1998). *Reach for the Summit: The Definite Dozen for Succeeding in Whatever You Do*. New York: Random House.

Krzyzewski, M., & Phillips, D. T. (2000). *Leading with the Heart: Coach K's Successful Strategies for Basketball, Business, and Life*. New York: Warner Books, Inc.

References

Barney, J. (1991). Firm resources and sustained competitive advantage. *Journal of Management, 17*(1), 99–120.

Bass, B. M. (1960). *Leadership, psychology, and organizational behavior*. New York: Harper Publishing.

Bass, B. M. (1985). *Leadership and performance beyond expectations*. New York: The Free Press.

Bass, B. M. (1988). Evolving perspectives on charismatic leadership. In J. Conger et al. (Eds.), *Charismatic leadership: The elusive factor in organizational effectiveness*. San Francisco, CA: Jossey-Bass Publications.

Bass, B. M. (1990). *Bass and Stogdill's handbook of leadership* (3rd ed.). New York: The Free Press.

Bass, B. M., & Avolio, B. J. (Eds.). (1994). *Improving organizational effectiveness through transformational leadership. Thousand Oaks, CA: Sage Publications.

Bennis, W. G., & Nanus, B. (2003). Leaders: Strategies for taking charge. New York: Harper & Row Publishers.

Bridges, F. J., & Roquemore, L. L. (2004). Management for athletic/sport administration: Theory and practice (4th ed.). Decatur, GA: ESM Books.

Bryman, A. (1992). Charisma & leadership in organizations. Newbury Park, CA: Sage Publications.

Burns, J. M. (1978). Leadership. New York: Harper & Row Publishers.

Chalip, L. (2001). Group decision making and problem solving. In B. L. Parkhouse (Ed.), The management of sport: Its foundation and application (pp. 93–110). Boston, MA: McGraw-Hill Higher Education.

Chelladurai, P. (1978). A contingency model of leadership in athletics. (Unpublished doctoral dissertation). University of Waterloo, Waterloo, Canada.

Chelladurai, P. (1993). Leadership. In R. N. Singer, M. Murphey, & L. K. Tennant (Eds.), Handbook of research on sport psychology (pp. 647–671). New York: Macmillan.

Chelladurai, P. (2009). Managing organizations for sport and physical activity: A systems perspective (3rd ed.). Holcomb Hathaway Publishers, Scottsdale, AZ.

Church, A. H. (1994). The character of organizational communication: A review and new conceptualization. The International Journal of Organizational Analysis, 2, 18–53.

Conger, J. A. (1989). The charismatic leader: Behind the mystique of exceptional leadership. San Francisco, CA: Jossey-Bass Publishers.

Conger, J. A., & Kanungo, R. (1987). Towards a behavioral theory of charismatic leadership in organizational settings. Academy of Management Review, 12, 637–647.

DiMaggio, P. J., & Powell, W. W. (1983). The iron cage revisited: Institutional isomorphism and collective rationality in organizational fields. American Sociological Review, 48, 147–160.

Fiedler, F. E. (1967). A theory of leadership effectiveness. New York: McGraw-Hill.

French, J., & Raven, B. H. (1959). The bases of social power. In D. Cartwright (Ed.), Studies of social power (pp. 150–167). Institute for Social Research, Ann Arbor, MI.

Hersey, P., & Blanchard, K. H. (1977). Management of organizational behavior: Utilizing human resources (3rd ed.). Englewood Cliffs, NJ: Prentice-Hall.

House, R. J. (1971). A path-goal theory of leader effectiveness. Administrative Science Quarterly, 16, 321–339.

House, R. J. (1977). A 1976 theory of charismatic leadership effectiveness. In J. G. Hunt & L. L. Larson (Eds.). Leadership: The cutting edge. Carbondale, IL: Southern Illinois University Press.

Kelman, H. C. (1958). Compliance, identification, and internalization: Three processes of attitude change. Journal of Conflict Resolution, 2, 51–56.

Kerr, S., & Jermier, J. M. (1978). Substitutes for leadership: Their meaning and measurement. Organizational Behavior and Human Performance, 22, 375–403.

Mintzberg, H. (1975). The manager's job: Folklore and fact. Harvard Business Review, 53, 49–61.

Nanus, B. (1989). The Leader's Edge: The seven keys to leadership in a turbulent world. Chicago, IL: Contemporary Books.

Osborn, R. N., & Hunt, J. G. (1975). An adaptive-reactive theory of leadership: The role of macro variables in leadership research. In J. G. Hunt & L. L. Larson (Eds.), Leadership frontiers. Kent, OH: Kent State University.

Pfeffer, J. (1981). Power in organizations. Marshfield, PA: Pittman.

Pfeffer, J. (1977). The ambiguity of leadership. Academy of Management Review, 2, 104–112.

Railey, J. H., & Tschauner, R. R. (1993). Managing physical education, fitness and sports programs. Mountain View, CA: Mayfield Publishing Company.

Vroom, V. H., & Yetton, P. W. (1973). Leadership and decision-making. Pittsburgh, PA: University of Pittsburgh Press.

Weber, M. (1997). The theory of social and economic organization. New York: The Free Press.

Stogdill, R. M. (1974). Handbook of leadership: A survey of the literature. New York: The Free Press.

Yukl, G. A., & Van Fleet, D. D. (1992). Theory and research on leadership in organizations. In M. D. Dunnette & L. M. Hough (Eds.), Handbook of industrial and organizational psychology (2nd ed.). Palo Alto, CA: Consulting Psychologists Press.

Yukl, G. A. (1989). Leadership in organizations (2nd ed.). Englewood Cliffs, NJ: Prentice Hall.

Yukl, G. A. (1998). Leadership in organizations (4th ed.). Englewood Cliffs, NJ: Prentice Hall.

5

An Introduction
to Sport Economics

Matthew T. Brown

WHAT IS ECONOMICS?

→ ever-changing (handwritten)

Economics is the *dynamic* study of collective human behavior. Typically, economics involves the study of the market system. Why individuals have money, the determinants of the cost of products, and the examination of the management of resources are all areas of study within economics. In sport, economists examine supply and demand within the sport industry, the market for sports broadcast rights, the relationship between team costs, profit and winning, and the value of sports talent (Fort, 2010). Additionally, economists often examine economic activity benefits accruing to a community hosting sporting events or building new stadia or arenas.

Sport mangers may apply economic theory without realizing so. For example, when calculating price for games, a ticket manager may decide to use a variable pricing model. If she decides to charge $35 for upper deck tickets on weekends and $20 for the same ticket Monday to Thursday, she is likely applying the economic principles of supply and demand. In this example, supply is fixed by the upper deck seating capacity of the stadium. Demand likely is higher for the product on the weekend versus weekdays. With a static supply and a shift in the demand curve on the weekends, the ticket manger can charge more for the same seat without negatively affecting attendance.

Learning Objectives
Upon completion of this chapter, students will be able to • Appreciate economic theory in sport; • Understand the laws of supply and demand; • Analyze competitive balance in professional sport leagues; • Understand the nuances of economic impact studies; • Explain the realities and myths of economic impact studies; • Identify the abuses of economic impact studies; and • Understand psychic income.

**"You want a bun, too? That'll
be another five bucks."**

In all, effective sport managers understand key economic principles such as opportunity and marginal costs, supply and demand, competitive balance, and economic impact. Managers with knowledge of these concepts will be able to anticipate the impact of financial decision making on the sport enterprise.

OPPORTUNITY AND MARGINAL COSTS

A key belief of economists is that individuals and groups of people choose based on the costs and benefits of their actions. Arlington, Texas used $325 million in public funding to help build AT&T Stadium, the home of the Dallas Cowboys and Cotton Bowl since 2009. The stadium when complete had the most modern amenities available, including a 120-foot-tall glass paneled wall that opens to let in fall breezes, a retractable roof, two 60-yard flat screens hanging above the field, and over 200,000 square feet devoted to a club seating luxury area (Hoffer, 2007).

Photo courtesy © Andy Gillentine

Critics may ask if there was or should have been a better use of taxpayer dollars. A missed chance is an **opportunity cost**. The opportunity cost of a decision is what you must give up to have what you wanted. Those in Arlington wanted a new football venue to attract an NFL team to their city. They gave up $325 million in public funds that may have been used to better community infrastructure or improve public schools. In Washington, D.C., the citizens were asked by Major League Baseball to publicly fund a new stadium for the Washington Nationals. The public's cost for the new stadium was $610 million. At the time Nationals Park was built, many students in the District's public schools were lagging significantly in academic achievement (McGuire, 2013). The choice of the stadium over K–12 education was one of opportunity cost.

Opportunity costs involve either **explicit** or **implicit** expenditures. In Los Angeles, if a fan decides to spend $100 to go to a Lakers game, he then has $100 less to go to a Kings game that week. This is an explicit expenditure, spending your money on the Lakers rather than the Kings. If a friend in Phoenix invites you to a Suns game on Monday night and another friend offers you tickets to a Coyotes game that same night, you obviously cannot be in more than one place at the same time. Your choice is an implicit expenditure. The cost is the intangible benefits you would have received by going to the game you chose not to attend.

Opportunity costs also affect owners of sport properties. In the 1990s several profitable National Football League franchises moved. The Rams moved from Los Angeles to St. Louis, the Browns from Cleveland to Baltimore (where they became the Ravens) and the Raiders from Oakland to Los Angeles and then back to Oakland. While these franchises were making profits in their original locations, they were operating at an economic loss due to the new or renovated stadia and revenue streams available elsewhere.

Sport managers, with an understanding of **marginal costs**, can predict human behavior through the examination of the benefits and costs of doing more. Another key rule of economic behavior is that people think about the marginal impact of their actions. Marginal cost is how much more an individual has to spend to acquire more of what he wants, without worrying about what already has been spent.

For the Los Angeles Angels of Anaheim, signing Albert Pujols to a 10-year, $240 million contract in 2012 drastically increased their payroll. The Angels' marginal costs were not changed, however. Baseball teams like the Angels sell tickets, which allow people to see the players on their roster. The Angels have to pay Pujols $16 million in 2013, $23 million in 2014, $24 million in 2015, and so on no matter how many people came to see him play in a given year. The team raised ticket prices approximately 4% after signing Pujols, not necessarily because they had to, but because they could (Plunkett, 2012). Pujols' signing excited the Angels fans as he was, at the time, one of the best players in the game. With him on the team, Angels fans were more willing to pay to see the Angels play. This in turn makes them more willing to pay a higher price to see the team play.

When Ken Griffey, Jr. returned to the Seattle Mariners in 2009 he and his agent understood this concept when negotiating his contract with the team. In addition to his $2 million base salary, Griffey could have earned a financial incentive if Mariners game attendance hit a preset threshold during the season. Griffey's presence on the team should have made the fans more willing to pay to see the team play, especially because the team only drew 2.32 million during the previous season. That attendance mark was the team's lowest total attendance since 1995 (Rovell, 2009). Attendance fell again in 2009, though, as Griffey only played in 117 games. Others have had attendance clauses in their contracts, too. Rovell stated that the 1998 attendance clause in Mark McGwire's contract with the St. Louis Cardinals earned him an extra $445,691. Roger Clemens earned $3 million from the Houston Astros in 2004 through his attendance clause as well.

SUPPLY AND DEMAND

If you are a fan of a baseball team and earn $4,000 a month you can afford to attend a certain number of games during the season based on the price of the team's tickets. If the team were to lower ticket prices suddenly in the middle of the year, you could then go to more games. This is the **Law of Demand**. The law states that when the price of an item declines the demand for that item increases. When the price goes down enough, people like you can now afford to buy more of the product, which means you can attend additional games.

The relationship between price and the amount of product people wish to consume is called the demand curve (see Figure 5.1). The demand curve slopes down because as price gets higher, the demand for a particular product decreases.

Supply is the quantity of a product that an owner is willing to offer or make available at a given price. The supply curve (see Figure 5.2) charts the relationship between the amounts of product a company or companies wish to sell and price. Usually, the supply curve slopes upward.

Going back to the example discussed in the opening section of this chapter, a ticket manager determining price could plot the demand and supply curve for her product on

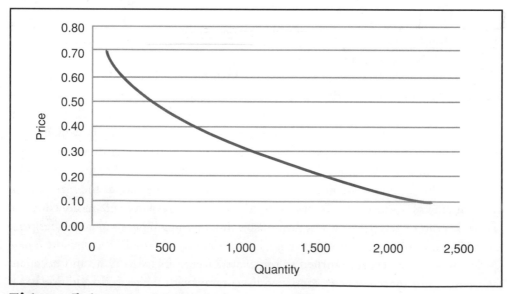

Figure 5.1. Demand Curve

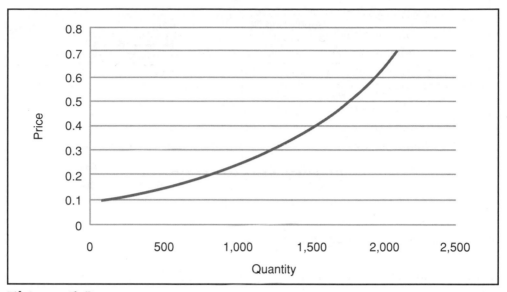

Figure 5.2. Supply Curve

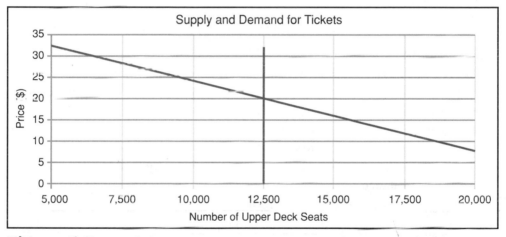

Figure 5.3. Equilibrium Point

one graph (see Figure 5.3). The point where the supply curve and the demand curve overlap is the **equilibrium price**. Here is where the amount of product demanded (tickets) equals the amount of product supplied (seats). Notice the supply curve is vertical. This is because the number of seats in the ballpark is fixed and does not change from game to game.

Changes in the demand curve also help explain why the ticket manager can charge $35 for tickets on the weekends and only $20 for those same seats on the weekdays. Figure 5.4 plots the supply curve for general admission seating at the ballpark. Again, the line is vertical as the number of general admission seats is fixed. The demand curve for games Monday to Thursday (D_1) intersects the supply curve at $20. On weekends, the demand for those seats increases and the curve shifts to the right. The weekend

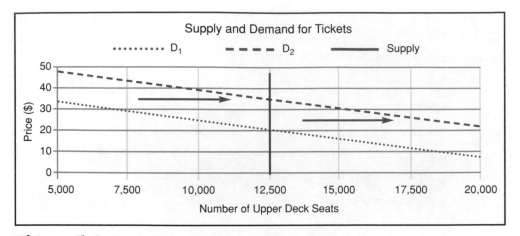

Figure 5.4. Demand Curve Shift for Weekend Games

curve (D₂) now intersects with the supply curve at $35. Because the demand for the product is greater on weekends, the ticket manager can charge more for seats because supply is fixed.

COMPETITIVE BALANCE

The National Football League (NFL) is likely the strongest league and sport property in North America. Most analysts attribute the league's strength to parity. In a given year, a last place team from the previous season has a realistic opportunity to compete for the Lombardi Trophy. Fourteen times in the last decade a team that finished last in its NFL division won the division title in the next season (Fox, 2013). The rise of the St. Louis Rams (2000) and the Baltimore Ravens (2001 and 2013) from has-beens to Super Bowl champions are perfect examples. In economic terms, the parity in the NFL is referred to as **competitive balance**.

The NFL is a league that shares a majority of its revenues between owners. These revenues include moneys generated via NFL Properties, NFL Enterprises, and nation-wide television packages. Owners keep a vast majority of locally generated revenues from items like stadium naming rights, concessions, parking, local radio, and sponsor-ship/advertising. Under this structure, the NFL has the highest central-to-local revenue percentage as compared to other professional leagues.

Formerly, the NFL salary cap was set based upon a percentage of all revenues. Under the most recent collective bargaining agreement, however, players share of league reve-nues must average 47% of all league revenues over the 10-year term of the 2011 Collec-tive Bargaining Agreement (CBA). The revenue varies by source, however, with players receiving 55% of national media revenue, 45% of NFL Ventures revenue and 40% of local club revenue ("NFL clubs approve," 2011). This change had the potential to affect competitive balance within the league. Small market owners and owners with stadia that did not generate a lot of revenue, who were at a disadvantage under the old agree-ment with the National Football League Players Association (NFLPA), now have some relief. Importantly, this could lead to greater parity within the league.

For example, under the old CBA Team A is a large market team and Team B is a small market team. Both teams receive $110 million from the league's central revenue pool. Team A generates an additional $100 million in local revenues and Team B generates $25 million. Therefore, overall revenues for Team A are $210 million and Team B $135 million. Next, total revenues per NFL team are estimated to be $170 million per team. Under the previous CBA, players receive 59% of total revenues, the salary cap for teams is set at $100.3 million. If both Team A and Team B are paying players at the maximum salary level, Team A spends 47.8% of its revenues on player salary while Team B spends 74.3% on player salary. With the non-player costs of operating an NFL franchise factored in with salary cap rules regarding the amortization of player signing bonuses, Team B is at a disadvantage in the free agent market. Team B also must worry about profitability as nearly all of its revenues are taken by player salary. This scenario explains, in some part, why the revenue sharing rules regarding local team revenues are set at 40% in the new CBA. It was hard for small market teams, in this example Team B, to remain competitive under the previous CBA. With the sharing of local revenue reduced, a greater opportunity now exists for small market NFL teams to be more competitive in building their franchise.

To further aid small market teams and thereby increase competitive balance, the NFL has implemented a local revenue sharing plan whereby a 10% tax is placed on local revenues of the highest-revenue teams. Money collected from this tax is then sent to the lowest-revenue teams (Florio, 2011). Between $10 and $15 million was shared in 2011 (Kaplan, 2012).

The NFL is trying to avoid Major League Baseball's small market situation. In baseball, where much less revenue is shared, where there is no salary cap, and where owners are willing to spend beyond Major League Baseball's luxury tax threshold (New York Yankees), competitive imbalance exists. Here, certain teams consistently win more games over time than the rest of the teams in the league. As an example, the New York

Yankees have won approximately one-in-three World Series since 1920. When one team is located in a market where fans will pay more for wins, the more profitable team will win more over time. Therefore, as seen in Major League Baseball, profit variation harms competitive balance (Fort, 2010).

MLB Commissioner Allan H. "Bud" Selig, however, argues that MLB now has the greatest competitive balance of any league. He points to the fact that since 2000 only a few teams have repeated as World Series Champions (Cardinals, Red Sox, and Giants) and none have won more than twice. Foster, Greyser, and Walsh (2006) state that competitive imbalance at the league level exists when one team dominates the sport over a number of years (dynasties), the same group of teams dominate the sport over a period of time, or the same group of teams remain at the bottom of the standings. Using the final regular season standings on NFL.com and MLB.com, which league, the NFL or MLB, has been more balanced over the past 10 years?

COMPETITIVE ADVANTAGE

Within the economic restrictions of a league, teams that are constantly successful understand competitive advantage. For example, to operate within the economic framework of the NFL while signing better players than other teams in the league, it helps to have a thorough understanding of the collective bargaining agreement and league rules. As stated previously, the Collective Bargaining Agreement (CBA) signed with the NFLPA regulates the amortization of player signing bonuses.

The NFL CBA rules state that a signing bonus paid to a player is allocated over the time of the contract (up to five years). So a player signing a 5-year, $10 million contract with a $10 million signing bonus would be paid $12 million in year one and $2 million per year in years two through five. However, the salary counted against the team's cap would be $4 million per year (Brown, Rascher, Nagel & McEvoy, 2010). Teams, like Team A above, with a new stadium filled with luxury seating in a large market, have access to unshared revenue that can be used to pay large signing bonuses, creating a competitive advantage on the field. Without revenue sharing between teams in the NFL, too many franchises would gain competitive advantage, thereby leading to competitive imbalance within the league.

ECONOMIC IMPACT

In sport, **economic impact** is defined as the net economic change in a host community that results from spending attributed to a sport event or facility (Brown et al., 2010). This economic change has both tangible and intangible benefits. The tangible benefits can be seen in Figure 5.5.

As Figure 5.5 depicts, the community benefits when the city subsidizes a sporting event or facility if that subsidy leads to new visitors coming to the community. These visitors bring new money into the community, which then leads to job creation. Job creation lowers unemployment and, therefore, the community as a whole benefits from its investment.

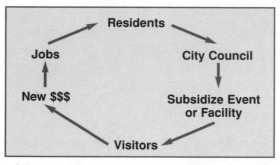

Figure 5.5. Tangible Community Benefits

Economic impact studies measure the benefits a community receives. The study measures total economic loss or gain after accounting for costs (Brown et al., 2010). These studies were initially developed by cities to determine the economic impact individual business had on a community. Later they were adapted to measure spending based on a sporting event or a facility. In most communities, sport economic impact studies are conducted by the Chamber of Commerce, or in larger cities, the sports commission.

The first to apply economic impact studies to sport was the Indiana Sports Corporation (ISC). The ISC used its economic impact studies successfully to gain governmental support to build facilities and provide resources for sport in central Indiana. Some of the early events the ISC attracted included the 1982 Olympic Sport Fest and the 1987 Pan Am Games. The ISC's economic impact studies indicated that sporting activities in the state generated 60,000 new jobs and created 7,400 new businesses. The ISC was able to get funding from the state to support their activities because they could prove that their activities created new jobs and brought new money to the region.

TYPES OF SPENDING

Economic impact studies measure three types of spending: direct, indirect, and induced. **Direct spending** measures actual dollars spent in the local community on the event. This spending can be both on site and off site. On site spending includes items like concessions, tickets, parking, and merchandise. Off site spending refers to all other spending in the local community such as spending on hotels, for fuel, to shop, and to dine. The key to measuring direct spending is that it has to occur in the local economy

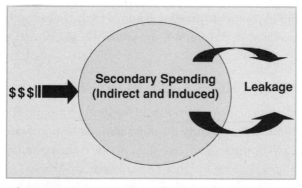

Figure 5.6. Community Cash Flow Model

as defined in the economic impact study.

Indirect and induced spending develops from direct spending (Brown et al., 2010). Direct spending creates secondary spending that circulates within the community (see Figure 5.6). This secondary spending includes indirect benefits like additional profits and incomes for local businesses and households.

These local businesses then spend some of these dollars on goods and services that support additional local businesses. This is **indirect spending**.

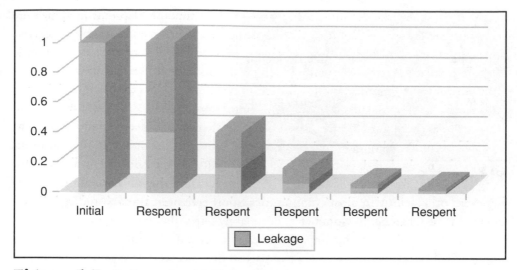

Figure 5.7. Mathematical Multiplier Model

At the same time, household wage earners receive additional income resulting from the increases in business spending. The wage earners spend some of their increased earnings on local goods and services. These expenditures are **induced spending**. Both indirect and induced spending are estimated using a regional multiplier.

The regional multiplier measures how many times money changes hands in the community before it leaves, or leaks out of the region (see Figure 5.6). It is the value multiplied by direct spending to estimate total spending, or economic benefit. The multiplier estimates the secondary spending (indirect and induced) in a region. Figure 5.7 depicts the method by which a multiplier is calculated.

In Figure 5.7, the initial dollar is spent in the local economy. Of that initial dollar, $0.40 is respent in the local economy. Of the $0.40, $0.16 is respent. Then of the $0.16, $0.06 is respent and so on. By adding together the initial $1.00 of spending to the amount of money respent each round, you can calculate the multiplier for the region. For this example, when the initial round of spending is added to the five rounds of respending, the total spending generated in the community would be $1.66; therefore, the regional multiplier is 1.66.

STEPS TO COMPLETING THE ECONOMIC STUDY

To conduct an economic impact study, the first step is to define the local economy. For instance, when conducting an economic impact study on the American Legion State Baseball Tournament held in Athens, Ohio, the researchers had to decide if the economy would be defined as the City of Athens, the area within the zip code of Athens, or Athens County. To define the local economy, the researchers must determine where the majority of impact will occur.

Second, the method for collecting data must be determined. In a basic economic impact study, direct spending is measured. Then the multiplier is applied to determine total impact. To measure direct spending, data can be collected directly from participants and spectators or from indirect sources like hotels and restaurants. In some instances, it makes sense to use indirect sources. When hosting a conference tournament, the organizing committee knows where teams are staying. The committee can contact these hotels and collect the exact amounts spent by team for the duration of the tournament.

In most instances, information will need to be collected directly from participants and spectators. Several data collection tools may be used, including self-administered questionnaires and logs or diaries. Most often, due to costs and efficiency of data collection, self-administered questionnaires are used.

Once the method of data collection is determined, the data must be collected. To accurately reflect the impact of an event, it is recommended that at least 350 surveys or diaries be collected. After the data collection, the results can be analyzed and direct spending determined.

Uses of Economic Impact in Sport

Economic impact studies are widely used in sport. As noted previously, the Indiana Sports Commission was the first to use economic impact studies to justify taxpayer subsidy. Other examples of the use of economic impact studies in sport vary widely. In the National Football League (NFL), it is estimated by the Maryland Department of Business and Economic Development that the impact of the Baltimore Ravens was $202 million in gross expenditures and $96 million in personal income, with 2,772 full time jobs being created. An economic impact study on the Buffalo Bills indicated that the team's impact was $111.5 million annually. A final NFL team, the Lions, generated $127 million in direct spending ("The fans," 2002). A recent study of the Carolina Panthers indicated that the team generated $361.5 million in direct spending, $636 million in total impact, and created 4,415 jobs in the local economy (Spanberg, 2013).

For the Olympics, it was estimated that the economic impact for London in 2012 was £9.9 billion (Blitz, 2013). The impact for the 2010 Winter Olympics in Vancouver was estimated to be $2.3 billion ("The games effect," 2010). In NASCAR, one study estimated that the Las Vegas Motor Speedway's annual NASCAR weekend has an annual impact of $240 million ("NASCAR weekend has," 2013).

The Reality and Myth of Economic Impact in Sport

Rosentraub (1997) examined several sport economic impact studies. In an era where new stadia were used to lure teams, these economic impact studies were used to justify the use of public funds to build the new sport venues. In the NFL, the Cleveland Browns went to Baltimore when the owner was promised a new stadium being built and paid for by taxpayers. The same can be said for the Houston Oilers when they moved to Nashville. In the NHL, the Winnipeg Jets moved to Phoenix and played for many years in the publicly funded Jobing.com Arena.

Rosentraub noted a problem with many of these studies, however. In several situations, studies were produced that gave the impression that for the right price you could get as large of an impact number you wanted. For a team moving to a city, two studies could differ by over $100 million.

Economic Impact Study Abuses

While economic impact studies are valuable estimates that can aid in planning, development, and the public decision making process, they can also be misused—sometimes through naïveté and unfamiliarity, and sometimes intentionally.

Professor John Crompton of Texas A&M University identified eleven sources of misapplication in a well-known 1995 article, which appeared in *Journal of Sport Management*. Crompton's list includes such mistakes as failing to use the correct type of multiplier; failure to correctly calculate the multiplier itself; the inappropriate inclusion of local residents, "time-switchers," and "casuals" (both refer to types of visitors who were not drawn in by the event being studied); and the failure to consider opportunity costs. Along with these categories of mistakes, all of which could be committed unintentionally, Crompton also notes that some mistakes, such as the use of "fudged" multiplier coefficients, can be and are committed willfully (Crompton, 1995).

The problems Crompton points out which are associated with multipliers are not minor ones. And within these problems, one of the potentially most profound is that there is no one set of multipliers universally agreed-upon and utilized by all researchers and critics. Commonly available commercial options include the RIMS II, IMPLAN, and REIM multipliers. Not only does the availability of competing multipliers contribute to the difficulty of making meaningful comparisons between studies, but it allows for the possibility of intentional misuse.

To illustrate this example, consider the case of a commercial firm with an interest in developing a downtown stadium complex in City A. The firm's best interests in this case would be promoted if an economic impact study demonstrated a large and sustainable return on the initial investment of City A in the project.

Thus in theory, the firm, and perhaps its supporters within City A's government, could contract a researcher to calculate the total economic impact for City A using all common commercially available multipliers. If differences between the estimates existed, the researcher could then select the results that indicated the most favorable outcome for City A. The cost of buying several commercially calculated multipliers could be subsumed into the total project costs and would likely prove to be only a very small percentage of the total study's expense.

While this scenario is hypothetical, and an approach such as the one described in it could be seen as cynical at best and completely unethical at worst, it is clearly possible—and the forces that could promote this kind of questionable decision making are present and powerful.

Intangible Benefits

Many American communities are in transition from more traditional economic bases of support, such as shipping and manufacturing, to new service-oriented industries, such as sport, entertainment, and tourism. And since all politicians must address issues related to employment and the economy, the ability to "create" jobs and wealth are often touted as reasons to support new initiatives and to vote for local tax and rezoning issues related to sport and tourism development.

Photo courtesy © bigstockphoto.com

Through new building, development, and policy changes, local government officials often hope not only to invigorate the private sector but also to increase sport tourism-related revenues through the collection of sales taxes, lodging/hospitality taxes, user fees, and even fines from the visitors who come to their cities. In addition to these multiple streams of revenue, which are often seen as potentially lucrative, many believe that more subtle reasons exist for supporting sport tourism development.

Billy Payne, CEO for the Atlanta Committee for the Olympic Games (ACOG), was one notable proponent of the transformative power of major sport infrastructure development and the hosting of special events. Always a champion of this power, his belief appeared to remain unshaken eight years after the 1996 Atlanta Olympics when he noted: "The Games vaulted Atlanta into a very elite group of cities, on a global scale. Naturally, I think it was worth every minute and every dollar that we spent bringing them here and hosting the world" (Yarbrough, 2000).

Not everyone shares Mr. Payne's exuberance, however. In considering the potential return from a proposed stadium renovation for the Miami Dolphins, Carlos Gimenez, Miami-Dade County mayor is reluctant to lend support to the project. Backlash remains in Miami after local officials voted to approve using taxpayer money to fund approximately 75% of the Marlins' new ballpark (Belson, 2013).

Experts claim, however, that while the Dolphins stadium project might not be a good investment from the perspective of achieving a real financial return, it might be worthwhile from the perspective of promoting the community's "psychic income" (Yarbrough, 2000). **Psychic income**, also sometimes referred to as "psychic capital," is increasingly referred to as a benefit of sport tourism development. This relatively new term refers to the real, yet intangible, qualities associated with community pride, prestige, and competitiveness, which may be associated with major sport and event hosting.

NATIONAL ASSOCIATION OF SPORTS COMMISSIONS

The National Association of Sports Commissions (NASC) in 2000 attempted to address the aforementioned abuses of economic studies when they published guidelines for computation of economic impact. The report stated, "The process of estimating the economic benefit of a sports event can become controversial" (NASC, 2000, p. 1). Because the bidding process on sports events is fairly competitive, owners of events have learned how to market their events in an attractive way. Examples from one event, according to the NASC, had economic impact estimates from $7.5 million to zero. Resulting from many discrepancies similar to this was the need to clearly estimate the return on investment of a host community.

The main problem with economic impact studies is that experts disagree on how to conduct the studies. As a result, economists, using different but legitimate methodologies, can derive far different values of economic impact. Sport organizing committees, wanting to inflate the value of their work, are therefore able to "shop" for the methodology that will show the greatest return on investment. This is affirmed by Crompton (1995) and Brown et al. (2010). These authors stated that economic impact studies are frequently used to justify a position or to create the appearance of a greater public benefit. Organizing committees, however, need to be cautious. Often bid fees or guarantees promised to an event are partially based upon the economic impact that the event generates. By shopping for an economic impact study with an inflated estimate of the true economic impact of the event, organizing committees and host communities are artificially inflating the cost of bidding for and hosting the event (NASC, 2000).

One of the issues leading to differences in computation of economic impact is the calculation of visitor spending. Visitor spending is defined as the dollars left in a community by persons that came to the community because of the event (Brown et al., 2010). Upon the examination of this definition, spending by local residents (those that live within the community which hosts the event) is excluded. Only new dollars brought into the community as a result of visitor spending should be counted in an economic impact study. But as Hudson (2001) noted, economic impact studies often include spending by local residents. Thus, the true impact of the event on the local economy is inflated.

The purpose of an individual's visit can also cause variations in the computation of economic impact. For example, an individual may be sent to a conference in Dallas, Texas. The purpose of her visit to Dallas was business—attending the conference. While in Dallas, if she learns that there is a Stars game and decides to go to the game, her money spent at the game would not be counted in the economic impact of that game. The purpose of her trip to Dallas was to attend the conference, not to go to a hockey game. Even if the event has appeal to business visitors looking for entertainment, the spending by that business visitor only would be counted when calculating the economic impact of the conference, not the sporting event.

Measuring Economic Impact

According to Brown et al. (2010) the first step to measure economic impact is to analyze direct spending. Because spending by local residents typically should not be counted in an economic impact study, it is very important that the analyst differentiate between event attendees who are visitors (those who live outside the geographic impact area) and those who are local residents (those who live inside the area). The goal is to measure the amount of spending in the geographic area of impact that goes to local businesses. For example, economic impact studies measure how much are people spending at sporting events, plus how much the visitors are also spending in local restaurants, retail establishments, on transportation, and so forth. Also, organizational spending is measured. Here, the spending by the team/organization, corporate sponsors, media, and other related entities is measured.

To measure direct spending, surveys are often used. The survey guides interviews with event patrons in order to determine whether they are local residents or visitors, how much money they are spending because of the event, etc. The data collected allows the researcher to estimate the amount of spending per capita per day for visitors for different spending categories. When enough spectators are surveyed, one can estimate how much the typical visitor spends and how long he or she stays (Brown et al., 2010). In addition to the visitor survey, the researcher may also survey the team/event management group, host committee, sponsors, and so forth to determine local corporate spending that is tied directly to the event.

Direct spending then impacts other industries and workers. For example, when attending a sporting event, you might eat in a local restaurant before the event. With the money you spend, the restaurant will pay its employees, purchase food, pay utilities, and so forth. The food distributor will pay the farmer who provided the produce. The farmer will then purchase supplies at a local feed mill. These expenditures continue to cycle through the economy and illustrate indirect economic impacts. Brown et al. (2010) define indirect economic impacts as impacts that occur in an area of impact under study that represent the circulation of initial visitor expenditures (direct impacts). Finally, direct and indirect impacts create induced impacts. Induced impacts are the effect of direct and indirect impacts on employment and earnings.

To measure indirect and induced impacts, a multiplier is used. A multiplier is a mathematical tool that measures economic input and output in a sector of the overall local economy. The multiplier describes changes in output resulting from changes in input (here, direct spending). Typically, the researcher does not actually create multipliers but instead purchases a regional multiplier model based on the USDA Forest Service IMPLAN (IMpact Analysis for PLANning) and data from the U.S. Bureau of Economic Analysis. Many vendors supply these multiplier tables too, including the Minnesota IMPLAN Group.

There are several types of multipliers including sales (output), income, and employment. Sales multipliers measure changes in economic activity resulting from the direct spending of a visitor to a community. The income multiplier measures the indirect and induced impact of new spending on household income while the employment multiplier examines the effect of new spending on local employment.

Total economic impact is then the sum of direct, indirect and induced impacts minus any costs associated with the event being measured. The following case analysis provides additional clarification.

Case Analysis Using Economic Impact Methodology

Brown et al. (2010) shows the economic impact of the MasterCard Alamo Bowl on the San Antonio, Texas economy. Figure 5.8 contains information on the direct economic impact of visitors to the game. In total, 28,542 visitors attended the game spending an average of $169 per visitor outside the game. These visitors spent an average of 3.2 days in San Antonio while also spending $73 at the game. The total direct spending of the visitors outside the Alamo Dome was $15.4 million ($169 × 3.2 × 28,542) while an additional $2.1 million was spend inside the Dome ($73 × 28,542).

Key Survey Data from Visitors	
Total number of visitors to MasterCard Alamo Bowl	28,542
Average expenditure estimates	
Daily per visitor outside Dome	$169
Average number of days stayed per visitor	3.2
Average visitor expenditure for entire trip outside Dome	$541
Average visitor expenditure inside Dome	$73
Total direct spending of visitors outside Dome	$15,435,514
Total direct spending of visitors inside of Dome	$2,083,566

Figure 5.8. Direct Spending Calucation at Alamo Bowl

Figure 5.9 shows total direct visitor spending by category, output (sales) multiplier by category and total impact by category. The total direct spending, including spending by visitors inside and outside the Alamodome and spending by teams, media, and corporate sponsors, was $22.0 million. With the multiplier used to calculate the indirect impacts of visitor spending outside the Alamodome, the total economic impact was $33.5 million.

Total Economic Impact			
Category	Direct Spending	Multiplier	Total
Transportation	$1685,852	1.79	$3,017,675
Retail	$2,613,793	1.69	$4,417,310
Lodging	$3,510,047	1.76	$6,177,683
Entertainment	$2,896,358	1.87	$5,416,189
Food & Beverage	$2,933,265	1.70	$4,986,551
Miscellaneous	$1,848,376	1.59	$2,938,918
Inside Alamodone	$2,083,566	–	$2,083,566
Corporate/Team/Media	$4,450,128	–	$4,450,128
Total Direct Spending:	**$22,021,385**	**Total Economic Impact:**	**$33,488,020**

Figure 5.9 Total Economic Impact Calculation

CONFLICTING STATEMENTS BY ECONOMISTS

It should come as no surprise that within the complex marketplace of ideas there exist conflicting statements by economists as to whether or not sport and sport tourism development projects are worthwhile.

There is certainly no shortage of experts who extol the virtues and benefits of these projects. Increasingly, though, many economists and other scholars are speaking out to challenge these assumptions. Among them, Art Rolnick has flatly stated that "if you want to try to make a case that we should invest public money in sport teams, it really shouldn't be based on what's good for this economy. You're going to lose that debate" (Horwich, 2004).

Still other researchers see questions about the value of sport-related projects as complicated, and not lending themselves to easy answers. One doctoral dissertation on the subject noted that while "mounting evidence suggests that sports stadia have only marginal economic impacts upon the metropolitan economy," economic impact studies have reached these conclusions largely by utilizing the entire metropolitan area as the unit of analysis, rather than the districts and neighborhoods, or "microareas," which are most proximate to these development projects. This study suggests that merely changing the focus, or level of analysis, of these economic studies has far-reaching implications for understanding the value and impacts of sport-related projects (Chapin, 2001).

Economics is a Social Science

It is worth remembering that the social science of economics has long been jokingly referred to as the "dismal science" perhaps partially because of the pessimistic historical predictions made by early economists such as Thomas Malthus. Malthus became famous for suggesting (over 200 years ago) that unchecked world population growth would accelerate exponentially and would soon result in widespread famine and strife.

Incidentally, most of Malthus' predications have failed to materialize due to what has been commonly seen as his failure to take new and emerging information into account. The lesson of Malthus should not be seen as a general criticism of the science of economics, but rather as a cautionary footnote to understanding the discipline's limitations.

Economic questions most often involve dynamic, rather than static, analyses of collective human behavior—and these analyses are not limited to discrete mathematical formulae, but also should include insights from psychology, sociology, geography, political science, and other fields. The bottom line: economic questions, and the ways in which researchers attempt to address them, are complex and always changing. Studies attempting to gauge the economic impacts of sport development are no exception.

While many researchers work hard to develop, standardize, and advocate appropriate methods for undertaking these studies, it may turn out that there is no one "best way" to design economic impact studies of sport-related developments due to the tremendous diversity of project types and settings. However, if this is a truism, then it is one that imposes very real limitations on our ability to meaningfully compare results between studies, and to think of any study as much more than a "best guess" based on the available information.

With that in mind, the only true problem with these studies may be our failure, unintentional or otherwise, to realize and accept these limitations.

SUMMARY

It should be quite apparent that measuring the economic impact of sport facilities, event operations, and team activities requires a solid understanding of economic theory. In this chapter you were exposed to the laws of supply and demand, opportunity costs, and how these theories are used in the sport industry.

The study of economic impact is an art, not a science. It is however, an essential part of the financial makeup of the sport industry.

Discussion Activities

1. Select a sport event and try to locate a related completed economic impact study. Look for inconsistencies, common errors, etc

2. Examine the money you spent on the last vacation you took. Calculate how the money may have been re-spent, both in and out of that community.

References

Belson, K. (2013, March 25). Anger in wake of Marlins' stadium deal threatens Dolphins' renovation plan. *The New York Times*. Retrieved from http://www.nytimes.com/2013/03/25/sports/football/miami-dolphins-stadium-refurbishment-plan-is-threatened.html?pagewanted=all&_r=0

Blitz, R. (2013, July 21). Olympics 2012: Cameron's claims over economic legacy questioned. *Financial Times*. Retrieved from http://www.ft.com/cms/s/0/009f532a-f207-11e2-8e04-00144feabdc0.html#axzz2dqvolOkq

Brown, M., Rascher, D., Nagel, M., & McEvoy, C. (2010). *Financial management in the sport industry*. Scottsdale, AZ: Holcomb Hathaway.

Crompton, J. L. (1995). Economic impact analysis of sports facilities and events: Eleven sources of misapplication. *Journal of Sport Management*, *9*(1), 14–25.

Florio, M. (2011). New revenue sharing plan features tax on highest-earning teams. *NBC Sports*. Retrieved from http://profootballtalk.nbcsports.com/2011/07/23/new-revenue-sharing-plan-features-tax-on-highest-earning-teams/

Fort, R. D. (2010). *Sports Economics* (3rd ed.). Upper Saddle River, NJ: Prentice Hall.

Foster, G., Greyser, S. A., & Walsh, B. (2006). *The business of sports*. Mason, OH: Thompson Southwestern.

Fox, A. (2013, August 15). Look for big turnaround by Chiefs. *ESPN.com*. Retrieved from http://espn.go.com/nfl/trainingcamp13/story/_/id/9569116/kansas-city-chiefs-year-worst-first-story

Hoffer, R. (2007, July 16). The king of Texas. *Sports Illustrated*, *107*, 64–72.

Horwich, J. (2004, April 7). *Financial experts see "psychic income," plenty of risk in stadium deal*. Transcript of Minnesota Public Radio. Retrieved from http://news.minnesota.publicradio.org/features/2004/04/08_horwichj_bizstadium

Hudson, I. (2001, February). The use and misuse of economic impact analysis: The case of professional sports. *Journal of Sport and Social Issues*, *25*(1), 20–24.

Kaplan, D. (2012, October 22). Revenue sharing among NFL clubs plummets. *SportsBusiness Journal*. Retrieved from http://www.sportsbusinessdaily.com/Journal/Issues/2012/10/22/Leagues-and-

McGuire, P. (2013). DC schools: Crediting success, confronting challenge. *The Huffington Post*. Retrieved from http://www.huffingtonpost.com/patricia-mcguire/dc-schools-crediting-succ_b_3704141.html

NASC. (2000). *Economic impact study*. Cincinnati, OH: Author.

NASCAR Weekend has pumped billions of dollars into the local economy. (2013, February 28). *Las*

Vegas Motor Speedway. Retrieved from http://www.lvms.com/media/news/630494.html

NFL clubs approve comprehensive agreement. (2011, July 21). *NFL Communications*. Retrieved from http://nflcommunications.com/2011/07/21/nfl-clubs-approve-comprehensive-agreement/

Plunkett, B. (2012, April 10). Angels "one of the best bargains in sports." *Orange County Register*. Retrieved from http://www.ocregister.com/angels/strong-423721-angels-ticket.html.

Rosentraub, M. S., (1997, April). The myth and reality of economic development from sports. *Real Estate Issues*, *22*(1), 24–30.

Rovell, D. (2009, February 23). Attendance clauses in contracts. *CNBC*. Retrieved from http://www.cnbc.com/id/29350397

Spanberg, E. (2013, February 28). As Carolina Panthers' stadium talks trudge on, a closer look at the economics. *Charlotte Business Journal*. Retrieved from http://www.bizjournals.com/charlotte/blog/queen_city_agenda/2013/02/as-carolina-panthers-stadium-talks.html?page=all

The fans, taxpayers, and business alliance for NFL football in San Diego (2002). Retrieved from http://www.ftballance.org/stadiums/impact.php

The games effect (2010, March 31). Retrieved from http://www.fin.gov.bc.ca/reports/pwc-olympic-report6.pdf

Yarbrough, C. R. (2000). *And they call them games: An inside view of the 1996 Olympics*. Atlanta: Mercer University Press.

6

Sport Finance

Tom Regan and Matthew Bernthal

INTRODUCTION

The sports industry has grown exponentially over the last few decades. A sport financial manager must be able to assess the operations of the team, league, conference, city, and the organization to make informed financial decisions. Financial managers must be able to compare the entity profits and operations with past performance and compare the organization to the other companies in the same sport. The following events are just a few examples of recent financial transactions in sport.

- Los Angeles Dodgers (MLB) purchased for $2 billion (May 2012).
- Chicago Cubs purchased for $845 million by the Ricketts family.
- Malcolm Glazer and his family took over the Manchester United soccer club in 2005 in a deal then valued at $1.47 billion.
- $425 million deal for World Cup television rights in the United States from 2007 to 2014.

NCAA CONFERENCE MEDIA AGREEMENTS

BIG12
- First-tier rights: $480 million, ESPN, eight years through 2015–16
- Second-tier rights: $1.17 billion, FOX, 13 years through 2024–25
- Per-year average: $150 million
- Per-school, per-year average: $15 million

Learning Objectives

After studying this chapter, the student should be able to
- Understand the relationship between accounting and finance;
- Identify the elements of a balance sheet, income statement, and budgets;
- Understand the relationship between the balance sheet, income statement, and the statement of cash flow;
- Understand the concept of time value of money;
- Understand the type of bonds that are used to fund public assembly facilities; and
- Discuss how to analyze financial information.

PAC-12
- First- and second-tier rights: $3 billion, ESPN/FOX, 12 years through 2023–24
- Per-year average: $250 million
- Per-school, per-year average: $20.8 million

SEC
- First-tier rights: $825 million, CBS, 15 years through 2023–24
- Second-tier rights: $2.25 billion, ESPN, 15 years through 2023–24
- Per-year average: $205 million
- Per-school, per-year average: $14.6 million

BIG TEN
- First-tier rights: $1 billion, ESPN, 10 years through 2016–17
- Second-tier rights: $2.8 billion, Big Ten Network, 25 years through 2031–32
- Select basketball rights (minimum of 24 games, men's tournament semifinal and championship games): $72 million, CBS, six years through 2016–17
- Football championship game: $145 million, FOX, six years through 2016
- Per-year average: $248.2 million
- Per-school, per-year average: $20.7 million

ACC
- First-, second-, and third-tier rights: $3.6 billion, ESPN, 15 years through 2026–27
- Per-year average: $240 million
- Per-school, per-year average: $17.1 million

BIG EAST
- First-tier rights: $200 million, ESPN, six years for basketball through 2012–13; seven years for football through 2013–14
- Second-tier rights: Basketball, $54 million, CBS, six years through 2012–13
- The NCAA announced $6-billion, 11-year contract with CBS Sports that will expand the network's exclusive right to televise the NCAA Men's Basketball Tournament.

In the past, the vertical integration of professional sport organizations made financial analysis very difficult to the casual observer. For example, Anaheim Sports (former owner of the Anaheim Angels, and current owner of The Mighty Ducks of Anaheim), owned by The Walt Disney Company, encompasses ABC, ESPN, and other media outlets. However, they sold to billionaire Arte Moreno for $180 million in 2005. In another example, The Tribune Company owned the Chicago Cubs and superstation WGN and operated extensive television, radio, and newspaper (thirteen) outlets throughout the world. However, The Tribune Company sold to the family trust of Joe Ricketts for $845 million in 2009. It is often difficult to understand the financial statements relative to the sport-related activities of these multi-national corporations. The trend appears to be that sole ownership and vertical integration in the sport industry has waned.

Some may think that finance and management of financial opportunities consist of sophisticated terms, techniques, and formulas. However, many companies and sport organizations practice financial management at a simpler level. Families, small enterprises, nonprofit organizations, and many large corporations practice fundamental finance. The essential element is the focus on cash entering and exiting the organization. **Cash flow** is the term associated with cash inflows and outflows in an individual's personal life and in various business enterprises.

For example, what is involved in the purchase of a car? One's thoughts may include the following: How much cash do I have on hand? Do I have a car to trade? What is my payment going to be? If I am going to borrow money, how much should I borrow? What is my income (cash inflow) going to be in order to make my monthly payment? Should I even buy this car? Do I need it? What benefit is it going to provide? Can I get by with a less expensive car? What if I lose my job? This process is part of **financial management**.

Let's take a look a sport finance situation. In the spring of 2013, Dwight Howard's deal with the Houston Rockets of the NBA was worth $88 million over four years. If he had stayed with the Los Angeles Lakers he could've made another $30 million and one more season. The contract negation involves aspects of federal, state, and local taxation. California has a state marginal tax rate of 10.3% and the state of Texas has no state income tax. Over the life of the Houston Rockets contract, Dwight Howard will pay almost $10 million less in state income tax. Therefore, the Houston Rockets' owner should consider the following: How much cash do I have on hand? Do we have players to trade? What is my payment going to be? If I am going to borrow money, how much should I borrow? What is my income (cash inflow) going to be in order to pay for Dwight Howard? Will season tickets and sponsorship increase? Should we even trade for Dwight Howard? Do we need him? What benefit is it going to provide? Can we get by with a less expensive player? What if he gets hurt? This process is part of business financial management.

IMPORTANCE OF FINANCE IN SPORT

The goal of this chapter is to introduce some of the concepts of business financial management in a sport environment. Sport finance utilizes the same business principals as any organization except it usually involves players in professional sport as assets. Sport also is highly integrated in the public sector (city, county, state, and federal governments to a degree). The objective of finance is to maximize profit to benefit the owners, which is accomplished by good financial decisions.

Global corporations now control professional sport. The past history of the entrepreneurial owner is quickly fading. Current owners are often part of large public corporations that will utilize the team, league, and community assets to produce a more valuable asset. Analyzing performance of professional sports teams is now more complex due to the integration of the teams into the other business opportunities of the owners.

College athletics is much easier to understand. The financial statements are usually public documents that can be obtained. It is easy to analyze teams in the same conference and specific NCAA division classification. The income statement is the dominant statement due to the agency relationship with a University. It should be stressed that major Universities are now trying to utilize the same revenue techniques implemented from professional sports into their organization.

Professional, college, and amateur sport are borrowing money at record levels. New facilities are being built, remodeled, and expanded at a record pace. It is essential for these organizations to have adequate capital and profit to provide assurances to creditors that the assets are secure. Banks, mortgage companies, and insurance enterprises do not want to repossess an arena or stadium. Think about that fact. What would a financial lending institution do with a new stadium with no team?

ACCOUNTING IS A PARTNER TO FINANCE

Financial analysis requires useful information. A company's suppliers, creditors, and shareholders have an interest in analyzing the performance. They need assurances that the sport enterprise has liquidity and solvency to meet short-term debts. Long-term creditors are concerned with projected profitability because they seek assurances that the company will be able to service its debt over several years. Public sport enterprises now must make financial decisions with the aspect of maximizing shareholder wealth. Sport stockholders, like public corporate shareholders, need to assess the potential cash flows and the adherent risks in order to estimate the future price of the common stock.

Analyzing financial performance begins with the sports enterprise's financial statements. The balance sheet, the income statement, and the cash flow statement are the starting point for evaluating the current condition and financial future of the company. Further explanation and examples of the financial statements will occur later in the chapter. A few questions should arise when looking at financial statements:

1. Can the current debts be satisfied from the current liquidity (cash) position?
2. Is company's long-term debt position overextended, or can the company borrow more money to alleviate liquidity problems?
3. What is the cash flow of the enterprise?
4. What is the debt to cash flow of the company?
5. Why is the sport enterprise more or less profitable than other comparable sport enterprises?

6. Is management aggressive or conservative concerning credit arrangements?
7. How does management's decision to enter the sport business compare to returns gained from non-sport-related business enterprises?

Each of the questions requires information to be gathered in order to make sound decisions. The balance sheet and income statements are essential to initiate an analysis of any business enterprise. Caution is necessary when reviewing financial statements. Audited financial statements have been compiled by a third party and are independent of the company's accountants and financial officers. Internal financial statements are the product of the financial officers and have not had the scrutiny of an independent auditor. Answers to the questions will involve analysis from financial statements, ratio, trend analysis, and cash flow interpretation.

Data Gathering

Fundamentally it is easy to say, "Get the financial statements and determine the financial performance of a sport enterprise." But how are internal financial statements obtained if the sport enterprise is not a public entity? Professional sport franchises will not provide a copy of the financial statements upon request. Therefore, it may be impossible to obtain the statements for the comparison to other teams or franchises. Publicly traded companies will have audited financial statements for shareholders to review and the potential investing public to access. Sounds great, but the reality is the sport-related business will be part of a larger asset on the balance sheet such as entertainment division or sport properties. It will not have the baseball or hockey team's financial statements broken out for review.

Gathering data is not a simple process. Public agencies are required by the Freedom of Information Act (FOIA) to provide data if requested. Following is a short synopsis of the law that will aid in gathering data on public colleges and universities, teams that are publicly traded, and other government agency involvement. "FOIA," or "the Act," is a law enacted in 1966 that established citizens' statutory right to access government records and information upon request. The basic purpose of FOIA is to "ensure an informed citizenry, vital to the functioning of a democratic society, needed to check against corruption and to hold the governors accountable to the governed." Basically, the public or any individual has the right to know or be informed about activities, decisions, and policies of U.S. federal agencies.

The financial statements and related summary material are part of the records. A record means any document, writing, photograph, sound, or magnetic recording, drawing, computerized record (disks, database), electronic mail, policies and decisions, or anything in which information can be retrieved and/or copied. The balance sheet, income statement, statement of cash flows, and specifically-stated financial document can be reviewed if it is not a confidential or privileged document.

Who can request such a document? U.S. citizens (and non-U.S. citizens), corporations, associations, public interest groups, private individuals, universities, and local, state, or foreign governments can all submit FOIA requests. The FOIA is a frequent vehicle for citizens to gain access to public records. Visit the site www.aclu.org/library/foia.html to access letters and other legal information that will be helpful in data gathering.

Other sources for data gathering include a request to the Chief Financial Officer for access to the financial information or a written request to Board of Directors (if available). These will probably be unsuccessful. Financial data may have to be gathered from third parties, league contracts that are public such as television and radio contracts, sponsorships, and revenue sharing. Next, a financial forecast will have to be completed to estimate revenue streams for the team and/or league. Elements necessary to complete a financial forecast include attendance figures, ticket prices, concession and merchandise sales estimates, parking data, luxury and club seating revenues, and other miscellaneous sales.

Third-party revenue and expense projections may also be available from regional newspapers, trade journals, and sport business journals. Net income and loss estimates of teams, conferences, and leagues are routinely done in *My Financial World*, *Sport Business Journal*, and *The Sporting News*. The NCAA produces the document "Revenues and Expenses of Intercollegiate Athletics Programs," an analysis of financial trends and relationships. This document is a very good basis for financial comparison of all NCAA division classifications.

Gathering financial data is time consuming and often frustrating. Professional sport organizations will not voluntarily provide proprietary information. They are in a competitive business to provide a rate of return to the shareholders or the owner. The owners may share the information with each other at league meetings, but the public is privy to the data. Remember that the owners are a select few in each sport and meet annually to discuss the status of the game. The status is usually financial in nature.

College sports data can be assessed. The FOIA may be required, but the information is available. Most major universities have booster clubs and they often act separately from the athletic department.

Therefore, without good accounting information, the finance manager is at a disadvantage in analysis. Accounting and finance are interrelated and depend on each other for proper business and financial management.

Organizational Structure

Sport, like any other business, has various organizational structures. The setup of the sport organization is vital to the financial analysis necessary to maximize profit. Sport companies exist in three major forms: sole proprietorship, partnership, and corporation.[1] Each differs in legal, tax, and business management and must be a concern when analysis occurs.

A **sole proprietorship** is a company owned by one person. Historically, many of the original professional sport franchises were proprietorships. This has changed due to the enormous capital necessary to finance a company. Now, sport franchises are usually smaller companies managed by one principal owner. A **partnership** is a company owned by two or more individuals who have entered into an agreement. A partnership agreement will determine each partner's share in the debt and profits of the company. Unless

Photo courtesy © dreamstime

specifically stated in the agreement, all partners will share equally in debt and profit. A **corporation** is a company formed by an agreement between the state and the persons forming the company, and the state requires legal documentation of the agreement. The agreement must be filed with the Secretary of State. A corporation (called a C corp) is a separately taxable entity. The profits and losses are taxed directly to the corporation. This can lead to double taxation on dividends that are paid out of corporate profits to the owners.

Special corporations exist in sport business. One special structure is called an **S corporation** which is simply a C corporation (also known as a standard business corporation) that files IRS form 2553 to elect a special tax status with the IRS. The articles of incorporation that are filed with the state are the same whether a corporation is a C corporation or an S corporation. The main difference is a pass-through tax entity—this means that the income or loss generated by the business is reflected on the personal income tax return of the owners. Another special company is called an LLC, or Limited Liability Company, which is a business entity formed upon filing articles of organization with the proper state authorities and paying all fees. LLCs provide the limited liability to their members and are taxed like a partnership, preventing double taxation. LLCs can be formed in every state. LLCs are now popular company structures in sport organizations.

Importance of Organizational Structure

The key to financial management is to structure the sport organization to maximize profit, limit liability, and provide opportunity for infusion of capital for growth. Each company has differences in tax issues, cash flow, and liability. Managing these companies requires knowledge of accounting, finance, and taxation issues. It should be noted that owners of corporations pay taxes twice. They pay taxes as the corporation, and the shareholders pay taxes on cash dividends they receive from the corporation.

REVENUE SOURCES

The high costs associated with operating professional sport franchises necessitates the generation and maintenance of a successful and consistent revenue stream in order to achieve profitability. As standard practice, revenues of franchises are generated through numerous sources, including ticket sales, sponsorship, luxury suites, club seating, media revenue, licensing/merchandising, concessions, and parking. These sources lead to big dollars in the world of sport. Annual revenue for the NFL currently stands at $9.7 billion (with a goal of $25 billion within 15 years), MLB at $7.5 billion, NASCAR at $4.1

billion, and the NBA at $4.0 billion (Isidore, 2013; Kaplan, 2013). Importantly, the annual revenue of a franchise is linked directly to its market value ("CEO Network Chat," 2003). The Dallas Cowboys, the NFL's most highly valued team at $2.1 billion in 2012, earned $500 million in revenue in the 2011 season ("NFL Team Values," 2012). The New York Yankees, MLB's most highly valued team at $2.3 billion in 2013, earned a similar amount of revenue, coming in at $471 million for the 2012 season ("MLB Team Values," 2013). Team revenue for all of the teams in the NFL, MLB, NBA, and NHL are provided in Table 6.1. The purpose of this section is to provide a brief introduction to the primary revenue sources for sport organizations.

Ticket Revenue

Photo courtesy © Andy Gillentine

Ticket revenue accounts for a significant portion of revenue for sport franchises, though the proportion that it contributes to total revenue varies by league. In general, ticket revenue accounts for a smaller proportion of total revenue for leagues with richer media rights deals (e.g., NFL) than it does for leagues with less valuable media rights deals (e.g., NHL). The significance of ticket revenue, often called the gate, can be seen in the steadily increasing ticket prices in sport. According to Team Marketing Report, the average ticket now costs $78.38 in the NFL, $50.99 in the NBA, $61.01 in the NHL, and $27.48 in MLB ("Fan cost experience," n.d.).

A regular practice for franchises is to engage in a strategy called variable ticket pricing to increase ticket sales and revenue. Variable ticket pricing refers to pricing different events at different levels based on fan demand. Many teams at all levels of sport, from professional to collegiate, have raised ticket prices for games that have higher demand due to factors such as playing a rivalry team or taking place during a prime time week or month of the year. As a collegiate example, the University of South Carolina Gamecocks football team charges significantly higher ticket prices for games against high-profile opponents such as The University of Florida, The University of Georgia, and Clemson, and lower prices for games against opponents such as Vanderbilt and non-Southeastern Conference opponents. The bottom line with variable pricing is to increase revenue by catering to fluctuating fan demand. Teams boost their revenue by capitalizing on high demand games and, in order to sell as many seats as possible, offering lower prices on less demanded games.

A relatively recent evolution of variable ticket pricing is dynamic ticket pricing. Teams that use dynamic ticket pricing utilize technology to increase their ability to match ticket price to demand by allowing ticket prices to fluctuate continuously based on a wide array of factors that can influence fan demand, including weather forecasts, team perform-

Table 6.1. Franchise Revenue							
NFL	Revenue ($MIL)	MLB	Revenue ($MIL)	NBA	Revenue ($MIL)	NHL	Revenue ($MIL)
Cowboys	500	Yankees	471	Knicks	243	Maple Leafs	200
Patroits	380	Red Sox	336	Lakers	197	Rangers	199
Redskins	373	Phillies	279	Bulls	162	Canadiens	169
Giants	326	Cubs	274	Heat	150	Canucks	143
Texans	304	Giants	262	Celtics	143	Bruins	129
Jets	299	Dodgers	245	Mavericks	137	Red Wings	128
Eagles	296	Rangers	239	Rockets	135	Blackhawks	125
Bears	286	Angels	239	Spurs	135	Flyers	124
Ravens	276	Cardinals	239	Cavaliers	128	Devils	122
Packers	269	Tigers	238	Warriors	127	Penguins	120
Broncos	276	Mets	232	Thunder	127	Kings	120
Panthers	269	Nationals	225	Magic	126	Flames	117
Colts	268	Braves	225	Pistons	125	Senators	113
Steelers	266	White Sox	216	Suns	121	Capitals	106
Dolphins	265	Mariners	215	Raptors	121	Oilers	106
Titans	262	Twins	214	Trail Blazers	117	Jets	105
Seahawks	260	Orioles	206	Jazz	111	Sharks	101
Chiefs	259	Blue Jays	203	Nuggets	110	Stars	100
Saints	259	Reds	202	Clippers	108	Wild	99
Buccaneers	258	Brewers	201	76ers	107	Sabres	96
Chargers	246	Rockies	199	Wizards	102	Avalanche	91
Cardinals	246	Astros	196	Hornets	100	Ducks	91
49ers	245	Diamondbacks	195	Hawks	99	Blues	89
Bills	240	Marlins	195	Pacers	98	Lightning	88
Falcons	239	Padres	189	Kings	96	Predators	88
Jaguars	238	Indians	189	Grizzlies	96	Panthers	87
Bengals	235	Pirates	178	Timberwolves	96	Hurricanes	85
Lions	231	Athletics	173	Bobcats	93	Blue Jackets	85
Rams	231	Royals	169	Bucks	87	Coyotes	83
Vikings	227	Rays	167	Nets	84	Islanders	66
Raiders	226						

Source: Compiled from http://www.forbes.com/nfl-valuations/list; http://www.forbes.com/mlb-valuations/list; http://www.forbes.com/nba-valuationslist; http://www.forbes.com/nhl-valuations/list

ance to date, injuries to star players on opposing teams, and the like (Fetchko, Roy, & Clow, 2013). Dynamic ticket pricing is an increasingly popular strategy. For example, its use by NBA franchises helped total ticket revenue pass the $1 billion mark for the 2012–2013 season, a record gate revenue for that league (Lombardo, 2013).

Sponsorship

Sponsorship can be broadly defined as investing in a sports entity (athlete, league, team, or event) to support overall organizational objectives, marketing goals, and promotional strategies (Shank, 2009). Sponsorship marketing represents an enormous revenue source for sport organizations. IEG estimates that North American sponsorship spending will rise 5.5% in 2013 to $19.9 billion, with nearly 70% of this amount spent on sport sponsorship (the other proportion being spent on entertainment, arts, and other types of entities) (IEG, 2013a). Sponsorship deals can be very significant. Anheuser-Busch, for example, spends an estimated $50 million per year on its NFL sponsorship, and is committed for six years (Schultz, 2012).

Sport organizations sell sponsorship in many forms, including but not limited to advertising (e.g., venue signage and programs), promotional opportunities tied to the sport property (e.g., the right to sample product at an event, the right to conduct sweepstakes in conjunction with the sport property), and naming rights to event facilities. Examples of naming rights deals for major and minor league stadiums and arenas, as well as for NCAA facilities, are provided in Table 6.2.

To an extent, sponsorship revenue is limited only by a sport organization's creativity. For example, sports teams can sell signage alone in numerous categories, including on scoreboards, marquees, the playing surface itself, the facility concourse, turnstiles, facility steps, game programs, media guides, team newsletters, and the backs of tickets, to name a few. Further, teams can sell sponsorship of fantasy camps, coach's clinics, ticket packages such as family packs, and the like. Sponsorship opportunities can range from the relatively small (e.g., John Deere sponsoring stolen bases by a collegiate baseball team) to the seemingly astronomical, such as the $20 million per year paid by Citigroup for naming rights to Citi Field, home of the New York Mets. Many sport organizations have seen growth in sponsorship revenue in recent years through better development of sponsorship categories. For example, Indianapolis Motor Speedway increased sponsorship revenue by 9% over each of the last two years in large part by signing sponsors in categories such as retail/personal grooming (Great Clips), construction/industrial (Caterpillar), and quick-service restaurants (Hardees) (Mickle, 2013). Strong sponsorship sales efforts by individual properties such as Indianapolis Motor Speedway lead to big spending within their respective sports. For example, North American companies were estimated to spend $3.76 billion on sponsorship of motorsports teams, tracks, and sanctioning bodies in 2013, a 3.9% increase from 2012 (IEG, 2013b).

Luxury Suites and Club Seating

Luxury suites and club seating provide another major revenue source for sport franchises. Luxury suites are special areas provided for premium seating and entertaining.

Table 6.2. Naming Rights					
Facility	City/School	Sponsor	Price ($MIL)	No. of Years	Expiration Year
Major League Stadiums					
MetLife Stadium	East Rutherfield, NJ	Metropolitan Life Insurance	425-625	25	2036
Citi Field	Queens, NY	Citigroup	400	20	2028
Reliant Stadium	Houston, TX	Reliant Energy	310	31	2032
Major League Arenas					
Barclays Center	Brooklyn, NY	Barclays PLC	200	20	2032
American Airlines Center	Dallas, TX	American Airlines	195	30	2030
Phillips Arena	Atlanta, GA	Royal Phillips Electronics	185	20	2019
Minor League Stadiums					
Chukchansi Park	Fresno, CA	Chukchansi Gold Resort/Casino	16	15	2021
Raley Field	Sacramento, CA	Raley's Inc.	15	20	2019
Huntington Park	Columbus, OH	Huntington Bancshares	12	23	2030
Minor League Arenas					
CenturyLink Center Omaha	Omaha, NE	CenturyLink	14	15	2018
KFC Yum! Center	Louisville, KY	Yum! Brands	13.5	10	2020
Wells Fargo Arena	Des Moines, IA	Wells Fargo	11.5	20	2025
Collegiate Facilities					
TCF Bank Stadium	U. of Minnesota	TCF Bank	35	25	2034
Comcast Center	U. of Maryland	Comcast Corporation	25	25	2026
Apogee Stadium	U. of North Texas	Apogee	20	20	2030
Source: Street & Smith's SportsBusiness Journal, Vol 14, Issue 21, pp. 22-23					

Club seats are premium seating areas that provide the fan with special amenities such as food and beverage service and special parking privileges. Indeed, it is the revenue potential of luxury suites, and to a lesser extent club seating, that has been the major catalyst in the boom of new sport venue construction and the remodeling of existing venues to accommodate the addition of such premium areas. Luxury suites and club seating have become such a critical revenue source that premium and club seating has grown from approximately 3% to nearly 20% of seating in stadiums and arenas in the last ten years (Ahlgren, 2012). The prices for luxury suites can be significant. For example, some suites at Yankee Stadium sell for over $800,000 per year, while some suites at Madison Square Garden sell for over $1 million per year. Indianapolis Motor Speedway brings in

		Suite	Suite	Club		
League	Suite Quantity	Low Price ($)	High Price ($)	Seat Quantity	Club Seat Low Price ($)	Club Seat High Price ($)
NFL	140	66,677	214,322	8,657	1,821	4,423
MLB	68	128,280	251,440	4,241	4,099	20,648
NBA	89	138,846	330,158	2,020	5,735	8,531
NHL	93	130,300	300,566	1,991	5,513	8,254

Table 6.3. Average Luxury Suite and Club Seat Prices and Quantities

Source: Revenues from Sports Venues (http://www.sportsvenues.com/rsv.php?menue=suites; http://www.sportsvenues.com/rsv.php?menue=clubs).

$110,000 per year for each Tower Terrace Suite sold (with three-year contracts for the suites) (Kane, 2012). Table 6.3 gives the average high and low prices for luxury suites and club seats for venues in MLB, the NFL, the NBA, and the NHL, along with the average quantity of suites and seats for each league. From these figures, one can see the significant amount of revenue provided by luxury suites and club seating.

Media Revenue

Media revenue is another major source of revenue for sports leagues and franchises, and new media deals in recent years have increased the proportion of total league and franchise revenue accounted for by broadcasting rights. The importance of media revenue, particularly from television rights, as a revenue source cannot be overstated in today's sports business climate. The NFL has nine-year contracts with Fox, NBC, and CBS that will take effect after the 2013 season and will bring in an average of $3.1 billion per year whereas ESPN has a contract with the NFL that is paying the league an average of $1.9 billion per year for broadcast rights (Flint, 2011). The NBA is also heavily supported by broadcast rights revenue, with current contracts with ESPN/ABC, TNT, and NBA TV worth $7.44 billion total from the 2008/2009 season through the 2015/2016 season (Ozanian, 2011). MLB has a deal with Fox and Turner Sports that will extend through 2021 and pay the league an average of approximately $800 million annually, while it has a $700 million per year deal with ESPN that runs from 2014 through 2021 ("MLB completes," 2012). The NHL has a ten-year deal with NBC that extends through the 2020/2021 season and pays the league approximately $200 million per year ("NBC and NHL," 2011).

Other sports organizations also benefit significantly from media revenue. NASCAR, for example, recently signed an extension with Fox that will pay the organization $300 million per year from the 2015 through the 2022 seasons (the current agreement is for $225 million per year) (Fixmer, 2012). NBC paid $894 million for all domestic media rights to the Beijing 2008 Olympic Games, $820 million for the Vancouver 2010 Games, and $1.18 billion for the London 2012 Games ("What NBC paid," 2012). Collegiate sports also benefits from broadcast rights, with the NCAA earning an astronomical $6 billion from CBS alone for the rights to broadcast the NCAA Men's Basketball Tournament as well as 66 other championships for eleven years (through the 2012–2013 season) ("2004 by the numbers," 2004).

Licensing and Merchandising

Licensing and merchandising provide yet another source of revenue to many sport properties. Licensing is a contractual agreement whereby a company may use another company's trademark in exchange for a royalty or fee (Shank, 2009). Within the sport industry, this most often takes the form of selling the right to use team names and logos to companies (termed the licensee) that sell logoed apparel and/or other logoed merchandise. Royalty fees paid by the licensee to the sport property (termed the licensor) usually range from 4% to 20% of gross sales at wholesale cost (Mullin, Hardy, & Sutton, 2007). Items beyond team names and logos, such as advertising slogans and terms and characteristics specifically associated with the sport organization, are also licensed in order to generate revenue and promote the brand. For example, the NFL secured the rights to the term "Dirty Bird" after it was popularized by the Atlanta Falcons during their Super Bowl season of 1998 (Irwin, Sutton, & McCarthy, 2002). As yet another example, there was a trademark battle for the term "Linsanity," a term that represented the recent excitement surrounding former New York Knicks point guard Jeremy Lin (with Lin ultimately prevailing).

Licensing is big business. Retail sales of licensed merchandise based on sports leagues and events were $12.79 billion in 2011 ("Sports on the rebound," 2012). In 2011, MLB and the NFL accounted for sales of $3.1 billion and $3.0 billion, respectively, the NBA accounted for $2.0 billion, and the NHL and NASCAR $887 million each ("Sports on the rebound," 2012). Another top player in the licensing business is Collegiate Licensing Co. (CLC), which handles licensing for nearly 200 universities/colleges, conferences, the NCAA, bowl games, and the Heisman Trophy, approximately 80% of the $4.6 billion retail market for collegiate licensed merchandise ("Collegiate Licensing Company," n.d.). Universities leading the licensing royalty race include the University of Texas at Austin, the University of Alabama, and the University of Kentucky. Licensing revenue can be significant for university athletic departments with top-tier programs. The University of Kentucky, for example, brought in $6.73 million in licensed merchandise royalties for the 2011/2012 fiscal year, aided, of course, by their basketball national championship that year (Novy-Williams, 2012).

Concessions

Food and beverage sales account for an additional source of team and venue revenue. The vast majority of teams outsource their concession services to organizations such as Centerplate and Aramark, and teams retain a percentage of concession sales dollars. For example, in 2010, the University of Louisville received $785,000 in concession revenues (30% of Centerplate's concession sales) from its home football games alone (Sayer, 2012). The trend in concessions has been to become smarter about marketing by catering to fan tastes. The result has been a boost in concession revenue achieved through the offering of more regional, local, and high quality cuisine. Not only do today's fans enjoy the standard fare such as hot dogs and burgers, they are now tempted by items such as crab cakes at Baltimore Orioles games, Latin cuisine at Tampa Bay Rays games, Anchor Beer at San Francisco Giants games, and Oyster Po' Boys (made with local oysters of course) at Seattle Mariner games (Boudevin, 2012). The result is increased spending by fans and more revenue to both concessionaires and teams.

In addition to enhanced concession revenue through more and better food choices, revenue is also being enhanced through technology that makes the purchase experience more convenient for fans. For example, Centerplate recently equipped the University of South Carolina's Williams-Brice Stadium concession stands with over 150 mobile computer tablets housing credit card readers. These tablets and their software allow for quicker and more efficient transactions, boosting sales (credit card sales at football games more than doubled) and resulting revenue for the school (Muret, 2012). With their mobility, the tablets can be moved to other University of South Carolina venues as well, enhancing concession sales for the university across a multi-sport platform. In sum, for many sport properties, the enhancement of both menus and transaction efficiency has revitalized concessions as a meaningful source of revenue. Indeed, for many minor league teams that have relatively low ticket prices and thus a smaller proportion of team revenue accounted for by ticket sales, concession sales can significantly impact profitability (Howard, 1998).

FINANCIAL STATEMENTS

Financial information is only as good as the statements or detail gathered from the company. Standards are set in most countries to conform to a set of common practices in accounting. In the United States, these common standards are called generally accepted accounting principles (GAAP). GAAP is a combination of authoritative standards (set by policy boards) and the accepted ways of doing accounting. Two private

Photo courtesy © Andy Gillentine

organizations, the American Institute of Certified Public Accountants (AICPA) and the Financial Accounting Standards Board (FASB), in addition to the Security Exchange Commission (SEC), an agency of the Federal Government, are the regulatory bodies that help determine GAAP.

A great source for quick financial data is Yahoo Finance. Go to Yahoo Finance and type in a symbol for a company; for example, KO for the Coca-Cola Company. You will see stock prices, financial statements, SEC reports (10K annual report), and 10Q –quarterly reports. The data can be extensive but provides the reader with essential financial elements to determine how the company is doing and the financial position at a specific date. The following are the standard financial statements that sport managers will utilize.

Balance Sheet

A balance sheet is a snapshot of a business's financial condition at a specific moment in time, usually at the close of an accounting period. A balance sheet comprises assets, liabilities, and owners' or stockholders' equity. Assets and liabilities are divided into short- and long-term obligations including cash accounts such as checking, money market, or government securities. At any given time, assets must equal liabilities plus owners' equity $(A = L + OE)$. An asset is anything the business owns that has monetary value. Liabilities are the claims of creditors against the assets of the business.[2] A quick synopsis for the balance sheet will help in your understanding. Assets—items of value owned by a company; total assets equal debt plus shareholder equity. Debt—money a company owes; debt equals total assets minus shareholder equity. Equity—owners' investment in a company; equity equals total assets minus debt.

Income Statement

An income statement, otherwise known as a profit and loss statement or an operating statement, is a summary of a company's profit or loss during any one given period of time, such as a month, three months, or one year. The income statement records all revenues for a business during this given period, as well as the operating expenses for the business.[3]

Cash Flow—The Statement

The **Statement of Cash Flow** shows the sources and uses of cash for your business over a certain period of time. This period coincides with the reporting period of the income statement. For example, if a cash flow statement covers the 12 months ended on Dec. 31, 2014, the associated income statement covers the same period.

A cash flow statement shows you how your business performs on a cash basis. An income statement shows how your business performs on an accrual basis. In this respect, a cash flow statement generally supplements the information provided in an income statement.

Financial statement analysis requires understanding the strengths and weaknesses of the company. A student of sport finance should be able to understand where problems may occur and what questions need to be addressed. It is often <u>more important to un-</u> <u>derstand the weaknesses than</u> to focus on the financial strengths of the enterprise. Data often must be forecasted and pro-forma statements generated to analyze a situation.

It is difficult to analyze financial information without understanding the relationship of the balance sheet and the income statement.

Cash Flow—The Concept

The statement of cash flow explains, "What happened to the cash?" This cannot be learned solely from the other financial statements (balance sheet and income state- ment). <u>The statement of cash flows reports the entity's cash receipts and cash payments</u> <u>during a period of time;</u> it <u>explains where cash came from and where cash was spent.</u> Analysis requires two periods of time, usually two fiscal years or calendar years, to com- pare the balance sheet and income statements. The following flowchart will provide a visual relationship.

The balance sheet is important, but it just reports the cash balance at the end of a pe- riod. Therefore, by comparing two consecutive balance sheets you can determine the cash increases and/or decreases during this specific time period. The curious student will inquire, "Why has cash changed?" <u>The income statement reports revenues and ex-</u> <u>penses, which results in net income or loss.</u> The income statement is often referred to as the statement of profit and loss, the statement of operations, or the statement of sources and uses. <u>However, the income statement alone doesn't answer why cash increased or</u> <u>decreased</u>. Analyzing the balance sheet and income statement in conjunction with the statement of retained earnings will provide the reader with the information to deter- mine why cash changed and explain the causes associated with this cash adjustment.

Cash dominates the sports industry, and therefore cash management is essential. Quickly consider sources of cash in a sports enterprise. Tickets, concessions, parking, merchandise sales, and sponsorships are only a few of the cash-generating categories in the sport industry.

The statement of cash flow is essential for the sport manager. They need to be able to make managerial and financial decisions based on cash availability. The purpose of cash flow is to:

1. **Predict the future cash flows.** Cash, not net income, pays the bills. Net income is not cash.
2. **Evaluate management decisions.** If the General Manager (GM) makes wise in- vestment decisions, the team and organization prospers. <u>If the GM makes poor</u>

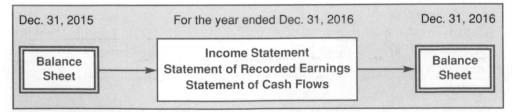

Figure 6.1. Financial Statements Flowchart

decisions, the team and organization suffers. For example, should the organization build a new stadium or facility (additions to property, plant, and equipment) with private or public funds? This management decision will impact the financial aspect of the organization for decades. A new facility will impact the ability of the organization to increase revenues. Factors that must be addressed include predicting the economy. If a recession is expected, will the new facility attract these anticipated revenues, or will the economy continue to expand and increase entertainment spending? Management's decisions impact investors' and creditors' cash-flow information.

3. **Determine the ability to pay dividends to stockholders as well as interest and principal to creditors.** Return on the stockholders' investment is necessary to maintain stock value and dividends produce cash to these owners. Creditors (bondholders or financial institutions) want to receive the interest and principal payments on time. The statement of cash flows assists the investors and creditors in determining the capability of management in making these payments.

4. **Analyze the business relationship between net income (income statement) and changes in cash (balance sheet).** Cash usually increases when net revenues increase; however, sport organizations must make sure the new facility will produce this anticipated result. It should be noted that cash could decrease when net income is high and increase when net income is low. Therefore, the need for accurate cash management is essential for management in the sport and entertainment industry. For example, if a bonus is to be paid to a new free agent, will the organization have the cash on hand to pay the player or will the bonus need to be borrowed from a lending institution?

THE LIFE CIRCLE OF A SUCCESSFUL BUSINESS

The sport and entertainment business is a special type of business. Sport organizations must invest in players, venues, facility upgrades, non-playing personnel, and technology to be successful (fixed assets). These expenditures are called capital expenditures and the venue (stadium, arena) is often the most expensive asset. In sport, players are assets and can be a significant investment for teams and organizations. The investments should produce greater revenue from ticket sales, sponsorships, concessions, parking, and all venue-related income streams.

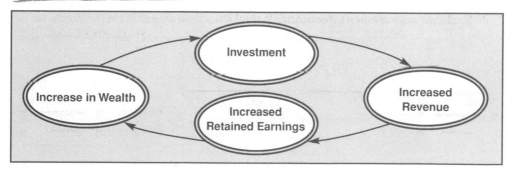

Figure 6.2. Life circle of a successful business

The increase in revenue will hopefully produce great net income (income statement) that will produce greater retained earnings (balance sheet) and then increase the owner's wealth. This is the circle of life for a successful business.

The increase in wealth then allows the ownership groups to invest in additional assets. These assets may be players, stadium upgrades, and additional technology in the stadium (video boards and social media). This all creates positive cash flow that completes this circle of life. In summary, capital assets should translate into greater wealth.

SUMMARY

Good financial planning is a roadmap to success. In this chapter we discussed the basic financial statements, terms, and concepts. The way accounting and finance work together to produce meaningful financial information was covered, along with the importance of organizational structure.

Sport is a service industry, and sport finance is a key component of the business that assists managers by producing tangible information for decision makers.

Discussion Activities

1. Identify the main expense categories in college, professional, and international sports
2. Conduct research into the broadcast rights deals of the four major North American professional sport leagues. Compare and contrast your findings

Endnotes

1. "Company" is a generic term identifying a group of people associating for some purpose. In this text we generally use the term "company" in place of corporation, proprietorship, or partnership. Corporation is too limiting because many of the concepts and procedures we describe are also applicable to proprietorships and partnerships. Source: Cooley and Roden, 1991
2. Streetwise Small Business Start-up
3. Streetwise Small Business Start-up

References

2004 by the numbers (2004). *Street & Smith's Sports-Business Journal, 6*(36), 10–14.

Ahlgren, A. (2012). Why the NFL stadium experience is dying. *Bleacher Report.* Retrieved from http://bleacherreport.com/articles/1191009-why-the-nfl-stadium-experience-is-dying

Boudevin, J. (2012). Foods of summer. *Venues Today.* Retrieved from http://www.venuestoday.com/news/detail/oyster-po-boy-0523""

CEO network chat on the business of sports (2003, February 10). *Forbes.com.* Retrieved from http://www.forbes.com/work/2003/02/10/cx_ml_0210sportschat.html

Club seats (n.d.). Retrieved from http://www.sportsvenues.com/rsv.php?menu=clubs

Collegiate Licensing Company (n.d.). Retrieved from http://www.clc.com/About-CLC.aspx

Cooley, P. L., & Roden, P. F. (1991). *Business financial management.* Dryden Press.

Fan cost experience. (n.d.). Retrieved from http://www.fancostexperience.com/

Fetchko, M., Roy. D., & Clow, K. (2013). *Sports marketing.* Upper Saddle River, NJ: Prentice Hall.

Fixmer (2012). Fox Sports signs eight-year extension of Nascar TV rights. *Bloomberg.* Retrieved from http://www.bloomberg.com/news/2012-10-15/fox-sports-signs-8-year-extension-of-nascar-tv-rights-contract.html

Flint, J. (2011). NFL signs TV rights deals with Fox, NBC and CBS. *Los Angeles Times.* Retrieved from http://articles.latimes.com/2011/dec/15/business/la-fi-ct-nfl-deals-20111215

Howard, D. (1998). Financial principles applied to sport management. In L. Masteralexis, C. Barr,

& M. Hums (Eds.), *Principles and practice of sport management* (pp. 70–71). Gaithersburg, MD: Aspen Publishers Inc.

IEG, LLC (2013a). 2013 Sponsorship outlook: Spending increase is double- edged sword. *IEG Sponsorship Report*. Retrieved from http://www .sponsorship .com/iegsr/2013/01/07/2013-Sponsorship-Outlook--Spending-In crease-IsDou.aspx

IEG, LLC (2013b). Motorsports sponsorship spending to total $3.76 billion in 2013. *IEG Sponsorship Report*. Retrieved from http://www.sponsorship.com/IEGSR/2013/02/25/Motorsports-Sponsorship-Spending-To-Total-$3-76-Bi.aspx

Irwin, R., Sutton, W., & McCarthy, L. (2002). *Sport promotion and sales management*. Champaign, IL: Human Kinetics.

Isidore, C. (2013). Why football is still a money machine. *CNN Money*. Retrieved from http://money.cnn.com/2013/02/01/news/companies/nfl-money-super-bowl/index.html

Kane, C. (2012). Most expensive luxury suites. *The Post Game*. Retrieved from http://www.thepostgame.com/blog/list/201205/most-expensive-luxury-suites#2

Kaplan, D. (2013). Slight revenue revision may raise NFL cap. *Street & Smith's SportsBusiness Journal*, *15*(44), 4.

Lombardo, J. (2013). Pricing helps NBA set record for gate revenue. *Street & Smith's SportsBusiness Journal*, *16*(3), 5.

Luxury suites. (n.d.). Retrieved from http://www .sportsvenues.com/rsv.php?menu=suites

Mickle, T. (2013). Sponsorship push starting to pay off for Indy. *Street & Smith's SportsBusiness Journal*, *16*(4), 7.

MLB completes new TV deals. (2012). *ESPN.com*. Retrieved from http://espn.go.com/mlb/story/_/id/8453054/major-league-baseball-completes-eight-year-deal-fox-turner-sports

MLB team values. (2013). *Forbes.com*. Retrieved from http://www.forbes.com/mlb-valuations/list/

Motorsports sponsorship spending to total $3.76 billion in 2013. (2013, February 25). *IEG Sponsorship Report*. Retrieved from http://www.sponsorship.com/IEGSR/2013/02/25/Motorsports-Sponsorship-Spending-To-Total-$3-76-Bi.aspx

Mullin, B., Hardy, S., & Sutton, W. (2007). *Sport marketing* (3rd ed.). Champaign, IL: Human Kinetics.

Muret, D. (2012). Centerplate launches entirely mo-bile point-of-sale system. *Street & Smith's SportsBusiness Journal*, *15*(29), 16.

Naming rights deals (2011). *Street & Smith's SportsBusiness Journal*, *14*(21), 22–23. Retrieved from http://www.sportsbusinessdaily.com/Journal/Issues/2011/09/19/In-Depth/Naming-rights-deals.aspx

NBA team values (2013). *Forbes.com*. Retrieved from http://www.forbes.com/nba-valuations/list/

NBC and NHL agree to 10-year TV rights deal (2011). *Reuters*. Retrieved from http://www.reuters.com/article/2011/04/20/us-nhl-nbc-idUSTRE73J02020110420

NFL team values (2012). *Forbes.com*. Retrieved from http://www.forbes.com/nfl-valuations/list/

Novy-Williams, E. (2012). Kentucky college basketball title brings 40% rise in royalties. *Bloomberg*. Retrieved from http://www.bloomberg.com/news/2012-08-06/kentucky-college-basketball-title-brings-40-rise-in-royalties.html

Ozanian, M. (2011). Higher NBA TV ratings mean at least a 30% increase in broadcasting fees. *Forbes*. Retrieved from http://www.forbes.com/sites/mikeozanian/2011/04/20/higher-nba-tv-ratings-means-at-least-a 30-increase-in-broadcasting-fees/

Sayer, B. (2012). Concessions: Quite the moneymaker for stadiums. *CPBJnow.com*. Retrieved from http://www.centralpennbusiness.com/article/20121107/SPORTS/121109844/-1/events_calendar/Concessions:-Quite-the-moneymaker-for-stadiums&template=sports

Schultz, E. (2012). Which marketers spend the most on sponsorships? *Advertising Age*. Retrieved from http://adage.com/article/news/marketers-spend-sponsorships/235112/

Shank, M. (2009). *Sports marketing: A strategic perspective* (4th ed.). Upper Saddle River, NJ: Prentice Hall.

"Sports on the rebound: Retail sales of licensed merchandise based on sports properties rises 5.3% in 2011" (2012). *The Licensing Letter*. Retrieved from http://www.epmcom.com/public/Sports_On_The_Rebound_Retail_Sales_Of_Licensed_Merchandise_Based_On_Sports_Properties_Rises_53_in_2011.cfm

What NBC paid for US Olympic rights over the years (2012). *Huffington Post*. Retrieved from http://www.huffingtonpost.com/2012/08/01/nbc-paid-us-olympics-rights_n_1729726.html

7

Sport Marketing

John Clark

"SPORT IS THE TOY DEPARTMENT OF HUMAN LIFE."

—*Howard Cosell*

INTRODUCTION

Think about the last time you attended or watched a professional sporting event on television. In addition to the game, you likely observed signs of companies throughout the arena or stadium, cheerleaders or a dance team, or a mascot roaming the sidelines or stadium rows entertaining fans. You may have heard the public address announcer talking about special offers or upcoming events and noticed entertaining elements on the scoreboard. If you were attending a professional baseball game and a hometown player hit a home run, there may have been a fireworks display. If you attended a baseball game in Milwaukee or Pittsburgh, in the middle of the game you may have seen mascots dressed as sausages or pierogies racing in the park. If you attended a National Basketball Association (NBA) game in Indianapolis, you may have seen "Boomer," the Pacers mascot, repel from the rafters at the beginning of the game, or don a mask of the Grim Reaper and stand behind the opposing team's bench late in the game.

Most things seen or heard at a professional sporting event are specifically designed to enhance our experience at that game. The same holds true for sporting events we watch on television or the Internet. Technological advances have allowed broadcast networks and production companies to enhance our viewing experience, making it easier to follow the action by providing the viewer with more information, increasing the number of cameras, and taking the viewer "into the action" with enhanced audio/visual capabilities. The end result, whether the game is viewed in person or from the comfort of our

---

Learning Objectives

Upon completion of this chapter, students will be able to
- Define marketing and its role in sport;
- Distinguish between marketing and promotions;
- Understand the need for market segmentation; and
- Identify the need for market research.

In the Bleachers © 2014 Steve Moore. Dist. by Universal Uclick
www.gocomics.com/inthebleachers

living room, is an elaborate strategy designed to keep the fans coming back. In essence, that is what sport marketing is all about—compelling customers to consume the sport product once, knowing that they will keep coming back if they have a good time and are more than satisfied with their experience.

SPORT MARKETING DEFINED

Ask several industry experts what sport marketing is exactly, and several different answers will emerge depending on the area of the industry in which the respondent works. Any all-inclusive academic definition of sport marketing would certainly include something about each of the four P's (product, price, promotion, and place) as they relate to the target consumers' behavior. It is beyond the scope of this chapter to tackle such a daunting task as creating *the* perfect definition for sport marketing; therefore, we will use a two-part definition from Mullin, Hardy, and Sutton (2000):

> Sport marketing consists of all activities designed to meet the needs and wants of sport consumers through exchange processes. Sport marketing has developed two major thrusts: the marketing of sport products and services directly to consumers of sport, and marketing of other consumer and industrial products or services through the use of sport. (p. 9)

The latter portion of the definition—marketing other products or services through sport—refers to promotional licensing or sponsorship, and will be dealt with extensively in the following chapter. As for the part of the definition that deals with the marketing of sport products and services, it bears exploring *why* the sport marketing specialty is needed. In other words, *how is sport marketing different than traditional marketing?*

PURPOSE OF MARKETING

An important caveat must be stated at this point. The primary purpose of marketing, both in the traditional and sport context, is ultimately to increase revenue for an organization. Certain marketing strategies may not lead to immediate sales (e.g., brand awareness strategies), but even these strategies have increased revenue as their ultimate goal. Aspiring sport marketers must remember that their efforts should pursue the objective of increasing revenue either in the short or long term.

Sport Consumers

In professional sport, all conceivable marketing strategies would not amount to a penny were it not for consumers. Both core and ancillary products in spectator and participatory sport rely on consumers for success. Sport is woven into the fabric of society—locally, regionally, nationally, and internationally. In the words of NBA Commissioner David Stern, as he watched the Houston Rockets and Sacramento Kings play a preseason game in China, "Fans are fans" (ESPN, 2004). As such, we learn to consume sport at a young age, both as participants and as spectators. For a sport marketer, two basic consumer characteristics exist that help differentiate types of sport consumers. These two characteristics are **involvement** and **commitment**. According to Mullin et al. (2000), involvement can be behavioral (the action of a sport activity), cognitive (seeking out information and knowledge about a sport), and affective (the feelings and emotions a sport consumer has for a particular activity or team).

Meanwhile, commitment refers to the frequency, duration, and intensity of involvement in a sport, or the willingness to expend money, time, and energy in a pattern of sport involvement (Mullin et al., 2000, p. 57). Sport is rife with examples of both of these consumer characteristics. For example, fans of the Major League Baseball's Chicago Cubs continue to pack Wrigley Field and drive the ratings for Cubs games on WGN-TV, WCIU, and Comcast SportsNet despite enduring over 100 years without a World Series title. Each spring, Cubs fans optimistically anticipate the upcoming season and the end of the alleged Cubs Curse. Some years, the franchise plays well enough to contend for a playoff berth, while other years, the Cubs' chances seem to diminish by mid-season. Nevertheless, Cub fans are highly committed to their franchise, and are heavily involved with each up and down of the season. For evidence, tune into a Chicago sport radio talk show any day between February and October to hear the Cub fans complain, suggest trades, disparage poor play, and, of course, deride the cross-town White Sox, or their arch-rival the St. Louis Cardinals. Researchers contend that highly

committed and highly involved sport consumers are more loyal than casual consumers; therefore, the sport marketer who can foster these characteristics in a consumer base will derive the benefits of a loyal customer base.

Involved and committed customers are important tenets of relationship marketing—a theory gaining increasing popularity in the sport world. According to Gordon (1998):

> [Relationship marketing is] the ongoing process of identifying and *creating new value* with individual customers and then *sharing the benefits* [italics added] from this over a lifetime of association. It involves the understanding, focusing and management of ongoing collaboration between suppliers and selected customers for mutual value creation and sharing through interdependence and organizational alignment. (p. 9)

Jeff Vinik, owner of the National Hockey League's Tampa Bay Lightning, and Shahid Khan, owner of the National Football League's Jacksonville Jaguars, are two excellent examples of professional sport managers who travel great lengths to ensure their customers are an integral part of the franchise by incorporating value-added strategies throughout the franchise operations. Both of these owners have created mechanisms opening up communication pathways with fans. More importantly, Vinik and Khan have incorporated customer feedback into the franchises' operations to improve the overall consumer experience. These men understand that each game attended by a customer is a vote of confidence for the franchise, as well as a product trial.

The fans are spending their disposable income on the Lightning or Jaguars and have certain levels of expectations about what their money will get them. Efficient, friendly service, comfortable seating in a clean facility, certain types of concessions, and an entertaining two to three hours are just some of these expectations. The key for a sport marketer to remember is that consumer expectations are unique to the individual, and whatever the consumer's individual perceptions may be, they are correct—at least for that individual consumer.

Consumer Expertise and Identity

One other important aspect of sport consumers is the familiarity that most consumers have with their chosen pastimes. Many consumers have actually participated with their favorite sport on some level—whether that level was during their formative years, in high school or college, or in some recreational capacity. Having played the game, consumers are better able to identify with the action on the field, court, or track. For example, Bill France, founder of NASCAR racing, was adamant that early racers drive stock cars available to the average person. Early racing fans actually witnessed drivers race the same model of car they would drive to church or to the grocery store (Hagstrom, 1998).

Of course, this level of familiarity is a double-edged sword for a sport marketer. In Pittsburgh, Sunday afternoons during the football season find thousands of people second-guessing every move the Pittsburgh Steelers make—from play selection to player personnel issues. Of course, Western Pennsylvania is a hotbed of high school football, so the level of familiarity with the sport makes it more likely that fans feel qualified to critique the Steelers organization. Whether the fans are actually qualified or not is irrelevant. It is each person's own perception they are qualified that heightens the individual and collective levels of commitment and involvement with the team. So, when a team starts to lose, these fans will voice their opinions.

THE FOUR P's OF MARKETING

The following section explains the four P's of marketing: Product, Price, Promotions, and Place. Each of these areas is common to every product or service, but in the sport industry, each requires the sport marketer to consider the unique aspects of sport when determining what marketing strategy to use.

[handwritten: ⟶ sometimes public relations]

The Sport Product

Imagine that immediately after class, you and your classmates go to the school gym to play basketball. You play for one hour and then go on with the rest of your day. Exactly one week later, after the same class, you and your classmates go to the gym to play basketball again. Imagine the weather was exactly the same, everyone was wearing the same clothes, and you all had the exact same breakfast food as the week before. You did everything within your control to replicate the conditions of that basketball game you played one week earlier. Even with all the efforts to ensure the game would be the same—will it? In the words of the famous John Wayne movie character Jacob McCandles (Big Jake, 1971), "Not hardly." Each and every sporting activity or game is different from one consumptive episode to the next. This is part of sport's appeal, but this characteristic is problematic for the sport marketer because the core product is largely out of the marketer's control.

What if you had a job marketing Dial soap? To be more specific, say your job was to market the bath-size, unscented bars of Dial soap. Due to production mechanisms and quality control programs, it is fairly certain that each bath-size, unscented bar of Dial soap was the same as the next. The same cannot be said for a marketer of the Minnesota

Vikings. One week, the Vikings may play flawless football, and the next, the Vikings offense may turn the ball over seven times. The crux of the issue is that the sport product is inconsistent and is largely out of the sport marketer's control.

Sport Production and Consumption

The next important difference between the sport product and traditional products deals with *when* the sport product is produced. Go back to the earlier example of the class playing basketball. The ball, the gym, the baskets, and the clothes people wear were all "produced" at a time before the actual game; yet those things combined do not create the experience. It is the actual

Photo courtesy © Andy Gillentine

game form that makes the experience or product. Sport activities, similar to hotel rooms and plane flights, are produced in the same moment they are consumed. Consequently, there is no inventory of the core product once the game is over. You cannot take empty seats and add them to the arena or stadium capacity the next home game; likewise, no one will buy tickets to yesterday's game or fight. That is why there is such a great emphasis in the industry to pre-sell the contest.

Core Product

If one were to list sport products, the first things to spring to mind would be spectator sporting events at all levels, participatory activities such as playing tennis or jogging, instructional lessons like karate or a session with a personal trainer, sporting goods (e.g., balls, golf clubs, equipment), and sport-related apparel (e.g., jerseys, hats). Most of these are usually considered part of sport's **core** product—the essential component to a sporting activity or event. These are all important aspects of the sport product, yet there are many more. Ticket stubs, programs, brochures, luxury suites, club seating, mascots, promotions, spirit squads, cheerleaders, broadcasts, and web pages are other components of the core product. In reality, a sport product can be anything related to a sport organization that has consumer demand, and in an industry where the ability to create new revenue streams is at a premium, sport marketers are always searching for new products to sell.

Pricing Sport

Potentially one of the most controversial issues facing a sport marketer is how to price an activity, event, or sponsorship. Compounding this problem, at least for spectator sport, is the previously mentioned fact about the inconsistent nature of the core product. For example, a Michigan–Ohio State football game will almost always be more attractive to a majority of the country than a Michigan–North Dakota game. Even so, sport marketers must devise a pricing strategy that appears fair to the paying public, while at the same time being careful not to set the price too low, thereby leaving the proverbial money "on the table." In addition, a wrongly priced product could potentially lower the perceived value of the product. It was previously mentioned that perceptions by individual consumers, be they correct or incorrect, often dictate consumption patterns. Similarly, consumer perceptions about the cost of an event or activity relative to its value also dictate consumptive behavior. The benefits for a sporting event or activity range from health benefits to psychological benefits or sociological benefits. In the fall of 2004, Master Card International extended its "Priceless" ad campaign to include the Major League Baseball (MLB) playoffs by running a commercial asking Boston Red Sox fans what it would be worth to see the Red Sox in the World Series. Fans' responses ranged from "My first born" to "My right arm." The spot ends with the Master Card catch phrase, "Seeing the Red Sox win the World Series—Priceless." Clearly for Red Sox fans, seeing their team win the World Series had a value far beyond any monetary figure.

Price vs. Total Cost

Conversely, the cost of a particular event or activity reaches beyond the actual dollar figure paid for a ticket or equipment rental. Also factored into the equation is the time it takes to travel to and from the activity or event, the cost of giving up something else to partake in the sporting activity or event, or the psychological or social cost of participating in an activity or event. In addition to these factors, a sport marketer also has to consider how frequently a particular activity or event is offered. NASCAR can charge more for a Nextel Cup race than a MLB franchise can charge for a regular season contest because the Nextel Cup race is only once a year, as opposed to the 81 home regular season dates for a MLB franchise. The National Football League (NFL) also enjoys the benefit of having a limited supply of home games when it comes to pricing strategy. The eight regular season home games in the NFL allow member franchises to charge, on average, higher ticket prices across the league, compared to their other professional league counterparts.

Additional Benefits

Another factor in pricing strategy is the amenities offered as part of the activity or event. Most professional sport franchises offer premium services and graduated benefits to season ticket holders depending on how many games are in the season ticket package and where the seats are located. An NFL season ticket holder purchasing club seats will receive access to a special area in the stadium with premium food, more luxurious surroundings, special parking privileges, the ability to purchase discounted merchandise at the team store, invitations to special season ticket holder parties, and other benefits. Meanwhile, the NFL fan who purchases season tickets in the upper level of the stadium may only receive the discounted merchandise and parking privilege benefits. Naturally, the club seating ticket package will cost more, as there are consumers who value those types of benefits and have no problem paying extra for them.

Variable Pricing

A recent pricing trend in the spectator sport industry has seen franchises and athletic departments incorporate variable pricing strategies into their marketing efforts. Variable pricing refers to charging higher amounts for more desirable games, and charging lesser amounts for the least desirable games. For example, assume the University of Wisconsin football team was to play Prairie View A&M one week and the University of Michigan the following week. The Badgers would be expected by their fans to beat Prairie View handily, which would impact the demand for tickets. On the other hand, the University of Michigan game, along with being a Big 10 match-up, would also be perceived as a "big game" by the Badger fans, which would drive demand for tickets. If the University of Wisconsin were to implement a variable pricing strategy, it would charge a lesser price for tickets to the Prairie View game than it would for the Michigan game.

Dynamic Pricing

Another recent trend employed in the professional spectator sport industry is *Dynamic Pricing* for single-game ticket sales. Long used in the airline and hotel industries, dynamic pricing, also called "real-time" pricing, allows a sport organization to maximize revenue from high demand games. To execute this pricing strategy, sport franchises must develop an algorithm which takes into account several variables such as the opponent, the day of the week, the weather, etc., and adjusts the ticket price higher or lower based on the demand using real-time data. Because dynamic pricing requires a sufficient number of events to accurately gauge the ebb and flow of demand, it is a strategy that is suited more for sports with a higher number of regular season games (like baseball).

Proponents of dynamic pricing argue that the strategy is a better gauge of market demand than variable pricing; therefore, more effective in maximizing ticketing revenue (Drayer, Shapiro, & Lee, 2012). The San Francisco Giants were one of the first professional franchises to use dynamic pricing, and according to Managing Vice President, Ticket Sales & Services, Russ Stanley, "All games are not created equal. We have seen an increase of 7% in the back to back years we implemented dynamic pricing. We have also been able to sell more tickets to lesser games because we can follow what the market will bear and accurately price tickets" (Rishe, 2012).

There are other benefits to dynamic pricing as well. Fans desiring the lowest guaranteed ticket price are driven to purchase a season ticket package, which in turn helps the franchise manage its ticket inventory. The strategy also allows the franchise to keep more of the ticketing revenue that was leaking to the secondary ticket market via scalpers or ticket brokers. However, for fans that only attend one to two games a year, the fluctuating ticket prices may leave them feeling confused or even angry, as happened to fans of the Anaheim Angels leading up to Opening Day after the franchise had adopted a dynamic pricing model (Moura, 2013).

Competition

A final consideration when determining a pricing strategy is the sport organization's competition in the marketplace. By setting a much higher price than the competition, a sport organization may create a perception of a high-quality product; however, this could occur only if the core product and ancillary product components are of high quality as well. For instance, the Green Bay Packers, the only major professional sport franchise in their market, can set prices much higher than the University of Wisconsin-Green Bay athletic program or local high school athletic programs, without experiencing any detrimental effect on attendance. This is due to the Packers' storied history of success and the affinity Wisconsin residents statewide have for the Packers franchise. In this case, the higher price is consistent with the image and value consumers place on the Packers.

On the other hand, in a market with many affordable entertainment options for consumers to choose from, a high price may have a negative impact on consumption levels, especially if there are not enough affluent consumers in the marketplace who value the core product offering. In this sense, a pricing strategy should consider the disposable income levels of both current and future primary consumer segments. To illustrate, consider the fans of the NBA. On average, NBA season ticket holders hold white-collar jobs and possess higher than average household income and education levels—in short, people who can afford to pay for tickets that may cost on average between $20 and $50. Yet, the NBA has many fans that are younger and live in urban areas with below average household income and education levels. From a long-term perspective, the NBA may have to develop alternative pricing strategies that will enable these customers to consume NBA basketball with more financial ease.

In conclusion, there is no universally accepted formula for pricing sport products. The shrewd sport marketer must consider all of the factors described above as well as conduct a thorough examination of the marketplace to ensure that the pricing strategy employed will generate sufficient levels of revenue without driving away large groups of consumers who are unwilling or unable to pay the price.

Promotions → media: TV, radio, print, internet, cross-promotions

While attending a minor league baseball game, fans, during the break between half innings, are likely to see some sort of contest involving fans on the playing field. This may have been a contest requiring contestants to place their forehead on a bat and spin around for several seconds before running to first base, or it may have required the contestants to throw a baseball through a target to win a prize. These contests are promotional contests. In general, the term promotion encompasses advertising, publicity efforts, personal selling, and sales promotion in all of their varied forms. Promotions can be categorized in two ways: **price promotions** and **non-price promotions**. To determine which type of promotion to use, sport marketers must first understand what they hope to achieve through the use of promotions. Once these objectives are clear, then the appropriate promotional strategy can be employed.

Price Promotions

As its name implies, a price promotion manipulates the actual cost of consuming a sport activity or event. Two-for-one ticket promotions are a popular promotional strategy used by many sport organizations on both the professional and amateur levels. Other popular price promotions involve coupons, a donation of canned goods in exchange for free or discounted tickets, children gaining free admission with the purchase of an adult ticket, and family packages in which a family of four receives four tickets and discounts at the concession stand for one packaged price. Price promotions are used to increase attendance and are most effective when a sport organization is in a market where consumer demand for the core product is not strong or the customer base is price-sensitive. Used properly, price promotions can increase attendance for activities or events that would usually not have great appeal to the public.

However, a sport marketer must exercise caution when contemplating the use of price promotions. If discounted tickets or admission through the use of price promotions becomes the standard fare for the sport organization, the danger exists of cheapening the core product as perceived by consumers. For example, if a minor league hockey team has a buy-one-get-one-free price promotion for every Friday home game, con-

[handwritten margin note: Family pack Friday]

sumers in that market may only consider attending a hockey game on a Friday, when they can get the tickets cheaper, as opposed to considering attending a hockey game on another night when the cost of admission is full price. Also, price promotions can anger full-paying season ticket holders who have already purchased their tickets and cannot take advantage of the discounted offer.

Photo courtesy © Andy Gillentine

Non-Price Promotions

The other type of promotions—non-price promotions—include all other activities designed to make the activity or event more attractive and enjoyable to consumers. Giveaways, fireworks, autograph signing sessions, and concerts are examples of non-price promotions used to increase interest and attendance at sporting events. Table 7.1 lists some of the more popular and successful non-price promotions used in professional sport.

Table 7.1. Top 15 Promotional Giveaway Items and Their Impact on Attendance in MLB, NBA, and NHL Teams

Giveaway	Change from Average (%)	Attendance	Additional Tickets Sold	Number of games
Jack-in-the-box	20.7	89,957	15,407	4
Travel Mug	19.8	156,828	25,939	6
Ring	14.3	142,653	17,863	4
Bobblehead	12.5	1,532,414	170,400	53
Stuffed Animal	11.3	127,344	12,920	4
Puzzle	10.8	172,369	16,805	5
Backpack	9.7	193,133	17,057	8
Notebook	9.1	304,391	25,292	8
Clock	8.9	98,085	8,035	4
Figure	8.3	659,520	50,460	22
Batting Helmet	7.2	187,479	12,590	5
Rally Towel	6.8	357,775	22,831	10
Cap	6.2	1,780,670	104,209	52
Ball/Puck	5.7	604,558	32,628	19
Wristband	4.9	138,778	6,441	4

This list does not include giveaways held by fewer than four teams, fan activities (ex. fireworks, concerts, etc.) or discounted ticket deals.

Source: Street & Smith's SportsBusiness Journal, October 18th–24th, 2004

Will revenue cover cost of promo?

From a sport marketing perspective, the question that must be answered is *how many people will we draw with this promotion and will the revenue generated from the additional people more than cover the cost of staging the promotion?* For instance, if a franchise were to contract with Justin Timberlake to perform after a game, will the attendance spike not only cover the cost of paying Timberlake's appearance fee, but also cover the advertising that will promote the concert, the cost of paying staff for the extended time at the event, and any other costs that accompany staging the promotion? Ideally, a promotion like this example will not only break even financially, but generate a profit for the franchise as well. One way to improve the chance for financial success is to have a third party (sponsor) pay for some or all of the costs associated with the promotion (see below, and Chapter 8).

BOMBS

Of critical import to the sport marketer is the question of *when* to use this type of promotion. One school of thought suggests that larger non-price promotions (including historically successful giveaways like bobblehead dolls) should be used on a date that the sport organization is not expecting a very large crowd. If used at this time, the non-

Photo courtesy © iStockphoto.com

price promotion should provide the desired spike in attendance, creating at least some business on a date that was anticipated to have very little business. The conflicting viewpoint is that larger non-price promotions should be used on more desirable dates in an effort to reach the capacity of the stadium or arena. Proponents of this view would argue for placing the concert on a Saturday evening (usually a well-attended date for most spectator sport franchises) against a good opponent in hopes of having a sell-out crowd. Sport teams have experimented year-by-year with these types of non-price promotions with varying degrees of success. Each marketplace is different, which underscores the need for sport marketers to understand their consumers so they might know what type of promotion will work at what time.

Fireworks and concerts are only one part of non-price promotions. The activities that occur during the down time in a game are also non-price promotions. Having a mascot shoot hotdogs into the crowd or deliver a pizza to a randomly chosen fan, or having sausages race around the ball park are also non-price promotions. These types of promotions add to the overall atmosphere and experience of attending a sporting event, especially for attendees who are only casual fans and are looking at the event more for its entertainment value. Moreover, these types of promotions are saleable. In other words, they can be built into a sponsorship package and generate revenue for the sport organization. The sausage race mentioned earlier is actually done by the Milwaukee Brewers franchise of MLB. This promotion has four people dressed up in over-sized sausage costumes race from the centerfield wall to home plate, and is sponsored by Usinger's—a maker of bratwurst and other processed meats in Milwaukee.

Clever and memorable non-price promotions of this sort help a sponsoring company as much as the franchise, as attendees to the event link the promotion back to the sponsor, which will ideally remain with consumers until it is time for them to make a purchase from the sponsor's category of products/services. Minor league sport franchises are often the testing ground for novel promotions of this sort, which, if successful, often make their way to the major league level.

Place

In traditional marketing, place refers to distribution of the product as well as the "place" of consumption. In that sense, sport marketers also consider the final "P" both place and distribution, since the physical setting (i.e., stadium, arena, health club) *is* where the sport product is distributed. Place can be an important factor in the purchase decision for many sport consumers. A facility that is both physically and aesthetically appealing enhances the core product and improves the overall sport consumptive experience. The place also is a major factor in consumers' initial perception of a sport organization. For instance, if a consumer walks into a stadium or club and is met with rude workers, litter, and poorly marked directions, they are most likely to have a negative perception toward the sport organization. It takes twelve positives to cancel out one negative

Photo courtesy © bigstockphoto.com

in a consumer's mind. If a sport organization does not cancel out the negatives, they may lose the consumer's business.

Today, newly constructed sport facilities are designed with amenities that provide additional revenue-generating streams for the sport organization, such as club seating, luxury suites, in-stadium retail stores, and a varied assortment of concessions and restaurants. Newer stadiums like the Pittsburgh Pirates' PNC Park and the Seattle Mariners' Safeco Field serve as attractions in-and-of themselves, which aid in driving attendance when the core, on-field product is perceived as substandard. The construction style is reminiscent of sport's Golden Age, evoking nostalgic emotions in older fans, while catering to fans' tastes for updated amenities. Even older facilities, with or without an update, can serve as attractions, drawing fans regardless of franchise performance. Wrigley Field in Chicago, Fenway Park in Boston, and Lambeau Field in Green Bay all are excellent examples of how a stadium exemplifies an experience and a franchise. Annually, thousands of fans visit these stadiums to experience the rich history associated with each one.

In sport, the amount of input a marketer has on the construction of a newer facility varies across the industry; however, every effort should be made in both new and existing facilities to accommodate fans and facilitate customer service. Such issues as the appropriate number and placement of restrooms, concession stands, customer service stations, and entrances should be thoroughly planned to anticipate the ideal customer experience. Merchandise kiosks, food stands selling locally flavored concessions, and in-stadium restaurants serve as another revenue-generating source for the sport organization, while offering more choices for the consumer base. Interactive zones are also commonplace in sport stadiums featuring activities for fans that tie entertaining activities with an organization's history to provide a richer experience for the consumer. Additionally, these areas serve as a mechanism to attract consumers with low involvement who may otherwise grow weary of just the core product. However you view it, the place in sport is an integral component of the marketing mix, and should be managed if a sport organization desires to stand out from the competition.

THE ROLE OF RESEARCH IN SPORT MARKETING

Earlier in this chapter, the involvement and commitment of sport consumers was discussed as a means of determining the best consumers of a sport organization. That discussion brings up the question, "How do you get that type of information?" Furthermore, in order to make calculated, strategic marketing decisions, a sport marketer requires additional information about the market, the competition, and the consumers. These issues can be addressed by incorporating a systematic marketing research agenda into the business practices of a sport organization. Market research is a topic with such sufficient depth that one semester of study barely touches all the issues involved in designing and analyzing research. Needless to say, a portion of a chapter can only introduce the aspiring sport marketer to the utility of research. Therefore, in this section, we will touch on consumer market research and its applicability for the sport marketer.

Sound market research helps the sport marketer understand who comprises the customer base, what characteristics are similar between customers, how they prefer consuming the sport product or service, when they are most likely to consume, and where the consumers reside. Once compiled, this information can be analyzed to divide the consumers into similar groups. This process is called **segmentation**. Segmentation is the process of dividing large, unlike groups of consumers into smaller, more defined groups of people who share similar characteristics (Mullin et al., 2000). The smaller groups of consumers allow a sport organization to communicate more effectively and efficiently because marketing communication messages can be constructed that appeal to the unique characteristics of the small groups. Two popular segmentation methods use **demographics** and **psychographics** to group consumers. Demographics describe consumers' state-of-being, including such factors as income level, education level, zip code, marital status, age, race, religious affiliation, occupation type, number of children in the home, and gender. Psychographics refer to consumers' state-of-mind, exploring the likes and dislikes of consumers and using the similarities to create the segments. Exhibit 7.1 at the end of this chapter displays a survey with both demographic and psychographic items from a minor league baseball franchise. Once collected, this information will allow the franchise to develop marketing strategies aimed at specific segments that appeal to the characteristics used in segmenting the consumers. For instance, if a sport organization conducts research and discovers a segment of its customer base is married with two children under the age of twelve, they may approach a local Chuck E. Cheese restaurant and develop a family package whereby consumers purchasing the package receive tickets to a game and discounted dinner at Chuck E. Cheese. This example brings up another important use of research: the ability to use the information to not only increase consumption levels of consumers, but to also sell corporate sponsorships.

When used correctly, market research helps the sport marketer make decisions that improve customer service, the type of merchandise or concessions sold, the number and type of promotions staged, as well as where marketing communications messages should be placed for maximum efficiency. Increasingly, sport organizations of all sizes and types are utilizing market research to improve their businesses, both from a revenue-generating and a customer service standpoint. As you progress through your academic career, you will be wise to learn as many market research techniques as you can, as they will be instrumental in your sport marketing career.

Developments in the Field of Sport Marketing

As one could imagine, the task of marketing a sport organization involves constantly altering the marketing mix to adjust to internal and external changes facing the organization. The caliber of team play, the state of a fitness facility, a downturn in the economy, or a new competitor entering the marketplace are but a small sample of events that force a sport organization to revisit and adjust its marketing strategy. In this section, we will briefly examine a few developing strategies sport organizations have employed to face such challenges.

Eduselling

Eduselling, a term first introduced by Sutton, Lachowetz, and Clark in 2000, refers to a process by which sport professionals approach new users of their products or services more as "teachers" than salespeople. Viewed primarily as a method to enhance sponsorship sales, the nine-step Eduselling framework moves beyond the traditional transactional exchange between organization and consumer, instead focusing on building a long-term relationship that benefits both parties. To that end, Eduselling advocates that the sport organization work with the potential sponsor in understanding all of that potential sponsor's wants and needs, as well as the particular objectives for entering into the sponsorship.

With that clear understanding in hand, the sport organization then develops a comprehensive sponsorship plan utilizing the relevant pieces of sport organization inventory to ensure successful achievement of the sponsor's objectives. Since many potential corporate sponsors may not fully comprehend all of the uses of certain pieces of team sport inventory, Eduselling calls for the sport organization to develop "how to" guides detailing exactly how the sponsor could best use aspects of their deal. Once the sponsor decides to commit to a deal with the sport organization, the sport organization must monitor the sponsor's activities and collect feedback from the sponsor to make the necessary adjustments to the deal. When carried out well, the sponsor will achieve its objectives and the sport organization will have a corporate customer for many years to come.

To illustrate the Eduselling concept, let us examine a hypothetical situation involving a Major League Baseball franchise and a regional bank with headquarters in the franchise's market. According to the Eduselling framework, before the baseball franchise can present the bank's marketing manager with a sponsorship proposal, the franchise should learn as much as it can about the bank's current business (market position, customer base, current marketing activities, etc.) and future business plans. The next step requires the franchise to meet with the bank's marketing manager to learn detailed information that will augment the research already conducted. Only then will the franchise be able to structure a sponsorship proposal that is likely to meet the wants and needs of the bank. Of course, some of the components of the proposal may be unfamiliar to the bank's marketing manager; therefore, the franchise should allow the marketing manager an opportunity to "sample" those components with the goal of the bank's marketing manager gaining a better understanding of how the various components fit together in the overall plan.

Once the deal is signed in our hypothetical situation, the franchise should not only schedule periodic meetings to gather feedback from the bank, but the franchise should also monitor the various components of the sponsorship to identify and correct any problematic issues before they are brought to the bank's attention. Then, after the annual sponsorship cycle is completed, the franchise will sit down with the bank's marketing manager and discuss the sponsorship program in detail, gaining valuable feedback for the next year.

Today, the Eduselling concept is being used by sport franchises not only in the sale of sponsorship agreements, but also in the sale of premium seating, broadcast contracts, and ticket packages. As the competition for customers' disposable income and a portion of businesses' marketing budget increases, the relational nature of Eduselling is an effective method to create partners for the sport organization, instead of just one time, transactional customers.

Loaded Tickets

Another recent development in the field of team sport marketing is the concept of "loaded tickets" utilizing stored-value technology. The loaded ticket is actually a normal ticket with an additional dollar amount "stored" into that ticket's bar code, which allows users to scan their ticket for purchases instead of paying cash or using their credit card. In this sense, the ticket is all a fan would need to enter into the stadium and enjoy the game.

One of the first team sport franchises to use the technology was Major League Baseball's Philadelphia Phillies as a means to increase the per capita consumption levels of fans (Muret, 2008). The additional cost of the loaded ticket is packaged into the total ticket price, and most franchises using the concept today offer the packages in special seating sections. The upside for the franchises is the increased spending by fans—the Phillies franchise claims fans with loaded tickets spend 70% more than fans without loaded tickets (Muret, 2008). The benefit for the fans is a hassle-free way to purchase concessions and merchandise without searching for an ATM or using a high-interest rate credit card. In certain instances where loaded tickets are purchased by a company and then given to employees or customers, the additional monetary value stored in the bar-code allows for a convenient, expense-free evening of entertainment.

While the loaded ticket concept has mostly been used in specially branded season ticket sections, additional uses are being explored by sport organizations in all of team sport. The loaded ticket may be a desirable feature for fans purchasing group tickets, or even for fans enjoying just an individual game.

All-Inclusive

Convenience for customers also is the focus of yet another sport marketing development: the all-inclusive concept. Common in the restaurant (think "buffets"), retail (Wal-Mart), and resort industries (e.g., Sandals resorts), the concept is being seen more both in spectator sport and the fitness industry. At its root, the all-inclusive package means providing the customer with everything they need or may want to ensure that they have the most enjoyable experience possible.

Spectator sport organizations have long had a similar concept in luxury suites where wealthy customers were sequestered from the masses while enjoying wine, veal medallions, and crème brûlée. But today, the general public can also experience the all-inclusive concept without breaking the bank. For instance, in the 2008 season, Major League Baseball's Pittsburgh Pirates unveiled a new seating section where for $30 ($40 if you purchased your tickets the day of the game), you not only received a game ticket, but license to an unlimited, all-you-can-eat game experience (alcohol not included). For the Pirates, the addition of this ticket option was most certainly in response to waning attendance due to poor team play, but the fact that the roll-out of the program coincided with a downturn in the economy certainly made the offer more attractive to cost-conscious fans. Since the Pirates unveiled the program, other team sport organizations both within MLB and without have announced they would offer a similar ticket.

In the fitness industry, the all-inclusive trend has also taken hold as a response to varying consumer wants and ever-changing fitness fads. For the fitness industry, the all-inclusive concept takes the form of providing one-stop health and fitness shopping for the club's members. These offerings range from the traditional (e.g., weight rooms, cardio equipment, fitness classes) to the latest developments (e.g., holistic healing, massage therapy, nutritional counseling). In these types of facilities, it would not be uncommon to find an area for members to enjoy a nutritious snack or light meal as well as a full-blown spa staffed by trained and registered professionals. According to the International Health, Racquet and Sportsclub Association (IHRSA), approximately one-quarter of the 41.3 million Americans belonging to some type of fitness club are members of one of these all-inclusive facilities (IHRSA/American Sports Data 2005 Health Club Trend Report). The obvious benefit for members of these clubs is that they are able to take care of all their health and fitness needs without traveling to various locations. For the club owners, the added amenities allow them to gain a larger share of their customers' health and fitness dollars. Of course, with new fads in the industry always on the horizon, the club owners have to carefully monitor the wants and needs of the membership so that the club is providing what the members desire.

Place: Bigger and Better

The new millennium seems to have ushered in a new gilded age of sport stadium construction, and the race is on between storied sport organizations to create the most fan-friendly, revenue-friendly facility. At the forefront of this race are the Dallas Cowboys and New York Yankees organizations. Both entities are in various stages of construction on facilities that will cost over $1 billion. The push to build new stadiums is linked back to the revenue a sport organization can generate—revenue that is often times excluded from any league-wide revenue-sharing agreements. The new stadiums boast the latest technology that supposedly will make the fans' experience better, but that experience will come at a price. For example, the new Dallas Cowboys stadium is home to the world's largest video screen (over 11,000 square feet); approximately 200 luxury suites (some only twenty rows from the field!); 15,000 club level seats; approximately ten acres of space in the end zones for gatherings; 280 concession areas; 1,600 toilets; and both the Dallas Cowboys Hall of Fame and Ring of Honor (Dallas Cowboys.com, 2008). The roughly 80,000 seat venue (with the capacity to add another 20,000 seats in the future) will be easier to get to as well, since the Cowboys and the City of Arlington, Texas are working to upgrade the interstate highway system leading to and surrounding the stadium. Experts contend that this grand stadium may set a record with its naming rights deal, with some experts predicting the Cowboys will receive over $20 million a year (Marta, 2008) (see Table 7.2). By all accounts, attending a Dallas Cowboys game is a trip into sport luxury, but if you plan on going, you had better make sure to bring lots of money. For those Cowboys fans who desire season tickets to the new stadium in one of the club levels, they must first purchase a 30-year seat license, which will cost them anywhere between $16,000 and $150,000. In addition, the fan must then pay for the actual game ticket, which will cost $340 (Exorbitant Prices, 2008). Revenue generation indeed!

The Cowboys and Yankees are not the only two sport franchises with new stadiums. In the metropolitan New York area alone, MLB's New York Mets, the NFL's Giants and Jets, the NBA's Brooklyn Nets, and Major League Soccer's New York Red Bulls all are in new facilities that allow fans to be closer to the action in more comfortable seats as they nibble on a more varied food selection—all of which will cost the fan more money. While franchises that have high demand for their product (e.g., the Cowboys and the Yankees) have little worry they will be able to sell the pricey seats in their new stadiums, other sport franchises that have a weaker brand must be careful they do not alienate their fan base and appear as if they are price-gouging their loyal customers.

Table 7.2. Top 10 Naming Rights Deals for Major League Sports

THE PRICE OF A NAME

Venue, City	Total	No. years	Annual	Exp
1. * Barclays Center, Brooklyn, NY Sponsor: Barclays PLC	$400 million	20	$20.0 million	2029
2. * Citi Field, Queens, NY Sponsor: Citibank N.A.	$400 million	20	$20.0 million	2028
3. ** Reliant Stadium, Houston Sponsor: Reliant Energy Inc.	$310 million	31	$10.0 million	2032
4. FedEx Field, Landover, MD Sponsor: FedEx Corp.	$205 million	27	$7.59 million	2025
5. American Airlines Center, Dallas Sponsor: AMR Corp.	$195 million	30	$6.5 million	2030
6. Philips Arena, Atlanta Sponsor: Royal Philips Electronics N.V.	$185 million	20	$9.25 million	2019
7. Minute Maid Park, Houston Sponsor: The Coca-Cola Co.	$178 million	28	$6.36 million	2029
8. University of Phoenix Stadium, Glendale, AZ Sponsor: Apollo Group Inc.	$154.5 million	20	$7.72 million	2025
9. Bank of America Stadium, Charlotte, NC Sponsor: Bank of America	$140 million	20	$7.0 million	2023
10. Lincoln Financial Field, Philadelphia Sponsor: Lincoln National Corp.	$139.6 million	20	$6.98 million	2022

SOURCE: *SportsBusiness Journal*

*Under construction
**Reliant has the naming rights to the entire Reliant Park, which also includes Reliant Arena.

Big Data and Social Media

As with most areas of the business world, the sport industry has been impacted by the latest trends in data analysis and social media. Just as you might have a personal Facebook or Twitter account, sport organizations and individual players are using these social media sights to gain followers (Pronschinski, Groza, & Walker, 2012; Witkemper, Lim, & Waldburger, 2012), which they then hope to monetize. This is done by utilizing user profile demographics and psychographics to present the user with the appropriate offer.

In team sport, this approach is effectively used to increase the sale of individual game tickets. For instance, a Major League Baseball team may want to increase its walk-up crowd for a Friday night game the following week that features a post-game concert performed by a band popular with local college-aged people. The franchise may buy an advertisement through Facebook that is directly targeted to users who have only liked the franchise, the band, or both. This method is more economical and efficient than traditional media buys. But it doesn't stop there. In the world of Big Data, a sport organization can capture information from unique visitors to its web site through an Internet Protocol (IP) address. This information can then be used to place special advertisements on web sites that person visits—even if it's not the site of the team itself.

The combination of technological advancements and the ease of obtaining detailed consumer information portends that sport organizations will be able to finely tune market segmentation efforts matching the right offer with each customer. Industry gatherings, like MIT's annual Sloan Sports Analytics Conference, will ensure that these practices become the norm in the sport industry.

Ticket Sales

The final development in the field of sport marketing is not really a development at all, but an area that has continued to remain vital to the spectator sport industry—ticket sales. Each professional sport league, both in the United States and abroad, as well as revenue-generating intercollegiate sports, relies on ticket buyers for financial stability. This is even true in the National Football League, where each franchise received more from the League's national television rights fees than in ticket sales. This is because sport organizations realize additional revenue from concession and merchandise sales, and in some cases parking fees when fans come to the stadium or arena. In addition, sponsors will not pay rights fees to a sport organization if the stadium is empty.

Poor attendance also hurts a sport organization's ability to negotiate television broadcast deals; poor attendance patterns usually indicate fan apathy for a particular team or sport. Consider the much-hyped XFL—a partnership between Vince McMahon's WWE and NBC. The opening games of the league saw reasonable attendance figures, which fell steadily through successive weeks of the season. Anecdotally, people find it hard to watch a sporting event on television when there is no one in the stands.

This brings us back to selling tickets. Aspiring sport marketers would enhance their careers if they had some experience selling tickets; whether that experience is with a professional, intercollegiate, or high school organization. The majority of entry-level jobs in professional sport are in the ticket sales department. Companies like The Aspire Group and IMG College have taken the same successful ticket selling principles developed at the professional level and applied them to the intercollegiate athletic setting, creating even more demand for people who can sell tickets. As the industry saying goes, ticket sales is the easiest way in and fastest way up in sports.

A number of opportunities exist for students to gain experience in ticket sales. Sales workshops, like the one hosted by Mount Union University, cater to aspiring ticket sellers. In this one-day workshop, students are mentored by sport industry professionals with experience in the ticket sales area. At many of these workshops, students are able to interview for internships or full-time jobs with the sport organizations represented. The Sales Combine is another opportunity to obtain a job selling tickets. Patterned after the NFL Combine, prospective ticket sales people spend two days in lectures, role-play, and actual ticket sales calls before interviewing for positions with various professional teams. Major League Soccer has elevated the concept of ticket sales training by creating a National Sales Center, where accepted candidates are exposed to ticket sales training while living in a campus-like atmosphere. From just these few examples, it should be apparent that the emphasis on tickets sales is here to stay.

SUMMARY

Any successful sport organization relies on its customers for stability and solvency. Sport marketing plays the primary role in acquiring and keeping customers. While the task may seem daunting at times, the great asset that many sport marketers enjoy is that they are marketing sport. As we have discovered, sport holds a special place in our society, where consumers' emotions are heightened and their involvement exceeds many other products or services. By utilizing sound market research to incorporate the proper mix of the marketing elements, sport marketers will be able to generate the revenue necessary to operate the organization, while creating fun and exciting experiences that will keep consumers returning game after game, season after season.

References

Dallas Cowboys new stadium. (2008). Retrieved from http://stadium.dallascowboys.com/

Drayer, J., Shapiro, S.L., & Lee, S. (2012). Dynamic ticket pricing in sport: An agenda for research and practice. *Sport Marketing Quarterly*, *21*(3), 184–194.

ESPN SportsCenter interview with NBA Commissioner David Stern. Aired October 17, 2004.

Exorbitant prices at new Dallas Cowboys Stadium haven't hurt sales one bit, says Dallas Cowboys management (2008). *Pegasus News Wire*. Retrieved from http://www.pegasusnews.com/news/2008/feb/03/exorbitant-prices-new-dallas-cowboys-stadium-haven/

Gordon, I. (1998). *Relationship Marketing*. New York: John Wiley & Sons.

Hagstrom, R. G. (1998). *The NASCAR Way*. New York: John Wiley & Sons.

IHRSA/American Sports Data (2005). Health Club Trend Report. Retrieved from http://cms.ihrsa.org/index.cfm?fuseaction=Page.viewPage&pageId=18890&nodeID=15

Marta, S. (2008). Dallas Cowboys stadium naming rights may top record deal. *Dallas Morning News*. Retrieved from http://www.dallasnews.com/shared content/dws/spt/football/cowboys/stories/033008 dnbusnamingrights.2b2caec.html

Moura, P. (2013). For some, Angels' dynamic pricing a ticket to confusion. *Orange County Register*. Retrieved from: http://www.ocregister.com/sports/tickets-499154-ticket-angels.html

Mullin, B., Hardy, S., & Sutton, W. A. (2000). *Sport Marketing* (2nd ed.). Champaign, IL: Human Kinetics.

Muret, D. (2008). Loaded tickets catch on among MLB teams. *SportsBusiness Journal*, p. 12.

Normann, R. (2000). *Service management* (3rd ed.). New York: John Wiley & Sons.

Pronschinske, M., Groza, M. D. & Walker, M. (2012). Attracting Facebook 'Fans': The importance of authenticity and engagement as a social networking strategy for a Professional Sport Team. *Sport Marketing Quarterly*, *21*(4), 221–231.

Rishe, P. (2012). Dynamic Pricing: The future of ticket pricing in sports. *Forbes*. Retrieved from: http://www.forbes.com/sites/prishe/2012/01/06/dynamic-pricing-the-future-of-ticket-pricing-in-sports/

Rothschild, P. C. (2011). Social media use in sports and entertainment venues. *International Journal of Event and Festival Management*, *2*(2), 139–150.

Sutton, W. A., Lachowetz, T., & Clark, J. (2000). Eduselling: The role of customer education in selling to corporate clients in the sport industry. *International Journal of Sports Marketing and Sponsorship*, *2*(2), 145–158.

Witkemper, C., Lim, C. H., & Waldburger, A. (2012). Social media and sports marketing: Examining the motivations and constraints of Twitter users. *Sport Marketing Quarterly*, *21*(3), 170–183.

Exhibit 7.1
Attendee Survey of Lake County Captains

Lake County Captains Fan Survey

Thank you for taking this survey about attendees of Lake County Captains games. Please carefully read each question, and mark the correct answer that is closest to your opinion about your experience a Captains' games. This is not a "test." There are no "correct" or "incorrect" answers. Most questions simply ask for your opinion and the results will be anonymous. Work quickly and record your immediate thoughts. Some of the questions may seem similar to you, or may not be worded exactly the way you would like them to be. Even so, give your best estimate and continue working through the survey. It is important that you answer all the questions. Your best response is far more valuable than an incomplete response.

Below are some statements regarding how you feel about the Lake County Captains. Please read each statement, and then circle the appropriate number printed on the right to indicate your level of agreement or disagreement with the statement.

	Strongly Disagree (1)					Strongly Agree (7)
The Captains' stadium is a clean, comfortable facility	1 2 3 4 5 6 7
There is ample parking around the Captains' stadium	1 2 3 4 5 6 7
The ushers are courteous and friendly	1 2 3 4 5 6 7
It is enjoyable to visit the Captains' stadium	1 2 3 4 5 6 7
I enjoy going to the stadium for Captains' games	1 2 3 4 5 6 7
To me, the Captains are the same as other franchises	1 2 3 4 5 6 7
On most nights, the Captains provide quality entertainment	1 2 3 4 5 6 7
Captain ticket-takers are courteous	1 2 3 4 5 6 7
I consider myself a loyal customer of the Captains	1 2 3 4 5 6 7
I enjoy the in-game promotions at Captains' games	1 2 3 4 5 6 7
There are many items to choose from at the concession stands	1 2 3 4 5 6 7
I think the price of concession items is fair	1 2 3 4 5 6 7
If I had to do it over again, I would not come to a Captains' game	1 2 3 4 5 6 7
I follow the Captains because they are my hometown team	1 2 3 4 5 6 7
It is important for me to support the Captains as my hometown team	1 2 3 4 5 6 7
The Captains are an important part of the community	1 2 3 4 5 6 7
I come to Captains' games because it is the best choice of entertainment for me	1 2 3 4 5 6 7
The Captains provide a rallying point for the community	1 2 3 4 5 6 7
The Captains do not have adequate in-game entertainment	1 2 3 4 5 6 7
I am proud to attend Captains' games	1 2 3 4 5 6 7
I care about the long-term success of the Captains	1 2 3 4 5 6 7
I am a loyal fan of the Captains	1 2 3 4 5 6 7
I feel a sense of belonging at Captains' games	1 2 3 4 5 6 7

Please provide answers to the following questions about the Captains and other area entertainment options.

1. Approximately how many Captains' games do you go to each season? _____

2. Please tell us how you hear about Captains' games and promotions?
   A. Newspaper/Circulars   B. Radio
   C. Television   D. Internet website
   E. Word-of-Mouth   F. Pocket Schedule
   G. Other (please specify)

3. Your decision to attend **today's game** was made within the past:
   A. 24 hours   B. 2–7 days   C. 8–14 days
   D. 15–30 days   E. 31+ days

(Continued on page 134)

Exhibit 7.1 *(Continued)*

4. How did you purchase/receive your ticket for today's event?
   A. Mail order
   B. Bought it today at the box office upon arriving
   C. Telephone order
   D. Ticket was given to me
   E. I have season tickets

5. For the following organizations, please indicate how many times a year you attend:
   _____ Cleveland Indians' games
   _____ Movies at a theater
   _____ Swimming at a public pool
   _____ Amusement Park
   _____ Eating out at a restaurant
   _____ Other Minor League Baseball games
   _____ Other Amateur baseball games
   _____ Plays/Symphony/Ballet

6. Please rank the following sport organizations according to your personal preference. Use #1 for your favorite organization, #2 for your second favorite organization, and so on.
   _____ Lake County Captains
   _____ Cleveland Indians
   _____ Cleveland Browns
   _____ Cleveland Cavaliers
   _____ Cleveland Barons
   _____ Cleveland Force

7. Are you at today's game as a member of a group?   YES   NO

8. Are you a Captains' season ticket holder?   YES   NO

Below are some more statements about the Captains. Please circle the number that best describes your opinion about each statement.

I feel the Captains franchise is . . .

| Very Undependable | | | | | | | | Very Dependable | |
| 1 | 2 | 3 | 4 | 5 | 6 | 7 | 8 | 9 | 10 |

| Very Incompetent | | | | | | | | Very Competent | |
| 1 | 2 | 3 | 4 | 5 | 6 | 7 | 8 | 9 | 10 |

| Of Very Low Integrity | | | | | | | | Of Very High Integrity | |
| 1 | 2 | 3 | 4 | 5 | 6 | 7 | 8 | 9 | 10 |

| Very Unresponsive to Customers | | | | | | | | Very Responsive to Customers | |
| 1 | 2 | 3 | 4 | 5 | 6 | 7 | 8 | 9 | 10 |

I feel the **EMPLOYEES** of the Captains are . . .

| Very Undependable | | | | | | | | Very Dependable | |
| 1 | 2 | 3 | 4 | 5 | 6 | 7 | 8 | 9 | 10 |

| Very Incompetent | | | | | | | | Very Competent | |
| 1 | 2 | 3 | 4 | 5 | 6 | 7 | 8 | 9 | 10 |

| Of Very Low Integrity | | | | | | | | Of Very High Integrity | |
| 1 | 2 | 3 | 4 | 5 | 6 | 7 | 8 | 9 | 10 |

| Very Unresponsive to Customers | | | | | | | | Very Responsive to Customers | |
| 1 | 2 | 3 | 4 | 5 | 6 | 7 | 8 | 9 | 10 |

For the prices you pay at a Captains' game, would you say the experience at a Captains' game is a . . .

| Very Poor Deal | | | | | | | | Very Good Deal | |
| 1 | 2 | 3 | 4 | 5 | 6 | 7 | 8 | 9 | 10 |

(Continued on page 135)

Exhibit 7.1 (Continued)

For the time you spend in order to get to the game, would you say attending a Captains' game is . . .

Highly Unreasonable   Highly Reasonable
1   2   3   4   5   6   7   8   9   10

For the effort involved in coming to a Captains' game, would you say attending a game is . . .

Not at all Worthwhile   Very Worthwhile
1   2   3   4   5   6   7   8   9   10

How would you rate your overall experience at a Captains' game?

Extremely Poor Value   Extremely Good Value
1   2   3   4   5   6   7   8   9   10

Please provide us with some demographic information about yourself.

1. Gender   A. Male   B. Female

2. Marital Status   A. Married   B. Single   C. Divorced   D. Widowed

3. How many children are living at home with you? _____

4. What is your Race?
       A. African American
       B. Aslan
       C. White
       D. Hispanic
       E. Other

5. What is the highest Level of Education you have completed?
       A. High School Graduate
       B. Trade School/Technical School Diploma
       C. Some College
       D. College Graduate
       E. Graduate Degree

6. What is your annual Household Income Level?
       A. Less than $25,000
       B. $25,001–$40,000
       C. $40,001–$60,000
       D. $60,001 $00,000
       E. $80,001–$100,000
       F. $100,001–$120,000
       G. More than $120,000

7. What is your age?
       A. 18–24
       B. 25–34
       C. 35–44
       D. 45–54
       E. 55–64
       F. 65 or older

8. What is your occupation? _____

9. What is the zip code of your primary residence? _____

Thank you for completing the survey! Please use the space below to share any additional comments or opinions with the Lake County Captains.

Case Study 7.1

What does a one-year-old minor league baseball franchise do to continue the success from its inaugural season into year two? How do they ensure that the fans continue to have a good experience and develop new revenue streams? The answer for the Lake County Captains, a Class A affiliate of the Cleveland Indians organization, is to use market research. The Captains organization plays games in a new stadium located in Eastlake, OH, just minutes from the parent club's home in downtown Cleveland; yet, the franchise routinely fills its stadium to near capacity. They do it with a mix of family entertainment off the field, and quality, developing players on the field. The first year of the franchise's existence was a success, but like any other business, the Captains' management felt they needed to keep a pulse on their consumers' wants and needs pertaining to their experience, so the Captains could alter their marketing strategy to meet those changing wants and needs. How did they know what the customers wanted? They asked them.

Exhibit 7.1 shows the survey the Captains disseminated to their customers. Because they already had information about ticket package holders, the vast majority of respondents were individual game attendees. Standard demographic questions (age, income levels, education levels, number of children at home, etc.) were asked of respondents to allow Captains management to obtain a clearer picture of their non-ticket-plan-holding fan base. These demographic questions, along with select psychographic questions (ex. how many times a year do you eat out at a restaurant), help the franchise determine business categories that should be pursued for sponsorship opportunities or other strategic partnerships.

Finally, certain survey items ask the respondents to indicate their opinion of the franchise's performance on several different elements. These items allow the franchise to gauge customers' attitudes toward operational and procedural elements of the franchise. If a particular area turns up lacking (based on fan responses) the franchise management can then make changes designed to improve fans' experience at a Lake County Captains game.

As you can see, market research plays an important role in the operation of a minor league baseball organization, as well as any sport organization. From an organizational perspective, it is important to regularly plan to collect data from your customer base. Survey research is only one method. Focus groups, stadium intercepts, and secret shoppers are other methods that allow a franchise to collect valuable information about their organization and fans. The important point to remember is that you cannot meet the wants and needs of your customer base if you do not know what those wants and needs are.

8

Sponsorship and Sales in the Sport Industry

Nancy L. Lough and Greg Greenhalgh

"A QUINTESSENTIAL NEED FOR ANY CORPORATION IS TO DIFFER-
ENTIATE ITSELF FROM ITS COMPETITORS VIA A COMPETITIVE
ADVANTAGE."

—*David Stotlar*

INTRODUCTION

Sport, as we have come to know it, could not exist without the financial support provided by corporate sponsorship. This practice of seeking a cash and/or in-kind fee paid
to the property (typically in sports, arts, entertainment, or causes) in return for access to
the exploitable commercial potential associated with the sport property, was once
thought to be the antithesis of all that was good about sport (Ukman, 1995). Yet,
throughout the last two decades, corporate investment in sponsorship became a key
indicator of a sport property's legitimacy. Sponsorship can make a sport, as is the case
with NASCAR. Within North American society, an unsponsored event is often viewed
as second rate and of little significance (Lamont & Dowell, 2007). Lack of sponsorship
can contribute to the dissolution of a sport entity, as was case for the Association of Volleyball Professionals who halted their 2010 season early partially due to a lack of interest
among sponsors. Similarly, participation in sport events relies heavily on sponsorship, as
illustrated when the 2011 Colorado Springs PRO XCT, a professional mountain biking
event, was canceled after failing to secure enough corporate support (Bate, 2011).

SPONSORSHIP

Sponsorship has many definitions and many potential benefits. The essence of any
quality definition includes reference to a relationship between a business and a sport
entity in which the business provides funding, resources, and/or services to the sport

In the Bleachers © 2014 Steve Moore. Dist. by Universal Uclick
www.gocomics.com/inthebleachers

"Stop! The promotions department screwed up! It's supposed to be 'Cap Night' …"

property in exchange for rights and privileges provided as a result of the association and/or affiliation with the sport entity. Pope (1998) provided the following definition:

> Sponsorship is the provision of resources (e.g., money, people, equipment) by an organization (the sponsor) directly to an individual, authority or body (the sponsee), to enable the latter to pursue some activity in return for benefits contemplated in terms of the sponsor's promotion strategy, and which can be expressed in terms of corporate, marketing, or media objectives.

Primary **benefits** sought by sponsors who invest in a sport relationship include generating brand awareness, image enhancement, improved business to business relations, enhanced employee relations, increased market-share, client acquisition, hospitality, product trials, and sales opportunities (Howard & Crompton, 2004; Stotlar, 2002; Seguin, Teed, & O'Reilly, 2005). Given the prospect for achievement of the aforementioned benefits, a sponsorship may appear to be an easy sell. Yet, the bottom line for the majority of businesses that invest in this type of communication vehicle is **return on investment** (Lough & Irwin, 2001). As the following substantiates, "Corporation bosses are increasingly having to justify their marketing investments to their shareholders and can no longer just say being associated with the Olympics is good for a company—they will have to prove it with hard facts" (Keeping the Olympics, 1997, p. 32). More recently, John Vaughn, manager of sponsorships and events with Advanced Auto Parts,

Inc. noted, "Properties (sport organizations) should justify prices by providing assets that help sponsors achieve meaningful return on investment" (International Events Group, 2011, p. 17).

Every business should have its own marketing plan that incorporates each of the Ps of sport marketing: product, price, place, and promotion. In order for a sport sponsorship to deliver a positive return on the investment made by the business, consideration must be made regarding integration of the sponsor's **marketing objectives** and the benefits provided via the sport affiliation. The International Events Group (IEG) noted sponsorship has been incorporated into the strategic planning of many corporations (IEG, 2011). Effective sport sponsorships can take advantage of the reach of traditional advertising as well as the emotional and experiential benefits of the partnership with a sport entity.

For example, the New York City Marathon signed ING, the Amsterdam-based financial services company, to become its title sponsor in 2003. ING opted for sponsorship of major marathons due to the fit between the services (product) they offer and the participants in major markets, such as New York City. With more than 25.5 million U.S. adults identifying as avid runners, ING research found that brand awareness was 15% higher among avid runners compared to the general public. The same study also indicated that 70% of avid runners own an investment and prefer to make informed financial decisions (Kaplan, 2007). Thus, the value (price) of the services offered may be of greater interest to marathon participants. To communicate with these potential consumers, the ING sponsorship activation plan starts with turning the event orange, through signage and cheering zones in quarter mile stretches. Fans are provided orange thunder sticks and signs. Meanwhile, street teams of ING employees also engage the "place" by offering refreshments to the crowd and generating excitement. Other promotional aspects of the sponsorship include exposure to the ING brand hundreds of times, from race registration to email updates in the months prior to the race, to race-day signage and water stops. Added promotion is available in the two-day race expo in which ING has a booth that showcases their financial services. Runners competing in the race receive orange "pace bands" to track themselves during the race. Still the communication and brand leveraging continues after the race with follow-up emails and the quintessential race "goody bag."

Recently, ING created the ING Runner's Nation Facebook tool allowing runners and their friends and family to create personalized e-postcards, and interact with events related to the marathon. The ING Runner's Nation Facebook page also provided a sort of digital lounge where runners could gather and interact, learn, and be engaged about running. Lastly, when publications such as *SportsBusiness Journal* and the *New York Times* publish articles (public relations) regarding ING's sponsorship of the race, all of the Ps suggested for a successful strategic marketing plan are addressed. This type of relationship illustrates the **symbiotic**, or win-win, nature of effective sponsorship in sport.

Has ING gained more investors as a result of this deal, which has continued for 10 years? Recent research supports the fit between ING and the marathon, suggesting those who take part in the New York City Marathon will be more likely to consider ING as their financial services provider. Eagleman and Krohn (2012) reported runners demonstrate high rates of recognition and recall, as well as purchase intention, for race sponsors. Nonetheless, an increase in sales remains the most critical method to measure return on investment and sponsorship effectiveness.

ADVERTISING ≠ SPONSORSHIP

Advertising may appear to serve the same purpose as sponsorship. Yet, upon analysis of the components of a sponsorship relationship, the limitations of advertising can be illuminated. In promotions such as advertising, one of the most common approaches is referred to as the **AIDA** concept. The goal of the AIDA (Awareness, Interest, Desire, and Action) approach is to move consumers along in the progression towards actual product purchase. Yet, this model stops short of acquiring the ensemble of benefits available via sponsorship. In advertising, little opportunity exists to gain access to a specific target market segment, and even less opportunity is available to create trust or enhance employee morale via an element such as hospitality. Still the most convincing argument for sponsorship versus advertising may be the potential for building loyalty and, thereby, **brand equity**. Dedicated marathoners and true running fans may perceive the success of major races such as the New York City Marathon as hinging on the success of the sponsors. For example, non-elite triathletes with higher levels of gratitude towards triathlon sponsors indicated a higher intention to purchase race sponsors' products (Kim, Smith, & James, 2010). In many cases, sport participants and sport fans have become loyal consumers of the products and companies that support their sport. They understand that without sponsors, they might not be able to compete or see their favorite athletes compete whether on television or in person.

Sponsorship Growth

Sponsorship prior to the late 1980s was typically simplistic in nature. Often the primary rationale for a company to sponsor a sport was the CEO's intent to "rub elbows" with elite athletes. However, the 1984 Olympic Games changed the landscape of sport sponsorship dramatically. After years of debt accruing to host cities for the Olympic Games, the Los Angeles Olympic Organizing Committee set out to prove that hosting this one-of-a-kind world class event could prove profitable for the city and others involved. A total of 32 companies agreed to pay between $4 million and $13 million in cash, goods, and services. At the previous Olympic Games in Montreal, 628 sponsors were involved for a total of $4.18 million. The result of the shift to category-specific sponsors and enhanced contributions was a net profit reported to be $222 million—equivalent to $490 million in 2013.

Today, corporate sponsors can be involved at various levels with the Olympic Games. For example, the sponsorship fee to be one of the 11 TOP (The Olympic Partner Program) sponsors has been reported to be approximately $100 million for the 2012 London Olympics. **TOP sponsors** sign up for a four-year contract that includes both the Summer and Winter Games. They are granted the right to Olympic affiliation in every participating country with worldwide **exclusivity** in their product category. Overall, sponsorship growth has been phenomenal following the example set by the success of the 1984 Olympic Games. In North America, corporations spent approximately $13 billion on sport sponsorship, more than what was spent sponsoring associations and membership organizations, festivals and fairs, the arts, charitable causes, and entertainment combined (IEG, 2013b).

Additionally, recent corporate scandals and a soft economy have created an enhanced need for corporations to demonstrate responsibility in all facets of a company's financial matters. Accountability for sponsorship investment is becoming commonplace in today's business environment, including some validation of the potential for increasing company profitability as a direct result of the sport sponsorship. The process of **evaluation** and servicing has taken on a new level of importance with regard to the likelihood of **renewal**. Those sport entities that fail to evaluate and/or quantify for the sponsor the value received, will likely find a higher rate of **defection** (current sponsors that decide not to renew).

Competition in the sport marketplace has proliferated at a rate commensurate with the growth of sponsorship in the sport industry. More sport products exist today in the form of tours, leagues, special events, participation based events, collegiate sport programs, and professional sport properties, than ever before. Measures of the industry demonstrate sports apparel, footwear, and equipment had sales totaling more than $285 billion in the US during 2009–2010. While estimates for the entire industry, including

Photo courtesy © Andy Gillentine

sport events, have trended toward $500 billion in the US alone. With this level of economic activity one can quickly appreciate the need for more sophisticated approaches to sponsorship and selling within the sport industry.

This has led to fierce competition among sport properties to secure sponsorship funding. Both US Airways and Verizon have reported receiving thousands of sponsorship requests each year. On a positive note, as the sport marketplace splinters, the opportunity to address specific target segments via lifestyle and affinity marketing opens the door for new and more creative sponsorship opportunities. As noted by Greenhalgh and Greenwell (2013), non-mainstream sports, or professional niche sports, in North America are able to provide sponsors with valuable commodities such as flexibility in assisting sponsors to achieve their objectives, a more targeted fan-base, decreased clutter, and a more cost effective sponsorship platform when compared to mainstream professional sports.

Similarly, growing sophistication resulting from competition and marketplace fragmentation has necessitated the growth of inventory that may be offered to potential sponsors. For example, many properties and athletes are adding social media to their sponsorship inventory components (Twitter, Facebook, etc). For example, Pizza Hut signed football quarterback Matt Barkley to do appearances and *tweet* about the brand. We have also seen the Los Angeles Kings change their Twitter profile photo to include "presented by" and the McDonald's golden arches logo, reflecting the sponsorship between the Kings and the fast food giant.

SPORT LEGITIMATIZATION

The 1999 Women's World Cup of soccer proved to be one of the most successful sport events ever held on U.S. soil. Yet, few realized the struggle event organizers experienced as they sought corporate involvement. Women's soccer had received needed exposure leading up to and following the 1996 Olympic Games. However, convincing corporate decision makers that investing in the Women's World Cup would provide substantial return on their investment was a hard sell. Few decision makers understood the value of associating with a women's sport property. Many companies who had committed to support the men's World Cup when the US hosted the event experienced disappointing results.

Two risks were apparent. First, the sport was soccer, which had yet to achieve significance in the U.S. sport marketplace. Second, it was women's sport, often considered outside the mainstream for appealing to typical sport fans. Yet, prepared with research suggesting that an enormous untapped market was available for those willing to sign on, event organizers managed to secure sufficient sponsorship dollars. This premier women's soccer event achieved unprecedented results including record crowds, unparalleled television ratings, and global media exposure. For the potential sponsors who neglected to sign on, what appeared to be a once-in-a-lifetime opportunity was missed.

Fortunately, the learning curve was short. In 2003, FIFA moved the Women's World Cup to the US due to an emergency situation. The SARS epidemic caused World Cup Officials to realize that China could not serve as the host. In less than four months, the U.S. Soccer Federation, with the help of corporate partners, created a tournament that turned a profit. The $7.5 million generated was more than triple the earnings from the 1999 World Cup.

SPORT FAILURE AND SPONSORSHIP

The Women's United Soccer Association was launched as a direct result of the phenomenal success of the 1999 Women's World Cup. Corporate backers saw potential and committed to building a league that would capitalize on the unprecedented interest. Organizers created the league with a solid vision and financial base of support. Yet, the long-term plan included increasing levels of corporate sponsorship as the years progressed. As time wore on, concern mounted due to unfulfilled goals. In the hypercompetitive sport marketplace, setting realistic, attainable goals is crucial. Missing an established target market often results in the need to return to the drawing board. As sponsors' needs went unmet, it became apparent that the WUSA was missing its mark.

Three primary concerns contributed to the defection of sponsors and ultimately dissolution of the league:

1. Diminishing television ratings
2. Decreasing on-site attendance
3. Pricing that did not equate to what the market delivered

Delivery of a realistic market estimate is vital to continued sponsorship. With teams competing in only eight markets, average attendance below 7,000, and television ratings of 0.1 (approximately 100,000 households), it was unrealistic to expect sponsors to contribute $2.5 million to sustain the league.

In contrast, Major League Soccer experienced similar challenges in the years following their 1996 initiation, yet recently added teams such as the Settle Sounders have demonstrated unprecedented success. While many have wondered if professional soccer will ever flourish in the US, this upstart team nearly doubled the league average of 16,120 fans per game. Their recent success prompted Major League Soccer to continue expansion into new markets. As the Seattle Sounders reached a new league high of over 30,000 fans per game, new sponsorship opportunities became available. For example, brands interested in appealing to the Hispanic demographic found success through MLS partnerships. These new relationships demonstrated how non-mainstream sports, or professional niche sports, are able to provide sponsors with value by reaching a more targeted fan-base, offering decreased clutter and providing a more cost effective sponsorship platform when compared to mainstream professional sports. Broadening the appeal has proven to be one strategy leading to more success for niche sports such as soccer. However, developing a sustainable women's professional soccer league has proven far more challenging. Ultimately, finding the fit between all the sport property has to offer and the image/goals of the corporate sponsor will lead to satisfaction and continued involvement for both parties.

HOT THEN NOT: The Case of the Association of Volleyball Professionals (AVP)

While sponsorship—through affiliation—can often establish a level of credibility for a sport, a lack of credibility in a sport product can rarely be altered, even with significant sponsorship. The AVP tour is a great example of a sport property able to attract big-name, high-value sponsors, yet they have been unable to maintain financial sustainability. Although the AVP saw success in the 1990s, their fortune changed significantly in the 2000s. Despite the success of American beach volleyball players in the Beijing Olympics, the AVP struggled and had to end their season early in 2010. One could argue the AVP floundered due to a substandard business model/plan opposed to the inability to attract sponsors.

In fact, prior to the 2010 season, which saw the AVP close its doors and file for bankruptcy, they were able to attract numerous high-profile sponsors. According to Lefton (2010), over $6 million in sponsorship was sold for the 2010 season with KFC,

Malibu Rum, and Progressive Insurance, plus a five-year $20 million title deal with Nivea. However, the Tour was unable to last through the entire 2010 schedule. Unfortunately for AVP, their business plan relied on sponsorship to contribute 80% of their revenue. This over-reliance on sponsorship and lack of emphasis on other revenue generators such as ticket sales and television rights set the AVP up for failure. A similar fate was experienced by the Women's Professional Soccer (WPS) league following its predecessor, the Women's United Soccer Association (WUSA). While sponsorship with the right sport property can often provide a sponsor with the **image enhancement** needed to shape or change the way the public views their organization, the same image enhancement is typically not reciprocated for the sport property. Clearly from the case of the AVP, no matter how reputable a sport property's sponsors may be, if the sport product has flaws, its days are numbered. It must be noted that at the time of this writing, the AVP was mounting a comeback and hopefully with a new business structure they will have positioned themselves as a viable and sustainable professional sport league within North America.

CREATING "BUY IN"

To create "buy in" for potential sponsors, the cost and value of a sponsorship deal must be equitable for both parties. The primary factor that contributes to the value for sponsors is the fit between the sport property and the corporate partner.

Fit is determined by the following criteria: a) the sport property's image should be compatible with the desired image of the brand, and b) a match needs to exist between the target market of the sport entity and the target market of the brand. The value of a sponsorship is often created by the sport entity's need for funding or resources. However, problems can arise when the value associated with a sponsorship is lower than the associated cost. In sport marketing, myopia is a common problem. In essence, myopia is the result of sport personnel focusing solely on the sport product and not considering the needs and wants of consumers. In sponsorship relationships, myopia occurs when sport representatives focus solely on the offerings associated through the sport sponsorship, yet neglect to consider the fit criteria that essentially establish the value or worth for the potential sponsor.

In a college town where an NCAA Division I program garners the majority of the sport media's attention, the concern for creating a fit between local sponsors and the athletic team or program is often neglected. The environment is one in which businesses commit to sponsorship deals more for the benefits associated with being perceived as a community leader or contributor to the university. Typically, sponsorships such as this lack the sophistication necessary in a more competitive marketplace and put the athletics marketing personnel in the dangerous position of becoming lulled into complacency. The creation of arbitrary sponsorship levels, which commonly occurs in these situations, results in a rigid menu of benefits available, with little room for focusing on the needs and wants of the sponsor. Thus, there is often a poor "fit," and, therefore, many of these types of sponsorships are ineffective at meeting the marketing needs of the sponsors. The only benefactor in this situation is the athletic program. Without a fair exchange of value and benefits, the sponsorship is at risk for non-renewal at any time.

Focus on Target Markets

When considering the aspect of buy in for sponsors that relates to their desired target market, a recognizable example can be seen in the relationship between FedEx and the PGA Tour's playoff points system. FedEx has experienced the benefits of communicating with a specific target market of golf fans, many of whom (45%) possess an average income over $75,000. The FedEx-sponsored playoff format was initiated in 2007 with tremendous success and resulted in an extended deal through 2017 before the original deal was set to expire in 2012. Reportedly, 48% of PGA fans said they were more likely to try FedEx products or services due to the sponsorship relationship. Similarly, about 70% reported they were more likely to try a PGA Tour sponsor's product. This deal exemplified the ideal fit between a target market for a company and the audience of a sport property. With a fit this clear, the effort needed to create buy in is reduced, therefore allowing more time to focus on enhancing communication platforms and promotional campaigns. Beginning in 2012, FedEx plans to increase their emphasis on the PGA Tour's international television broadcasts, where they can reach fans in over 200 countries.

Beyond the cost and value factors, there remains the need to protect companies who commit to sport sponsorship. Increasing competition to get a promotional message across has resulted in diminished value in certain situations. The three primary concerns that arise from competition in the marketplace include clutter, noise, and ambush marketing. **Clutter** is the result of too many sponsors being associated with a sport entity. No single brand image stands out as the sponsor. Spectators are less able to distinguish competing brands in this instance, thereby diminishing the value for all. Clutter commonly occurs when no specific sponsorship categories are designated. Consider the typical 5k road race t-shirt. On the back is a conglomeration of company names and tag-lines. Yet, no single brand stands out or gains significantly from association with race participants.

Noise can be considered very similar to clutter. The average person is exposed to hundreds, possibly thousands, of selling messages/advertisements each day. Whether they are radio, television, Internet, billboards, or print advertisements, the "noise" from each begins to desensitize the consumer to all messages. This explains the yelling car salesman who is trying to break through the noise by being the loudest, or most annoying. Yet, the result is often a consumer who tunes out the message. Public address, or PA, announcements at stadiums and arenas come complete with sponsor mentions. Yet, very often these messages go unnoticed because of the "noise" factor.

Ambush Marketing

Still the most challenging element of competition to handle in sponsorship is the deliberate attempts to ambush another sponsor's association with a sport entity. Take for example Pepsi's decision to buy a food truck, the Twisted Cuban, wrap it in a Pepsi Max cover, and park it in a Sears parking lot directly across from the Daytona International Speedway during the week of the Coke Zero 400, a major race in the NASCAR Sprint Cup schedule. Pepsi gave away free tacos before the race and had Jeff Gordon, who drives the Pepsi Max car, visit the truck and interact with fans. Pepsi also had a slogan on the truck: "Free Food. The other guys give you zero." Clearly, this was a dig at Coke Zero. Pepsi also sponsored the flags on the light poles on International Speedway Boulevard, guaranteeing fans would see the Pepsi Max logo before exposure to Coke Zero could make an impression. Pepsi was also certain to promote this effort via the Twitter accounts of the Twisted Cuban, Jeff Gordon, and Pepsi Max (Thiel, 2012). While Pepsi officials would likely insist there was no intent to ambush, this example exhibits the very definition of **ambush marketing**: a direct competing brand in the same product category staging a presence to create confusion in the mind of the consumer regarding who is the official sponsor. Clearly, new or non-seasoned race fans may have confused the title sponsor of the race (who paid millions for the official rights) with the ambush company who bypassed the official payment but still used the event to potentially impact tens of thousands of race fans and potential consumers.

Increasingly, sponsors are requiring some assurance that ambush will be prevented by the sport property. Part of the bid process for the Olympic Games requires host cities to describe how they will ensure that official sponsors are protected from ambush marketing. Typically, special legislation is passed within the host nation to assist organizers in curbing ambushing efforts around the Games. According to Jacques Rogge, IOC President, "We have to protect the sponsors because otherwise there is no sponsorship, and without sponsorship there are no Games" (Davis, 2012). Therefore, the IOC and the host committee closely monitor advertising activities around the Games. The IOC requires a "Clean Field of Play" where advertising within the Olympic venues is limited; this is also extended to all areas immediately surrounding the venues. The IOC and organizing committee closely monitor the television broadcasting and Internet coverage of the event. Any companies found associating themselves with the Games who are not official partners are sent cease and desist orders and could be subject to legal actions. Even with these very strict rules, some companies have been able to creatively skirt these regulations and possibly cause confusion as to their official status with the Olympic Games. For example, during the 2012 London Olympics, Beats Electronics gave their popular headphones to athletes for free. These headphones were given primarily to swimmers and divers as these athletes commonly wear headphones out to the pool deck where millions of fans watching the Games on TV could see the athletes wearing the Beats headphones. Furthermore, a number of these athletes Tweeted about receiving the gift, tying Beats even closer to the Games. Clearly, this incident did not please Panasonic, the official audio provider of the Games (Grady & McKelvey, 2012).

Emotion and Loyalty

Just as the previous scenario points out, when creating buy in for potential corporate partners, nothing appeals quite as strongly as the example of NASCAR fans. It was not by accident that NASCAR was one of the fastest growing sports in the industry. In this sport that incorporates sponsorship into every conceivable element, fans are famous for their degree of emotional commitment to each of their favorite driver's sponsors. Some fans have gone so far as to say that they will only buy the products from companies that sponsor "their" driver. This may seem logical if the sponsor happens to be involved in auto parts or a similarly linked product; however, products such as *Tide* laundry detergent have also been cited as chosen for purchase directly due to their sponsorship involvement with a race car driver. Few sports can claim this degree of emotional commitment and loyalty, yet it remains the ultimate goal of all who create sponsorship deals.

Sponsor Rationale

The most desirable strategies are those that create a win-win situation. A win for both the sponsor and the sport entity can best be achieved by meeting sponsors' objectives, including those that replace direct funding or dollar allocation with trade-outs or in-kind services. A familiar model in which this strategy is evident is the gift-in-kind of shoes and apparel to a collegiate sport team by a company such as Nike, Adidas, or Under Armour. The company in many instances provides little or no financial contribution to the athletic program. Instead, a trade is made in which the company agrees to provide their branded product for the right to be affiliated or directly associated with the team or program. The benefit for the shoe company is reaped when local fans become consumers and possibly develop loyalty to the brand as a result of the sponsorship for their favorite team. Additionally, if the team happens to receive significant media coverage, the brand then benefits from the university's success. When a university team appears on ESPN, March Madness on CBS, or a football bowl game on network television, then the return on investment is significantly increased. Recruits and the general public often judge coaches and teams as legitimate if they have a significant sponsorship deal.

Photo courtesy © Andy Gillentine

Under Armour has utilized this strategy by sponsoring over a dozen college athletic departments. By showcasing their wares on elite college athletes and gaining mainstream media attention, specifically via football and men's basketball, Under Armour has gained legitimacy within the athletic footwear, apparel, and equipment market. The rapid success realized by Under Armour can be attributed to their unorthodox, creative uniform and shoe designs provided to the collegiate programs they sponsor. Specifically, uniforms designed by Under Armour for the University of Maryland's football program garnered substantial press when they played the University of Miami in a nationally televised game on ESPN in 2011. The uniforms, designed to look like the state flag of Maryland, garnered an abundance of free publicity for both Under Armour and Maryland football ("Turtle Power," 2011).

Employee Motivation

While return on investment is arguably always a primary motivation, other motives can impact sponsorship decisions and lead to the accomplishment of many of the same objectives. Consider the sponsorship involvement of FedEx and NASCAR. Through their sponsorship of Joe Gibbs Racing team, specifically the number 11 car driven by Denny Hamlin, FedEx has been able to provide a number of benefits for their employees. FedEx also holds naming rights for the FedEx 400 NASCAR race held in June at Dover International Speedway. FedEx partners with the charity Autism Speaks to raise awareness and education about autism. During this race Hamlin's car has a paint scheme honoring the Autism Speaks organization (Dover Motorsports, Inc., 2012). Not only are FedEx employees involved in volunteer activities during the events leading up to and including the race, this affiliation with such a noble cause on a national scale is intended to instill a sense of pride and goodwill within FedEx employees company-wide. The media attention depicting the relationship between FedEx, NASCAR, and Autism Speaks through coverage by local and national newspapers as well as television exposure paints FedEx in a very positive light. As part of their partnership with Denny Hamlin, FedEx also arranged for him to visit one of their main shipping hubs in Alaska and sort packages alongside FedEx employees (IEG, 2013a). Based on this example, the assortment of benefits available to the sponsor and the ensuing rationale for involvement with the sport event/property are both realized.

Awareness

Most often companies engage in sport sponsorship to create brand awareness and enhance their brand image. The Mountain Dew action sports sponsorships have been most effective in illustrating aspects such as lifestyle and affinity marketing. In **lifestyle marketing**, the company is attempting to cut through all the other selling messages by appealing to consumers who have or desire the lifestyle depicted in the sport sponsorship relationship. Action sports such as skateboarding, snowboarding, and motocross represent an edgy, risk-taking, youthful lifestyle considered to be attractive to a large target market. Lifestyle marketing often cuts across demographic lines, appealing to people who already have an affinity for the activity or lifestyle represented by the sport sponsorship.

Mountain Dew has been involved in action sports for over 20 years, transforming the brand from something focused on being "country cool" to being edgy and celebrating individuality (Mickle, 2013). During the late 1990s Mountain Dew was sponsoring three action sports properties: X Games, Vans Triple Crown, and the Gravity Games. The image of Mountain Dew as a drink presumably chosen by extreme-minded opinion leaders illustrates the magnitude of effectiveness the X Games has provided for their top tier sponsors. Without their sponsorship of action sports, Mountain Dew would have continued to struggle for a place in the soft drink market. Instead, Mountain Dew (the brand) has become synonymous with the "extreme" image and action sports. In 1999, the brand became the third most popular soft drink in the US, surpassing Diet Coke, and in 2005, Mountain Dew was the only carbonated soft drink to increase its volume.

In a survey conducted by ESPN Research, 96% of respondents recognized Mountain Dew as a sponsor of the X Games and Winter X Games (Fuse Marketing, n.d.). By 2005, they had started their own series of events, the Dew Tour, and by 2007 Mountain Dew ceased their relationship with the X Games as it was becoming too commercialized (Mickle, 2013). Mountain Dew wisely realized that action sports fans were not all about the competition; hence, they became involved in the art, culture, music, and local shops in the cities where their tour stopped. This was an effort to fully ingrain the brand in the action sports lifestyle. The strategy has paid off as data shows those people aware of the Dew Tour are two times more likely than those unaware to think that Mountain Dew is a "brand for me, this is a brand that helps me express myself, this is a brand that I'm about, this is a brand I love" (Mickle, 2013). Through their sponsorship of action sports, Mountain Dew has clearly become part of the action sports lifestyle, a feat not often accomplished but very powerful when properly executed.

Image

There can be a negative side to sponsorship relationships, however, when ethical concerns are not addressed. The Washington Nationals made a very concerted effort to ensure their facility, Nationals Park, was built and managed to be as environmentally friendly as possible. However, the Nationals received significant backlash from many of

Photo courtesy © bigstockphoto.com

their fans, including protestors, when they signed Exxon Mobile to be the official sponsor of the seventh inning stretch. Exxon Mobile had a negative reputation with respect to the environment stemming from oil spills significantly affecting the Gulf region, including wildlife. In short order, Exxon Mobile was replaced as the sponsor for the seventh inning stretch. This exemplifies the notion that not all money makes good business sense with respect to sponsorship, and sport properties need to ensure they stay true to their values when signing sponsors or the consequences could be severe, as demonstrated by the Nationals.

Clearly, opportunities arise in which the sport entity would be wise to back away from sponsorships that create ethical dilemmas. An example that better illustrates a positive link of brand image with a sport that has a lifestyle all its own is Roxy and surfing. The brand Roxy was created by Quicksilver to appeal to the women's surf market. Roxy has been so successful in associating with top women surfers and surf competitions, that Roxy is synonymous with the surfing lifestyle among women.

Sales Objectives

Perhaps the most clear, rational, and measurable benefit in a sport sponsorship is meeting sales objectives. The case of the FIFA World Cup in South Korea illustrates this rationale well. Product purchase intentions are most often considered a key sales objective that can be measured. When consumer purchase intentions were examined, as influenced by the 2002 FIFA World Cup in Korea/Japan, a significant relationship was found. Consumers felt more positively about the image of the companies that sponsored the event, they were more accurate at recognizing the actual sponsors, and they indicated that they would be more likely to buy the products of the sponsors (Shin, 2002). To the companies involved, this indicates a successful sponsorship relationship due to the likely return on investment.

Selling Sponsorships

One of the most important factors to recognize relative to sponsorship in sport is that those who can sell well advance quickly. With this in mind, a focus on a few of the methods that enhance success in sales is provided. There are seven rules for effective personal selling according to Mullin, Hardy, and Sutton (2007):

1. The utilization of a marketing database generates leads that are likely to have a greater interest and/or ability to become consumers.
2. Communicate with consumers based on a shared interest in the sport product. Consider the potential consumer as a potential friend.
3. The LIBK rule needs to be adhered to. This means to "let it be known that" you are proud and enthusiastic to be selling a product you believe in.
4. Be prepared for the most common objections used. Be flexible in your approach and capable of providing examples that show how current consumers once had similar objections.
5. Be an effective listener, then be prepared to react with points that address the consumer's concerns.

6. Take the consultant approach. Approach the consumer as though you are proposing possible solutions to the consumer's needs and wants, not just trying to make a sale.

7. Just as "fit" is critical to success in sponsorship, "fit" is key to success in sales. Match the consumer to a product that is appropriate for his or her budget and lifestyle.

When selling sponsorship, the most desirable measure from a sponsor's perspective is a return on investment (ROI). According to the IBM Global Chief Marketing Officer (CMO) Study from 2011, nearly two-thirds of CMOs said that ROI will be the primary measure of marketing effectiveness by 2015. Hence, the impact that a sponsorship investment has on sales is the best indicator that the sponsorship was a success. Sales objectives are most often expressed in three ways:

- Increase in traffic at retail points of purchase
- Resulting number of new sales leads
- Actual increase in sales connected with a sponsorship

Actual sales can be measured by tracking coupon redemptions or ticket discounts given with a proof of purchase of the sponsor's product. Similarly, a comparison of sales during a three-month period corresponding with the event and the sales for a comparable period can be calculated to measure actual increases.

The AIDA concept for promotions was previously discussed relative to meeting sponsor's objectives. Yet, this concept can be extended to assist in the enhancement of sales. The **product adoption process** is an extension of the AIDA concept that awareness builds interest and knowledge of a brand's associated benefits, which, in effect, creates an image in the mind of the consumer. When the image is congruent with an image the consumer desires, then a product trial is likely. Evaluation is being conducted in the mind of the consumer both before and after the product purchase. The goal is to move the consumer to purchase the product. Following the consumer's experience with the product, the option exists to repeat the purchase, re-evaluate and consider alternate brands, or discontinue the process.

If the consumer chooses to repeat their purchase, then product adoption has been attained. At this point, the levels of branding suggest that consumers have progressed from **brand recognition** to **brand preference**. Once brand preference has been achieved, loyalty builds as the consumer refuses to purchase any other company's product in that category. Ultimately, the consumer then moves into **brand insistence**, which is the creation of **brand loyalty**. As we have seen from NASCAR and other similar examples, sponsorships are often sold because of the potential for brand loyalty as exemplified in sport.

Take, for example, the recent sponsorship between Lexus and the Atlanta Braves. One of the attributes of the Lexus sponsorship was the provision of parking spaces at Atlanta Braves games free of charge for Lexus owners. This approach was intended to reward Lexus owners and encourage their loyalty to the brand while also creating an opportunity to expose Atlanta Braves fans to new Lexus models. This strategy illustrates another important concept in selling, which is the **consumer escalator**. With the consumer escalator model, the goal is to move consumers from non-aware/non-consumers onto the consumption escalator and ultimately up each level from light to medium to heavy users. Heavy users are known to be responsible for up to 80% of all purchases. This is significant, especially considering that heavy users may represent as few as 20% of all consumers. This **80/20 principle** suggests that a focus be made on moving consumers up the escalator while keeping the existing heavy user segment content.

In sales, finding new consumers or leads is far more difficult than prompting the existing consumers to increase their level of consumption. In addition, existing consumers provide invaluable promotion through word of mouth. Many consumers step onto the escalator as a direct result of influence by a friend or colleague who happens to be a consumer. Increasingly, with the proliferation of social media, professional sport teams, participant sport events and brands are using this medium to enhance existing relationships with consumers as well as reach new consumers.

WHY SPONSORS DEFECT

Sponsors defect or discontinue their relationship with a sport entity for two primary reasons: (1) their goals and objectives were not met and/or (2) they have chosen a new marketing approach that may focus on a new target market or a different direction altogether. Little can be done when the second rationale is given; however, failure to meet objectives or company marketing goals rests with the company as well as the sport entity. The key strategy that must be incorporated is a leveraging or activation plan.

Leveraging involves developing an integrated plan that specifies the role promotional tools will play and the extent to which each will be used. Unless a company invests in these additional means to amplify the intended message, their initial sponsorship fee will likely be a wasted investment. Sponsorship offers a unifying theme that needs to be exploited to communicate with a specific target market through the use of a full array of promotional tools. **Sponsorship activation** means that for every dollar spent on a sponsorship fee, an equivalent dollar is typically spent in the promotion of the sponsorship. This 1:1 ratio was once considered an industry standard. Today, many elite sponsors say the ratio is more likely to be 1:5 for a sponsorship that will be short-term (one year or less). When the contract includes multiple years, the ratio can be closer to 1:2 or 1:1, with an extended period of time to create a strong association between the sport entity and sponsor to build the message and enhance loyalty. Thus, one of the surest ways to see a sponsorship fail is to neglect allocating funding to activate the sponsorship.

Take, for example, Izod returning to golf in 2013. With the theme "Izod is color," the brand decided to jump back into golf by securing deals with players such as U.S. Open champ Webb Simpson. The initial step was to "take Augusta by storm" by making a big splash though multiple activation outlets. To create an initial presence, Team Izod golfers Simpson, Spencer Levin, and Scott Piercy were represented in wall wrap images (measuring 69 by 19 feet as well as 97 by 19 feet) on side walls. The placement chosen was the hospitality structure near the corner where the heaviest traffic flows on the way to the event. Similarly, Izod established a social media hub in a 2,500 square foot property across the street from the Augusta National entrance. Bloggers, journalists, and social media team members were allowed to work in the hub while referencing the Izod social media studio throughout the event. The brand also invested heavily in advertising including a presence on NBC/Golf Channel and print ads in *Golf Digest*, *Maxim*, *Men's Health*, and *GQ*. According to industry accounts, the onsite activation of multiple sponsors at Augusta has become prolific, largely due to their reputation as the mecca of golf in the US. The aggressive plan launched by Izod was in response to the bright colors being worn by players, and the age of the golfers reflecting a younger demographic. Even though Izod spent the previous five years as title sponsor of the IndyCar series, brand representatives indicated "golf has always been in Izod's DNA" (Smith, 2013, p. 4).

SPONSORSHIP EVALUATION AND MEASUREMENT

Generally, the one aspect in which many sport entities fall short in regard to corporate sponsorship is in the area of measurement and evaluation. Historically, the only means for communicating with sponsors following the event ended up being a quickly written thank you note with a picture of their sign or logo at the event. Seldom were sponsors informed of the *impact* of their sponsorship—for example, the number of people in attendance and who they were. What was the extended audience reach? The profile of the audience reach incorporates the media outlets that covered the event and the amount of coverage/publicity given by each. Most media outlets have data on their audiences that can assist in determining if the target market was reached. Yet, as simple as this type of feedback may seem, many of the best means for providing information can be acquired with equally simple recognition and recall techniques.

Recognition has occurred when a spectator can correctly identify the brand of a sponsor from a list. **Recall** equates to a higher level of effectiveness. In recall, a spectator can remember and correctly identify a sponsor's brand without input or prompting. It is still considered a key measure, as recall forms the top of a funnel leading to purchase of the brand, along with triggering brand or product consideration, trial, repeat, and advocacy. Since many sponsors continue to rely on logos and signage, recall continues to be considered the most "fair" measure. Still, key considerations should include the factors of asset location, incremental levels of investment, and even the time period in which the logo or sign is visible. The downside to recognition measuring is that oftentimes consumers identify brands that were not official sponsors, indicating ambush has occurred. In the case of the 2002 FIFA World Cup, most spectators surveyed indicated that Nike (63.7%) was an official sponsor. In reality, the official partner was Adidas. Nike had contracted to supply uniforms for the Korean team, in addition to Brazil, Portugal, Russia, and Nigeria. Nike also had several well-planned promotions that confused consumers as to who was the official sponsor. Nonetheless, on a similar measure, the sponsorship by Adidas proved to be effective. Purchase intentions towards the sponsoring company's products increased 41.5% for Adidas due to their sponsorship of the FIFA World Cup. Purchase intention has been found to have a significant relationship with corporate image, prior use experience, and sponsor recognition accuracy (Shin, 2002).

Given the common omission of feedback provided by sport entities, specialized companies have emerged for the sole purpose of evaluating sponsorship effectiveness. One such company, Joyce Julius and Associates, created a model in which each and every second that a sponsor's brand was recognizable during a television broadcast was counted. An accumulation of hours and seconds that the brand was visible then was utilized to calculate the equivalent dollar amount that such visibility would have cost if the corporate sponsor had chosen to simply buy advertising time on that station at that particular time on that particular day. Surprisingly to some, the accumulation of minutes often equated to hundreds of thousands of dollars. More often than not, the cost paid by the sponsor was significantly less than the equivalent "value" attributed by this evaluation technique. Similar measurements can be calculated in print media coverage by measuring column size in inches, number of company mentions, and location within the print publication (i.e., newspaper sports section). A photo with the brand of the sponsor prominently displayed is often attributed a higher value than being mentioned in the text of an article.

Overall, sponsorship evaluation should be designed to meet two primary purposes: (1) measuring the accomplishment of the sponsor's objectives and (2) generating information that can be utilized when selling future sponsorships.

SUMMARY

There are five primary concerns that need to be addressed to create success when selling sport sponsorships:

1. Benefits sought by potential sponsors are framed as specific, measurable objectives.
2. A good "fit" equates to a shared image between the corporate sponsor and the sport property with target market access.
3. Integration with other communication vehicles around a unifying theme should be incorporated with promotional actions that reinforce the sponsor's desired message.
4. Protect clients from ambush, clutter, and noise (perceptual distortion).
5. Time/longevity of a sponsorship relationship contributes to improved recall, recognition, and product purchase intentions among consumers, thereby improving sponsorship effectiveness.

Sponsorship is one of the most valuable tools sport managers have to work with. Future sport professionals will need to understand and be capable of utilizing this essential tool.

Discussion Activities

1. Consider for a moment the sport events you have attended or consumed through some form of media. Next consider recent purchases you have made. Did sponsors of the sports you consumed influence these purchases? If so, why?

2. Look through some recent issues of *Street and Smith's SportsBusiness Journal*. Based on what you've learned in this chapter, select a few sport properties and match them with potential corporate sponsors.

Suggested Reading

Davis, J.A. (2012). *The Olympic Games Effect: How Sports Marketing Builds Strong Brands* (2nd ed.). Singapore Pte Limited: John Wiley & Sons.

Kahle, L. R., & Close, A.G. (2011). *Consumer Behavior Knowledge for Effective Sports and Event Marketing*. New York, NY. Routledge: Taylor & Francis.

References

Batc, J. (2011). Colorado Springs PRO XCT race axed. Retrieved from http://singletrack.competitor.com/2011/02/news/colorado-springs-pro-xct-race-cancelled_13562

Dover Motorsports, Inc. (2012). FedEx, Denny Hamlin to have strong presence at Dover International Speedway on race weekend. Retrieved from http://www.doverspeedway.com/news_content/fedex-denny-hamlin-to-have-strong-presence-at-dover-international-speedway-on-race-weekend/

Eagleman, A., & Krohn, B. (2012). Sponsorship awareness, attitudes and purchase intentions of road race series participants. *Sport Marketing Quarterly, 21,* 210–220.

Fuse Marketing (n.d.). *Case study: Mountain Dew.* Retrieved from http://www.fusemarketing.com/modules.php?name=CaseStudies&ServiceID=1&TacticID=1&CaseID=19

Grady, J., & McKelvey, S. (2012). Ambush marketing lessons from the London Olympic Games. *SportsBusiness Journal,* October 22–28, *15*(27), 25.

Greenhalgh, G., & Greenwell, T. C. (2013). Professional Niche Sport Sponsorship: An Investigation of Sponsorship Selection Criteria. *International Journal of Sport Marketing and Sponsorship, 14*(2), 77–94.

Gwinner, K. P., & Eaton, J. (1999). Building image through event sponsorship: The role of image transfer. *Journal of Advertising, 28*(4), 47–67.

Howard, D., & Crompton, J. (2004). *Financing Sport* (2nd ed.). Morgantown, WV: Fitness Information Technology.

International Events Group, LLC (2011). Best practices: How to justify rising fees. *IEG Sponsorship Report.* Retrieved from http://www.sponsorship.com/IEGSR/2011/11/21/Best-Practices—How-To-Justify-Rising-Fees.aspx

IEG, LLC (2013a). Sponsorship hot buttons: Logistics companies. *IEG Sponsorship Report.*

IEG, LLC (2013b). 2013 Sponsorship outlook: Spending increase is a double-edged sword. *IEG Sponsorship Report.* Retrieved from www.sponsorship.com/IEGSR/2013/01/07/2013-Sponsorship-Outlook—Spending-Increase-Is-Dou.aspx

Kaplan, D. (2007). Running up big numbers. *Street & Smith's SportsBusiness Journal, 10*(27), 18–23.

Kim, Y. K., Smith, R., & James, J. D. (2010). The role of gratitude in sponsorship: The case of participant sport. *International Journal of Sports Marketing & Sponsorship, 12*(1), 53–75.

Keeping the Olympics Ideal. (1997, April). *Sport Business,* 32–33.

Lamont, M., & Dowell, R. (2007). A process model of small and medium enterprise sponsorship of regional sport tourism events. *Journal of Vacation Marketing, 14*(3), 253–266.

Lefton, T. (2010). Marketers question value left in AVP brand. *SportsBusiness Journal.* Retrieved from http://www.sportsbusinessdaily.com/Journal/Issues/2010/08/20100830/This-Weeks-News/Marketers-Question-Value-Left-In-AVP-Brand.aspx?hl=AVP

Lough, N., & Irwin, R. (2001). A comparative analysis of sponsorship objectives for U.S. women's sport and traditional sport sponsorship. *Sport Marketing Quarterly, 10*(4), 202–211.

Maxwell, N., & Lough, N. (2009). Signage vs. no signage: An analysis of sponsorship recognition in women's college basketball. *Sport Marketing Quarterly, 18*(4), 188–198.

Mickle, T. (2013). How they Dew it. *SportsBusiness Journal.* Retrieved from www.sportsbusinessdaily.com/Journal/Issues/2013/02/25/In-Depth/Dew-Tour.aspx?hl=fans support sponsors&sc=0

Mullin, B. J., Hardy, S., & Sutton, W. A. (2007). *Sport Marketing* (3rd ed.). Champaign, IL: Human Kinetics.

Pope, N. (1998, January). Overview of current sponsorship thought. *The Cyber-Journal of Sport Marketing.* Retrieved from http://www.cad.gu.edu.au/cjsm/pope21.htm

Seguin, B., Teed, K. C., & O'Reilly, N. J. (2005).

National sports organizations and sponsorship: An identification of best practices. *International Journal of Sport Management and Marketing*, *1*(1/2), 69–92.

Shin, H. (2002). The effects of sport sponsorship on consumer purchase intentions. (Unpublished master's thesis). Illinois State University, Normal, IL.

Smith, M. (2013). After drifting from golf, Izod attracted to sport's younger face. *SportsBusiness Journal*. Retrieved from http://www.sportsbusiness daily.com/Journal/Issues/2013/04/08/Marketing -and-Sponsorship/Izod.aspx

Stotlar, D. (2002). Sport sponsorship: Lessons from the Sydney Olympic Games. *International Journal of Applied Sports Sciences, 14*(2), 27–45.

Thiel, S. (2012). Ambush marketing—Pepsi Max at the Coke Zero 400? Retrieved from http://de vosstudents.blogspot.com/2012/07/ambush-mar keting-pepsi-max-at-coke-zero.html

Turtle power? Maryland's unique Under Armour uniforms draw nation's attention (2011). *SportsBusiness Journal*. Retrieved from http://www .sportsbusinessdaily.com/Daily/Issues/2011/09 /07/Marketing-and-Sponsorship/Maryland-Uni forms.aspx

Ukman, K. (1995). *The IEG's complete guide to sponsorship: Everything you need to know about sports, arts, event, entertainment and cause marketing.* Chicago, IL: Intl Events Group.

9

Sport Facility Management

Bernard Goldfine and Tom Sawyer

"THE OLDEST STANDING BUILDING IN ROME IS THE COLOSSEUM."
—*Red Smith*

INTRODUCTION

Have you ever been a spectator at a sporting event or concert and left with the feeling you had just experienced something that was incredibly special? Conversely, have you ever had a miserable experience at a highly anticipated event? Your experiences could very easily have been influenced by the manner in which the facility was managed. If you have ever wondered how you would organize or manage a facility differently, perhaps facility management might be a career path to consider.

To embark upon such a career, you have to be someone who likes organization, order, advanced planning, leading others, and does not mind being assertive and aggressive (Solomon, 2002). Specifically, some of the attributes successful facility managers must possess are (1) interpersonal and leadership skills (i.e., inspiring others to perform effectively and calmly under pressure); (2) proactive thinking, (i.e., anticipating problems and having contingency plans ready when obstacles present themselves) (Walker & Stotlar, 1997); (3) organizational skills (such as when and how to delegate tasks); and (4) the ability to think quickly on one's feet when crises emerge. Also, this field calls for individuals who do not mind working nontraditional and extended hours.

Learning Objectives

Upon completion of this chapter, the reader should be able to
- Discuss the skills necessary for sport facility management;
- Identify models used in the management of facilities;
- Understand the importance of operational philosophies and mission statements regarding the management of sport facilities;
- Address the elements of public and media relations;
- Explain the risk management considerations in the management of venues;
- Identify revenue streams in facility management;
- Recognize the role of marketing and budgeting in sport facility management.

There are many opportunities for sport management graduates to use facility/venue management skills, including working for a large, prominent organization that specializes in event management, such as TSE Sports and Entertainment or Jack Morton Worldwide (www.jackmorton.com). Or you could work for a company, which oversees concessions (such as Aramark), merchandising, ticketing, maintenance, security, sponsorships, and complete venue management.

The skills required for facility management are also advantageous for individuals seeking employment in sport-related organizations that manage their own facilities or run their own events. For example, sport organizations that do not outsource their operations need individuals whose focus is game day operations or event management. In **participant-oriented organizations**, individuals with very specialized skill sets often manage municipal parks, YMCAs, recreation departments, collegiate recreation settings, and special events. The aforementioned organizations' facilities, in addition to some **public assembly sport facilities** that are often run by the municipalities themselves, require competent personnel to operate them in the most cost-effective and safe manner.

SPORT FACILITY MANAGEMENT

"Whatever you do, do it with all your might. Work at it, early and late, in season and out of season, not leaving a stone unturned, and never deferring for a single hour that which can be done just as well now."

—P. T. Barnum

Sport facility management is a coordinated and integrated process of utilizing an organization's resources to achieve specific goals and objectives through the managerial functions of planning, organizing, leading, and evaluating. Sport facility management also includes effective booking and scheduling, provision of security and safety for fans and participants, and maintenance of the venue.

Sport venues can be classified into sub-categories. Examples of outdoor facilities could include, but are not limited to:

- Aquatic Centers
- Baseball and Softball Parks
- Football and Soccer Stadiums
- Motor Sport Tracks
- Golf Courses and Practice Facilities
- Tennis Stadiums and Complexes
- Recreational Sport Fields for Football, Lacrosse, Rugby, and/or Soccer
- Parks and Playgrounds

Indoor venues could include, but are not limited to:

- Basketball Arenas
- Bowling Alleys
- Domed Stadia
- Field Houses
- Gymnastic Sport Facilities
- Fitness Centers
- Family Centers
- Football, Lacrosse, and/or Soccer Facilities
- Water Parks
- Miniature Golf Facilities
- Ice Hockey and Skating Rinks
- Natatoriums

SPORT FACILITY OWNERSHIP AND MANAGEMENT

Sport facilities are either publicly or privately owned. Public ownership requires management to operate the sport facility within regulations and procedures established by the governing body. Recently, both publicly and privately owned sport facilities have moved toward private management companies, yet their different objectives have a direct impact on a facility manager's decision making process.

Table 9.1 depicts four eras and shows that there has been a substantial shift over time in responsibility for funding these types of facilities (Crompton, 2004).

Table 9.1. Comparison of Public and Private Sector Financing by Funding Era

Combined Costs for Stadiums and Arenas

Era	% Public	% Private
Gestation (1961–69)	88	12
Public Subsidy (1970–84)	93	07
Transitional Public-Private Partnerships (1985–94)	64	36
Fully-Loaded Public-Private Partnership (1995–2003)	51	49
Future Partnership (2004–2015)	33	67

Modified from Crompton, J. L. (2004). Beyond Economic Impact: An Alternative Rationale for the Public Subsidy of Major League Sports Facilities. *Journal of Sport Management, 18*(1), 41.

Public Ownership

The local government and/or government entities operate publicly owned sports facilities such as Citi Stadium and MetLife (NY Giants and Jets) in New York, Soldier Field in Chicago, and Lucas Oil (Indianapolis Colts) and Bankers Life Field House (Indiana Pacers) in Indianapolis. The objective of these governmental agencies is to provide a service to the community while generating enough revenue to break even. All revenue beyond expenses goes back into operation of the sport facility.

Private Ownership

A number of individuals privately own sports facilities (e.g., Forum Arena, Pro Players Stadium, Texas Stadium, and Wrigley Field); others are owned by stockholders (e.g., Green Bay Packers, Green Bay, WI) or by partnerships (e.g., New York Yankees, Los Angeles Dodgers); and others still are owned by corporations (e.g., Disney). The primary objective of a privately owned facility is to deliver a profit for the owners and/or stockholders. The management focuses on maximum return on investment.

Sport Authorities

These are not-for-profit entities generally operated by a commission or board of directors appointed by a governmental body. Sport authorities control a number of sport facilities, such as Bank One Ballpark (Arizona Diamondbacks), 3 Com Park (San Francisco Giants), Coors Field (Colorado Rockies), ThunderDome (Tampa Bay Devil Rays), Turner Field (Atlanta Braves), Philips Arena (Atlanta Hawks), U.S. Cellular Field (Chicago White Sox), and Camden Yards (Baltimore Orioles), among others.

Naming Rights in Sport Facilities

One of the major sources of finance for sport facilities is sponsorship through naming rights in large, public assembly sports facilities. This phenomenon was referred to in Chapter 6 (Sport Finance) and in Table 6.2 (page 103). Tables 9.2 (pages 162–165) and 9.3 (pages 166–168) demonstrate the extent to which primary naming rights (naming of the facility) and secondary naming rights (parts of the sports facilities such as club levels, hospitality suites, etc.) are being used in today's sports facilities:

Private Management (Privatization or Outsourcing)

When sport facility operations are privatized or outsourced, the owners pay a private organization to manage the day-to-day operation of the facility. There are five major private sport facility management companies including Centre Management, Global Spectrum, Leisure Management International (LMI), Ogden Allied, and Comcast Spectator Management Group. These companies manage sports facilities worldwide. The first sport facility to be privatized or outsourced was the Louisiana Superdome. This type of management enables the owner to maintain control over the sport facility and simultaneously (1) reduce or eliminate an operating deficit, (2) improve services, (3) increase the quality and quantity of the events scheduled, (4) join a larger national and interna-

Photo courtesy © Andy Gillentine

tional network of sport facilities that will expand opportunities for future booking of events, (5) provide greater flexibility concerning policies, procedures, and overall operational structure, (6) improve concessionaire (food service and pouring rights) and full-service restaurant agreements, and (7) expand the sale of licensed merchandise (Mulrooney & Farmer, 2001; Sawyer, Hypes, & Hypes, 2004; Sawyer, 2005, 2009, 2012). According to the International Association of Venue Managers (IAVM) and the International Facility Management Association (IFMA), there are six easy steps in selecting a private management company. The steps include (1) preparing a request for proposal (RFP), (2) distributing the RFP to all major management groups, (3) providing sport facilities tours for all prospective bidders, (4) reviewing proposals, selecting the top five, and interviewing the top five bidders, (5) selecting the finalist and negotiating the contract, and (6) gaining final approval from both sides (Mulrooney & Farmer, 2001; Sawyer, 2005, 2009, 2012).

TYPES OF SPORT FACILITIES

A simple and effective way to classify facilities is by the types of events held within them. Table 9.4 describes the various sport facilities based on events. Most of the facilities below include administrative and staff offices, bars, ballrooms, concession and merchandising spaces, daycare facilities, dressing, locker, and shower areas, lobby, lounge, and reception spaces, maintenance areas, parking, press and interview spaces, public restrooms, restaurants, spectator seating (e.g., general admissions, club seats, private license seats [PSLs], and luxury [VIP] boxes), and ticket sales spaces.

Arenas, centers, coliseums, field houses, pavilions, palaces, and domes are indoor sport facilities that can be utilized for a variety of activities and events including circuses, concerts, shows, graduations, political rallies, and sporting events. Other specialized facilities include adventure areas, fitness centers, ice arenas, natatoriums, and skate parks. An adventure area might provide a ropes course (high and low), a challenge (or confidence) course, and/or a rock-climbing wall. A fitness center might include activity

Table 9.2. Primary Naming Rights of Professional Sport Venues

PRIMARY NAMING RIGHTS—MLB

Facility	Location	Teams	Sponsor	Sponsor HQ	Category
AT&T Park	San Francisco, CA	San Francisco Giants	AT&T Inc.	San Antonio, TX	Communications
Chase Field	Phoenix, AZ	Arizona Diamond-backs	JPMorgan Chase & Co.	New York, NY	Financial
Citi Field*	Flushing, NY	New York Mets	Citigroup, Inc.	New York, NY	Financial
Citizens Bank Park	Philadelphia, PA	Philadelphia Phillies	Citizens Financial Group Inc	Providence, RI	Financial
Comerica Park	Detroit, MI	Detroit Tigers	Comerica Inc	Dallas, TX	Financial
Coors Field	Denver, CO	Colorado Rockies	Molson Coors Brewing Co.	Golden, CO	Food & Beverage
Great American Ball Park	Cincinnati, OH	Cincinnati Reds	Great American Insurance Co.	Cincinnati, OH	Insurance
McAfee Coliseum	Oakland, CA	Oakland Raiders	McAfee Inc	Santa Clara, CA	Software
Miller Park	Milwaukee, WI	Milwaukee Brewers	Miller Brewing Co.	Milwaukee, WI	Food & Beverage
Minute Maid Park	Houston, TX	Houston Astros	The Coca-Cola Co.	Atlanta, GA	Food & Beverage
PETCO Park	San Diego, CA	San Diego Padres	Petco Animal Supplies Inc.	San Diego, CA	Retail
PNC Park	Pittsburgh, PA	Pittsburgh Pirates	The PNC Financial Services Group Inc.	Pittsburgh, PA	Financial
Rogers Centre	Toronto, Canada	Toronto Blue Jays	Rogers Communications	Toronto, Canada	Communications
Safeco Field	Seattle, WA	Seattle Mariners	Safeco Corp.	Seattle, WA	Insurance
Tropicana Field	Tampa, FL	Tampa Bay Devil Rays	Tropicana Products Inc.	Bradenton, FL	Food & Beverage
U.S. Cellular Field	Chicago, IL	Chicago White Sox	U.S. Cellular Corp.	Chicago, IL	Communications

PRIMARY NAMING RIGHTS—NHL

Facility	Location	Teams	Sponsor	Sponsor HQ	Category
BankAtlantic Center	Sunrise, FL	Florida Panthers	BankAtlantic	Fort Lauderdale, FL	Financial
Bell Centre	Montreal, Canada	Montreal Canadiens	Bell Canada	Montreal, Canada	Communications
Sommet Center	Nashville, TN	Nashville Predators	Sommet Group	Franklin, TN	Conglomerate
General Motors Place	Vancouver, Canada	Vancouver Canucks	General Motors	Detroit, MI	Automotive
HP Pavilion at San Jose	San Jose, CA	San Jose Sharks	Hewlett-Packard Co.	Palo Alto, CA	Technology

Continued on page 163

Table 9.2. Primary Naming Rights of Professional Sport Venues

PRIMARY NAMING RIGHTS—MLB

Inception	Price	Term	Price/Year	Exp.	Other Events/ Tenants
2000	$50,000,000	24	$2,083,333	2024	NCAA Emerald Bowl
1998	$66,000,000	30	$2,200,000	2028	—
2006	$400,000,000	20	$20,000,000	2026	—
2004	$95,000,000	25	$3,800,000	2029	—
2000	$66,000,000	30	$2,200,000	2030	—
2005	$15,000,000	Indefinite	NA	Indefinite	—
2002	$75,000,000	30	$2,500,000	2032	—
1998	$11,800,000	10	$1,180,000	2008	Oakland A's
2000	$41,200,000	20	$2,060,000	2020	—
2001	$170,000,000	28	$6,071,429	2029	—
2003	$60,000,000	22	$2,727,273	2025	USA Sevens (Annual Rugby Tournament)
2001	$40,000,000	20	$2,000,000	2021	—
2004	$17,736,000	10	$1,773,600	2014	Toronto Argonauts (CFL)Int'l Bowl (NCAA)
1999	$40,000,000	20	$2,000,000	2019	—
1996	$46,000,000	30	$1,533,333	2026	—
2002	$68,000,000	23	$2,956,522	2025	—

PRIMARY NAMING RIGHTS—NHL

Inception	Price	Term	Price/Year	Exp	Other Events/ Tenants
2005	$27,000,000	30	$2,700,000	2035	—
2002	$60,000,000	20	$3,000,000	2023	—
2007	NA	NA	NA	2018	Nashville Kats (AFL)
1995	$18,500,000	20	$925,000	2015	—
2001	$47,000,000	15	$3,133,333	2016	San Jose Saber-Cats (AFL)San Jose Stealth (NLL)ATP SAP Open

Continued on overleaf

Table 9.2. Primary Naming Rights of Professional Sport Venues (continued)

PRIMARY NAMING RIGHTS—NHL (continued)

Facility	Location	Teams	Sponsor	Sponsor HQ	Category
Honda Center	Anaheim, CA	Mighty Ducks	Honda	Tokyo, Japan	Automotive
HSBC Arena	Buffalo, NY	Buffalo Sabres	HSBC USA Inc.	Hong Kong	Financial
Jobing.com Arena	Glendale, AZ	Phoenix Coyotes	Jobing.com	Glendale, AZ	Online
Mellon Arena**	Pittsburgh, PA	Pittsburgh Penguins	Mellon Financial	Pittsburgh, PA	Financial
Nationwide Arena	Columbus, OH	Columbus Blue Jackets	Nationwide Insurance	Columbus, OH	Insurance
Pengrowth Saddledome	Calgary, Canada	Calgary Flames	Pengrowth Mgmt.	Calgary, Canada	Financial
Prudential Center*	Newark, NJ	New Jersey Devils	Prudential Financial	Newark, NJ	Financial
RBC Center	Raleigh, NC	Carolina Hurricanes	RBC Centura Banks Inc.	Halifax, Canada	Financial
Scotiabank Place	Ottawa, Canada	Ottawa Senators	Scotia Bank	Toronto, Canada	Financial
St. Pete Times Forum	Tampa, FL	Tampa Bay Lightning	St. Petersburg Times	St. Petersburg, FL	Media
Xcel Energy Center	Minneapolis, MN	Minnesota Wild	Xcel Energy	Minneapolis, MN	Energy

PRIMARY NAMING RIGHTS—MLB

Category	Amount	% of Total
Financial	5	31%
Food and Beverage	4	19%
Communications	3	12%
Insurance	2	12%
Software	1	7%
Retail	1	5%
Total	**16**	**100%**

Sources: Collected by Adam Powell from *SportsBusiness Journal* research, Wikipedia.com, Ballparks.com, and company websites.
*Not yet opened
**Will be razed after the 2009 NHL Season

PRIMARY NAMING RIGHTS—NHL

Category	Amount	% of Total
Financial	7	44%
Insurance*	2	13%
Automotive	1	6%
Communications	1	6%
Technology	1	6%
Online	1	6%
Conglomerate	1	6%
Media	1	6%
Energy	1	6%
Total	**16**	**100%**

Continued on page 165

spaces for cardiovascular exercises, free weights, gymnastics, martial arts, walking or jogging, racquetball courts, strength training, tennis, swimming, and aerobics. Ice arenas have been constructed for figure skating competitions, ice hockey, curling, and instructional and recreational skating. A natatorium is an aquatic center constructed to provide for swimming and diving, synchronized swimming, water polo competition, and instructional and recreational swimming and diving. Finally, skate parks have been designed as safe areas for kids to practice and compete in skateboarding activities. The number of parks nationwide has grown dramatically over the past decade.

			Table 9.2. Primary Naming Rights of Professional Sport Venues *(continued)*		
			PRIMARY NAMING RIGHTS—NHL *(continued)*		
Inception	**Price**	**Term**	**Price/Year**	**Exp.**	**Other Events/ Tenants**
2006	$60,000,000	15	$4,000,000	2021	—
1996	$22,500,000	30	$750,000	2026	Buffalo Bandits (NLL)
2006	$25,000,000	10	$2,500,000	2016	—
NA	NA	NA	NA	NA	—
2000	$135,000,000	Indefinite	NA	Indefinite	Columbus Destroyers (AFL)
2000	$20,000,000	20	$1,000,000	2020	—
2007	$105,300,000	20	$5,265,000	2027	Seton Hall (basketball)
2002	$80,000,000	20	$4,000,000	2022	NC State (basketball)
2006	$200,000,000	15	$1,330,000	2021	—
2002	$30,000,000	12	$2,500,000	2014	Tampa Bay Storm (AFL)
2000	$75,000,000	24	$3,125,000	2024	Minnesota Swarm (NLL)

SPORT FACILITY ORGANIZATION

All successful sport facilities have an established organization model to guide operations. The model outlines the personnel required for operations, an organizational philosophy, a mission statement, and goals and objectives based on the organization's philosophy and mission statement.

The Management Team and Personnel

A sport facility director, general manager, chief executive officer, or executive director heads the management team for a sport facility. The head of the management team is ultimately responsible for sport facility planning and management. Further, he/she is responsible for negotiating major contracts pertaining to the sport facility, often including events being scheduled in the sport facility. Other members of the management team oversee marketing, public relations, customer relations, advertising, sales, and operations (Mulrooney & Farmer, 2001; Sawyer, 2005, 2009, 2012).

The **director of operations** is the primary assistant to the head of the management team. This individual has a wide variety of departmental responsibilities, including event coordination; engineering; security, safety, and medical services; and maintenance and housekeeping. The **director of marketing** is responsible for market planning,

Table 9.3. Secondary Naming Rights of Professional Sport Venues

NFL STADIUMS (SECONDARY)

Facility	Team	Sponsor	Category	Branded Area
Jacksonville Municipal Stadium	Jacksonville Jaguars	Crown Royal	Food & Beverage	Crown Royal Touchdown Club (Luxury Suites)
		Budweiser	Food & Beverage	Bud Zone (Sports Bar)
		Pepsi	Food & Beverage	Pepsi Plaza (Entertainment Zone)
Edward Jones Dome	St. Louis Rams	Budweiser	Food & Beverage	Budweiser Brew House
Ford Field	Detroit Lions	Comcast	Media	Comcast Family Fun Zone
Gillette Stadium	New England Patriots	Fidelity Investments	Financial	Fidelity Investments Clubhouse
		Bank of America	Financial	Bank of America access ramp
		uBid.com	Online	uBid.com access ramp
Heinz Field	Pittsburgh Steelers	Coca-Cola	Food & Beverage	Coca-Cola Great Hall (retail/entertainment area)
		McDonalds	Food & Beverage	McDonalds Steelers KidZone Show
Sports Authority Field at Mile High	Denver Broncos	Budweiser	Food & Beverage	Budweiser Champions Club
		United Airlines	Airlines	United Club Level (Suites)
M&T Bank Stadium	Baltimore Ravens	Budweiser	Food & Beverage	Backyard Bash (Hospitality)
		Miller Lite	Food & Beverage	Beer Garden Tents
Candlestick Park	San Francisco 49ers	Budweiser	Food & Beverage	Bud Light Goldmine (entertainment)
		Coca-Cola	Food & Beverage	Coca-Cola Red Zone (exclusive ticket package)
Qwest Field	Seattle Seahawks	Wells Fargo	Financial Club	Wells Fargo Lounges
		Fox Sports Net (FSN)	Media	FSN Lounge
Reliant Stadium	Houston Texans	Miller Lite	Food & Beverage	Miller Lite Entrance
		Ford	Automotive	Ford Entrance
		Coca-Cola	Food & Beverage	Coca-Cola Entrance
		Gallery Furniture	Retail	Gallery Furniture Entrance
		Budweiser	Food & Beverage	Budweiser Plaza
U of Phoenix Stadium	Arizona Cardinals	Insight Enterprises	Software	Insight Club East

NBA ARENAS (SECONDARY)

Facility	Team	Sponsor	Category	Branded Area
Air Canada Centre	RaptorsMaple Leafs	TD Waterhouse	Financial	TD Waterhouse Platinum Club (Restaurant)
American Airlines Arena	Miami Heat	Dewar's	Spirits	Dewar's 12 Lounge
		Grey Goose	Spirits	Grey Goose Lounge
American Airlines Center	Dallas Mavericks Dallas Stars	AT&T	Network	AT&T Plaza
		Jack Rouse Associates	Energy	TXU Concourse

Continued on page 167

Table 9.3. Secondary Naming Rights of Professional Sport Venues

NBA ARENAS (SECONDARY) (continued)

Facility	Team	Sponsor	Category	Branded Area
US Airways Center	Phoenix Suns	Bud Light	Food & Beverage	Bud Light Paseo (Venue and Bar)
		Lexus	Automotive	Lexus Club (Lounge and Seating)
		Levy Restaurants	Food & Beverage	Levy Restaurant
		Verizon Wireless	Communications	Verizon Wireless Jungle (Jungle gym and Arcade for kids and families)
		Bacardi	Spirits	Bacardi Rum Bar
AT&T Center	Spurs	AT&T	Communications	The AT&T Center "Star" (East entrance)
		AT&T	Communications	AT&T Center FAN SHOP and "Atomic Spur"
		Ashley Furniture	Retail	Ashley Furniture Saddle and Spurs Club
		Frost Bank	Financial	Frost Bank Saddle and Spurs Club
		HEB	Retail	HEB Fan Fiesta
BankAtlantic Center	Florida Panthers	Lexus	Automotive	Lexus Club Level/Lexus Lot
		Spirit Airlines	Airlines	Spirit Gateway
		WCI Communities	Real Estate	WCI Communities Private Club
		BankAtlantic	Financial	BankAtlantic Chairman's Club
		Patron Tequila	Spirits	Patron Tequila Platinum Club
		Budweiser	Food & Beverage	Budweiser Terrace
Bradley Center	Milwaukee Bucks	Cambria	Quartz Surfaces	Cambria Club (Premium seating and Lounge)
Continental Airlines Arena (Meadowlands)	Nets, Devils	Marquis Jet	Airlines	Marquis Jet Locker Room
		Vonage	Communications	Vonage Press Club
Conseco Fieldhouse	Indiana Pacers	Krieg DeVault	Attorney	Kreig DeVault Club Level (Premium Seats)
Energy Solutions Arena	Utah Jazz	Lexus	Automotive	Lexus Club
		All Star Catering	Food & Beverage	All Star Catering
Jobing.com Arena	Phoenix Coyotes	Lexus	Automotive	Lexus Level
Madison Square Garden	New York Knicks	WaMu	Banking	WaMu Theatre
Nationwide Arena	Columbus Blue Jackets	Bud Light	Food & Beverage	Bud Light Arena Pub
Oracle Arena	Golden State Warriors	Smirnoff	Food & Beverage	The Plaza (Smirnoff) Club (Lounge and cocktails)
		Corona	Spirits	880 (Corona) Club (Lounge and cocktails)
Palace of Auburn Hills	Detroit Pistons	Jack Daniels	Spirits	Jack Daniels Old No. 7 Club (Restaurant)
		Captain Morgan	Spirits	Captain's Quarters (Restaurant)

Continued on overleaf

Table 9.3. Secondary Naming Rights of Professional Sport Venues

NBA ARENAS (SECONDARY) *(continued)*

Facility	Team	Sponsor	Category	Branded Area
Pepsi Center	Denver Nuggets Colorado Avalanche	Lexus	Automotive	Club Restaurant
		Denver Post	Media	Lounge
Philips Arena	Atlanta Hawks	Ciroc	Spirits	Ciroc Bar
		First Horizon	Banking	First Horizon Club (Suite and Club seats)
Rose Garden	Trailblazers	Lexus	Automotive	Lexus Level
Tampa Bay Times Forum	Lightning	Bud Light	Food & Beverage	Bud Light Party Deck
		Coors Light	Food & Beverage	Coors Light Between the Pipes Bar
Staples Center	Lakers	Fox Sports	Media	SkyBox Restaurant
Target Center	Timberwolves	US Bank	Financial	US Bank Theater
TD BankNorth Garden	Celtics	New Balance	Apparel	Sports Museum
United Center	Bulls	Ketel One	Spirits	Ketel One Club (Club and Banquet)
		Jose Cuervo	Spirits	Jose Cuervo Cantina
		Budweiser Select	Food & Beverage	Budweiser Select Brew Pub and Carvery
Verizon Center	Washington Wizards	Lexus	Automotive	Lexus Suite Level
		Acela Express	Travel	Acela Club Seating
		Dewar's	Spirits	Dewar's 12 Coaches Club
		Captain Morgan	Spirits	Captain Morgan Party Pavillion c
Wells Fargo Center	76ers	Holt's Cigars	Tobacco	Holt's Cigars Club
		Bud Light	Food & Beverage	Bud Light Zone/ Bud Light Block Party
		Lexus	Automotive	Lexus Club (Restaurant)
		Cingular	Communications	Cingular Pavilion (Food & Beverage)
Xcel Energy Center	Minnesota Wild	Treasure Island	Casino	Treasure Island Resort and Casino Club Level

SECONDARY NAMING RIGHTS

Category	Amount	% of Total	Category	Amount	% of Total
Food & Beverage	17	23%	Building Products	1	1%
Spirits	14	19%	Casino	1	1%
Automotive	9	12%	Energy	1	1%
Financial	9	12%	Online	1	1%
Communications	5	7%	Real Estate	1	1%
Media	4	5%	Software	1	1%
Airlines	3	4%	Tobacco	1	1%
Retail	3	4%	Travel	1	1%
Attorney	1	1%			
Totals	**Amount: 73**			**Percent: 100**	

Sources: Collected by Adam Powell from the *SportsBusiness Journal* research, Wikipedia.com, Ballparks.com, and company and facility websites

The number of personnel needed to manage a venue depends on the size of the venue and the number of events scheduled annually. Commonly, the following positions are present within a venue:		
Venue Director/General Manager/Chief Executive Officer/Executive Director	Housekeepers	Coordinator for Advertising
Director of Operations	Maintenance Workers	Coordinator for Sales
Concessionaires	Coordinator of Events	Ticket Sellers
Parking Attendants	Coordinator of Security (Emergency Management, Risk Management and Safety)	Retail Sales Associates
Ticket Takers	Security Officers	Director of Finance
Ushers	Emergency Medical Technicians	Accountants
Coordinator of Maintenance	Director of Marketing	Director of Customer and Public Relations

Figure 9.1. Typical Venue Personnel

advertising, and sales (i.e., sponsorships, merchandise, and tickets). The **director of finance** is responsible for fiscal accountability, budgeting, cost control, contract negotiations, and financing.

Mission Statement

The **mission statement** provides guidelines that outline the parameters for operating the sport facility and is the basis for the development of goals and objectives for the sport facility. **Goals** are achievable statements provided by management, ideally developed through consultation with all stakeholders in the sport facility. The goals are based on the mission statement and are used to justify the fiscal resources requested in a budget document. **Objectives**, sometimes called action strategies, are the activities to be implemented to reach the overall goal. Each objective should be measurable using assessments to evaluate whether or not the outcome has been met. A mission statement should be purposefully broad and vague, with more specific goals and objectives in support of the mission. Following is the mission statement of the Sports and Exhibition Authority of Pittsburgh and Allegheny County:

> The Sports & Exhibition Authority (SEA), formerly known as the Public Auditorium Authority, of Pittsburgh and Allegheny County was incorporated on February 3, 1954 pursuant to the Public Auditorium Authorities Law Act of July 29, 1953. As a joint authority for the City of Pittsburgh and Allegheny County, the SEA's mission is to provide sport facilities for sporting, entertainment, educational, cultural, civic, and social events for the benefit of the general public. The SEA currently owns and operates the Civic Arena, leases the Benedum Center to the Pittsburgh Cultural Trust, and is responsible for the management of the David L. Lawrence Convention Center. (Sports and Exhibition Authority, 2011)

Policies and Procedures

Policies should be developed with the mission statement in mind. A policy, although formal in nature, should be designed with some flexibility. Policies are general statements that serve to guide decision making and prescribe parameters within which certain decisions are to be made. Policies set limits but are subject to interpretation because they are broad in nature (Sawyer & Smith, 1999; Sawyer, 2012).

Procedures are a series of related steps that are to be followed in an established order to achieve a given purpose. Procedures prescribe exactly what actions are to be taken in a specific situation. They are similar to policies, as both are intended to influence certain decisions, but differ in that they address a series of related decisions (Sawyer & Smith, 1999).

All policies and procedures should be written and compiled into a policy and procedures manual or operations manual. This manual should be revised regularly to reflect changes or current practices within the organization. Finally, the manual should be provided to all employees so that they may familiarize themselves with all aspects of the operation.

SPORT FACILITY OPERATIONS

Operating a sport facility is challenging, complex, and requires knowledge of all managerial functions. There are important operational areas critical to the successful functioning of the sport facility, including booking and scheduling; customer and public relations; security, safety, and medical services; maintenance and housekeeping; retail sales; financial management; and risk management.

Booking and Scheduling

Revenue generated from holding events is the main source of income at most sport facilities. The mission of the venue will determine what types of events are booked and scheduled. Facilities that are home to an NFL franchise often utilize the facility for other events beyond the ten home football games per year. Each sport facility relies on shows, concerts, and events to shape its image. A public assembly facility is obligated to provide for the scheduling of community events (e.g., charitable activities, home and garden shows, non-profit functions, or political rallies) whereas a private sport facility, depending upon its formation agreement, may limit charitable and non-profit activities. Ticketing activities often fall under the auspices of the booking and scheduling departments.

Booking is the act of engaging and contracting an event or attraction. The mechanics of booking include reserving a specific space within a specific sport facility for a specified date at a specific time for an agreed-upon amount of money. **Scheduling** is the reservation process and coordination of all events to the sport facility's available time. The reservation process involves scheduling a series of events and providing the best possible event mix to fit the venue's usage. Written contracts with specific penalties for cancellation, revenue sharing, and other concerns are part of booking and scheduling.

Tickets are sold through the box office, one of the most important areas in the sport facility. It is the first contact the public has with the sport facility. Tickets account for a large amount of revenue for the sport facility. There are many ticketing variables, including venue capacity, types of seating (e.g., reserved and general admission), and type of ticket (e.g., computerized tickets or rolled tickets). Finally, there are specialized seating contracts, including luxury boxes, club seats, and **private seat licenses (PSLs)**.

Public and Media Relations

> "PUBLIC SENTIMENT IS EVERYTHING. WITH PUBLIC SENTIMENT,
> NOTHING CAN FAIL; WITHOUT IT, NOTHING CAN SUCCEED."
>
> —*Abraham Lincoln*

A **public relations** program is designed to influence the opinions of people within a target market through responsible and acceptable performance based on mutually satisfactory two-way communication. In order to gain public sentiment, sport venue managers must be in touch with a wide variety of constituents, including booking agents, promoters, sponsors, risk management experts, fans and patrons, employees, government officials, and the public in general. An effective public relations program will open communication lines with various publics and effectively utilize the media in a manner that competently presents the objectives of the organization to the public at large. Further, it will modify the attitudes and actions of the public through persuasion and integrate them with those of the organization.

In modern society, with its sophisticated communications media, citizens are virtually bombarded by thousands of messages per day. It is critical for the sport facility operator to make his or her message stand out among all the "noise."

Security, Safety, and Medical Services

The security, safety, and medical services usually are under the jurisdiction of the department of operations. Larger sport facilities generally have some full-time safety personnel, but generally hire part-time help—usually police officers and EMS personnel to assist with particular events. Often, private crowd management firms like Contemporary Services Corporation (CSC), Tenable, and Landmark are retained to help with crowd control at events. All employees should be trained in CPR and first aid. The sport

An opportunity for you to learn more about facility management is also a great way to raise money for your sport management student organization. Sport management students at Slippery Rock University in Pennsylvania work for Landmark Event Services at Pittsburgh Steelers and University of Pittsburgh games to raise money for the Sport Management Alliance. These funds offset some of the costs associated with annual sport management trips to Ireland, Costa Rica, Italy, and other international sites.

facility should also have an emergency response plan. Examples of potential emergency situations are bad weather, fire, bomb threats, medical emergencies, terrorism, an airplane crash, loss of power, and hazardous material leakage.

The majority of patron problems involve excess consumption of alcohol. This problem can be minimized by enforcing strict guidelines pertaining to alcohol distribution during events (e.g., no beer sales after the seventh inning in baseball, the beginning of the third quarter in football, or the beginning of the third period in ice hockey). The quantity of beer sold to any one patron at a time (e.g., no more than one beer per patron per sale) should be regulated. Finally, all beverage sellers and other staff should be taught to recognize signs of unacceptable intoxication and the steps to be followed to limit further abuse.

Maintenance and Housekeeping

Studies have shown that a well maintained sport facility encourages repeat patronage. Maintenance and housekeeping are functions designed to keep a sport facility clean, safe, and appealing for patrons. The maintenance and housekeeping staff work together cooperatively to keep the sport facility clean and in good repair. The housekeeping crew is responsible for all seats, stairways, stairwells, restrooms, offices, tile, concrete, carpet floors, walls, ceilings, elevators, upholstered seats, and much more. The maintenance crew is responsible for setup and breakdown of events, replacing filters, maintaining the seating area, as well as operation of equipment, restroom facilities, doors, HVAC, and much more.

Retail Sales

This area is responsible for food services, pouring rights, and merchandise sales. The food service is the business operation that prepares, delivers, and sells food to customers. A concessionaire provides the food service. Various teams manage their own food and beverage service, but often sport facilities contract with a private vendor. The main concessionaires in the sport industry are Ozark Food and Beverage, Inc., Ovation Food Services, Aramark, Levy Restaurants, Sportservice (Delaware North Company), and Centerplate. Sport facilities may have two concessionaires working the same event, including one servicing the fans in the general concourse areas and a premium concessionaire servicing the club level and luxury suites.

Revenue from concessions and pouring rights plays a vital role in the success of any sport facility. Coca-Cola and Pepsi regularly compete for the pouring rights in professional and collegiate sport facilities. **Pouring rights** are the exclusive ability to sell soft drinks, bottled water, and beer in a facility. Pouring rights in multi-purpose sport facilities, with upwards of 250 event nights per year, can be very lucrative.

Merchandise sales are another vital revenue stream for any sport facility. Gift shops, team stores, and vendors sell novelties and licensed products including tee-shirts, jerseys, sweat shirts, caps, blankets, cups, pens, pins, players cards, autographed balls or bats, disposable cameras, and more to patrons. Concessions, pouring rights, and merchandise sales can generate at least 60% of a sport facility's operating revenue

Parking

Fees generated from selling parking spaces can be another source of revenue, even when it is shared with local parking vendors. Parking fees can range from $5 per vehicle for minor league stadiums to $35 per vehicle at downtown major league stadiums. Additional sources of parking revenue can be generated from selling preferred, personalized parking spaces, like the Atlanta Braves did in 2004 by creating Lexus-only parking spaces (sponsored, of course, by Atlanta-area Lexus dealers) for season ticket holders driving Lexus vehicles. Premium parking spots are often sold to season ticket holders at professional sport facilities and major athletic donors at colleges and universities. Parking lots can also be rented for new or antique car shows, carnivals, food festivals, driver's safety school, and other events.

Financial Management

Efficient financial management is essential to the successful operation of a sport facility. Large sport facilities have an in-house staff and smaller sport facilities outsource fiscal duties. Financial managers are concerned with developing and monitoring the operational budget, ordering equipment and supplies, paying accounts payable, collecting accounts payable, developing a capital budget, seeking financing when necessary, managing all internal accounting, working with internal and external auditors, establishing and maintaining bank accounts, and payroll.

Risk Management

Risk management is a process to reduce or limit risk exposure in a sport facility. The goal of risk management is to reduce or eliminate all types of risk the sport facility could be exposed to during operation. Every sport facility, large or small, should have a risk management committee and a person on staff directly assigned to risk management. The risk management committee should establish policies and procedures for identifying and assessing foreseeable risks faced by the sport facility. The risks should be classified into (a) high, moderate, or low loss potential and (b) high, moderate, or low frequency of exposure. After the risks are classified, an action strategy should be devel-

Photo courtesy © Andy Gillentine

oped for each risk ranging from avoidance to modification to transferring a portion of the risk to a third party (e.g., insurance company). Finally, the risk management committee and the risk management director or coordinator should annually conduct a risk audit to identify progress made and new risks that surface.

Sport Event Security Management

There is a major concern regarding sport event security issues existing in today's society. These can include the concern of potential natural disasters (e.g., earthquakes, hurricanes, and tornadoes) and man-made (e.g., fan/player violence, spectator injuries) emergencies. Further, the existence of weapons of mass destruction (e.g., chemical, biological, radiological, nuclear, and explosive) and the identified lack of training and education of key scholastic and collegiate personnel responsible for sport security operations have resulted in The Department of Homeland Security identifying high-profile sporting events in the United States as potential terrorist targets (Lipton, 2005). Terrorist incidents in the sporting world, such as Munich in 1972, Atlanta in 1996, and when an Oklahoma University student prematurely detonated a bomb strapped to his body outside the 84,000-seat stadium in October 2005 (Hagmann, 2005), are examples of events with the potential for catastrophic consequences.

All sport event security management personnel should be trained in alcohol, crowd, and emergency management. The manager of this area should be concerned about all personnel being able to

- Understand sport terrorism activity
- Explain homeland security national strategies and principles
- Identify federal, state, and local roles in the event of a terrorist incident, natural disaster, or crowd management issue (e.g., alcohol management, fan/player violence, or spectator emergency)
- Detect critical infrastructure protection systems
- Identify key assets as a sport facility
- Analyze sport business preparedness, continuity, and recovery systems
- Demonstrate the importance of organizing and building a multi-disciplinary vulnerability assessment team and assessing local sport facilities
- Evaluate potential threat elements
- Determine local vulnerable targets
- Identify potential countermeasures and strategies to improve security at a sport facility
- Assess the importance of contingency planning
- Identify and analyze components of an emergency response plan
- Develop an emergency response plan for a sport facility
- Appraise physical security measures
- Evaluate perimeter and access controls
- Analyze incident/crisis management processes
- Evaluate vendor and contractor management strategies

Alcohol Management

The focus on patron safety relating to alcohol consumption began in 1983 with the *Bearman v. University of Notre Dame* case. This was a landmark case because the court determined that intoxicated persons could pose a general danger to other patrons. This determination flew in the face of previous decisions that placed the responsibility of duty of care on the individual or group, not on the event organizers. The Court determined that foreseeability dictated that Notre Dame had a duty to protect its patrons from the potentially dangerous actions of intoxicated third parties. This case set the standard for duty of care for the management of alcohol at events (Sawyer, 2005, 2009, 2012).

Photo courtesy © bigstockphoto.com

In a number of states, there are dram shop statutes that allow injured plaintiffs to bring suit against restaurants, bars, and other establishments that allow the defendant to become drunk. In some states, the court allows recovery through common negligence actions. There are a few states that allow recovery using both methods. In addition to the dram shop statutes, there is another statute known as the social host liability. This statute provides the injured plaintiff an opportunity to sue based on a social host knowingly serving alcohol to individuals who become intoxicated and cause injury or damage to property (Sawyer, 2005).

Sport facility managers should have an alcohol management plan in their liability tool bags. This plan should be coordinated with the crowd control management plan. The plan should include procedures to check age restrictions, restrictions on the number of beers served, terminating beer sale at a specific point during the event (i.e., basketball, end of third period; football, beginning of third quarter; ice hockey, end of the second intermission; and baseball, end of the seventh inning), deploying trained personnel to watch for trouble, and incorporating a designated-driver program (Sawyer, 2005, 2009, 2012).

Miller Brewing Company, in combination with previous research and encouragement from its legal department, provided the following suggestions regarding an effective alcohol sales strategy (modified from Ammon, Southall, & Blair, 2004, pp. 188–189):

1. Decide whether or not to sell alcohol. If the decision to sell alcohol is made, then an alcohol management plan must be developed.
2. Develop procedures to stop outside alcohol from entering the sport facility.
3. Establish crowd management procedures for alcohol management for day and evening events and for weather.

4. Install appropriate signage to enlightened patrons about responsible and irresponsible drinking and its consequences.

5. Establish a strong ejection policy.

6. Do not promote or advertise drinking during the event.

7. Make sure that security personnel are aware of the demographics of the crowd in each section of the sport facility (e.g., gender, white-collar, blue-collar, families, senior citizens, under 21, etc.).

8. All staff (not just security and servers) should complete regulated alcohol management training.

9. Establish consumption policies (e.g., number of beers per patron at one time, termination of sales prior to conclusion of the event).

10. Tailgating only permitted in parking lots under strict supervision of security personnel.

11. Establish non-alcohol sections within the sport facility (i.e., family sections).

12. Develop a designated-driver program.

One example of a league-wide minimum alcohol policy was implemented by the National Basketball Association in 2005 and includes the following provisions: alcohol can be served only until the start of the fourth quarter; serving size is restricted (24 ounces); a maximum number of two alcoholic beverages are sold per individual customer, and there must be training of arena personnel in effective alcohol management (NBA Media Ventures, LLC, 2005).

Crowd Management

Crowd management is an organizational tool that can assist sport facility directors and/or event coordinators in providing a safe and enjoyable environment for patrons. The crowd management plan is an integral part of the larger risk management plan and includes training programs for staff; drills and procedures to be used to in an emergency; procedures to eject disruptive people; a proper signage system; an efficient communication network; a security response plan; and measurable performance objectives. The personnel are either in-house or outsourced by the sport facility. Smaller sport facilities often utilize on- or off-duty police in uniform. Larger sport facilities have an in-house security force composed of part- and full-time officers. A number of sport facilities have outsourced the security function.

Management can attempt to be proactive in their approach to educate fans and encourage decorum in their sport facilities. For example, the NBA implemented a Fan Code of Conduct in 2005 after the infamous altercation which took place at the Palace of Auburn Hills during a game between the Detroit Pistons and Indiana Pacers, which spilled into the arena stands. This code of conduct sets forth expected standards of behavior for all players and fans in attendance at NBA games, which are posted prominently and announced over the PA system at each NBA game. These crowd management guidelines were prepared in consultation with NBA teams and arena operators, crowd management and security experts, law enforcement officials, members of the

Table 9.4. Common Traits of Sport Facility Managers	
• Preparing and managing a checklist of activities	• Excellent time manager
• Projects a positive attitude	• Effective negotiator
• Working independently or as a team member	• Finance and budget conscious
• Accurate and quick at details	• Possesses good typing, word processing, and other office skills
• Articulate on the telephone and in written and oral communication	• Leadership ability
• Creative, flexible	• Quick problem solve
• Working under extreme pressures for long hours	• Good motivator
• Working with all levels of people including volunteers	• Desire to learn and grow
• Effective at balancing multiple projects simultaneously	

concessions industry, and representatives of TEAM (Techniques for Effective Alcohol Management) (NBA Media Ventures, LLC, 2005).

A relatively new attempt to curb unruly crowd behavior involves text messaging and has been implemented by the National Football League (NFL) and Major League Baseball (MLB). If there is an incident of bad fan behavior that is perceived to be out of control, fans may text or call for security to their seating area to confront abusive fans, rather than having fans confront one another, which might incite fan-on-fan verbal abuse or fighting (Kohl, 2011).

Medical Emergencies

The sport facility should have an emergency management plan as part of the larger risk management plan. Emergencies can range from localized medical emergencies (e.g., slips and falls, heart attacks, diabetic complications) to mass casualty situations (e.g., collapse of bleachers, roof, or walkway) and large disasters (e.g., hurricane, tornado, earthquake, or fire). The plan should include training programs for staff (e.g., CPR, first aid, AED), drills, and communication links with outside emergency agencies. Evacuation strategies, security procedures, and measurable performance objectives should also be included.

Parking Management

Management of a parking operation can be profitable, but it has liabilities. The manager, before charging for parking, must be sure to accomplish the following:

- Purchase adequate liability insurance
- Provide adequate surfacing for the proposed traffic
- Ensure safe entrance and exit areas
- Provide adequate lighting
- Plan for immediate snow and ice removal
- Establish an emergency plan for the space
- Ensure that adequate supervision and security is available
- Provide for the safety of the pedestrians
- Plan a graphic system that makes it easy to find customers' cars at the conclusion of the event
- Provide an adequate number of cashiers and attendants

After the manager has accomplished the above, it is time to decide how many spaces will be allocated for the handicapped (i.e., review state and federal handicapped guidelines for actual number of spaces), VIPs, and regular customers (Sawyer, 2005, 2009, 2012).

According to Russo (2001), the following controls should be implemented to ensure a smooth operation: "(1) sensors or loops buried in each entrance line, (2) a single pass lane, (3) a cashier or checker watching the sellers and authorizing passes, (4) spot checks on sellers, (5) different colored tickets for different events, days, or hours, (6) cash registers, (7) TV monitors, and (8) clean graphics and signs indicating special entrances."

The parking operation is second only to the box office in terms of direct contact between the facility and the patron. A well-designed and managed parking operation will ease crowd tension and allow for sufficient time for patrons to buy a snack, enter the sport facility, and still be in their seats on time. There is no question that the ease of access and parking is a major factor in increased public acceptance and attendance at events (Sawyer, 2005, 2009, 2012).

SUMMARY

The purpose of this chapter was to introduce the segment of the sport management field dealing with sport and facility management. The major concepts presented in this chapter include

- The skill set necessary for facility management
- The differences in public and private ownership of public assembly facilities, in addition to approaches to management (in-house versus outsourcing)
- An overview of the wide array of participant-oriented facilities
- The management and personnel required in facility management
- The concepts of planning, organizing, leading, and evaluating relative to facility management
- The importance of risk management
- Marketing, budgeting, and public relations in facility management
- Post-event evaluation

Discussion Activities

1. If you had to initiate, organize, and oversee a four-person team co-ed volleyball tournament, what steps would you take to ensure its success?

2. As director of operations for women's basketball at Eagle University (a Division I program), you are charged with running the end-of-the-season conference tournament. The college does not outsource any of the facility functions. How will you manage this process? What considerations have to be made as far as preparing and managing the facility? What will you do to enhance the entertainment value, minimize the risk, and market the tournament?

References

Ammon, R. Jr., Southall, R. M., & Blair, D. A. (2004). *Sport facility management: Organizing events and mitigating risks*. Morgantown, WV: Fitness Information Technology.

Crompton, J. L. (2004). Beyond economic impact: An alternative rationale for the public subsidy of major league sports facilities. *Journal of Sport Management, 18*(1), 41.

Hagmann, D. J. (2005). Black hole in America's heartland. *Northeast Intelligence Network*. Retrieved from http://www.homelandsecurityus.com/site/modules/news/article.php?storyid=16

Horine, L., & Stotlar, D. (2003). *Administration of physical education and sport programs* (5th ed.). Boston: McGraw-Hill.

Howard, D. R., & Crompton, J. L. (1995). *Financing sport*. Morgantown, WV: Fitness Information Technology.

Kohl, G. (2011). How Text Messaging Helps your Security Department. *Security Info Watch*. Retrieved from http://www.securityinfowatch.com/article/10481286/how-text-messaging-helps-your-security-department

Lipton, E. (2005). U.S. report lists possibilities for terrorist attacks and likely toll. *New York Times*, Sec. A, p. 1.

Mulrooney, A., & Farmer, P. (2001). Managing the facility. In B. Parkhouse (Ed.). *The management of sport: Its foundation and application* (3rd ed.) (33–36). Boston: McGraw-Hill.

NBA Media Ventures, LLC (2005). NBA Establishes Revised Arena Guidelines for All NBA Arenas. *NBA.com*. Retrieved from http://www.nba.com/news/arena_guidelines_050217.html

Russo, F. (2000). Marketing events and services for spectators. In H. Appenzeller & G. Lewis (Eds.), *Successful sport management*. (2nd ed.) (151–162). Durham, NC: Carolina Academic Press.

Sawyer, T. H. (2005). *Facility design and management for health, fitness, physical activity, recreation, and sports facility development*. Champaign, IL: Sagamore Publishing.

Sawyer, T.H. (2009). *Facility management for physical activity and sport*. Urbana, IL: Sagamore Publishing.

Sawyer, T.H., & Judge, L.W. (2012). *The management of fitness, physical activity, recreation, and sport*. Urbana, IL: Sagamore Publishing.

Sawyer, T. H., Hypes, M. G., & Hypes, J. A. (2004). *Financing the sport enterprise*. Champaign, IL: Sagamore Publishing.

Sawyer, T. H., & Smith O. R. (1999). *The management of clubs, recreation, and sport: Concepts and applications*. Champaign, IL: Sagamore Publishing.

Silvers, J. R. (2003). *Event management body of knowledge project*. Retrieved from http://www.julia silvers.com/embok.htm#Event_Management_as_a_Profession

Smith, S. (2008). Hawks lose win over Heat to statistical error. Teams forced to replay last minute of December game. *Atlanta Journal Constitution*, Sec. A, p. 1.

Solomon, J. (2002). *An insider's guide to managing sporting events*. Champaign, IL: Human Kinetics.

Sports and Exhibition Authority. (2011). Retrieved from http://pgh-sea.com/history.htm

Walker, M. L., & Stotlar, D. K. (1997). *Sport facility management*. London, UK: Jones & Bartlett, Inc.

10

Event Management

Heather Lawrence and Bernard Goldfine

INTRODUCTION

Event management is an exciting and fast-paced segment of the sport industry. The definition of a sport event is continually expanding, creating new opportunities in the industry. Today, sport event managers can work for sport franchises such as a professional team or league, for sport facilities, recreational leagues, colleges and universities, extreme sport events, or even for niche event brands (e.g., Warrior Dash). Historically, the job of an event manager was merely to ensure that sport events occurred and satisfied the needs of the participants. Today, the job requires the event manager to be knowledgeable in almost all areas of

In the Bleachers © 2014 Steve Moore. Dist. by Universal Uclick
www.gocomics.com/inthebleachers

"These are *great* seats!!"

sport, from parking cars to security planning to high-level sponsor activations. In a single day, an event manager might change from a business suit to meet with a sport execu-

---

Learning Objectives

Upon completion of this chapter, the reader should be able to
- Discuss the skills necessary for event management;
- Understand the event management process;
- Determine necessary documentation for successful event execution;
- Describe how events can be most effectively organized for success; and
- Recognize the role of marketing and budgeting in event management.

tive into shorts and a T-shirt to help prepare a facility for an event, and maybe even into the unofficial event management uniform of khakis and a polo shirt to supervise a baseball game. In essence, the event manager is a "jack of all trades" charged with making all the pieces of the event puzzle come together, resulting in a high-quality experience for event participants and spectators alike.

While creating and managing an event is often viewed as a linear process in which exact steps are followed, the reality is that many issues occur simultaneously, requiring managers to handle multiple tasks proficiently (Solomon, 2002). Plus, no two events are exactly the same. Event managers must be able not only to anticipate problems and have contingency plans in place, but also to think quickly on their feet when unforeseen crises arise. In fact, event managers do well to refer to several corollaries of Murphy's Law:

- Everything takes longer that you plan.
- If several things could go wrong, the one that will do the most damage will—and often at the last possible moment.
- Left to themselves, things tend to go from bad to worse.
- Human beings tend to regress toward meanness.
- Every solution creates new problems.
- And, finally, the scientific consensus on Murphy's Law: Murphy was an optimist. (Kelly, 1985)

Examples of sporting events that have been altered by circumstances beyond the organizers' control abound: the lighting outage at the 2013 Super Bowl in New Orleans, the two-day rain delay in the 2008 World Series between the Philadelphia Phillies and the Tampa Bay Devil Rays, the 1989 earthquake that delayed the World Series between the Oakland A's and San Francisco Giants. Event organizers must be prepared with contingency plans when facing these occurrences. The main point here is that individuals who pursue a career in event management must be flexible and able to adapt to setbacks or changes. Event managers also must remain calm when faced with crises and convey a sense of confidence to those under their direction.

This chapter will introduce the basic components of event management and is divided into two sections: (1) The Event Management Process and (2) People and Event Management. Entire textbooks, as well as undergraduate and graduate courses, focus specifically on the nuances of sport event management for those interested in learning more. The intent of this chapter is to highlight the critical pieces of event management as well as identify areas that are rapidly growing and evolving.

THE EVENT MANAGEMENT PROCESS

Similar to other forms of management, event management entails directing, collaborating, monitoring resources, and motivating professional spirit and cooperative efforts toward the fulfillment of organizational goals (Horine, 2003). Essential elements of successful event management include, but are not limited to, seamless organization, the ability to plan from event inception to execution, effective leadership, and attention to detail. Any event, regardless of scope, requires more than one person to be successful.

Therefore, effective leadership is at the heart of successful production of events. All individuals—including volunteers, interns, and paid staff—must have a clear understanding of their responsibilities, be treated with respect, and encouraged to do whatever is necessary to make the event a success.

The types of events that can be run are as varied as one's imagination. They can be mega-events such as the Olympics or small, local tournaments that exist strictly for social interaction. Event management authority and educator Julia Rutherford Silvers (2003) created an excellent classification scheme for categorization of the events based upon their respective purposes (see Table 10.1). Despite the varied types of events, a common series of elements are found and must be examined in order to successfully organize and conduct the event.

Table 10.1. The Event Genre of Event Management	
Business & Corporate Events	Any event that supports business objectives, including management functions, corporate communications, training, marketing, incentives, employee relations, and customer relations, scheduled alone or in conjunction with other events.
Cause-Related & Fundraising Events	An event created by or for a charitable or cause-related group for the purpose of attracting revenue, support, and/or awareness, scheduled alone or in conjunction with other events.
Exhibitions, Expositions, & Fairs	An event bringing buyers and sellers and interested persons together to view and/or sell products, services, and other resources to a specific industry or the general public, scheduled alone or in conjunction with other events.
Entertainment & Leisure Events	A one-time or periodic, free or ticketed performance or exhibition event created for entertainment purposes, scheduled alone or in conjunction with other events.
Festivals	A cultural celebration, either secular or religious, created by and/or for the public, scheduled alone or in conjunction with other events. (Many festivals include bringing buyer and seller together in a festive atmosphere.)
Government & Civic Events	An event comprised of or created by or for political parties, communities, or municipal or national government entities, scheduled alone or in conjunction with other events
Marketing Events	A commerce-oriented event to facilitate bringing buyer and seller together or to create awareness of a commercial product or service, scheduled alone or in conjunction with other events.
Meeting & Convention Events	The assembly of people for the purpose of exchanging information, debate or discussion, consensus or decisions, education, and relationship building, scheduled alone or in conjunction with other events.
Social/Life-Cycle Events	A private event, by invitation only, celebrating or commemorating a cultural, religious, communal, societal, or life-cycle occasion, scheduled alone or in conjunction with other events.
Sports Events	A spectator or participatory event involving recreational or competitive sport activities, scheduled alone or in conjunction with other events.
(Silvers, 2003)	

Event Purpose

The foundation of any event is to first establish the purpose of the event. Establishing and clarifying event goals gives organizers a framework from which to manage their event. Examples of event goals are:

1. To make a profit or raise funds.
2. To achieve a specific attendance or fan support for a sport team or event.
3. To raise awareness, sensitivity, and/or money for a particular cause (e.g., children's cancer).
4. To improve an organization's image and visibility in order to foster a positive image or overcome a negative one.
5. To expose an entity (e.g., community or organization) to a specific type of entertainment or sport. (Goldfine & Schleppi, 1997)

The purpose and goals of an event will determine the emphasis to be placed upon various aspects of event management. For example, if the purpose of an event is to raise awareness and funding for the Special Olympics, then it follows that event literature and a portion of the event itself will be aimed at educating attendees or participants as to the nature of Special Olympics competition and the challenges it faces.

Event Bidding

Not all events require a bid process, but some do. Event bidding is the process by which an event host is chosen through a competitive process prescribed by a rights holder. Rights holders are defined as "any entity, including national governing bodies (NGBs), which controls an event through ownership" (Lawrence, 2009, p. 23). The process of bidding on an event can range from a simple one-page document that the potential host submits to a multi-year, multimillion-dollar effort, as in the case of the Olympic Games. Table 10.2 lists common content items required by rights holders during the bid process.

Photo courtesy © Dreamstime

Table 10.2. Sample Bid Requirements			
I	General Stadium Information		
	A	Owner/address	
	B	Management	
	C	Year opened	
	D	Renovation information	
II	Stadium Specifics		
	A	Size of main stadium floor	
	B	Storage space for equipment	
	C	Field surface	
	D	Field lighting	
		i	Foot candles
		ii	Warm-up time of lights
		iii	Shutters availability
		iv	In-stand spotlight locations
	E	Number of Seats	
		i	Permanent seating in main seating bowl (non-premium)
		ii	Permanent club seats
		iii	Suites (number and seats in each)
		iv	Ability to add temporary suites/club seats
		v	ADA seats available and location in stadium
	F	Stadium availability for practice	
	G	Description of union contracts	
III	Media		
	A	Number of working media seats in press box	
		i	Type of work set up (internet access, telephone, power)
	B	Number and location of working media seating	
		i	Type of work set up (internet access, telephone, power)
	C	Size and location of post-event press conference room	
	D	Size and location of post-event media work room	
		i	Type of work set up (internet access, telephone, power)
	E	Media lunch/dinner location	
IV	Television/Radio		
	A	Domestic broadcast abilities/compound	
	B	Network broadcast abilities/compound	
	C	Interview areas	
	D	Photographers areas	

Continued on overleaf

\multicolumn{3}{l}{**Table 10.2.** Sample Bid Requirements *(continued)*}		
V	\multicolumn{2}{l}{Sound/Scoreboards/Signage}	
	A	Press box sound system
	B	Stadium scoreboard screens (number, location, and size)
	C	In-stadium electronic message boards (number, location, and size)
	D	Exterior stadium electronic message boards (number, location, and size)
	E	Nature of all existing advertising contracts (including naming rights)
VI	\multicolumn{2}{l}{Hotels}	
	A	Number of available rooms in vicinity
	B	Anti-gouging agreements
	C	Rights holders headquarters hotel
	D	Media headquarters hotel
	E	Participants headquarters hotel
VII	\multicolumn{2}{l}{Ancillaries}	
	A	Club/restaurants in stadium
	B	Existing stadium stores
	C	Novelty vending
	D	Concessionaire
		i Name and contact
		ii Terms of agreement
		iii Other relevant information
		iv Any differences with suite catering
	E	Security
		i Name and contact
		ii Terms of agreement
		iii Other relevant information
	F	Relevant alcohol laws
	G	Parking
		i Stadium owned/controlled spaces (number and location)
		ii Regular prices charged
		iii Availability of disabled parking spaces
	H	Sponsor tent location
VIII	\multicolumn{2}{l}{Host committee description}	
	A	Members
	B	Mission

Source: Lawrence, 2009.

Understanding why the rights holder is using a bid process to select a location to hold the event is a critical component to bidding success. For rights holders with revenue as a primary motive, the eventual winning host will have to demonstrate the ability to make money for the rights holder. In other situations, a primary purpose might be to find a locale and facility willing to host the event. Many events operate at a financial loss, so attracting bidders to compete for the privilege of losing money is often difficult. But the bidders might have motives that allow for some financial loss. For example, if it is a youth event that will bring outside money into the city through hotel nights, shopping, and restaurant spending, a financial loss for the event is often acceptable. It all depends on the rights holder's motivations for bidding out the event and the event organizer's purpose for bidding on the event. When a match is found between the rights holder and the bidder, the event is awarded to the bidder and the planning process commences.

Facilities and Equipment

Traditional sport venues such as stadiums and arenas are designed to host sport events, but more and more events are taking place in nontraditional venues such as roads, parks, waterways, or mountains. As a result, the event manager must be diligent in ensuring the selected venue is appropriate and meets the needs of the event. In a large-scale event such as the Olympics, chosen cities often are in a race against the clock to build their venues in time for the opening ceremonies. For other events, preparation usually includes some modifications—even if temporary.

In preparing any facility or site for a sport event, a number of concerns are common. For traditional venues, one concern is confirming that the facility does not require impossible alterations or repairs before the event. What would happen if a facility was scheduled to host a wheelchair basketball event, but the locker rooms were not capable of accommodating wheelchairs? Nontraditional venues also pose a variety of hurdles in preparing for a sport event, such as obtaining permits to close a road for a race or acquiring temporary seating for spectators on a ski racecourse. If these seem like big issues, they are.

After addressing any major facility adaptations, the best method to assure that a site is adequately prepared for an event is to use facility and equipment checklists. These checklists should be comprehensive and include the following, depending upon the type of event being held:

- Site-preparation tasks, such as providing adequate parking
- Testing the public address equipment and lighting
- Ensuring proper signage for pedestrian and vehicular traffic
- Providing sufficient ticket-taker areas
- Making proper provisions for concessions and merchandise stands
- Inspecting seating
- Stocking the restrooms adequately

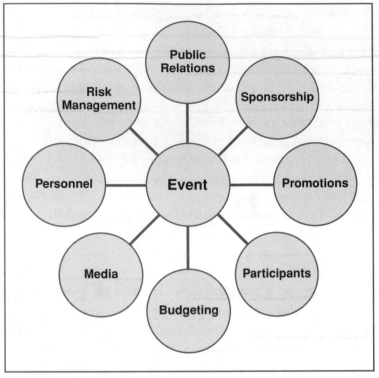

Figure 10.1.

- Providing for on-site storage and repair of equipment
- Setting aside hospitality areas for sponsors and game officials
- Addressing the needs of the media
- Developing a system for on-site communications among personnel, etc.

Event Planning Documents

Once the primary purpose and goals for an event have been established, the planning begins. During the planning of an event, a variety of organizational documents are used to keep the event on track. At a minimum, the planning timeline, field of play diagram, and event checklist are required for the successful operation of the event. In most cases, documents associated with policies and procedures marketing and sponsorship, budget, staffing, and risk management/safety/security must also be generated. For some events, the organizational documents may number thousands of pages and take years to successfully plan and implement.

Events run much more smoothly when guidelines are provided to organizers, paid staff, and volunteers, ensuring that communication and understanding among staff is clear. These planning documents help the event process by (1) limiting or avoiding the duplication of effort, which may lead to internal conflict; (2) increasing cooperation among event staff; (3) standardizing worker training; and (4) promoting enhanced customer service. When all those involved in the planning and execution of an event are aware of their roles, the event's goals, how the event is being marketed, and the dead-

Table 10.3. Planning Timeline					
Road Race Planning Timeline					
Days Out	Due Date	Task	Functional Area	Task Owner	Date Completed
−240	21-Mar-13	Initial course drive-thru	Events	Lawrence	
−1	9-Nov-13	Final pre-event course drive-thru	Events	Lawrence	
−150	19-June-13	Sinage design first draft	Creative	Goldfine	
−75	2-Sept-13	Sinage design final/sent to print	Creative	Goldfine	
−45	2-Oct-13	Course split timing mat locations tested for interference	Timing	Wells	
−45	2-Oct-13	Exact course split timing mat locations noted on drive-thru	Timing	Wells	
−8	8-Nov-13	Course split timing locations marked with spray paint	Events	Lawrence	
−3	12-Nov-13	Music band power tested-Final	Ancillaries	Gillentine	
−1	15-Nov-13	Registration area set	Events	Lawrence	
5	21-Nov-13	Recap report format sent out	All	Smith	
10	26-Nov-13	Recap reports due	All	Smith	

Note. Adapted from Wells, 2000.

lines for the various tasks, there is a great likelihood that the event will be a success (Goldfine & Schleppi, 1997).

Providing detail on all of the referenced planning documents is beyond the scope of this chapter, but the planning timeline (see Table 10.3), field of play diagram (see Figure 10.2), and event checklist deserve special attention. If any of these documents are improperly structured, the event quickly disintegrates.

The planning timeline gives organizers an overview of what needs to be accomplished by specified dates; therefore, organizers can gain a clear sense of priority and task order. For example, if all the sponsors for a given event are supposed to be listed on T-shirts, then it is essential that a deadline for soliciting sponsors be established in time for the production of T-shirts so they will be ready for distribution and sale on the day of the event. The timeline can be as detailed as the event mangers choose. Or there might be one overall planning timeline with separate timelines for each functional area. For example, the overall event timeline might list major tasks, and the marketing staff might have a separate and more detailed timeline for its specific assignments.

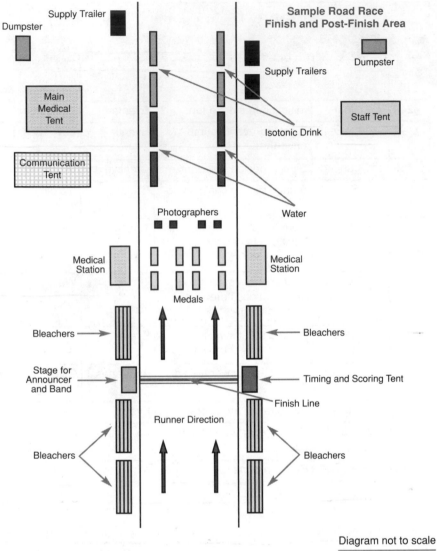

Figure 10.2. Field of Play Diagram

Diagram not to scale
Source: Wells, 2009.

The timeline is the event manager's handbook because it is akin to a countdown calendar or check-off list of when various tasks should be completed. A planning timeline should feature information about the task, the date the task should be completed, the functional area responsible for the task (e.g., marketing, operations, etc.), and the person responsible for completing the task, as well as an area to be filled in with the task completion date. The timeline also could list "days out" of the number of days prior to the event by which the task must be completed. The "days out" information is a simple way for all of the event staff to see critical items and the order in which they must be completed.

The timeline's structure is influenced by the time available leading up to the event. For annual events, the preliminary planning should transpire during the 7- to 12-month period prior to the event date (Goldfine & Schleppi, 1997). An event season planning timeline might apply to a high school football season; this would list things that need to be done to prepare for the season. Because every game has some similarities, the planning timeline can be abbreviated for each week leading up to the game. The season timeline provides the event manager and their team a sense of progress in their efforts to keep the event on schedule without glitches.

The field of play diagram illustrates the physical layout of the space (see Figure 10.2). The complexity of the diagram is dictated by the complexity of the event. For some events, a sketch might be sufficient; for others, specific computer software might be needed to ensure the accuracy of the diagram. Event organizers might choose to diagram only the primary space (e.g., football field, racecourse, etc.) or also diagram each ancillary space (e.g., tailgate areas, hospitality function space, parking lots, etc.). Because most events require a team to set up the event space, diagrams allow for easy communication between event organizers and those responsible for setup.

When the day of the event finally arrives, the event manager and his/her team must have their proverbial ducks in a row. The event manager should develop a master event checklist that includes the time by which a task must be completed along with who is responsible for each task. This master checklist can then be coordinated with checklists for each of the key areas of the event planning, such as parking, registration/ticketing, program and merchandise sales, security, concessions, etc. (Walker & Stotlar, 1997). If all personnel know their assigned responsibilities, there is an increased probability that the event will be a success.

Event Marketing

Event marketing is similar to sport marketing in general and follows the same principles (see Chapter 7). For events, the marketing plan delineates the event's purpose, timelines, budget, target audience, means of promotion, advertising, public relations, media plan, sponsorship plan, and list of targeted sponsors. The marketing plan needs to be carefully thought out because it is the blueprint for the event's success.

An event must be properly marketed and promoted to ensure it is successful. Attracting customers (participants, fans, or both) requires research to determine if a proposed event has appeal. Ideally, the event management team can outsource the task of gauging

customer interest for an event. However, outsourcing is often cost prohibitive, so the event team must conduct research to determine event viability. Regardless of personnel involved in conducting the research, it is essential that the information collected and analyzed accurately portray potential customers' sociodemographic data (age, income, gender, etc.) and psychographic data (interests, attitudes, etc.) in order to attract customers and spon-

sors to an event. Promotions, when properly timed, draw attention to an event and enhance anticipation (Goldfine & Schleppi, 1997).

Event Sponsorship

Obtaining event partners or sponsors is expected in contemporary event management
to help absorb some of the expense of the event. As with marketing, event sponsorship
is similar to general sport sponsorship principles (Chapter 8). The key for event organizers is to attract sponsors with values and goals that align with the event. Potential
sponsors must be able to identify or estimate their return on their investment, should
they choose to sponsor a particular event. The local donut shop is probably not a likely
sponsor of a fun run established to fight childhood obesity. On the other hand, a nutri-
tion brand or store, daycare center, dance or gymnastics studio, or sporting goods store
might be excellent targets as event sponsors for the fun run. Sponsors can support the
event either by providing money for the event to use on expenses or by providing in-kind
trade by providing products or services (e.g., equipment, food and beverage, advertising
space) that the event would otherwise have to purchase. For example, a trophy and
award company might agree to an in-kind sponsorship in which they receive exposure
in exchange for supplying awards to the winning participants of an event. Once a sponsor is secured, the event is responsible for ensuring there is value in the sponsorship for
the sponsoring entity.

Event Budgeting

Another key element of the event process is making sure that the budget is carefully
developed (for additional information on budgeting, please see Chapter 5). The potential revenues from ticketing, participant registration, sponsorship, merchandise, concessions, etc. must be estimated and balanced against the cost of holding the event, such as
facility rental, maintenance, personnel, and anything else that carries any cost. On the
revenue side, ticket or user fees costs must be analyzed carefully, as does the development of a sponsorship package. The value of research into similar events and developing
a profile of the potential demographic and psychographic participants/fans is key to
being able to secure financially sound sponsorships.

The budget for any event should be based on the goals established at the outset of
planning. Some events are held specifically to make large sums of money (e.g., celebrity *(gala)*
flag football game to raise funds for new turf for a football stadium). On the other side
of the ledger, some events operate at a financial loss but achieve their goal of increasing
visibility for an institution or a cause.

To determine expenses and identify sources of revenue, the event manager should do
some comparative research, seeking the advice of others who have run similar events.
For an inaugural event, the event manager and committee coordinators should priori-
tize the various event-related expenses and determine if any could be diminished through
in-kind sponsorships or trades. It is important for the event management team to meticu-
lously analyze all potential expenses and have them reflected in the budget. The expenses should be estimated on the worst-case, most-expensive scenario to help alleviate.

any potential budget shortfalls. For recurring events, revenue streams from tickets/user fees, sponsorships, ancillary events, merchandise, concessions, parking, and any other potential cash generators will be easier to estimate.

Once a budget has been established, several important items must be clarified and conveyed to the appropriate personnel. For example, everyone should know who is directly overseeing the budgetary processes, such as purchasing authorization, bill paying, petty cash oversight and distribution, insurance purchasing, contingency fund disbursement for emergencies, receipts processing, and accounting. Expenses also may be incurred for promotions, venue rental, equipment purchase or rental, transportation, accommodations, performers' fees, printed materials, gifts, advertising, and personnel.

Events operating on a limited budget can maximize funds through the aforementioned in-kind trades. To save on advertising and publicity costs, various media can sponsor each other. For example, a newspaper may sponsor a local radio or television station and vice versa, thus providing each exposure through print and electronic media at no cost to the event's organizers (Goldfine & Schleppi, 1997).

Sponsorships are often the largest percentage of total revenue for many events; therefore, care must be taken to make sure that the packages being offered to potential sponsors are attractive and that the various levels of sponsorship (title, presenting, official, etc.) are internally consistent—in other words, that the difference in benefits for the presenting sponsor are significantly higher than those of an official sponsor. The event manager and committee coordinators should identify every potential source of revenue based on the main product extensions (e.g., concessions, merchandise, ancillary event, etc.). For example, organizers of a charity golf event might want to include a pre-event putting and chipping contest to generate additional revenues beyond greens fees and sponsorships.

Finally, an important consideration: the farther out the planning of an event is from its actual date (such as one or two years), the greater the likelihood that costs will exceed the initial budget. Therefore, contracts for purchases or services (such as hotels) to be received later at current prices should be well understood at the outset, and contingency funds can be set aside to help meet the rising costs of goods and services (Goldfine & Schleppi, 1997). Those charged with budgeting for an event should carefully consider and designate a specific line item for every imaginable expense, and estimate revenue on the low side to stay within an allotted preliminary budget.

Event Risk Management

Keeping everyone associated with the event safe and secure is the top priority for any event manager. Risk is inherent in sport and in any location where large groups of people gather (see Chapter 11 for additional info). It would be impossible to eliminate all risk for sports events, so the job of the event manager is to manage risk and reduce the likelihood of any safety or security issues during the event. This is easily demonstrated by a review of major sporting events around the world that, despite years of planning and preparation, were unable to avoid emergency situations (see Case 10.1 and Case 10.2).

Event risk management should be viewed as an evolutionary process; that is, each event should be examined to assess how risks could be mitigated during succeeding

events. Four major aspects of risk management for event managements are (1) insurance, (2) facility inspection and monitoring, (3) crowd management, and (4) first aid
and emergency services. A risk management plan for an event should be documented
carefully and updated continually based upon data regarding problems, potential haz-
ards, and injuries. Recommended solutions to these problems should also be recorded
(Goldfine & Schleppi, 1997).

Technology

Only a few years ago, the use of technology was optional for event managers. Today,
technology and social media are an integral part of daily life. Consider this: how would
an individual find information on a local 5K run? The current likely response is, "Google
it." What if the Internet search revealed no website or information available? For many
people, that would be the end of their effort to seek out information. It is expected that
sport events have a website and that participant-driven sport events provide the ability
for participants to register online. Continuing with the 5K example, assume a website
is found and online registration is possible. What now? The frequent answer is to "Like"
the Facebook page and follow the event on Twitter.

Technology can be used for information dissemination, information management,
and revenue generation. Websites, social media, online chats, e-mail, and text messaging all provide a very inexpensive way for event managers to communicate with the
marketplace. Users must seek out the information on websites, social media, and online
chats, while information can be pushed to users through e-mail and text messaging. Of
course, for e-mail and text messaging, the event property has to have access to a database of emails and cell phone numbers. Many people find text messages to be too inva-
sive as a marketing and communication technique (and it is possible the user is paying
per text received), so it is recommended that text messaging be used only to communicate with individuals who sign up to receive texts. In addition to communicating basic
event information, these avenues are clearly effective marketing platforms as well (see
Chapter 7).

There is a lot of information needed for effective event management that must be organized in a useful way. Information management refers to the mechanism used to capture, organize, categorize, and retrieve pieces of information. The type of information
that might be used by event staff includes planning timeline documents, budgets, vendor contracts, participant registrations, participant waivers, and customer data from
ticket purchases. Of course this list is not exhaustive, but the idea is that there must be
a structure through a custom database or a simple spreadsheet that enables pieces of
information to be retrieved quickly and easily.

All events—even charitable events—must generate revenue to sustain operations.
Technology is a great addition to traditional revenue streams such as ticket sales, registrations, sponsorships, event programs, concessions, and merchandise sales. According
to Pfahl (2009), "monetization describes the efforts made to utilize website space for
revenue generation, even if revenues are not for profit purposes" (p. 77). Think about
how this might work during an intercollegiate basketball season. A university could

idea

place 25 replica jerseys at various sponsor locations in the locale; fans would need to visit the website to get clues as to the location of the jerseys. Each jersey has a special code on it that represents a prize. Individuals who find the jerseys then go to the athletic website to enter the code to see what they won. There might even be a big prize such as free tuition for a semester or a vacation package provided by an athletics sponsor. The end result is that the promotion got people excited about the jersey hunt, encouraged visits to the athletic website (where they viewed athletic information as well as sponsor information), and drove traffic to sponsor locations in search of the jersey. In other words, there is value through online opportunities. It is this type of online/offline initiative that is the future of event management and marketing. Whether it is creating a simple informational website about the event or launching complex experiences with sponsors, technology is becoming more and more important by the day in our society.

PEOPLE AND EVENT MANAGEMENT

The quality of an event will only be as good as the people who are associated with it. Ideally, the primary leader overseeing the event from the top possesses all of the desirable qualities of any good event manager, including but not limited to the ability to see the big picture of how the event will unfold and to convey that vision clearly to staff; to inspire and motivate those charged with executing the event; to organize the behind-the-scenes operations to ensure the most efficient and effective staging of an event; and to solve problems calmly when faced with unexpected circumstances.

Leadership

Identifying and securing excellent leadership for events goes a long way toward ensuring that an event will be successful. An example of one of the most successful people to run an event was Peter Ueberroth, president of the Los Angeles Olympic Organizing Committee that staged the 1984 Los Angeles Olympic Games. Under Ueberroth's innovative and inspiring leadership, the first privately financed Games resulted in a surplus of $238 million, which continues to support youth and amateur-related sports programs throughout the United States (Degun, 2013). To provide some perspective of the enormity of this accomplishment, most nations incur debt when hosting the Olympic Games simply due to the sheer magnitude of this type of endeavor. Due to his success with the Olympics, Ueberroth was selected as *Time* magazine's 1984 Person of the Year and his business model has been duplicated in many subsequent Olympics. Words used to describe his leadership highlight his creativity, his ability to energize people, his natural leadership and teaching abilities, and his ability to make unpopular decisions (Anderson School of Management, 2011).

Event Organizational Structure

Establishing an organizational structure for the event is essential. The purpose, magnitude, and complexity of the event will dictate the overall structure. If the event is large enough to warrant committees, each committee should be headed by a committee leader/coordinator. This person preferably has experience with the type of assignments

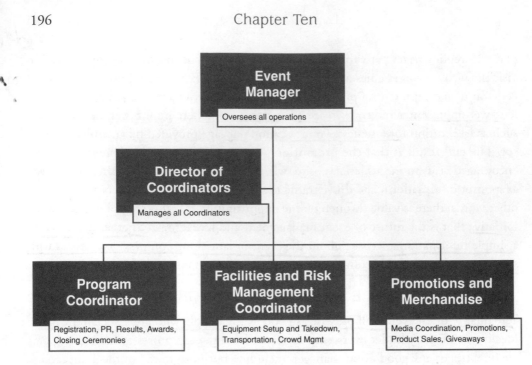

Figure 10.3. Organizational Chart

the committee is charged with, or at the least is highly driven and willing to take charge of the group to ensure that its objectives are accomplished in a timely manner. Organizational charts can clarify the roles and committees and help to avoid overlap and duplication of responsibilities (Figure 10.3). Use of technology to aid in communication and information management along with sufficient face-to-face meetings among committee members is essential to confirm that the committee is indeed accomplishing its goals in accordance with the event timelines.

Event Staffing

Another key aspect of the overall event process is staffing (i.e., gathering the key human resources for successful execution of the event). Once event leadership has been established, event managers need to select and train both paid personnel and volunteers. Being able to get the right people placed in key roles is essential to delegating responsibility. The degree of delegation of key, substantive responsibilities will depend on the experience of the staff recruited for an event. Also, job descriptions need to be clearly stated so people know their roles and responsibilities. Jerry Solomon—one of the leading sport event managers in the country—says that successful event managers "create a team atmosphere and a sense of camaraderie that energizes others to go any length in making the event a success" (Solomon, 2002, p. 165).

The event manager must assign a high priority to recruitment, selection, training, supervision, motivation, and evaluation of both paid personnel and volunteers. Recruitment of experienced personnel, especially those familiar with a previous similar event, increases the odds that the event will run smoothly. However, experienced personnel are not always available, which entails a higher degree of training and less likelihood that aspects of the event can be completely delegated without concern.

The quality of individuals the top leadership is able to recruit as paid personnel will depend in part on the time available prior to the event. Ideally, job descriptions should be advertised through the local media (including newspapers, radio, on local college campuses, and cable-access channels) as well as on the Internet. Furthermore, job descriptions can be posted at service organizations (e.g., university clubs) and other highly visible community locations. If a job requires leadership or complex technical skills, the selection process must be rigorous, including requests for résumés, interviewing, and reference checks. Jobs that do not require specific expertise (such as parking attendants) should also have a selection process. Although the selection process may be less rigorous, it should still screen based on past experience, include brief interviews, and require employment or character references.

The event manager must screen for certain qualities when recruiting personnel. For example, ushers should possess excellent interpersonal skills. The most frequent problems ushers encounter are customers who are in the wrong seats or who are disrupting other customers' enjoyment of the event. Therefore, event managers should seek diplomatic, quick-thinking individuals who can find solutions to these types of problems (Goldfine & Schleppi, 1997). Individuals charged with parking, concessions, or sales of merchandise or programs need to possess solid math skills as well as knowledge of how to process credit cards quickly. If these individuals can quickly calculate and dispense change for cash transactions as well as process credit card transactions, then lines will move quickly. Hawkers (roving vendors) are part of the personnel team at some events, and they must have pleasant and outgoing dispositions if sales in the stands are to be lucrative. Finally, more specialized paid personnel need to possess the qualities necessary to fill their roles. For example, public address announcers should have excellent public-speaking skills and be knowledgeable of the event or contest; scoreboard operators should have a thorough understanding of basic computer operations; and electricians should have industry-standard certifications and be familiar with a venue's power supply and wiring.

For most sports events, volunteers are a necessary component to the staffing model. In addition to using the staffing techniques to attract volunteers, local community service organizations such as Rotary Clubs, church groups, and university groups are often fantastic places to seek individuals interested in volunteering. Another way to attract group of volunteers (instead of individuals) is through revenue sharing:

> Often, a group will volunteer to help out at the event if they concurrently can do some fundraising for their organization. For example, a local high school team may be willing to come and clean up the stands after an event in exchange for the event making a donation to the team. This creates a positive for both groups, as they both get something they need from the relationship: the venue gets cleaned and the team earns money. Another example would be when a group staffs the concessions areas in exchange for a percentage of the profits from the sales they make during the event. (McGlone, Wells, & Lawrence, 2012, pp. 225–226)

Volunteers must be treated well and shown appreciation, especially if an event is going to occur on a regular, annual, or semi-annual basis. Creative gifts of recognition such as mugs or T-shirts and good food (which can be supplied by a sponsor) can be very motivating. In fact, if volunteers enjoy their experience, they can become informal recruiters in persuading others to volunteer the next time the event is held. Organizers of large-scale events, such as the U.S. Open Golf Championship, utilize well over 5,000 volunteers to help manage the event.

Committees

Due to the wide array and complexity of tasks necessary to run an event successfully, committees or subgroups need to be formed to address specific areas of managing the event. Each committee/subgroup must have a well-defined mission, such as participant registration, media relations, hospitality, facility setup and takedown, concessions, security, sponsorship, programming, or marketing. Each committee should have a coordinator/chairperson who has experience in those specific areas, or at the very least leadership abilities, organizational skills, and a passion for the event. Ideally, they are good at managing human resources, especially given that guiding volunteers to perform effectively can be a daunting task. These committee leaders can be recruited from sponsoring organizations, city governments, the corporate community, and local universities.

Although there is no definitive code of operations for committees, some general guidelines for such groups (Goldfine & Schleppi, 1997) include:

1. Keep the number of committees to a minimum. A good small group is always preferable to a large, unwieldy one.

2. Allow committee coordinators to select the people with whom they work. Given autonomy in the selection process, committee coordinators are likely to recruit volunteers with whom they can work well. This ability of the committee to interact well facilitates the accomplishment of its given tasks. Moreover, committee chairs should be allowed to set up their own chain of command.

3. Prepare written outlines of committee responsibilities, including the dates and times tasks are to be accomplished. Chairs must maintain close contact with their committee members to ensure that all assigned tasks are completed in accordance with the event timetable.

Photo courtesy © iStockphoto.com

4. Regular meetings of the event manager and committee coordinators (the executive event team) should be scheduled for the purposes of planning, assessing progress toward event preparation, and coordinating efforts between committees.

Develop a calendar of tasks to be completed. This master calendar should begin with the first day the event is confirmed and continue through the execution and final wrap-up of the event.

Event Wrap-Up and Evaluation

The final aspect of the event process is the wrap-up and evaluation. First and foremost, gratitude must be clearly expressed to all attendees/participants, sponsors, volunteers, paid staff, and any ancillary support personnel. The process for evaluation needs to be in place well before the event is finished, and a timetable for this evaluation should be established. The following are several criteria to consider when evaluating the relative success of the event:

Was the event successful in accomplishing its stated purpose and goals (e.g., fund-raising goal reached)?

a. Check against written purpose and goals.
b. What were the successes?
c. What were the mistakes or what specifically could be improved?
d. How can the event be better marketed and promoted next time?

This post-event evaluation can be accomplished in one or several ways including open-ended written questions; objective questions or check sheets; and brainstorming and/or post-event interview or surveys with participants, sponsors, or other stakeholders. As demonstrated, the process of event management entails specific steps to ensure the event is set up for success. From appropriate planning timelines all the way to realistic budgeting, the event manager is required to be able to gather all of the information needed while also managing the people associated with the event.

SUMMARY

The management of sports events is an exciting and evolving aspect of the sport business industry. From local charity events to the Olympic Games, the principles of solid event management are the same. Common aspects of event process for most events include establishing a purpose, bidding on the event, facilities and equipment issues, generating planning documents, marketing, sponsorship, budgeting, risk management, technology integration, and event evaluation. Relating to the people involved in event management, establishing the event leadership, providing an organizational structure for the event, staffing and acquiring volunteers, and effectively using committees all fall under the event manager's purview.

Differences between types of events in purpose, scope, and complexity drive the event manager's approach to each aspect of the event management process. Event managers are charged with bringing the pieces of the event process together with the people needed to run the event. For students with a desire to manage projects, do something different every day, be involved in many pieces of the sport industry, and have fun while doing it, event management might be a great segment of the sport industry to explore.

Discussion Questions

1. Describe what you think a day in the life of an event manager is like on an event day and a non-event day, respectively. What do you think event managers spend their time doing?

2. Your university is seeking to bid on a large collegiate cross-country meet. What would you include in the bid so that your institution would be awarded the event?

3. You are planning a large youth soccer tournament utilizing multiple venues. Unfortunately, the day of the event is preceded by four days of nonstop rain, making some of the grass fields unplayable. You still have two artificial turf fields available, but six of the teams you have scheduled on grass cannot play due to field conditions. Discuss solutions for this problem and contingency planning that might ameliorate the problems you are now facing.

4. Develop a planning timeline for a 5K race on your college campus. Identify the specific tasks that must be planned for and then determine the day by which each task must be completed.

Event Case Study 10.1

Vancouver Winter Olympic Games Marred by Death of Luge Athlete

Before the 2010 Winter Olympic opening ceremonies in Vancouver, Canada, the unthinkable occurred: Nodar Kumaritashvili, a 21-year-old Georgian luge athlete, died tragically during a training run at the Whistler Sliding Center. This was the first luge fatality in 35 years (Longman, 2010). How exactly did this accident occur and was anyone at fault for this fatality?

While on a training run, Kumaritashvili lost control toward the end while traveling nearly 90 miles per hour and slammed into vertical steel supports that held lights over the course. The accident immediately raised questions about the track's safety. Although luge is not new to the Olympic Games, technology and track design have rapidly pushed luge speeds higher (Branch & Abrams, 2010).

So how did Olympic organizers and the sport's international governing body handle this tragedy? Approximately 10 hours after this tragedy, the International Luge Federation issued a statement saying that the accident was caused by Kumaritashvili's errors —not by "deficiencies in the track" (Branch & Abrams, 2010). However, while insisting that the track was safe, Olympic and luge officials announced that the men's competition would start lower on the track at the original women's start, shortening the track by 577 feet to drop the luge sliders' speed by 6 miles per hour. Also, the wall at the crash site (Curve 16) was raised and padding was placed around the metal posts where Kumaritashvili met his death (Stone, 2010).

Many had raised concerns about the Whistler track for months leading up to the games—particularly after several countries, including the US, were upset over access restrictions for everyone but Canada, with some noting it could lead to a safety issue (Wilson, 2010). Some sliders, especially those from small luge federations, saw the world's fastest track only days before the opening ceremonies for the first time (Reynolds & Withers, 2010).

Case Questions:
- Do you believe this tragedy could have been prevented?
- Was the course really safe?
- Did the Olympic officials and International Luge Federation handle this incident properly?

Event Case Study 10.2

The Night the Super Bowl Lights Went Out

It was an event manager's nightmare: a partial power outage during a live sporting event. This actually happened during Super Bowl XLVII hosted in New Orleans at the Mercedes Benz Superdome on February 3, 2013. On the surface it seems like a simple fix—just flip the switch and turn the lights back on. But there is a lot more to it. The game was attended by 71,024 fans, watched on television by an estimated 108.4 million people, and the subject of 47.7 million social media posts during the game (Belson, 2013; ESPN, 2013). With that type of media focus on the game, any event management problem is magnified in the eyes of all involved.

This case can be analyzed in multiple areas, but for the purposes of event management, we will briefly consider three: safety and security, venue operations, and communications and public relations. All three areas have an impact on the overall event experience for fans in the stadium and viewers at home.

Safety and security is always at the forefront of event planning and management. Long before the power failure occurred, the facility and event managers, along with local and federal emergency response and law enforcement, prepared, trained, and practiced responses to a variety of possible emergency situations. Although each and every eventuality cannot be accounted for, the group certainly had a plan in place for a power outage. Thus, immediately after half of the Mercedes Benz Superdome lights went out, "the FBI quickly ruled out terrorism and the New Orleans Fire Department dismissed reports that a fire might have been the cause" (Associated Press, 2013, para. 10). The reaction was probably automatic for the response team, with the first priority being the safety and security of everyone in the venue.

Once it was established that there was not a major safety issue and that the backup generators were operating as intended, the focus turned to systematic restoration of power and resumption of normal operations (Belson, 2013). Major sporting venue lights are not the same as household light switches. It is not uncommon for stadium lights to take 15 or 20 minutes to warm up before they are operational. In addition to lighting, power was needed to operate the sideline coaching communication headsets, support the television broadcast, operate concession stands, and run the air conditioning in the building.

Communication to internal constituents such as CBS as the broadcaster, spectators in the venue, and spectators at home is also a priority to suppress possible panic and dismiss any rumors that may start related to the cause. Given the current prevalence of social media, it is even more critical to communicate effectively to manage the message. Announcements were made over the public address system to inform fans of the problem, although some reported that the announcements were muffled and hard to understand (Belson, 2013). Because the sideline and press box power was affected, CBS "lost numerous cameras and some audio powered by sources in the Superdome" (Belson, 2013, para. 8) and quickly switched to backup power. Even with good communication, social media took on a life of its own. Twitter became the go-to place for spreading both accurate and inaccurate information on the situation at the Super Bowl. Parody Twitter accounts were set up within minutes of the power failure, such as #SuperBowlLights, which boasted 18,500 followers within an hour (the account has since been removed).

Although the 34-minute blackout is the most recent example of a Super Bowl event problem, there is a history of problems during the game. Issues have included halftime performers flipping a middle finger at the TV camera, 400 ticketed fans being displaced due to "unusable" seats, and the infamous Janet Jackson wardrobe malfunction (Abrotsky, 2013). Through it all, it is often the event manager who has a plan in place to respond if and when something goes wrong, is immediately responsive to the problem, and quickly returns the event back to normal.

Case Question:

- In order of importance, which areas of operations would you connect to backup generator power if you were in charge of a major sporting event?

References

Abrotsky, J. (2013, February 4). Past super bowl mishaps and accidents. *USA Today*. Retrieved from http://www.usatoday.com/story/gameon/2013/02/04/super-bowl-outage-wardrobe-malfunction-middle-finger-seats-rain-traffic-mishaps/1889587/

Anderson School of Management (2011, May 11). UCLA Anderson School of Management to honor former baseball commissioner and Olympic organizer Peter Ueberroth with John Wooden Global Leadership Award. *UCLA Media Relations*. Retrieved from http://www.anderson.ucla.edu/media-relations/2011/peter-ueberroth-x36810

Associated Press. (2013, February 3). Superdome power outage delays Super Bowl XLVII. *NFL.com*. Retrieved from http://www.nfl.com/superbowl/story/0ap1000000134895/article/superdome-power-outage-delays-super-bowl-xlvii

Belson, K. (2013, February 3). Before game is decided, Superdome goes dark. *The New York Times*. Retrieved from http://www.nytimes.com/2013/02/04/sports/football/power-outage-in-superdome-delays-super-bowl.html?_r=0

Branch, J., & Abrams, J. (2010, February 10). Luge athlete's death cast pall over game. *The New York Times*, Retrieved from http://www.nytimes.com/2010/02/13/sports/olypmics/13luge.html

Degun, T. (2013, January 1). Ueberroth honoured by United States Olympic Foundation. Retrieved from http://www.insidethegames.biz/1012280-ueberroth-honoured-by-united-states-olympic-foundation

ESPN (2013, February 4). Super bowl just shy of TV record. *ESPN.com*. Retrieved from http://espn.go.com/nfl/playoffs/2012/story/_/id/8913211/2013-super-bowl-falls-short-television-ratings-record

Goldfine, B., & Schleppi, J. (1997). Events. In M. L. Walker & D.K. Stotlar (Eds.), *Sport facility management*. London, UK: Jones & Bartlett, Inc.

Horine, L. (1991). *Administration of physical educa-tion and sport programs* (2nd ed.). Dubuque, IA: Wm. C. Brown.

Kelly, J. R. (1985). *Recreation Business*. New York: Wiley.

Lawrence, H. J. (2009). Event feasibility. In H. J. Lawrence & M. Wells (Eds.), *Event management blueprint: Creating and managing successful sports events* (pp. 23–40). Dubuque, IA: Kendall Hunt.

McGlone, C., Wells, M., & Lawrence, H. J. (2012). Event staffing. In H. J. Lawrence & M. Wells (Eds.), *Event management blueprint: Creating and managing successful sports events* (pp. 37–38). Dubuque, IA: Kendall Hunt.

Pfahl, M. (2009). Technology and event planning. In H. J. Lawrence & M. Wells (Eds.), *Event management blueprint: Creating and managing successful sports events* (pp. 69–80). Dubuque, IA: Kendall Hunt.

Reynolds, T., & Withers, T. (2010, February 12). Winter Olympics Luge Crash: Nodar Kumaritashvili dies. *Huffington Post*. Retrieved from http://www.huffingtonpost.com/2010/02/12/winter-olympics-luge-cras_n_460575.html

Silvers, J. R. (2003, October 26). Event management as a profession. *Event management body of knowledge project*. Retrieved from http://www.juliasilvers.com/embok.htm#Event_Management_as_a_Profession

Solomon, J. (2002). *An insider's guide to managing sporting events*. Champaign, IL: Human Kinetics.

Stone, M. (2010, February 13). Changes made to Olympic luge track after Nodar Kumaritashvili crash. *Examiner*. Retrieved from http://www.examiner.com/article/changes-made-to-olympic-luge-track-after-nodar-kumaritashvili-crash

Wilson, S. (2010, February 12). Nodar Kumaritashvili, Olympic luger, dies after crash. *Huffington Post*. Retrieved from http://www.aolnews.com/2010/02/12/nodar-kumaritashvili-luger-in-near-fatal-crash/

11

Sport Industry and the Law

Paul J. Batista, JD

"[I]N AMERICA THE LAW IS KING. FOR AS IN ABSOLUTE GOV-
ERNMENTS THE KING IS LAW, SO IN FREE COUNTRIES THE LAW
OUGHT TO BE KING; AND THERE OUGHT TO BE NO OTHER."
—Thomas Paine, Common Sense (1776)

INTRODUCTION

Most Americans became enamored with the pleasures of sports as youngsters, but as adults we see that law permeates sports as much as it does other areas of society. We look for the day's scores, but instead we find out that today's game takes second billing to the activities of judges, mediators, arbitrators, prosecutors, defense attorneys, investigators, and police officers. In their 1986 publication, *Sports Law*, Smith, Schubert, and Trentadue noted that "attorneys and judges are more than idle spectators at sporting events" (as cited in Appenzeller, 1998).

We read and hear of athletes involved in criminal activities, illegal drug use, and domestic violence. There are free agents to sign and contracts to negotiate, collective bargaining agreements to finalize in order to avoid strikes by players, or lockouts by management. Athletes and coaches file suit, claiming they are victims of discrimination

Learning Objectives
Upon completing this chapter, students should be able to: • Define "the law" • Identify three primary ways to resolve disputes • Describe the philosophical basis for American law • List the three general classifications of law • Explain the four main sources of law in the United States • Identify the eight content areas of sport law

based on race, gender, religion, age, or disability. Most occurrences of legal intervention in sport receive attention from the media:

In the Bleachers © 2014 Steve Moore. Dist. by Universal Uclick
www.gocomics.com/inthebleachers

"It's a ruling on the field, your honor. It rose through the appellate process and now players, coaches and millions of viewers are awaiting your decision."

- The NFL is having to deal with domestic abuse charges, concussion and long-term disability lawsuits, and negotiating with the players' union to make changes to the drug policy in the Collective Bargaining Agreement;
- The NCAA is under fire in numerous lawsuits relating to concussions, athletes' rights of publicity fees, pay-for-play, and full cost of tuition. There is also a movement to undermine the NCAA ideal of "amateur athletes," with Northwestern University football players considering invoking workers' rights under federal labor law by attempting to organize themselves into a union in order to collectively bargain for terms and conditions of their "employment;"
- The ongoing legal issues at Penn State University relating to the Jerry Sandusky sexual assault incident has cost the University over 100 million dollars, and resulted in allegations of cover-ups by University administrators resulting in the firing of the former president and athletic director, who are also facing criminal charges arising from the scandal;
- Lawsuits filed by both the University of Maryland and the Atlantic Coast Conference seeking to enforce (ACC) or avoid (UM) a breach of contract based upon Maryland's exit from the ACC to move to the Big Ten Conference. An interesting issue is which court will hear the case since the ACC filed suit in North Carolina where the ACC is headquartered, and UM filed suit in state court in Maryland;
- The Texas Supreme Court has agreed to hear a case filed by high school cheerleaders in Kountze, Texas, asking the Court to decide that holding signs with Bible scripture for the players to run through prior to games does not violate the First Amendment religion clauses;
- Hazing continues to be a problem in both interscholastic and intercollegiate settings, with courts considering both criminal and civil cases resulting from these hazing incidents; and
- The use of social media sites like Facebook and Twitter by both professional athletes as well as college student-athletes has raised concerns about Free Speech issues.

Clearly, despite accepted conduct such as the "chin music" delivered when a hitter digs in, or the unwritten rules enforced by the "goon" in hockey, law has permeated sport in the same manner that it has affected society as a whole. It is not surprising, then, that the sport management curriculum includes a study of the legal aspects of sport. You will note that the subject is called both "sport law" and "sports law" depending on the preference of the individual author. In this chapter, it will be referred to as "sport law," except when used in direct quotations.

This chapter is designed to introduce you to general principles of law involved in sport management, including:

- A basic understanding of "the law" and how it works,
- The sources of law in the United States,
- The different methods of resolving disputes, and
- The body of law that applies to sport in America.

WHAT IS "THE LAW"?

While virtually every student will have an idea of what "the law" is, the student's perception most likely developed through the media via reading newspapers and magazines or watching television or movies. The study of any subject, and particularly law, should begin with a discussion of the basics, so let's start with a description of "the law."

Although there are hundreds of definitions of **law**, a reasonable description would be a body of enforceable rules, established by the lawmaking authorities of a society, governing the relationships among individuals, and between individuals and their government. The New Jersey Legislature has defined law as "all the official rules and codes that govern citizens' actions, including the Constitution, statutory laws enacted by the Legislature, case laws established by court decisions, and administrative law as set forth by executive branch agencies" (New Jersey Office of Legislative Services, 2008).In the simplest terms, the fundamental purpose of laws is to resolve (or avoid) conflicts. In ancient days, and indeed in parts of the world today, law was defined by the phrase "might makes right," where the strongest person/group made the laws and enforced them. As we have become more civilized, society has generally agreed that mortal combat is not the appropriate manner of resolving disputes. Therefore, laws have been established to resolve conflicts without physical battle.

Photo courtesy © iStockphoto.com

There are three primary methods of resolving conflicts. The first (and most widely used) is negotiation. While most people do not stop to think about how they resolve disputes, it is true that most disputes are resolved through negotiation. **Negotiation** is a process involving formal or informal discussions in order to reach an agreement. The Collective Bargaining Agreements of the various professional sport leagues are examples in which negotiation was used to reach a contractual agreement. The second way to resolve disputes is through **alternative dispute resolution** (ADR). ADR may be defined as resolving a dispute through any means other than litigation or negotiation. The primary forms of ADR are mediation and arbitration. **Mediation** is the submission of a dispute to a disinterested third person who intervenes between the parties in an attempt to settle their dispute without going to court. In mediation, the third party (**mediator**) communicates with all parties to the dispute, presents proposals from each party to the other, and facilitates resolution of the dispute, if possible. The mediator makes no ruling and has no authority to enforce his/her judgment on any party. **Arbitration** is the submission of a dispute to a neutral third party (**arbitrator**) who listens to all parties, considers the legal position of each, then renders a decision to resolve the dispute. The arbitrator acts much like a judge. The arbitrator's decision may not be binding on the parties, or may be binding if there is a prior agreement of the parties, or required by applicable law. Disputes in Major League Baseball are resolved by specially appointed arbitrators under the terms of the MLB Collective Bargaining Agreement. The final manner of resolving disputes is **litigation**, which is the process of filing a lawsuit so that a court can resolve the disagreement. In the US, all citizens have access to the court system and have the right to petition courts to settle disputes.

THE STUDY OF LAW

As you progress through your career in sport management, you will undertake a more detailed study of the legal aspects of sport. Undoubtedly, you will be required to read court cases, and thereby be exposed to this "**case study method**" of learning. The case study method presents students with the opportunity to read previously decided cases in order to learn how courts make legal decisions by applying relevant law to the facts of the case. In this manner, law students learn not only "the law," but also gain an understanding of the reasoning courts use in deciding disputes. The purpose of case study is to equip you with the knowledge you need to (hopefully) avoid situations that put your participants, your employer, or you at risk. Further, it will give you the vicarious experience of being involved in the dispute. Finally, it should alert you to the situations that need the intervention of your attorney.

CLASSIFICATIONS OF LAW

Although law affects every person sitting in college classrooms, most students have a limited exposure to, and understanding of, how the legal system works. In an effort to simplify and distinguish the differences among various types of law, it is helpful to divide law into three general classifications and distinguish the characteristics within each of the three classifications.

Substantive v. Procedural

All court cases involve both substantive and procedural law. **Substantive law** is the law that defines, describes, or creates legal rights and obligations—it is *WHAT* the law is. In contrast, **procedural law** is the method of enforcing rights and obligations given to citizens by substantive law—it is the step-by-step mechanics concerning *HOW* the rights are enforced. Parties must carefully follow relevant procedural rules in order for the courts to have the authority to determine whether a plaintiff's substantive rights have been violated.

Public v. Private

Generally, **public law** governs the relationship between citizens and their government while **private law** governs the relationship among private citizens. In many cases, these categories are not always easily distinguishable. Generally, public law includes areas such as criminal, tax, environmental, constitutional, and administrative law, as well as protection of rights of the general public. Private law includes most other areas of law including contracts, property, personal injury, products liability, insurance, etc.

Example

The First Amendment to the U.S. Constitution states, "Congress shall make no law respecting an establishment of religion, or prohibiting the free exercise thereof." In *Santa Fe ISD v. Doe* (2001), the U.S. Supreme Court held that Santa Fe ISD's policy authorizing prayers before high school football games violated this clause, but also affirmed an individual student's right to engage in religious activities at public schools. Both the Constitutional provision and the Court's interpretation as it relates to the facts in *Santa Fe* are substantive law because they declare what the law is.

However, before the Supreme Court could hear and rule on the case, the plaintiffs were required to comply with the procedural prerequisites, such as filing the case in the proper court, giving notice of the suit to the school, completing **discovery**, engaging in alternative dispute resolution, trying the case before a judge and jury, properly appealing it to the appellate court, then ultimately asking the Supreme Court to resolve the dispute. In order to enforce rights given by substantive law, parties must comply with the rules of procedural law in the respective courts.

Example

There is a federal statute governing workplace safety that is enforced by the Occupational Safety and Health Administration (OSHA), a regulatory agency established by the U.S. Congress. The workers in professional sport stadiums are provided certain protections by this law and have the right to file claims with OSHA for violations. Enforcement of this statute would be considered in the "public" domain. On the other hand, although the professional athletes are also workers, they are represented by unions who collectively bargain terms and conditions of players' work with the owners, and ultimately enter into a contract called a **Collective Bargaining Agreement** (CBA). In the event that either party violates this agreement, the parties have the "private" right to enforce its provisions without government intervention.

Criminal v. Civil

Criminal law deals with unlawful acts committed against the public as a whole, in which a defendant is accused of violating a statute defining a criminal act, thereby committing a **crime**. Congress and the individual state legislatures create these criminal statutes, which authorize the government to punish the violator by either a fine or incarceration. It is the government seeking to impose the penalty that defines the violation as a criminal act. **Civil law** includes everything that is not criminal law. It should be noted, however, that a single fact situation could include both criminal and civil cases, e.g., the Michael Vick case where the government sought to send him to prison for dog fighting, while the Falcons sued for return of his roster bonuses. Although these categories appear to make a clear distinction among the classifications, it is important to note that the divisions are not always as simple as they may appear. It is also important to note that most cases feature one of the characteristics from each category.

SOURCES OF LAW IN THE UNITED STATES

All law in the US comes from one of four sources: (1) Constitutions, (2) statutes, (3) administrative rules and regulations, and (4) court cases. If you will review the definition of law by the New Jersey legislature cited above, you will see that it includes all these sources in the definition. These primary sources of substantive law are listed in hierarchical order starting with Constitutions, which carry the most weight.

Constitutions

The "**Supreme Law of the Land**" is the United States **Constitution**. It takes precedence over any other law in the US. Each state also has a constitution, but it is subordinate to the U.S. Constitution. If the terms of a state constitution violate a provision in the U.S. Constitution, the state provision will be declared unconstitutional. Constitutional questions raised in sport settings include issues relating to religion, criminal search and seizures, due process, equal protection, drug testing, persons with disabilities, etc.

Statutes

Statutes are particular laws passed by the U.S. **Congress** or a state **legislature**. These legislative bodies have the power to declare, command, or prohibit some conduct, or require citizens to act in a certain manner. Violation of these statues normally creates various kinds of penalties for acting in a manner contrary to the law, such as going to jail for driving while under the influence of drugs or alcohol. Legislatures can essentially institute whatever statutes they desire, so long as they do not violate provisions of an applicable constitution. Examples of statutory enactments include Title IX, the Americans with Disabilities Act, the Sherman and Clayton Antitrust Acts, the Bankruptcy Act, and state Athlete Agent Acts.

Administrative Rules and Regulations

When Congress or state legislatures pass statutes regulating some industry or activity, frequently they will also establish administrative agencies to oversee enforcement of the legislation. These agencies are granted authority to establish directives in order to carry out the legislative body's intent in passing the statute. These directives are known as **Administrative Rules and Regulations**. They generally carry the force of law as if Congress or the state legislature passed them, and violators of the rules and regulations are subject to the penalties provided in them. Examples of Administrative Agencies that establish such Rules and Regulations include the Internal Revenue Service (IRS) that regulates income taxes, the Federal Communications Commission (FCC) that regulates television and radio, the Occupational Safety and Health Administration (OSHA) that regulates workplace safety, and the Office for Civil Rights (OCR) that administers Title IX.

Case Law

The final source of law in the United States is law established within the court system. The US adopted the **common law** system from England, which allows courts to create rules of law. Under this system, appellate courts announce a rule of law that applies to the facts of a particular case. The rules established in this manner are called **case law**. Once case law is established, other courts will usually adhere to the opinion of the original court and follow its holding, citing the original case as a **precedent**. This is an important concept because it allows for consistent outcomes among cases that share similar facts. Courts are not required to follow the precedent unless it is announced by a higher court within that court's system. For example, a California intermediate appellate state court must follow a precedent established by the California Supreme Court, but is not required to follow a precedent of the Florida Supreme Court. Further, appellate courts on the same level may have different opinions on the same issue, with the issue remaining unresolved until a higher court establishes the precedent for all inferior courts. Courts may also change their precedent and issue a new opinion changing the previous rule, although this is not a routine occurrence. An example of this is the 1954 U.S. Supreme Court decision in *Brown v. Board of Education*, which desegregated public schools. The existing educational system was based on a Supreme Court decision in an 1896 case that established the principle that a "separate but equal" system segregating races was constitutional. In *Brown*, the Court changed its precedent and held that such systems violated the Equal Protection clause of the 14th Amendment. Each of these areas supplies various laws affecting sport. Let's look at some specific examples of the legal aspects of sport.

PRACTICE AREAS IN SPORT LAW

Sport law is just one of the many subjects encompassed by sport management programs taught across the country. While there are a virtually endless number of legal aspects related to sport law, the following discussion will be limited to the eight legal aspects of sport provided by the Commission on Sport Management Accreditation (COSMA).

Legal System

Although the legal system encompasses law from all four sources discussed earlier in this chapter, this portion will be limited to the court system and litigation. You will remember that one of the ways to resolve disputes is through litigation, or filing a lawsuit. Court systems have been established to handle these lawsuits. There are two court systems in the United States: one federal system and one system comprised of 50 independent state systems. The U.S. Constitution established the federal system, and the state systems are created by the respective state constitutions or statutes.

State Court Systems

State court systems generally hear matters that occur within the boundaries of the state, and resolve disputes that involve state (as opposed to federal) law. Examples of cases normally heard in state courts are cases involving personal injury and other negligence claims, contracts, family disputes, defamation (libel and slander), products liability, workers' compensation, and state criminal matters.

Most state court systems have three levels. The first level where the case is initially filed is the **trial court**. This is the court where the parties actually "try" the case, presenting evidence to a jury and legal arguments to a judge. This is the type of court that is shown in most movies and television shows. The jury will render a **verdict**, and then the judge will enter a ruling, or **judgment**, in favor of one party or the other.

If one of the parties thinks the judge made a mistake in the way he/she tried the case (such as applying the wrong law), that party can **appeal** to the next court level, the **intermediate appeals court**. Most of these courts are called "**Courts of Appeal**," although they have different names in various states. Litigants are not required to seek permission of these courts to process the appeal to the intermediate appellate level. The function of these courts is to determine if the judge followed the law (both substantive and procedural) when trying the case.

Appellate courts normally enter one of three results in a case:

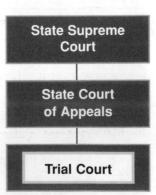

Figure 11.1. Typical State Court System

- **Affirmed**—The trial court made no significant mistakes, and the ruling stands.
- **Reverse and remand**—The trial court made a significant mistake and the case should be tried again, but correctly this time. For instance, if the court allowed testimony that should not have been heard, the appellate court will order the case tried again, this time without the improper testimony.
- **Reverse and render**—The trial court made a significant mistake, but there is no need for another trial

because when the correct law is applied, the winning party in the trial court cannot prevail. If a court entered a judgment holding a state university liable for negligence, even though that state's sovereign immunity law protects the state from liability in negligence cases, the appellate court will reverse and "render" the judgment that should have been entered (that the plaintiff cannot recover from the university).

After the Court of Appeals has rendered its judgment, any of the parties (but usually the losing party) may take an appeal to the **highest appellate court** in the state, usually called the **Supreme Court**. In order to have a case heard, the litigant must file an application with the court asking that the case be heard. In most states, the Supreme Court can hear or refuse to hear any case it chooses, at its sole discretion. If the court refuses the application, the case is finished, with the result in the intermediate court being the final ruling in the case. If the Supreme Court accepts and decides the case, it will enter one of the same rulings as the intermediate appellate court.

Federal Court System

The federal system is established in Article III, Section 1, of the U.S. Constitution, which states: "The judicial power of the United States shall be vested in one Supreme Court and in such inferior Courts as the Congress may from time to time ordain and establish." Congress has used this constitutionally-granted authority to create a court system similar to what is found in the states (Administrative Office of the U.S. Courts, 2013).

In order to file a case in a federal court, the litigant must establish that a law specifically allows such a case to be filed in federal court. The four categories primarily used to establish that cases should be heard in federal court are (1) when a litigant is seeking to enforce rights created under the U.S. Constitution or a federal statute (this is called a **federal question**), (2) when the dispute is between two states, (3) when the United States is a party to the lawsuit, and (4) when there is **diversity of citizen-**

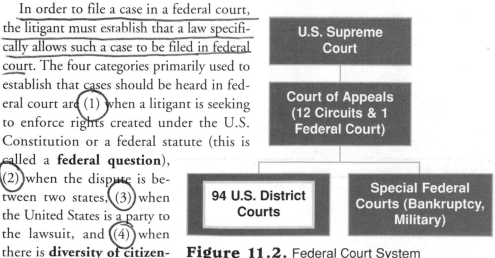

Figure 11.2. Federal Court System

ship, meaning that the parties are citizens of different states and the amount in controversy is more than $75,000.

The **federal trial courts** are called **U.S. District Courts**, followed by a geographical description of the location of the court (e.g., United States District Court for the Western District of Pennsylvania). There are 94 throughout the country, with at least one located in every state. These courts operate essentially the same as state trial courts, providing a trial of the case before a judge and jury. When a judgment has been entered, either party has the right to pursue an appeal to the federal intermediate courts, called **Courts of Appeals**.

The Courts of Appeals are divided into 11 regional groups, called **circuits**, as well as a circuit for the District of Columbia and a specialized federal Court of Appeals. These courts are normally referred to by their circuit number, so that cases from Louisiana, Mississippi, and Texas are heard in the "**5th Circuit**," while cases from Alabama, Florida and Georgia are decided in the "**11th Circuit**," etc.

In the event that a litigant wants to appeal a decision of a Circuit Court, the appeal would be taken to the **United States Supreme Court** by filing an **Application for a Writ of Certiorari**. If the Court grants the application, the Supreme Court will issue a **Writ of Certiorari**, ordering the lower court to forward the case to the Supreme Court for its consideration. It takes a vote of four justices to issue the Writ and hear a case.

The Supreme Court is not required to hear any case, and may refuse to hear a case for any reason. A refusal to hear the case is not considered a decision by the Supreme Court. Therefore, the ruling of the Circuit Court becomes final. Further, a refusal by the Supreme Court to hear a case is not considered a comment on the Circuit Court's opinion.

In the most recent Supreme Court reporting period, the 2012–2013 Term of Court, 7,509 applications were filed, 77 cases were argued before the Court, and the Court issued 73 written opinions (2013 Year End Report, 2013). If a litigant is dissatisfied with the result in the Supreme Court, there is no other avenue of appeal in the court system.

Contract Law

Of all the elements of sport law, the most publicized subject deals with issues related to player contracts. Think of the regularity that sportscasters talk about free agency, trades, contract extensions, bonuses, suspensions, options, and other contractual matters. When you discuss sport law with your friends, most will immediately think of these contractual issues. With the amount of money involved in professional and amateur sports, contracts are common in every facet of sport. Simply stated, a **contract** is an agreement, or exchange of promises, that creates legally enforceable duties and obligations for all parties to the contract. Except under certain circumstances, contracts are not required to be in writing to be enforceable. However, it is wise to remember the words of movie producer Samuel Goldwyn: "A verbal contract isn't worth the paper it's written on." Reducing a contract to writing not only establishes proof of an agreement, it also provides reliable evidence of the terms of the contract. Four elements are required to form a valid contract: (1) legal capacity, (2) agreement, (3) consideration, and (4) legality.

1. ***Legal Capacity.*** Each party to a contract must be legally competent to enter into the contract. The courts are concerned with the relative strength of bargaining power, and if there is a great discrepancy among the parties, the courts will protect the party with much lower mental capacity. In this manner, contracts with **minors** (persons under age 18) and people with significant mental disabilities are normally not enforceable against them, and courts will allow those parties to avoid the terms of the contract.

2. ***Agreement.*** An agreement is reached through a process called **offer** and **acceptance**, which involves the parties making a series of proposals to the other until the negotiations culminate with an agreement. The normal pattern for negotiating player contracts is a classic example of the offer and acceptance scenario. The team will make a contract proposal to a player, who then presents a **counteroffer** to the team, and this process continues until the parties reach agreement on the terms of the contract. The final component of agreement is that all of the essential terms of the contract must be agreed upon, so that the parties have a "meeting of the minds" on all aspects of the contract.

3. ***Consideration.*** Once the parties have agreed to the terms of the contract, there must be an exchange of something of value for the contract to be valid. Each party must get and give consideration, but it does not have to be equal. In most instances, **consideration** is the payment of money by one party to the other, who in turn provides something of value. However, promises to perform an act or service, or even refrain from performing acts or services, will be sufficient to establish consideration. When a baseball player signs a contract with a team, the team promises to pay the player for playing, and the player promises to play, follow team and league rules, refrain from dangerous activities, etc.

4. ***Legality.*** Courts will not enforce contracts that require performance of an illegal act. If the contract is the subject of an illegal act, the contract is void.

Constitutional Law

Many provisions contained in the U.S. Constitution (and to a lesser degree, state constitutions) have become the focus of litigation in sports. Among the constitutional issues that have been raised are

- Establishment or expression of religion in public schools (locker room or pre-game prayer),
- Free speech (wearing items of clothing as a political protest),
- Search and seizure (drug testing),
- Due process (right to notice and a hearing prior to suspension or job termination),
- Equal protection (discrimination based on race, ethnicity, gender, religion, age, etc.),
- Freedom of association (discrimination by private clubs or societies), etc.

This list could continue indefinitely, but the examples listed above are representative of the issues sport managers and participants have dealt with in the past. The first topic to consider in constitutional issues is to determine if the plaintiff has been deprived of his/her rights by **state action**. The U.S. Supreme Court has said state action means "the State (federal or state government) is *responsible* for the specific conduct of which the plaintiff complains" (*Brentwood Academy v. Tennessee Secondary School Athletic Association*, 2001), meaning that the state has caused the harm suffered by the plaintiff. Virtually all of the rights established in the U.S. Constitution are designed to protect citizens from actions by the government. Under most circumstances, if the state is not involved, then there is no violation of the Constitution. Clearly, statutes passed by Congress or state legislatures, ordinances passed by city governments, or policies of public schools are state action, and subject to the provisions of the Constitution. In *Santa Fe ISD v. Doe* (2001) the public school district established a policy that enabled a student chosen by the student body to say a prayer over the public address system before a high school football game. The Supreme Court held that the school was a state actor, and that the school's policy violated the **Establishment Clause** of the First Amendment.

Administrative and Statutory Law

As discussed in the sources of law section, Congress and state legislatures create law by passing "statutes." Frequently, these laws establish agencies to enforce the laws that have been passed. Many agencies are more commonly known by their acronyms. The following are some of the agencies that sport managers are most likely to encounter during their careers, and the matters they regulate:

- Equal Employment Opportunity Commission (**EEOC**)—workplace discrimination issues,
- Occupational Safety and Health Administration (**OSHA**)—workplace safety,
- Office for Civil Rights (**OCR**)—Title IX,
- National Labor Relations Board (**NLRB**)—labor laws,
- Internal Revenue Service (**IRS**)—tax, and
- Social Security Administration (**SSA**)—retirement.

This is a representative list of federal agencies, but there are hundreds more. Additionally, sport managers should be familiar with state agencies in the state in which they are employed. As previously stated, statutory laws are generated from both Congress and state legislatures. As a sport management student, you will complete a more thorough examination of many of the applicable statutes later in your studies. However, a cursory exposure to some of these statutes is appropriate in an introductory course. (Note: The descriptions are for general informational purposes only, and are not an exhaustive coverage of the particular statute. Detailed study will come in later courses.) Federal statutes dealing with sport include (in no particular order):

1. ***Title IX of the Education Amendments of 1972, ("Title IX").*** (20 USC § 1681 et. seq.) Probably the most discussed statute relating to sport is Title IX. When it was passed in 1972, it was a one-sentence law that stated: "No person in the United States shall, on the basis of sex, be excluded from participation in, be denied the benefits of, or be subjected to discrimination under any education pro-

gram or activity receiving Federal financial assistance." The intent of Congress was to prohibit **gender discrimination** in educational activities. There was no mention of sport or recreation in Title IX. However, this is a good example of Congress authorizing an administrative agency to enforce the laws it has passed. The **Office for Civil Rights** (OCR) division of the **Department of Education** has been charged with enforcing Title IX. OCR has passed administrative regulations governing the implementation of Title IX, and has determined that both interscholastic and intercollegiate athletics is an educational activity subject to Title IX.

2. *Title VII of the Civil Rights Act of 1964, ("Title VII").* (42 USC § 2000e, et. seq.) The Civil Rights Act of 1964 is a comprehensive set of laws that address discrimination issues in a wide range of circumstances. Title VII of the Act protects employees (and prospective employees) from **discrimination** by making it unlawful for an employer to discriminate against a person in employment activities (hiring, firing, compensation, promotion, classification, etc.), based on "race, color, religion, sex or national origin." Courts are given wide-ranging powers to address and remedy violations of this Act.

3. *Americans with Disabilities Act of 1990, ("ADA").* (42 USC § 12101, et. seq.) The purpose of the ADA is "to provide a clear and comprehensive national mandate for the elimination of discrimination against individuals with **disabilities**." The ADA not only encompasses issues of accessibility to facilities, but also prohibits discrimination against disabled persons in employment, subject to some specific exceptions. The overriding feature of this law requires "**reasonable accommodation**" of disabled persons.

4. *Sherman Antitrust Act.* (15 USC § 1, et. seq.) As American business developed during the Industrial Revolution, the advances in manufacturing, transportation, and communication created a model of business operation that effectively created monopolies. This was accomplished by consolidating all existing companies in an industry into a single business entity called a **monopoly**, and allowing all former companies to have an ownership interest in the new, single entity. The effect of removing all competition was deemed detrimental to American citizens. In response, Congress passed the Sherman Antitrust Act, which declared any contract, combination or conspiracy "in **restraint of trade** or commerce" to be illegal. Although the U.S. Supreme Court, in the 1922 case of *Federal Baseball Club v. National League*, has held that major league baseball was not involved in commerce and was not an interstate business enterprise, and, therefore, was not subject to this Act, all other major sports are subject to antitrust laws. In your later studies, you will find out that this Act (coupled with later legislation called the **Clayton Antitrust Act**) ultimately caused a change in the relationships between management and players, resulting in familiar scenarios such as unions, free agency, strikes, lockouts, and collective bargaining agreements.

5. *Sports Agent Responsibility and Trust Act, ("SPARTA").* (15 USC § 7801). Since its enactment in 2004, this is the only federal statute that imposes certain

duties on sports agents in order to ensure that they do not jeopardize the NCAA eligibility of student-athletes or their schools. Violations of these statutory duties can result in liability for the agent.

Individual states have passed legislation that affects sport managers. It is impractical to list all, or even a small percentage, of state statutes. However, a few subjects are appropriate to mention.

1. ***Athlete Agent statutes.*** Since 1981 when California adopted the first statute attempting to regulate athlete agents, at least 41 states have adopted laws seeking to protect prospective professional athletes (National Collegiate Athletic Association, 2008). Due to the differences in the various state statutes, there was no consistency among the acts in those states that attempted to regulate athlete agents. The NCAA and other organizations sought to standardize the various state provisions, ultimately culminating in the passage of the "**Uniform Athlete Agents Act**" on November 30, 2000, by the National Conference of Commissioners on Uniform State Laws. It should be noted that this is not a federal statute, but merely a model for states to use in passing legislation.

2. ***Recreational Use statutes.*** Acknowledging the social benefits of recreational activities, state legislatures became concerned by the upsurge in lawsuits against owners of recreational facilities by injured participants. Reacting to the threat that lawsuits would cause these facilities to close, state legislatures in virtually every state have passed laws that provide liability protection to the owners and operators. The statutes protect them by placing responsibility for injury on the participant who voluntarily assumed the risk. Generally, as long as the assumed risk is inherent to the activity, the injured party cannot sue for damages.

3. ***Charitable Immunity.*** In addition to the benefits of recreational activities, legislatures have recognized the value of charitable organizations such as youth sport programs that provide services and activities to citizens. Many states (and the federal government) have passed statutes that provide liability protection for **charitable organizations** that operate sports or recreational activities. For states that do not have such statutes, the federal **Volunteer Protection Act** (42 USC § 14501, et. seq.) provides protection (for individuals, only, not organizations) unless the state has specifically chosen not to be covered by the Act. Most of these statutes provide protection to volunteers, employees, and the organization, so long as the organization has insurance in the amount required by the statute to cover losses sustained by injured participants.

Tort Law

A **tort** is a civil wrong (other than a breach of contract) for which an injured party can recover damages. The basic premise of tort law is that a person who is damaged by the unlawful acts of another is entitled to recover his/her losses (**damages**) from the person causing the harm. In other words, the person responsible for the harm bears the financial loss. There are three primary categories of torts: intentional torts, negligence, and strict liability. **Intentional torts** occur when the party acting wrongfully (called the "**tortfeasor**") intends to cause the harm by committing the act that causes the injury. For example, a group of experienced players engages in hazing activities to initiate their new teammates. A team member who sustains an injury has grounds to file a lawsuit against those who caused his/her injury. (Incidentally, not only is **hazing** an intentional tort, but most states have enacted statutes making hazing a criminal offense.) Other intentional torts include assault, battery, defamation (libel and slander), invasion of privacy, etc. **Negligence** is described as the failure to exercise ordinary care, or the degree of care that the law requires, by acting differently than a person of ordinary care would have acted under the same or similar circumstances. Negligence is an unintentional tort, where the responsible party acted without the intent to commit the act, or to cause harm or injury to the plaintiff. Most tort lawsuits are prosecuted under this theory by alleging that the defendant has acted negligently, thus causing harm or injury to the plaintiff.

To decide whether the defendant has acted with ordinary care, the court will apply the **standard** known as the "**reasonably prudent person**" standard. The court will determine if the defendant acted as a reasonably prudent person would have acted under the same or similar circumstances. If so, then there is no negligence. If not, then the defendant acted negligently (assuming the other elements of negligence are present). For example, when a player is injured by lightning when a coach fails to end soccer practice after several nearby lightning strikes, the coach has not acted as a reasonably prudent coach would have acted under those circumstances. Even though being struck by lightning is normally considered an "**Act of God**," the coach may be negligent and liable for the injuries the plaintiff sustained. In addition to negligence, you will study gross negligence, which falls somewhere between the standards of intentional torts and negligence. **Gross negligence** is acting in such a reckless manner that the court will consider that the defendant exhibited a conscious indifference toward the safety of the plaintiff, even though the defendant did not intend to injure the plaintiff. Driving while under the influence of alcohol or drugs is the classic example of gross negligence. **Strict liability** is the tort theory of liability without fault. This theory is usually associated with products liability discussed in a later section of this chapter.

You will also study various defenses to tort liability. One of the most important to understand is the concept of **sovereign immunity**. The theory of sovereign immunity has existed for thousands of years and can best be summed up by the maxim that "the king can do no wrong." Under this theory, the state cannot be held liable for any act unless it agrees to accept liability. While some states retain this protection, other states have **waived** (or given up) the right to be immune from liability. Most of these statutes are referred to as "**tort claims acts**," indicating that the state has agreed to accept liability for certain tort claims. The state laws vary widely, from states that have waived liability in all cases to those that have waived liability only under limited circumstances. Other defenses to tort liability include: Assumption of risk, waivers and agreements to participate, indemnification agreements, procedural noncompliance, sovereign immunity, charitable immunity, and recreation and Good Samaritan statutes protections.

Risk Management Procedures

Risk management includes identifying and reducing potential risks for participants, spectators, owners, operators, and organizations. Successful organizations incorporate various liability concerns into a **risk management plan**, which may include policies regarding employment and personnel practices, supervision, security, emergency care, crisis management, insurance, transportation, and legal issues involved in the operation and administration of the organization. There is a more detailed discussion of risk management in the facility and event management chapter of this book.

Crowd Control and Security

Although crowd control and security is a component of risk management, it is a separate content area under COSMA. There is a more detailed discussion of crowd control and security in the facility and event management chapter.

Products Liability

A person who is injured by a product may be allowed to recover for his/her injuries under the concept of **products liability**. The theory is that a person who places a defective product into use is liable for the harm it causes. Virtually everyone involved in the design, manufacture, distribution, or sale of the product might be held liable.

Products liability encompasses three distinct concepts: (1) negligence, (2) breach of warranty, and (3) strict liability. The first theory asserts negligence in the manufacture or design of the product, or negligence for failure to warn purchasers of the dangers associated with the product. One case held the manufacturer liable for injuries sustained by a baseball player when his sunglasses were hit by a ball and shattered, causing loss of his eye, because the lenses were designed and manufactured to be too thin (*Filer v. Rayex Corp.*, 1970). The second concept involves a **breach of warranty** by the defendant. A **warranty** is a promise or guarantee that products will comply with a certain standard. In such a case, the plaintiff alleges that the goods do not comply with the guaranteed standards. The "Golfing Gizmo" (a golf ball attached to an elasticized string) included in the instructions the statement "completely safe ball will not hit player." While hitting the ball, a 13-year-old suffered head injuries. The court held that the plaintiff should recover because the manufacturer/seller was liable for breaching its warranty that the gizmo was completely safe (*Hauter v. Zogarts*, 1975). The Supreme Court of New Mexico has described the purpose of **strict liability** "to allow an injured consumer to recover against a seller or manufacturer without the requirement of proving ordinary negligence. Its goal is to protect the injured consumer" (*Aalco Manufacturing Co. v. City of Espanola*, 1980). In this case, the plaintiff was injured by a falling volleyball net, and the court held that the manufacturer was liable even though it did not negligently cause the injury. The strict liability theory also applies to the manufacture and sale of items that are unreasonably dangerous to the user of the product.

SUMMARY

There is no area of sport management that is not impacted by "the law." Hopefully, this chapter has opened your eyes to all of the legal obstacles and hurdles that exist in the field of sport management. For every category within the discipline, there is a special set of rules and regulations that affect virtually every decision you will make. Neither this chapter, nor your further study of the legal aspects of sport, will make you a lawyer. However, if you can learn to identify legal issues before they arise, you will be able to greatly reduce the cost of operating your organization. The best money you will ever spend is the cost to avoid problems before they arise.

POSTSCRIPT—REPRESENTING PROFESSIONAL ATHLETES

"Show me the money!" has become the mantra of agents and those who dream of representing professional athletes in negotiating their contracts, coordinating their business and financial dealings, and basically acting as a clearinghouse of information for the player. An **agent** is a person who is authorized to transact business or manage some affair for another person. The perceived glamour, prestige, and financial reward of being an agent attracts many students, who envision themselves as a real-life Jerry Maguire.

In *The Agent Game*, one of the earliest books examining the agent business, author Ed Garvey highlighted the criteria to become an agent: "How does someone become an agent? The answer is simple: find a client. If you have an athlete as a client who wants to play professional football, basketball, soccer, tennis, baseball or hockey, **you are an agent**. Congratulations" (Garvey, 1984). Unfortunately, while a student may eventually become certified as an agent, successfully recruiting a client or securing employment with a player representation firm is extremely unlikely. As the Executive Director of the National Football League Players Association at the time, Garvey wrote his book in an effort to educate prospective professional athletes about the perils of dealing with agents. He outlines some of the realities of dealing with agents ("each agent has to out-promise the competition") and some of the unethical tricks-of-the-trade used to sign players, then reaches the conclusion that for agents, "recruitment, not performance, is the key" (Garvey, 1984). In the 30+ years since Garvey's book was published, all of the professional players' associations have adopted strict rules regulating the actions of agents representing players, but recruitment of clients remains the most important aspect of being an agent. It is unrealistic to expect that a recent college graduate would be able to out-recruit established agents, with their impressive client lists, previous experience, and financial investments in the recruiting process. The opportunity to secure employment with an established firm is also rare for newly graduated students. One well-known agent (who represents dozens of clients in various sports) has said that he and his partner received an average of more than 200 letters a month from students (including undergraduate, graduate, and law students) seeking a job or internship with his firm. In over 20 years, this two-man firm had hired only secretarial employees, and not a single prospective agent.

Taking into account the perils of seeking employment as an agent, the student should proceed at his/her own risk, acknowledging that the odds against you are monumental. One Internet source asserts that there are over 25,000 individuals who act as sport agents in the US, and about 4,000 of those agents are certified (Pro Sports Group, 2010). As Garvey said, "The number of agents is astounding . . . How can so many agents make a living in this business? The answer is, they can't," (Garvey, 2008).

Follow your dreams, but understand the challenges ahead. The purpose of this section is not to discourage you, but to present relevant information so that you can make educated choices. Good luck!

Suggested Reading

Clement, A., & Grady, J. (2012). *Law in Sport: Concepts and Cases*. Fitness Information Technologies; 4th Ed.

Cotten, D., & Wolohan, J. (2013). *Law for Recreation and Sport Managers*. Kendall Hunt Pub Co; 5th Ed.

Epstein, A. (2013). *Sports Law*. South-Western, Cengage Learning.

Mitten, M. Davis, T., Shropshire, K., Osborne, B., & Smith, R. (2013). *Sports Law Governance and Regulation*. Wolters Kluwer Law & Business.

Sharp, L., Moorman, A., & Claussen, C. (2007). Sport Law: *A Managerial Approach*. Holcomb Hathaway, Publishers.

Shropshire, K. & Davis, T. (2008). *The Business of Sports Agents*. University of Pennsylvania Press; 2nd Ed.

Yasser, R., McCurdy, J., Goplerud, C. & Weston, M. (2001) *Sports Law Cases and Materials*. Matthew Bender & Co; 7th Ed.

References

Aalco Manufacturing Co. v. City of Espanola, 618 P.2D 1230 (NM 1980).

Administrative Office of the U.S. Courts. (2013). *Jurisdiction of the Federal Courts*. Retrieved from http://www.uscourts.gov/FederalCourts/Understandingthe FederalCourts/Jurisdiction.aspx

Appenzeller, H. (1998). *Risk Management in Sport*. Durham, NC: Carolina Academic Press.

Brentwood Academy v. Tennessee Secondary School Athletic Assoc., 531 U.S 288, 295 (2001).

Brown v. Board of Education, 347 U.S. 483 (1954).

Commission on Sport Management Accreditation. Retrieved from http://www.cosmaweb.org/

Federal Baseball Club v. National League, 259 U.S. 200 (1922).

Filer v. Rayex Corp., 435 F.2d 336 (7th Cir. 1970).

Garvey, E., (1984). *The Agent Game: Selling Players Short*. Washington, DC: Federation of Professional Athletes.

Hauter v. Zogarts, 534 P.2d 377 (CA 1975).

National Collegiate Athletic Association. (2008). Uniform athletes agent act (UAAA) history and status. *NCAA.org*. Retrieved from http://www.ncaa.org/

New Jersey Office of Legislative Services. (2008). *Glossary of Terms*. Retrieved from http://www.njleg.state.nj.us/legislativepub/glossary.asp#L

Pro Sports Group (2014). Sport Agent Directory. Retrieved from http://prosportsgroup.com/products-and-services/sports-agent-directory/

Santa Fe ISD v. Doe, 530 U.S. 290 (2000).

United States Supreme Court Public Information Office. (2013). 2013 Year-End Report on the Federal Judiciary. Retrieved from http://www.supremecourt.gov/publicinfo/year-end/2013year-endreport.pdf

12

Sport Governance

Dennis Phillips

> "SPORT IS BEST GOVERNED AUTONOMOUSLY. LIKE UNIVERSITIES
> AND THEATRES, SPORTS ARE INTERMEDIATE SOCIAL INSTITUTIONS
> WHICH NEED PROTECTION FROM DAY-TO-DAY PARTISAN POLITICAL
> PRESSURES—BUT THEIR AUTONOMY IS ONLY VALUABLE IN SO FAR
> AS IT HELPS THEM TO PROMOTE AND PROTECT THE PUBLIC GOOD
> WHICH THEY GOVERN."
>
> —*Sunder Katwala, 2000*

INTRODUCTION

As you race to the cafeteria to grab a quick bite of breakfast before your morning class, you notice the headline in the local newspaper stating that an Olympic athlete lost his or her medal because of a positive drug test for a banned performance-enhancing substance. Between classes you hear two athletes discussing a new financial aid rule passed by the National Collegiate Athletic Association (NCAA). Walking across campus you see a bulletin board flyer announcing an organizational rules meeting for all teams interested in participating in the intramural flag football league. After classes you go to the swimming pool for a workout and see signs on the wall from the Red Cross explaining mandatory safety procedures and CPR techniques. At dinner you flip the remote to ESPN's *Sports Center* and hear about a new National Football League (NFL) disciplinary rule governing helmet-to-helmet contact and safety regarding concussions. In one

---

Learning Objectives

After studying this chapter the student will have an understanding of:
- The origin and purpose of governing bodies;
- Differences between governing bodies;
- Benefits of membership in a governing body;
- The governance legislative process in sport;
- The principles and bylaws of the NCAA; and
- Legal issues associated with governing bodies.

In the Bleachers © 2014 Steve Moore. Dist. by Universal Uclick
www.gocomics.com/inthebleachers

"I don't believe it's a concussion, but out of an abundance of caution, I've called for an attorney."

day you have seen several indications of governance and policy development at work within the sport industry.

It is difficult to imagine the world of sport without organization or rules. What would sport be like without referees, league officials, commissioners, event managers, sport medicine personnel, scoreboard operators, or timekeepers making policy, enforcing rules, or following guidelines? Even children playing wiffle ball in a back yard establish an agreed-upon set of rules and boundaries to enjoy play. The sport continuum runs from relatively unstructured recreational play, through the various levels of club and youth sport leagues, to the more highly controlled contests of interscholastic and intercollegiate competition, and finally the elite level of amateur and professional athletic achievement. As different as the participants and goals may be, they all share at least one thing in common: their actions are governed by someone or group with authority, control, and power.

IMPORTANCE OF SPORT GOVERNANCE

A practice used by some sports reporters when writing a game summary is known as the "5 W's and an H." A report of *What, Why, Who, How, When,* and *Where* will "cover all the bases" of content needed to explain the story. That same technique may be used to explore the importance of governance in sport.

What

Let's first start with the *What.* What do we mean by the term "governance"? The Merriam-Webster Dictionary (2004) definition of governance is "to control and direct the making and administration of policy" (p. 313). Other descriptors could include "direct," "influence," "determine," "regulate," and "restrain." Authors Hums and MacLean (2004) operationally defined sport governance as "the exercise of power and authority in sport organizations, including policy making, to determine organizational mission, membership, eligibility, and regulatory power, within the organization's appropriate local, national, or international scope" (p. 5).

Governance is usually recognized in terms of the power and authority vested in amateur and professional sport organizations at the municipal, state, national, and international levels. Local sport groups such as the Hattiesburg, Mississippi Youth Soccer Association (HYSA) and the Oak Grove, Mississippi Dixie Youth Baseball Association administer youth sport programs in the local community. The Pennsylvania Inter-scholastic Athletic Association, Inc. (PIAA) is an example of a state level organization that develops policy and enforces rules governing athletic competition among nearly 350,000 athletes at approximately 1,420 public and private schools.

At the national level, amateur sport agencies such as the Amateur Athletic Union (AAU), the National Federation of State High School Associations (NFHSA), USA Track and Field (USATF), and the National Intramural-Recreational Sports Association (NIRSA) regulate sport and recreational activities. Examples of professional sport organizations include Major League Baseball (MLB), the Professional Golf Association (PGA), the Women's National Basketball Association (WNBA), and the National Association for Stock Car Auto Racing (NASCAR). International governing organizations include the International Olympic Committee (IOC), the Federation Internationale de Football Association (FIFA), which governs soccer (football), and the Federation Internationale de Gymnastique (FIG), the organization for international gymnastics competitions.

Why

It is apparent, then, that governing agencies are a common and extremely important part of the sport industry, but *Why* study it? For those who wish to engage in sport as their vocational pursuit there are many reasons why knowledge of organizational governance will prove beneficial. A sport manager at the community level will need knowledge of local government structures and politics in order to effectively achieve budgetary approval for community recreational programs. An athletic administrator involved in intercollegiate athletics will need to know the legislative process of the National Collegiate Athletic Association (NCAA) in order to enact new rules and regulations. Detailed knowledge of the rules and regulations regarding eligibility, financial aid, and recruiting will enable the organization to act ethically in the pursuit of competitive excellence and avoid costly and embarrassing rule violations.

Awareness of governing principles of organizations will promote a smooth working relationship with your superiors and an understanding and appreciation of the functions of various committees and departments within your company. You will also appreciate the "big picture" of how various agencies within and outside of your industry segment relate and effectively interact with one another.

Who

The *Who* of sport governance focuses on the leadership positions within an organization. Sport governing agencies, like all businesses, rely heavily on top-level management leadership to strategically plan for the future, formulate and implement policy, and communicate the mission and goals of the organization. The leadership methods used by governing bodies of sport come in a variety of packages; however, there are some common practices familiar to most sport organizations. All organizations have membership requirements with specific dues, application documents, regulations, and minimal qualifications for acceptance in good standing with the group. When the large group of members gathers together for meetings, conventions, or special events—such as conference tournaments, The Final Four, College World Series, etc.—the body is frequently called a General Assembly, General Business Meeting, or Congress. Organizational business is conducted and policies developed and voted upon by the membership after a "quorum," or majority, of available attendees has been established.

The membership representatives are selected according to the by-laws and constitution guidelines of the organization, and the sessions are conducted under a set of established procedures common to most "official" business meetings called "**Robert's Rules of Order**." These procedures assure legislative fairness, maximum participation, and an orderly process by participants, while protecting individuals from domination by certain vocal sub-groups. Membership can revise the by-laws or constitution by an overwhelming ⅔ vote of the assembly.

While most General Assemblies are composed of volunteer members of the organization, there is often a need for permanent, paid staff to conduct the business of the organization in between convention and business meetings. These full-time staff members are often referred to as the Executive Staff, which is frequently led by a person with a title such as Executive Director, Chairman of the Board, President, Chief Executive Officer (CEO), or Chief Operating Officer (COO). The staff assisting the leader usually consists of functional managers in charge of such areas as membership services, eligibility, marketing and sponsorship, finance and budgeting, publications and printing, media and public relations, administration, conference and special event planning, legislative advocacy, and educational services. These individuals are paid employees, located at a centralized headquarters to perform the tasks of the daily organizational business. Generally they work through committees comprised of selected membership with specific expertise and responsibilities, who gather together periodically to conduct particular tasks.

Annual or continuous tasks are completed by permanent "*standing*" committees. Finance, budget, championship, enforcement, legislative action, and appeals committees usually fall under the "standing" category. Single use, temporary committees assigned with a specific responsibility are frequently called "*ad hoc*," or "*single-use planning*" or "*task force*" committees. Tasks that require special problem-solving for non-programmed

Photo courtesy © Andy Gillentine

events such as dealing with recruiting scandals, internet gambling abuse, penalties for distribution and use of an illegal performance-enhancing substance, or security plans for a sport venue following terrorist threats, are examples of directives assigned to a task force. Upon completion of the assigned responsibility, the committee will permanently disband.

How

Next is the question of *How*; specifically, how do sport groups get things done, and how are they structured in order to be effective and efficient? We may have leaders and staff who guide the organization and membership, and who participate and financially support it, but how is it all organized? Are there management principles that help organize a sport unit in the process of delegating, coordinating tasks, and distributing human, financial, and informational resources to achieve objectives? The answer to the preceding question, of course, is yes. These principles guide the governance of a sport body by establishing the scope of authority, clarification of an individual's responsibility, coordination in task completion, and supervision of employees. The principle of **Unity of Command** states that an employee should only have one boss to which he or she reports. The **Scalar Principle** refers to the Chain of Command that denotes a clear line of authority from top to bottom of the organization. This principle shows who your immediate boss is, as well as those whom you supervise. Another principle is the **Division of Labor**, a directive that shows the separation of departments by function or specialization such as Marketing, Finance, Accounting, Event Management, Media Relations, or Athletic Training. The **Span of Management** principle refers to the number of employees reporting to a specific manager. Factors that affect this principle include the complexity and safety of the task, the experience and competence of the employees, the experience and competence of the manager, and the size of the organization. The greater the *Span of Management*, the broader the organizational chart. Lower level managers tend to supervise a larger number of employees, with a narrower span of management the higher one ascends (Lussier & Kimball, 2009).

An organizational chart is generally used to represent a business structure. Lussier and Kimball (2009) defined an organizational chart as a "chart [that] lays out the organization's management hierarchy and departments, and their working relationships" (p. 129).

How can organizational charts help the sport management graduate entering their first job, or starting a new job in the sport industry? Organizational charts can provide great insight into the kind of organizational environment in which you are employed. For example, if the chart appears to be very steep, with many levels of management, then it is probably a "Tall" organization with a bureaucracy that involves many levels of managers or committees and decision-making centralized at the top levels of leadership. If, however, the chart appears to be shallow and broad, it is probably a "Flat" structure, characterized by few levels of management and de-centralized decision-making. Immediate and effective response to customer service is critical in today's sport industry, and "Flat" organizations are often able to respond more quickly to the needs of their sport customers.

A recent example of this occurred during a "mystery shopper" adventure conducted by a consulting firm at a National Football League game. The "mystery shopper" played the role of a fan claiming to have lost his ticket and needing help from the guest services personnel to find a seat for the game. The NFL team customer service employee had the authority to make rapid decisions without going through many management channels in order to best serve the customer. The "shopper" was pleased at the rapid resolution to his problem and gave a positive report to executives of the team (R.B. Crow, personal communication, September 2, 2004).

Sport governing bodies can be organized in a variety of ways, the most common of which are:

- By function
- By geographic location
- By product line
- By customer segment

For example, Benjamin Russell founded the Russell Corporation in 1902 in Alexander City, Alabama. From humble beginnings with only eight knitting machines and ten sewing machines, the company has grown to become the largest supplier of athletic team uniforms in the United States. Today, with annual sales of over $1 billion in team uniforms and active-wear, the company employs over 15,000 people worldwide. The Russell Corporation is best known for its apparel brands of Russell Athletic team uniforms, JERZEES casual-wear, Mossy Oak hunting and outdoor-wear, Cross Creek and Three Rivers promotional clothing, Moving Comfort high performance athletic-wear for women, and DeSoto Mills socks (Russell, 2004). There are several ways the Russell Corporation could be organized:

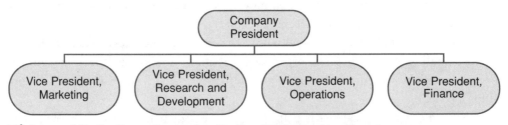

Figure 12.1. Sport Governing Bodies Organized by Function

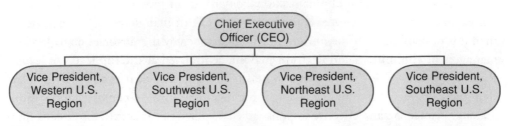

Figure 12.2. Sport Governing Bodies Organized by Geographic Location

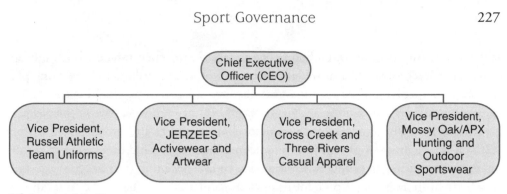

Figure 12.3. Sport Governing Bodies Organized by Product Line or Brand

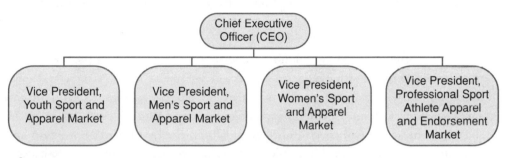

Figure 12.4. Sport Governing Bodies Organized by Customer Segment

Each method of departmentalization can become a separate entity in itself and can lead to various management styles, work force division, formal or informal authority lines, and line and staff chain of commands. *Line employees*, like those shown in the above charts, issue orders and relate directly to the objectives of the organization. *Staff employees* assist and support line employees and relate indirectly to the organization's objectives. Staff employees can have titles such as "secretary," "administrative assistant," "equipment manager," "athletic trainer," "academic adviser," or "assistant strength and conditioning coach." They are often shown under or on the side of the supervision authority of line employees. If they have an "informal" relationship to another line employee or different departmental unit, they may have a "dotted line" attached to their position within the organizational chart.

When

The question of *When* governance began in American sport can only be answered by going back to the historical foundations of organized amateur sport in US organizations like the Young Men's Christian Association (YMCA), the Amateur Athletic Union (AAU), the National Collegiate Athletic Association (NCAA), and the National Federation of State High School Associations (NFHSA), which were extremely influential in the development of amateur sport in the United States. Each association faced challenges in developing rules, regulations, and policies during the early stages of its organizational life. Eligibility, amateurism, financial support, administrative and coaching leadership, equipment conformity and safety, and legislative control were just a few of the issues these early governing bodies had to face during their infancy. It became apparent that each organization needed a statement of its core values and operating philosophy in order to provide a compass for the direction the group would take.

For many sport associations, a "*Mission Statement*," or "*Vision Statement*," helped provide that direction. A "**Mission Statement**," according to Bridges and Roquemore (2000), is "the broadest of objectives and defines the purpose and uniqueness of the organization regarding its products, services, markets and revenues" (p. 124). Every governing body of sport has a purpose for its existence and a quality that makes it unique. A brief summary of a few of the early governing bodies of sport and their origins, mission, growth, and present day influence will help us discover when sport governance began.

The National Strength and Conditioning Association

The National Strength and Conditioning Association (NSCA) is a non-profit organization dedicated to the growth of elite strength coaches, personal trainers, and educational researchers. The national headquarters is located in Colorado Springs, CO and features a 6,000-sq. ft. Performance Center for training novice and elite athletes.

Nebraska head football coach Bob Devaney hired the first full-time strength and conditioning coach in 1969; this decision produced such success that the team became a leader in the formation of the NSCA. The NSCA formally began in 1978 with 76 strength coaches from across the nation in order to further the knowledge, unity, and development of strength and conditioning. The organization has grown from those humble beginnings to a strong international community of 30,000 members in 72 countries (NSCA, 2013).

During the 1990s, the NSCA-Certified Personal Trainer credential was launched, followed by the Registered Strength and Conditional Coach (RSCC) and the Tactical Strength and Conditioning (TSAC) coach. Each year, a national convention is held, as well as several conferences for the TSAC. Alliances have been formed with the National Interscholastic Athletic Administrators Association (NIAAA), the National Collegiate Athletic Association (NCAA), and the National Federation of State High School Associations (NFHSA).

The NSCA is governed by an eight-member Board of Directors with an additional member representing the general public. In addition, an Executive Director and permanent staff members conduct and administer membership and event management duties for the association.

The NSCA mission statement is: "As the worldwide authority on strength and conditioning, we support and disseminate research-based knowledge and its practical application to improve athletic performance and fitness" (NSCA, 2013).

The Amateur Athletic Union (AAU)

The Amateur Athletic Union (AAU) is one of the oldest and largest multi-sport governing bodies in the United States. Formed in 1888, its original purpose was to bring uniformity and standards to amateur sport. The AAU quickly became the dominant sport organization in America and the driving force in representing our country in all international sport competitions including the Olympic Games. The role of the AAU changed, however, following the enactment of the Amateur Sports Act of 1988 that established an official governing body for international sport, The United States Olympic Committee (USOC). The AAU then focused on the programming of the largest grassroots venture for sport competition with over 50,000 volunteers helping administer over 30,000 age division events, and 250 national championships for over 500,000 participants. In 1996, the Disney Corporation and the AAU formed a strategic alliance to further the goals of each organization. The outgrowth of their partnership was *Disney's Wide World of Sports* complex, which is home to more than 40 national AAU events each year (AAU, 2008). The AAU mission is "to offer amateur sports programs through a volunteer base for all people to have the physical, mental, and moral development of amateur athletes and to promote good sportsmanship and good citizenship" (AAU, 2013).

National Federation of State High School Associations (NFHSA)

The National Federation of State High School Associations (NFHSA) is a prime example of an organization formed to meet the needs of a growing program of interscholastic athletic competition. Interscholastic sport developed quickly in America during the late 1800s. Football became a very popular spectator and participant sport in the 1890s, but suffered from some of the same ills as its intercollegiate counterparts. Problems such as increasing violence and injury, the overemphasis on winning, the use of ineligible players, and financial mismanagement were rampant (Rader, 1999). The need for adult supervision and a centralized organization with the authority to set minimum, consistent standards was apparent to many state association leaders. In 1902, the Fifteenth Conference on Academies and High Schools met and issued basic recommendations to initiate faculty and state association control of interscholastic sports. Upper Midwest states such as Illinois, Wisconsin, and Michigan had already organized state associations by the first decade of the 1900s, and rules governing minimum course loads, satisfactory progress, participation standards, and even basic rules controlling play were enacted to ensure fair and equitable competitions (Covell, 1998).

In 1920, the Midwest Federation of State High School Athletic Associations was formed when representatives of Illinois, Indiana, Iowa, Michigan, and Wisconsin met to discuss high school athletic competitions. Student athlete welfare issues were discussed as well as consistent rules for competitions across state boundaries. By 1923, the organization changed its name to accommodate new state associations, and the group became known as the National Federation of State High School Athletic Associations. The name remained unchanged until fine arts were added during the 1970s and the word "*Athletics*" was dropped from the organizational title (NFHSA, 2013a).

Today, the organization represents 51 state associations and 9 Canadian Associations. The NFHSA works with over 20,000 high schools, 500,000 officials and judges, 11 million students, and 500,000 coaches and sponsors. The organization promotes educational programs in areas such as sportsmanship, citizenship, gender equity, sexual harassment, concussion studies, hazing prevention, drug and alcohol prevention, academic eligibility and participation standards, and eating disorders. The NFHSA also publishes sports and rules books for over 16 interscholastic sports (NFHSA, 2013a).

The governance power of high school sports, according to Wong (1994), rests in state and local agencies. School Boards, State Education Associations, State Legislatures, and Coaching Associations yield regulatory power over the conduct of sport programs. The NFHSA is a service provider that assists state associations with programs, rather than a sanctioning body with enforcement personnel and penalty provisions. High school extracurricular programs are voluntary and therefore participation is legally and financially viewed as a *privilege* rather than a *right*.

The NFSHA organizational chart consists of several committees that determine the direction of the governing body. At the top is the membership represented by each state association. The *National Council* is the equivalent to a Senate legislative governing body, as it consists of one member from each state association meeting twice each year to enact legislation and consider by-law and constitution revisions. The *Board of Directors* is composed of one member from each one of the eight geographic sections of the country, and four additional at-large members for a total of twelve members. The Board conducts the business and financial affairs of the organization, approves committees, and oversees the annual budget. The *Executive Director* and *Executive Staff* support the daily activities of the Indianapolis headquarters including marketing, publications, information and member services, convention planning, certifications, educational training, and financial services. The organization has several member associations that strongly influence the state of interscholastic sport and activities: The Coaches, Officials, Spirit, Music, and Speech/Debate/Theatre Associations help develop rules and regulations that govern the extracurricular competitive experience for young men and women.

The National Interscholastic Athletic Administrators Association (NIAAA) is another group under the National Federation umbrella that has a tremendous impact on high school and junior high sports. One of the most important roles of the NIAAA is to provide management and leadership skill development through continuing education opportunities in their more than 30 Leadership Training Courses (LTCs). Graduate degree programs specializing in Interscholastic Athletic Administration at Ohio University, Indiana University, Purdue University at Indianapolis, and the University of Southern Mississippi utilize LTC materials to further the professional growth of present and future interscholastic athletic administrations. The rest of the organizational structure consists of the standing and special committees that administer the various programs and professional organizations of the NFHSA. The mission of the NFHSA is as follows:

> The National Federation of State High School Associations serves its members, related professional organizations and students by providing leadership for the administration of education-based interscholastic activities, which support academic achievement, good citizenship and equitable opportunities. (NFHSA, 2013b)

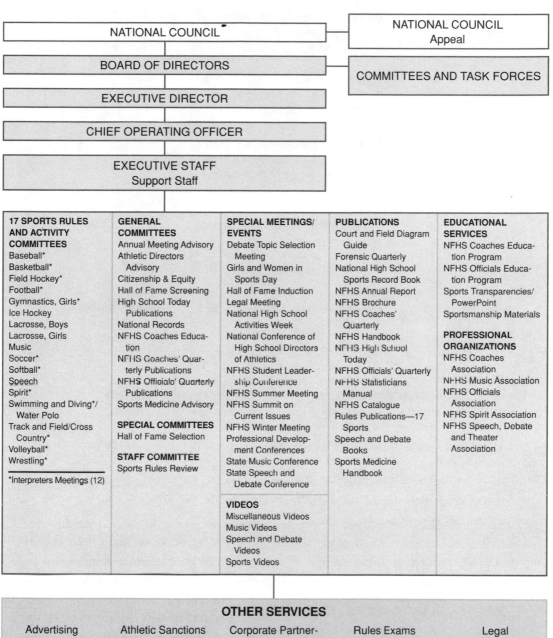

Figure 12.5. NFHS Organizational Chart

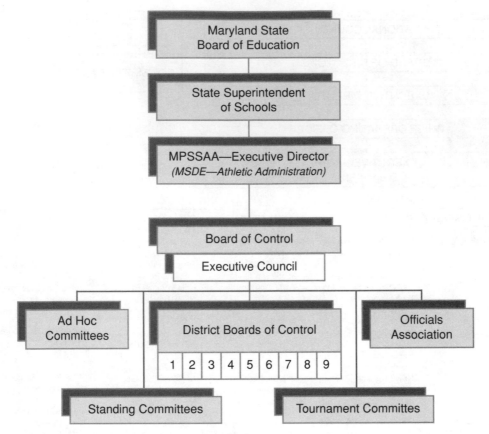

Figure 12.6. Maryland Public Secondary Schools Athletic Association Organizational Chart

State Governing Body of Interscholastic Sport

The Maryland Public Secondary Schools Athletic Association (MPSSAA) was founded in 1946 and consists of 184 public high schools. The MPSSAA is under the authority of the Maryland State Department of Education and 24 local school systems, which are divided into nine districts. The legislative powers of the association are entrusted to a

Board of Control made up of one delegate from each county, three superintendents, and representatives from each of the counties based on school enrollment in grades 9–11. The structure of this Board is similar to the House of Representatives in Congress as the number of representatives (1–5) is based on the enrollment of students in the member schools of that county. The elected officers of the association include a President and a President-Elect. Standing Committees include Nominating,

Finance, Constitution, Tournaments, Classification, Appeals, and Officials (MPSSAA, 2013). The mission of the MPSSAA is "to promote and direct public high school inter-scholastic activities in order to assure that those activities contribute toward the entire educational program of the state of Maryland" (MPSSAA, 2013).

National Collegiate Athletic Association (NCAA)

One of the most powerful sport governing agencies in the United States is the National Collegiate Athletic Association (NCAA). Prompted by the numerous injuries and deaths occurring in football during the early 1900s, President Theodore Roosevelt called 13 college presidents and athletic leaders to the White House in 1905 to discuss needed reforms in the game. The outgrowth of that and subsequent meetings was rule reform and the formation of a group to organize college athletics. The Intercollegiate Athletic Association of the United States (IAAUS) was founded in 1906 with 62 members. Four years later, the association changed its name to the present day name of the National Collegiate Athletic Association (NCAA, 2013).

The organization evolved over time from a service-oriented, facilitative group based on the philosophy of "*Home Rule*," or local college control of all aspects of the athletic program, to a sanctioning body with enforcement and policy-making authority and responsibility. Factors that prompted the philosophical change in governance included eligibility and academic fraud, recruiting scandals, financial aid abuse, and amateurism violations. Following World War II, A "*Sanity Code*" was adopted to try to regulate and prevent further abuse in those areas. By 1973, the organization divided into three divisions of competition in order to promote unity of like-minded institutions in athletic contests. The NCAA began to administer championships and programs for women in 1981–82, and the organization grew dramatically (NCAA, 2013).

The organization took a major step forward in 1997, however, when it reorganized the governance structure. Upon recommendations by the Knight Commission on Inter-collegiate Athletics, more autonomy was given to each division for specific division-only matters, and presidential authority was required at all levels of policy making. The new Division I chart included a Board of Directors composed of 18 college or university presidents charged with the responsibility of dealing with all legislative proposals. A Division I Management Council, composed of 49 members, most of whom were Athletic Directors, received reports from special cabinets beneath them and recommended policy to the Board of Directors (NCAA, 2013).

Further reorganization of the NCAA structure was proposed in October 2007 and was approved in January 2008 for implementation in September 2008. The revised organization replaced the Management Council with two 31-member bodies: the Leadership Council and the Legislative Council. The Legislative Council is straightforward in name and deed; it will be responsible for final action on more routine legislative matters. The Leadership Council is expected to have a national focus on current and emerging issues in intercollegiate athletics. They will be the primary advisory group to the Board of Directors on strategic and policy issues (Hosick, 2008). The current Academics/

Eligibility/Compliance Cabinet and the Championship Cabinet were eliminated and replaced by six 21-member Cabinets focused on Championships, Administration, Academics, Student-Athlete Awards, Benefits, and Financial Aid, Recruiting, and Amateurism (Philippi, 2008).

The 1997 NCAA governance restructuring mixed two objectives: presidential control and a representative form of governance with voting control given to the major football conferences (Knight Commission on Intercollegiate Athletics, 2010). While support for presidential control of intercollegiate athletics has remained strong, concerns have grown over the issues of coaches' salary escalation, loss of institutional academic integrity, increasing focus on revenue and facility expansion, lack of fiscal restraint, and the rise of the Bowl Championship Series (BCS). The Knight Commission further revealed that there was a general loss of confidence in the NCAA governance process—from both the membership institutions and the general public—in wake of perceived inefficiencies of the organization to effectively react to crisis and scandal situations at Pennsylvania State University, University of Miami, Rutgers University, and Oklahoma

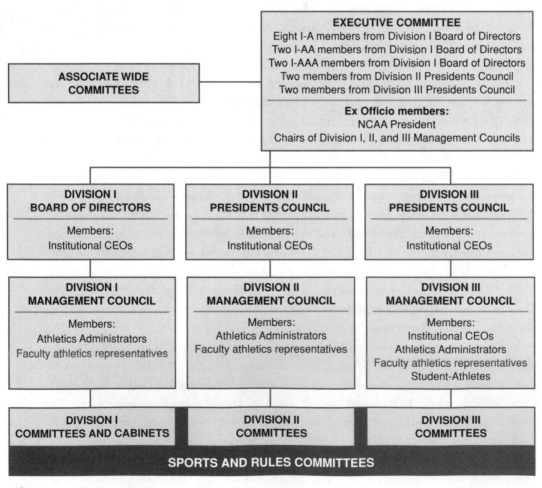

Figure 12.7. NCAA Governance Structure

State University. The NCAA is in a state of further evolutional development, as organizational debate and discussion concerning further reorganization entails. The divisional structure may continue to change in order to meet the needs of high-budget football conferences and their financial interests in financial support of its student athletes and governance rules that pertain only to their financial landscape (Knight Commission on Intercollegiate Athletics, 2013). The mission of the NCAA is as follows: "The NCAA is devoted to the expert administration of intercollegiate athletics for its membership. The purpose of the NCAAA is to provide programming and deliver national championships for intercollegiate athletes" (NCAA, 2013).

The United States Olympic Committee (USOC)

One of the most visible sport competitions in the world is the Olympic Games. What is the governing body that administers the team and individual programs that compete for the United States in major international events? The International Olympic Committee (IOC), headquartered in Lausanne, Switzerland, was founded in 1894 and is the umbrella organization that organizes the summer and winter Olympic Games. The IOC is comprised of National Olympic Committees (NOCs) from each country that sends athletes to the Games. The NOC of the United States is the *United States Olympic Committee* (USOC).

The USOC was formed in 1978 when the U.S. Congress passed the Amateur Sports Act (now called the Ted Stevens Olympic and Amateur Sports Act), and gave them overall authority to manage and promote the Olympic, Pan American, and Paralympic Games. The USOC is composed of over 78 member organizations categorized by Olympic Sport, Pan American Sport, Affiliated Sport, Community-Based Multisport, Education-Based Multisport, and the Armed Forces. Headquartered in Colorado Springs, Colorado, the USOC employs more than 500 staff, but also relies heavily upon additional volunteers to run their extensive activities (USOC, 2013).

The USOC underwent the most sweeping changes in its history because of allegations of Code of Ethics violations, fighting within the organizational leadership, the forced resignation of the President due to résumé misstatements, and scandals involving illegal payments to IOC members. An independent commission was appointed by the U.S. Congress, as well as an internal Governance and Ethics Task Force created to investigate actions that had tarnished the image of the USOC.

The process began in 2003, as Bill Martin was named acting President and charged with leading the organization through a difficult time of reform, and culminated in recommendations to develop a more efficient governance structure. Peter Ueberroth, former President of the Los Angeles Olympic Organizing Committee (LAOOC) 1984 Olympic Games, was the initial Chair of the reorganized Board of Directors for the USOC. Ueberroth developed the financial and organizational model currently used by the USOC by managing the first privately financed games in Los Angeles that netted over $238 million profit. He later became Commissioner of Major League Baseball. The new structure (1) reduced the size of the Board of Directors from an unwieldy 125 to 16, (2) reduced the number of standing committees from 23 to 4, (3) eliminated an

Executive Committee from the governance structure, (4) refined the Mission statement to emphasize support for the U.S. athletes, and (5) created an Olympic Assembly (USOC, 2013a).

Currently, in addition to the 16-member Board of Directors, there is a 16-member Executive Team, an Athletic Advisory Council (AAC), a National Governing Bodies Council (NGBC), a Multi-Sport Organizational Council (MSOC), a Paralympic Advisor Council (PAC), and Working Groups for Safe Training Environments, Diversity, and Athlete Career Development. According to former Secretary General Jim Scherr, "the new governance structure will enable the USOC to better fulfill its mission while reaffirming for the American public that its confidence and trust in our organization is well-placed" (2004, p. 5). The USOC Mission Statement is: "To Support United States Olympic and Paralympic athletes in achieving sustained competitive excellence and preserve the Olympic ideals, and thereby inspire all Americans" (USOC, 2013b, p. 4).

Professional Sport Organizations

Professional sport in America has a long and varied history beyond this chapter's discussion. The governance structure of the four major professional organizations, Major League Baseball (MLB), The National Football League (NHL), The National Basketball Association (NBA), and the National Hockey League (NHL), have many similarities. All four have a storied history, with MLB's National League the earliest to form in 1876 (Scully, 1989).

The first professional football league was the American Professional Football Association, created in 1920, which later became the National Football League (NFL) in 1922. The American Basketball League (ABL) was the first pro basketball league and was

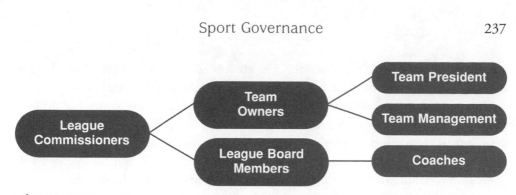

Figure 12.8. Organizational Structure of the NBA

founded in 1924. After the ABL went out of business, two rival leagues, the Basketball Association of America (BAA) and the National Basketball League (NBL), came into existence, only to join together to become the National Basketball Association (NBA) in 1949. The NHL began in 1917 with four Canadian teams, and it expanded to the United States in 1924 (Quirk & Fort, 1992). All of the established leagues have withstood challenges by rival leagues such as the Players and Federal Leagues in Baseball, American Basketball League, the American Football League and XFL, and the World Hockey League.

The "Big 4" professional leagues all have a number of teams divided into conferences and divisions of competition, usually based on geographical location. MLB has 30 teams divided into the National and American Leagues, each with East, Central, and West Divisions. The NFL has 32 teams divided into the American Football Conference (AFC) and the National Football Conference (NFC). The teams are further divided into North, South, East, and West Divisions. The NBA has 29 teams in an Eastern and Western Conference that is further divided into Atlantic, Central, Midwest, and Pacific Divisions. The NHL has 30 teams in the Eastern and Western Conferences. Northeast, Southeast, Atlantic, Central, Northwest, and Pacific Divisions provide competitions based on proximity (Hums & MacLean, 2004). Further similarities abound in the central governance of these leagues. All of the leagues have a league commissioner, a Board of Governors made up of team owners, a central office to administer daily business, a player's association, and individual teams—each with its own unique structure. All four leagues are headquartered in New York City.

Centralized league functions include security, marketing, policy development, dispute resolution, rule-making, disciplinary actions, licensing, public relations, officiating, media coordination and production, and international business operations. De-centralized team functions (see organizational chart of NBA below) cover some of the same areas, but with a local orientation. Teams usually have departmental units that focus on individual and group sales, facility security and management, marketing and promotions, concessions and merchandise sales, player development, finance and business operations, community outreach, and legal services (NBA.com, 2013).

Where

The *Where* can be answered in two ways: *Location* and *Future*. Where is the location of the "governance of sport"? A simple answer is it is *everywhere*! It is impossible to imagine organized sport without "organization." Governance gives us consistency with the past and guiding principles for the future. However, where does that future lead us?

Each level of governance has current and future challenges to overcome. Local, state, and national levels of amateur sport face issues of increasing costs of participant health care, increased insurance and product costs involved with the demands of a litigious society, unethical behavior by management, spectators, and players, and the safety of athletes. In interscholastic sport, fund raising and sponsorship issues, hazing, funding for extracurricular activities, facility renovation and improvement, homeschool athlete eligibility, sportsmanship and character development, and a shortage of qualified coaches and officials present hurdles to overcome. In intercollegiate athletics, issues include:

1. Maintaining (and in some cases establishing) academic integrity
2. Reducing operational costs
3. Title IX compliance
4. Meeting the increased demands of television
5. Justifying runaway coaching salaries
6. Combatting the use of illegal performance enhancing substances
7. Dealing with financial aid and amateurism issues
8. Curtailing athletes' involvement with agents
9. Increasing awareness about gambling and point-shaving scandals
10. Reducing early entrance into professional leagues by student athletes

SUMMARY

Sport as we know it today would not exist without the formal organizational structure under which teams, leagues, conferences, and governing bodies operate. There are many career opportunities within governing bodies in sport, all of which can be both financially and personally rewarding. As you've undoubtedly read elsewhere in the text, the best way to prepare yourself for these jobs is through volunteering and performing internships. Developing an understanding of the complexities of these various governing bodies will assist you as you prepare for a career in the industry.

Discussion Activities

1. Why do we need governance in sport? Review the "5 W's and an H" and add a new reason in each area.
2. Locate the mission statement from your local university and compare it with the mission statement of the athletic department at that school. What are the similarities? What are the differences? Are they in agreement with each other?
3. Visit the NCAA web site (www.ncaa.org) and examine the organizational diagrams. Who (whom) is located at the top of the chart? Why is it structured in this manner?
4. Is the need for governance greater or less in professional sport organizations? Defend your answer.

References

AAU. (2013). *About the AAU*. Retrieved from www.aausports.org/

Bridges, F., & Roquemore, L. (2004). *Management for athletic/sport administration: Theory and Practice* (4th ed.). Decatur, GA: ESM Books.

Covell, D. (1998). High school and youth sport. In A.L.P. Masteralexis, C.A. Barr, & M.A.

Hums (Eds.), *Principles and practice of sport management* (pp. 137–163). Gaithersburg, MD: Aspen Publishing.

Hums. M., & MacLean, J. (2004). *Governance and policy in sport organizations*. Scottsdale, AZ: Holcomb Hathaway Publishing.

Hosick, M. B. (2008, Winter Ed.). Governance Split Adds Value. *Champion, 1*(1), 63. Indianapolis, IN: NCAA Publishing.

Knight Commission on Intercollegiate Athletics. (2013). Knight Commission Memorandum to the NCAA. Retrieved from http://www.knightcommission.org/resources/press-room/833-august-6-2013-knight-commission-memorandum-to-ncaa-president-mark-emmert-and-ncaa-board of-directors-on-ncaa-governance-and-related-issues

Knight Commission on Intercollegiate Athletics. (2010). Restoring the Balance. Retrieved from www.knightcommision.org

Lussier, R., & Kimball, D. (2004). *Sport Management: Principles, applications, skill development*. Mason, OH: Thomson Learning South-Western Publishing.

Merriam-Webster. (2004). *The Merriam-Webster Dictionary* (11th ed.). Springfield, MA: Merriam-Webster Inc.

MPSSAA. (2013). MPSSAA Organization. *MPSSA.org*. Retrieved from www.mpssaa.org/intro/organization

National Basketball Association (2013). *About the NBA*. Retrieved from www.nba.com

National Strength and Conditioning Association (2013). *Organizational structure*. Retrieved from www.nsca.org

NCAA. (2013). *About the NCAA: Purposes and goals*. Retrieved from www.ncaa.org.

NFHSA. (2013a). *About the NFHSA*. Retrieved from www.nfshsa.org/about.htm.

NFHSA. (2013b). *National federation of state high school associations 2012–2013 Handbook*. Indianapolis, IN: NFHSA.

Philippi, R. (2008). *Division I Governance Changes*. Conference USA Memorandum to Directors of Athletics.

Rader, B. C. (1999). *American sports: From the age of folk games to the age of televised sports* (4th ed.). Upper Saddle River, NJ: Prentice Hall.

Russell Athletic Corp. (2004). About Russell Athletic. Retrieved from www.russellathletic.com

USOC. (2004). USOC Pressbox. Retrieved from www.usolympicteam.com

USOC. (2013a). About the United States Olympic Committee. Retrieved from www.usolympicteam.com

USOC. (2013b). United States Olympic Committee Bylaws, Article II. Retrieved from www.usolympicteam.com

Wong, G. M. (1994). *Essentials of sport law*. Westport, CT: Praeger.

YMCA. (2013). *YMCA History*. Retrieved from www.ymca.net/index.jsp

13

Ethics in the Sport Industry

Lynn L. Ridinger and T. Christopher Greenwell

INTRODUCTION

In 2012, several events unfolded that illustrated some of the questionable decisions made by athletes, coaches, and administrators. Here are a few of the more notorious examples:

- Lance Armstrong was stripped of his seven Tour de France titles due to the use of performance-enhancing drugs.
- New Orleans Saints coach Sean Payton was suspended for the entire season for his role in what the NFL deemed a "bounty" program where it is alleged that players earned incentives for injuring opposing players.
- University of Southern California Coach Lane Kiffin had a player change jersey numbers during a game against Colorado, a clear violation of the American Football Coaches Association's Code of Ethics.
- The Badminton World Federation disqualified eight women from China, South Korea, and Indonesia from the 2012 London Olympics after an investigation determined teams were purposely losing to manipulate the seeding in the next round of the tournament.

Learning Objectives

Upon completion of the chapter, the student will be able to
- Define and understand key terms associated with ethics;
- Demonstrate a basic knowledge of ethical theories;
- Examine his or her personal value system;
- Acquire an appreciation of the role that personal values and professional ethics play in the management of sport organizations;
- Identify the progressive stages of moral development and reasoning;
- Apply the steps of ethical decision-making to help resolve ethical dilemmas;
- Understand the role of codes of ethics and understand how codes of ethics are formulated; and
- Gain an appreciation for the impact socially responsible organizations have on key stakeholder groups.

- Both Ohio State and Penn State were ineligible to compete in the Big 10 championship game and were banned from competing in bowl games due to unethical behavior by coaches and administrators.

In the Bleachers © 2012 Steve Moore. Dist. by Universal Uclick

www.gocomics.com/inthebleachers

"All righty, then ... We'll give it another minute, and if your parents are still brawling we'll resume the game without them."

In sport, we see numerous other incidents such as teams using ineligible players, hiring discrimination against women and minorities by sport organizations, coaches cheating to gain a competitive advantage, professional teams circumventing salary caps, and boorish behavior of athletics both on and off the playing field. These incidents are problematic as the sport industry prides itself on providing wholesome entertainment, promoting positive values, building character, and creating good role models, but unethical behavior threatens all of the positive benefits.

ETHICS AND MORALS

Ethics is a branch of philosophy dealing with right and wrong and with moral duties and obligations. The terms "ethics" and "morals" are sometimes used interchangeably, but they are different. Ethics deals with theories or principles whereas morals have a more practical base and take into account social values, motives, and attitudes (DeSensi & Rosenberg, 2010). **Ethics** can be defined as a set of principles or values that are used to determine right and wrong. **Morals** are the fundamental baseline values that dictate appropriate behavior within a culture or society (Solomon, 1992). For example, most societies have the moral value that murder is wrong. Other types of conduct, however, may not be as clear. Providing a token of appreciation as a means to gain favor may be viewed simply as a gift in some societies whereas that same token might be considered a bribe in another culture.

Billington (1988) identified six characteristics of ethical or moral questions:

1. Dealing with questions of ethics and morals is unavoidable. As long as one lives among and interacts with others, moral issues will arise and ethical decisions will need to be made.
2. Moral decisions involve other people; there is no such thing as a private ethics.
3. Not all decisions have ethical implications. Moral decisions are reserved for those ideals that matter most to a society such as honesty, fairness, respect, and integrity.
4. Ethical decisions offer no final answers. Philosophers usually do not provide definitive right or wrong answers. Some ethical theories and actions may be shown

to be more reasonable and correct than others, but rarely can a completely satisfactory solution be achieved.

5. A central element of morality is choice. Ethical dilemmas are associated with a variety of options or actions that can be taken.

6. The aim of moral reasoning is to discover the right or correct form of behavior. Because there are a variety of competing ethical theories and none without some weakness, no action can be declared as absolutely correct or incorrect. Nevertheless, through moral analysis, an appeal to ethical principles can be made and certain decisions may be deemed more justifiable than others.

ETHICAL THEORIES

The most widely accepted ethical theories are either teleological, deontological, or some combination of the two (Branvold, 2001). Theories based on **teleology** (from the Greek *telos* meaning "end") focus on the consequences of an action and weigh the benefits against the costs. A popular teleological theory is utilitarianism. Morality is assessed by whether or not the action creates the greatest good for the greatest number of people. In applying utilitarianism to decision making, the good of the group supersedes the good of the individual. For example, a coach may decide to play a star athlete to increase the chance of victory for the team despite the fact that the player is not fully recovered from an ankle injury.

Deontology (derived from the Greek *deon* for "duty") is based on the idea of absolute rules of moral behavior. Immanuel Kant provided the foundation for this approach with his categorical imperative statements. According to Kant, moral action is (1) universal and would make sense to everyone in a similar situation, (2) demonstrates respect for the individual, and (3) is acceptable to all rational beings. Critics feel that this theory is too vague and it does not address the issue of conflicting individual rights. In the previous example, would the action be considered moral under Kant's theory? Would all coaches in a similar situation keep the injured star in the game? Was respect shown for the individual? Would all rational beings agree that this was the appropriate action? For a more detailed discussion of ethical theories, refer to DeSensi and Rosenberg (2010).

VALUES

It is often said that sports builds character, provides positive role models, and teaches valuable lessons in teamwork, discipline, and sportsmanship, but there is little evidence to support this belief. Participation in sports does not automatically produce better or worse people (Weinberg & Gould, 2003). Character development is a learned process that involves the adoption and application of various virtues such as compassion, fairness, sportsmanship, and integrity (Shields & Bredemeier, 1995). These virtues are based on values that are instilled by socializing agents such as parents, teachers, coaches, and friends. Societal influences such as culture, religion, educational institutions, and the media also contribute to the formation of values, character, and moral development.

Values provide the foundation of ethics. A description of a person's ethics would revolve around his or her set of values (Hitt, 1990). According to Rokeach (1973), values are enduring beliefs that provide guidance for personal goals and behavior. He classi-fied values into two categories: (1) **terminal values** that relate to end-states of existence (goals) and (2) **instrumental values** that relate to one's mode of conduct (behavior). Ter-minal values can be viewed as the ends toward which one is striving whereas instrumen-tal values are the means that one will use to achieve the ends. The ends and the means would be consistent and mutually reinforcing in a unified value system (Hitt, 1990).

Values Clarification Exercise

Listed below are a set of terminal values and a set of instrumental values from *The Nature of Hu-man Values* by Milton Rokeach. To help clarify your own values, analyze the lists in terms of *their relative importance to you*. Choose the five most important values and the five least important val-ues from each list.

#	Terminal Values	#	Instrumental Values
1	A comfortable life—a prosperous life	1	Ambitious—hard-working, aspiring
2	An exciting life—a stimulating, active life	2	Broadminded—open-minded
3	A sense of accomplishment—lasting contribution	3	Capable—competent, effective
4	A world at peace—free of war and conflict	4	Cheerful—lighthearted, joyful
5	A world of beauty—beauty of nature and the arts	5	Clean—neat, tidy
6	Equality—brotherhood, equal opportunity for all	6	Courageous—standing up for your beliefs
7	Family security—taking care of loved ones	7	Forgiving—willing to pardon others
8	Freedom—independence, free choice	8	Helpful—working for the welfare of others
9	Happiness—contentedness	9	Honest—sincere, truthful
10	Inner harmony—freedom from inner conflict	10	Imaginative—daring, creative
11	Mature love—sexual and spiritual intimacy	11	Independent—self-reliant, self-sufficient
12	National security—protection from attack	12	Intellectual—intelligent, reflective
13	Pleasure—an enjoyable, leisurely life	13	Logical—consistent, rational
14	Salvation—saved, eternal life	14	Loving—affectionate, tender
15	Self-respect—self-esteem	15	Obedient—dutiful, respectful
16	Social recognition—respect, admiration	16	Polite—courteous, well-mannered
17	True friendship—close companionship	17	Responsible—dependable, reliable
18	Wisdom—a mature understanding of life	18	Self-controlled—restrained, self-disciplined

Discussion Questions

1. Do you have a unified value system? In other words, do your instrumental values support your terminal values?
2. Do you have a good understanding of your own value system? Was it easy for you to determine which values are most and least important? Why or why not?
3. Compare your value selection with one or two of your classmates. Do you agree on which val-ues are most and least important? Why or why not?

VALUES IN SPORT

There has been a growing concern that the value system of some sport participants, managers, and spectators is in decay. In an effort to combat moral transgressions and emphasize the important role that sports can play in contributing to positive values of society, nearly 50 influential sport leaders gathered for a conference in May of 1999 and issued the **Arizona Sports Summit Accord**. The Accord encourages greater emphasis on the ethical and character-building aspects of athletic competition. The goal of formulating this document was to establish a framework of principles and values that would be adopted and practiced widely by those involved with sport organizations. According to the Accord, "the essential elements of character-building and ethics in sports are embodied in the concept of sportsmanship and six core principles: trustworthiness, respect, responsibility, fairness, caring, and good citizenship" (Arizona Sports, 1999, p. 2). A sample of the declarations of the Accord is listed below:

- It is the duty of sports leadership, including coaches, athletic administrators, and officials, to promote sportsmanship and foster good character.
- Sports programs must be conducted in a manner that enhances the mental, social, and moral development of athletes.
- Participation in sports is a privilege, not a right. Athletes and coaches have a duty to conduct themselves as role models on and off the field.
- The academic, emotional, and moral well-being of athletes must be placed above desires and pressures to win.
- Coaches and athletes must refrain from disrespectful conduct such as verbal abuse, taunting, profane trash-talking, and unseemly celebrations.
- Sports programs should adopt codes of conduct for coaches, athletes, parents, spectators, and other groups that impact the quality of athletic programs.
- Relationships with corporate sponsors should be continually monitored to ensure against inappropriate exploitation of the sport organization's name or reputation and undue interference of influence of commercial interests.

Following are some questions to consider related to the above list of the declarations of the Accord:

- Do these ideals apply only to youth sports or are they applicable to all levels of sport?
- What strategies could sport managers implement to promote these ideals?

Go to http://www.charactercounts.org/sports/strategies.htm to see how your answers compare to the strategies suggested on the website.

PERSONAL AND PROFESSIONAL ETHICS

Personal values and professional standards of right and wrong do not exist in a social vacuum, nor are they mutually exclusive (Beauchamp, 1988). All organizations, including sport organizations, are guided by beliefs or values that communicate what is important to the organization. A healthy organizational culture is characterized by congruence between the organization's statement of values and the daily behavior of its members (Hitt, 1990). Sound professional ethics begins with good moral behavior of the people associated with an organization. An individual's personal values of honesty, fairness, and integrity will have a social effect through the decisions that he or she makes as a member of an organization. It is important for leaders within sport organizations to clarify the parameters of professional conduct and set the tone for merging personal and professional ethics through their own words and actions. Sport managers should express expectations about ethical and moral conduct in the workplace and define acceptable and unacceptable behavior for members (DeSensi & Rosenberg, 2010).

MORAL DEVELOPMENT AND REASONING

Even when guidelines for ethical behavior have been established, real-life ethical dilemmas are often complex and require some degree of moral reasoning. The capacity for moral reasoning is dependent upon an individual's level of moral development. **Moral development** refers to a process of growth in which a person's capacity to reason morally is developed through cognitive maturation and experiences. **Moral reasoning** is the decision process in which an individual determines whether a course of action is right or wrong. **Moral behavior** is the execution of an act deemed right or wrong (Weinburg & Gould, 2003).

According to Kohlberg (1987), a leading scholar on moral development, children and adolescents progress through distinct stages of moral reasoning. Kohlberg's model, comprised of three levels, each with two stages, is based on the relationship between the individual and the rules and expectations of the society. Level I, preconventional, is characterized by a separation between conventions and the individual. This is the moral level of most children under age 9 and many adolescent and adult criminals. Level II, conventional, is based on a person's conformance to society's rules and is the level of most adolescents

Photo courtesy © Andy Gillentine

and adults in societies. Level III, postconventional, is where the individual's values are formed independently of social norms. This final level is reached by a minority of adults and is usually attained only after age 20 (Kohlberg, 1987).

Level I: Preconventional

Stage 1—*Heteronomous Morality.* At this stage, what is right is to avoid breaking rules that will lead to punishments. Individuals at this stage have a very egocentric point of view and do not consider the interests or intentions of others.

Stage 2—*Individualism, Instrumental Purpose, and Exchange.* What is right is to follow rules only as a means to achieve one's own interests and let others do the same. At this stage, the person is aware that others may have different interests, so sometimes a deal or agreement must be reached. What is right in this case is a fair or equal exchange.

Level II: Conventional

Stage 3—*Mutual Interpersonal Expectations, Relationships, and Interpersonal Conformity.* What is right is to be good, to have others recognize this goodness, to show concern for others, and abide by the Golden Rule. An individual at this stage moves beyond self-interest to recognize the feelings and expectations of others.

Stage 4—*Social System and Conscience.* What is right is to perform duties, adhere to laws, and contribute to groups, institutions, and society. Someone at this stage views individual relations in terms of their place in the social system.

Level III: Postconventional or Principled

Stage 5—*Social Contract or Utility and Individual Rights.* What is right is being aware that others may hold different values, accepting those differences, and upholding basic fundamental rights like life and liberty in all societies.

Stage 6—*Universal Ethical Principles.* Right is based on self-chosen ethical principles such as justice, equality, and respect for the dignity of individuals. These principles are universal; they are comprehensive, consistent, and can be justified to any moral rational individual. A person at this stage believes that most laws and social agreements are valid because they rest on such principles; however, when laws violate these principles, one acts in accordance with the principles.

In her work on teaching sportsmanship and values, Weiss (1987) outlined five levels of moral development that progress in similar fashion to Kohlberg's model. Keep in mind that not everyone reaches the highest level of moral reasoning and oftentimes adults operate at lower levels of moral reasoning despite their cognitive capacity to think at higher levels. Level 1, the lowest level of moral reasoning, is based on external control. In other words, "It's okay as long as I don't get caught." At this stage, a child determines whether an action is right or wrong based on self-interest and the outcome of his action. If Billy is penalized for tripping his opponent, then the action must be wrong. On the other hand, if the official does not see the intentional trip, then the action is deemed okay.

In Level 2, one will compromise and rationalize to maximize self-interest. This "eye for an eye" orientation is often used in defending questionable actions. For example, Billy may feel justified in tripping his opponent because the opponent had previously tripped him. This type of moral reasoning is evident when athletes think that it is okay to use performance-enhancing drugs because everyone else is using them.

In Level 3, the child begins to take a more altruistic view and treats others like they would like to be treated. Billy may choose to not intentionally trip his opponent because he does not want to be tripped. A coach may insist that his players not taunt the other team because he wants his team treated with respect.

Level 4 of moral reasoning involves following external rules and regulations. At this stage, a child realizes that rules were made for the common good because not everyone can be trusted to do the right thing. Self-interest is no longer the driving force because the child can now understand the bigger picture and the importance of everyone playing by the same rules. In this case, Billy would not trip his opponent because it is against the rules.

Level 5 focuses on doing what is best for everyone involved whether or not it is in accordance with the official rules and regulations or not. This is considered the most mature level of moral reasoning because a person seeks to maximize the interests of the group by taking action that does not violate anyone's fundamental rights as a human being. Thus, Billy would reason that he should not trip his opponent not just because it is against the rules, but because it would create an unsafe playing environment and could cause harm.

ETHICAL DILEMMAS

An **ethical dilemma** occurs in situations where the course of action is not clear due to the presence of (1) significant value conflicts among differing interests, (2) real alternatives that are equally justifiable, and (3) significant consequences on stakeholders in the situation (McNamara, 1999). Sport managers face ethical dilemmas on a regular basis. Examples of situations associated with ethical dilemmas are reported in the sports media every day. For each of the following situations, decide if an ethical dilemma exists and discuss what, if any, action should be taken by sport managers.

- An athlete is under investigation for the use of performance-enhancing drugs and has just qualified for the Olympic team.
- You are interested in joining a private golf club, but you learn that club policies ban women from becoming members and restrict their tee times on the course.
- Sales of luxury suites in a new ballpark are slow so the owner attempts to create an incentive to buy by falsely advertising that there are only a few suites left to purchase and they are selling fast.
- A star player is accused of sexual assault just prior to the playoffs.
- A college basketball coach has been very successful in leading her team to the NCAA tournament for the past several seasons, but the graduation rate of her players is 0%.
- A NASCAR driver intentionally spins out to bring out a caution flag.
- In searching for a new coach, qualified minority candidates are excluded from the interview pool.
- The parents of players in a youth soccer league have become increasingly verbally abusive toward officials and opponents.
- A baseball pitcher intentionally hits a batter in retaliation for his teammate being hit by a pitch in the previous inning.
- The highest bid for naming rights for a new sports facility at a university is a beer company.
- During the last few seconds of a high school football game, there is confusion and the home team ends up winning on 5th down. The mistake is not detected at its

occurrence, but becomes apparent the next day while reviewing the game film.

- The team mascot, an Indian chief, has caused controversy. Some people are offended by this symbol, but most of the alumni and financial donors associate the symbol with school pride and do not want the mascot changed.

ETHICAL DECISION-MAKING

Trying to decide on the best alternative to resolve an ethical dilemma can be a challenging task for sport managers who often deal with various stakeholders with different interests.

Photo courtesy © iStockphoto.com

Ethical analysis and decision-making should incorporate a systematic process of reasoning. McNamara (1999) recommends that organizations develop and document a procedure for handling ethical issues. He suggests that organizations form an ethics committee comprised of top leaders, board members, and staff to resolve ethical dilemmas. There are various models for ethical analysis that are built on the foundations of basic ethical theories. They are not designed to provide absolute answers, but do provide guidelines for assessing ethical issues and evaluating alternatives.

An adaptation of a model suggested by Zinn (1993) and presented by Crosset and Hums (1998, p. 129) outlines the following steps in the ethical decision-making process:

1. Identify the correct problem to be solved.
2. Gather all the pertinent information.
3. Explore codes of conduct relevant to your profession or to this particular dilemma.
4. Examine your own personal values and beliefs.
5. Consult with your peers or other individuals in the industry who may have experience in similar situations.
6. List your options.
7. Look for a "win-win" situation if at all possible.
8. Ask the question, "How would my family feel if my decision and how and why I arrived at my decision were printed in the newspaper tomorrow?"
9. Sleep on it. Do not rush to a decision.
10. Make your best decision, knowing it may not be perfect.
11. Evaluate your decision.

Managing Ethics

"The integrity of college sports has always been first priority. If it weren't for the integrity of the sport, no one would be interested—players, fans, media." (NCAA President Myles Brand, as cited in *Barnhouse*, 2004, p. 1D)

While this may seem like a tedious process, keep in mind that ethical dilemmas and ethical decisions involve complicated problems. The decisions of sport managers are often publicly scrutinized and may receive more media attention than other types of businesses. It is therefore important to have a logical approach to deal with ethical issues and to develop a sound game plan for managing ethics in the workplace.

Considering the importance of protecting the integrity of their respective sports, many sport organizations and governing bodies have developed **codes of ethics** to guide the actions of their constituents. By providing guidelines, organizations hope to both encourage ethical behavior and discourage unethical behavior by assisting individuals in making the right ethical choices.

Sport organizations and governing bodies incorporate codes of ethics to meet a variety of needs, therefore the content and purposes of these codes of ethics will vary from organization to organization. For example, the purpose of the International Olympic Committee (IOC) Code of Ethics is to stress commitment to the fundamental principles of the Olympics and the Olympic ideal (IOC , 2004). Their code focuses on four key themes: dignity, integrity, use of resources, and relations with states. The National Association of Sport Officials (NASO) publishes a code of ethics for the purpose of guiding the professional conduct of its members. Their code covers themes such as impartiality, conflict of interest, professional courtesy, and other themes that are important to sports officials. The USA Gymnastics Code of Ethics is written with the intent to "guide and to affirm the will of all of USA Gymnastics' members to safeguard the best interests of the sport by acting ethically at all times" (USA Gymnastics, 1996, p. 1)

Codes of ethics will target different stakeholder groups depending on the organization or governing body. For example, The New Jersey Sports and Exposition Authority is a state agency operating sports and convention venues. Therefore, their code of ethics has been written to define acceptable behavior for their members and employees. The National Youth Sports Coaches Association has a much different mission; therefore, they publish three codes of ethics: one for coaches, one for players, and one for parents. Some organizations take their codes a step further and address their fans. This is the case in the NFL where the league and several of its teams have developed codes of conduct in an attempt to eliminate inappropriate fan behaviors such as public intoxication, foul language, and harassment of other fans. Similarly, in 2012, the city of Los Angeles adopted a uniform fan code of conduct to apply to Southern California sporting events in order to provide a better and safer fan experience (Muret, 2012).

Ideally, these codes are developed in advance to promote positive behavior and prevent problems. However, sometimes codes of ethics are developed in response to growing controversies. For example, members of the National Association of Basketball Coaches (NABC) agreed to adopt codes of ethics for their basketball programs. This movement stemmed from unethical incidents involving basketball coaches at St. Bonaventure, Georgia, Baylor, Fresno State, and Iowa State, that tarnished the image of the coaching profession (Moran, 2003). Similarly, the International Skating Union (ISU) adopted a code of ethics in 2003 in response to the judging scandal at the 2002 Olympics where French judge Marie-Reine Le Gougne voted in favor of Russian skaters under suspicious circumstances ("ISU adopts," 2003). More recently, the Fiesta Bowl, in response to a scandal related to political contributions, adopted a code of conduct to discourage future issues (Smith, 2011).

Criteria for Good Codes of Ethics

Considering the importance of encouraging good conduct, it is important to take care in developing a code of ethics to ensure the code will be effective in meeting its stated purpose. The mere existence of an ethical code does not ensure people will act ethically (Helin & Sanstrom, 2007; Kaptein, 2011). A code of ethics must be part of the organization's culture, embraced by leaders, and relevant to the stakeholders addressed in the code (Stevens, 2008; Wood & Rimmer, 2003).

Mahony, Geist, Jordan, Greenwell, and Pastore (1999) identified several factors related to constructing an effective code of ethics.

- Codes of ethics should avoid being too vague or too specific. When codes are too vague, individuals are provided little guidance as how to make ethical decisions. However, codes that are too specific are limited in that they may not apply to a wide variety of situations. For example, think of what happens when a new performance-enhancing drug is introduced that is not expressly prohibited by a governing body's code of ethics. Athletes may be tempted to use it because it is not expressly prohibited, even though it gives the athlete an unfair advantage.
- Effective codes of ethics are founded on a few themes that can be used to guide individuals' decisions in a variety of situations. These themes represent the organization's values and will vary from organization to organization. In a study of intercollegiate conference codes of ethics, several themes emerged as being important. **Sportsmanship**, **welfare** of participants, **compliance** with institutional and conference rules, **equitable treatment**, and professional **conduct** of employees were themes commonly found in codes of ethics (Greenwell, Geist, Mahony, Jordan, & Pastore, 2001).
- Organizations developing codes of ethics should communicate what is in the code of ethics to those individuals addressed in the code. The NCAA realizes this as they call for each member institution to continuously educate their stakeholders about policies related to sportsmanship and ethical conduct (NCAA, 2003). The NBA and NFL do this by hosting orientation events for rookies that focus, in part, on ethical behavior (Broussard, 2003).

- Codes should be clear as to whom they apply. This can be especially challenging in sport contexts due to the large number of stakeholder groups affected. The behavior of coaches, administrators, athletes, and fans can all impact the organization.
- Consequences for violating ethical standards should be established (DeSensi & Rosenberg, 2003; Lere & Gaumnitz, 2004). Without some sort of penalty, the code is simply a suggestion and is not likely to influence behavior. These penalties should be clear, should identify who is in charge of enforcing penalties, and identify methods of appeal. In terms of common penalties, Greenwell et al. (2001) found intercollegiate conferences included penalties ranging from reprimands and probation to player and team suspensions. For the most serious violations, penalties included institutional fines and institutional expulsion.

> Select a sport organization. Who should be addressed in its code of ethics? What values should be highlighted in their code? How should those participants be encouraged to follow what is in the code?

- Finally, in order for codes to be effective, codes must be relevant to the stakeholders addressed in the code (Wood & Rimmer, 2003). In order to encourage increased acceptance, codes should be developed with input from those who will be impacted by the standards (DeSensi & Rosenberg, 2003; Stead, Worrell, & Stead, 1990). This type of participatory approach to developing codes of ethics should lead to better understanding of what coaches and athletes desire from each other, which should ultimately lead to effective codes of ethics.

SOCIAL RESPONSIBILITY

"... THE PUBLIC IS FOCUSED NOW MORE THAN EVER ON WHAT FIRMS ARE SAYING ABOUT THEIR CORPORATE SOCIAL RESPONSIBILITY."
(Snider, Hill, & Martin, 2003)

Sport organizations often impact multiple stakeholder groups including employees, coaches, athletes, spectators, the business community, and the local community in general. Further, sport organizations often rely on these stakeholder groups for the resources they need to operate successfully. For example, organizations may utilize government money to fund programs like city recreation leagues or tax revenue to build stadiums and arenas. They may require other resources from the community such as volunteers to staff an event or local media to promote events. Similarly, the actions of sport organizations impact the community in many ways, both positively and negatively. On the positive side, sport organizations contribute to the local economy and citizens are provided opportunities to participate in activities or enjoy sports performances. Negatively, bad acts by an organization can harm the reputation of the community, and bad acts by athletes can provide poor role models to the youth of the community. These points illustrate an inextricable relationship between the organization and its stakeholders, therefore sport organizations' responsibilities toward their stakeholders is an important issue.

Corporate Social Responsibility

Corporate social responsibility is the term most often used to refer to the role an organization has within the community. Due to the media exposure sport organizations receive and the celebrity status of their athletes, sport often has greater opportunities to impact their communities than other organizations (Babiak & Wolfe, 2006). Smith and Westerbeek (2007, p. 43) state, "Sport offers a bridge across social and economic gaps, an opportunity to improve the quality of life, and a stimulus to encourage large and profitable businesses to share a little of their prosperity."

According to Carroll (1999), socially responsible businesses have four main responsibilities—economic, legal, ethical, and philanthropic—all of which responsible organizations will seek to achieve.

Economic responsibilities require organizations to produce goods and services and sell them at a profit because that is how a capitalist society operates (Carroll, 1999). At first this definition seems to imply that organizations should act in their self-interest without regard to other stakeholder groups, but Carroll (1999) argues that economic viability also influences other parts of society. For example, professional sports teams have a responsibility to make wise fiscal decisions, since the local economy may benefit from jobs, tourist dollars, and tax revenue generated by the existence of a team. In intercollegiate athletics, administrators are entrusted with funds from the university, donors, and corporate sponsors. These administrators have a responsibility to use these funds efficiently to maximize the experience of the student-athletes and contribute to the university.

Under this definition, socially responsible professional teams should strive to produce the best product. This would seem to be the goal of every team, but it is not always the case. After the 2012 season, the Miami Marlins traded several of their better, higher-salaried players, which angered their fan base (Levinson & Matuszewski, 2012). This followed a season where the team moved into a $515 million, retractable roof ballpark that was 80% financed by taxpayer money. Considering how much the community had invested in the team, both economically and psychologically, was team owner Jeffery Loria justified in his actions?

Legal responsibilities require organizations to reach goals within legal constraints. Sport organizations are often under the scrutiny of contract laws, labor laws, criminal laws, etc., and socially responsible sport managers are expected to adhere to these laws. Further, legal responsibility also applies to organizational rules and procedures. For example, Olympic athletes have numerous eligibility and anti-doping rules to adhere to, and colleges are expected to adhere to rules in the NCAA manual.

The competitive nature of sport often provides challenges to organizations, coaches, and athletes who are tempted to "bend the rules" for their advantage. For example, the New England Patriots were caught using video to spy on the New York Jets, and Formula One's McLaren team was caught with secret technical data from rival Ferrari (Powers, 2007). In both cases, the offending parties argued they really had not done anything against the rules of their respective sports. We also see this in college sports where coaches bend recruiting rules to land top athletes. These coaches may feel that winning is what is important, and that they should win at all costs. Socially responsible coaches also want to win, but they see more value in "winning within the rules."

Ethical responsibilities require organizations to operate by established norms defining suitable behavior. In other words, ethical responsibilities represent what organizations are expected to do above the rule of law. For example, in 2009 NFL teams began printing the message "Fans Don't Let Fans Drive Drunk" on their beer cups to curb drinking-related problems. Although teams are not legally required to do so, they do out of a legal responsibility. Conversely, organizations may act within the rules, but not meet ethical standards. The NFL's "Rooney Rule" requires teams to interview at least one minority candidate when hiring head coaches. However, this rule does not apply to assistant coaches. In 2012, only one minority coach among the league's 32 teams was calling offensive plays (Florio, 2012). Although teams are not breaking NFL rules, can it be considered ethical to have only one minority in a position considered to be a key qualification for those wanting to be head coaches?

Philanthropic responsibilities require organizations to give back to their communities. Bill Veeck, who owned the Cleveland Indians Baseball team in the 1950s, exemplified philanthropic responsibilities. Contrary to most baseball owners at the time who felt the city owed them something, Veeck surmised that his team was dependent on the facilities of the city and the goodwill of the citizens (Veeck & Linn, 1962). Due to this belief, the Indians were active in philanthropy, inviting community groups to attend for free and contributing gate receipts to community charities and youth sports programs. This trend continues today as many professional sports teams have established charitable foundations to contribute to their communities. In addition to financial contributions, many sport organizations contribute other resources to their community. Many universities create programs like the University of Louisville's Cards Care program. The Cards Care program organizes activities for student athletes to donate their time to various community projects such as pen pal programs with local schools, visits to children's hospitals, shifts serving food at soup kitchens, etc.

Individual Social Responsibility

Social responsibility applies to individuals as well as organizations. Individual athletes, coaches, and administrators have a responsibility to their communities and to their peers. Administrators bear the weight of knowing their decisions affect many stakeholder groups ranging from owners, employees, athletes, to fans. Coaches are often responsible for teaching values in addition to skills, and these coaches often hold a high public profile in the community. Former Indianapolis Colts head coach Tony Dungy was one of many coaches who actively used his stature in the community to make a positive impact. While coaching, Dungy was actively involved with Big Brothers/Big Sisters, Boys and Girls Clubs, and several faith-based initiatives. Conversely, negative incidents involving coaches can send entirely different messages to their athletes and to the people who follow their teams. Two recent examples involved high profile coaches. University of Arkansas head football coach Bobby Petrino was entangled in a scandal where it was revealed he had been having an affair with a university employee, and University of Kentucky head basketball coach Billy Gillespie was arrested on drunk-driving charges. In both cases, the coaches' actions were starkly opposed to the values they tried to communicate to their athletes and their fans. Both coaches were subsequently fired.

In addition to coaches, athletes impact their communities in many ways. Like it or not, athletes serve as role models for young kids who often emulate their heroes. This is why brands such as Nike and McDonald's are willing to pay LeBron James millions of dollars in endorsement deals. They do this knowing kids will want to wear what LeBron wears and eat what LeBron eats. This influence can be both positive and negative. On one hand, role models such as Mia Hamm and Lisa Leslie have encouraged girls to get involved in sports and to lead healthier lives. Many kids have taken up soccer to be like David Beckham. On the other hand, much of the boorish behavior seen in youth sports can be attributed to kids emulating professional athletes. What do children learn about sportsmanship when they see athletes argue with officials, taunt opponents, or start brawls? Although many athletes may want to shun this responsibility, high profile athletes have to realize they are always being watched and emulated.

Many athletes feel a responsibility to use their fame to have a positive impact on their communities. For example, professional football player Matt Birk is involved in several initiatives beyond the playing field. His "Ready, Set, Read!" program reaches nearly 100,000 children in the Baltimore area. Additionally, he agreed to donate his brain and spinal cord tissue to help research the effects of head trauma. He received the 2012 Walter Payton Man of the Year award in recognition of his off-the-field community service. The 2007 winner, Warrick Dunn, established the Homes for the Holidays program, which assists single mothers in purchasing homes. He started the program to give back to the community in the way others had supported him and his siblings following his mother's death. According to the Warrick Dunn Foundation, through 2012, Dunn had helped 120 single parents and 322 children obtain affordable homeownership. Major League Baseball recognizes the power athletes have in their communities and encourages athletes to be active by awarding the Roberto Clemente award each year to recognize devotion to work in the community. The 2012 winner, Clayton Kershaw of the Los Angeles Dodgers, was recognized for his community work with Kershaw's Challenge which supports an orphanage in Zambia and at-risk youth in Los Angeles and Dallas.

Often this responsibility extends beyond the local community. American speedskater Joey Cheek provides a great example. After winning a gold medal at the 2006 Winter

Olympics in Turin, Cheek donated his gold medal bonus to Right to Play, an international humanitarian organization. In addition, he used his influence as an athlete to encourage Olympic sponsors to do the same (Crouse, 2006).

Benefits of Being a Good Corporate Citizen

Just as socially responsible organizations deliver benefits to their stakeholders, they may also reap benefits, as organizations contributing to the **public good** often enjoy business success as customers reward organizations for their roles in the community (Besser, 1999). There is some evidence to suggest that socially responsible activities can boost an organization's image, generate increased business, and keep organizations out of trouble. In addition, customers are more likely to buy from organizations that are socially responsible and less likely to purchase products from companies whose practices are viewed as being less socially responsible (Creyer, 1997; Sen & Bhattacharya, 2001). Good corporate citizenship often helps sport organizations attract fans and corporate sponsors (Babiak & Wolfe, 2006).

Socially irresponsible organizations can suffer negative effects. A good example of how irresponsible activities can have negative effects on an organization comes from the Salt Lake City Olympics scandal. In 1999, while Olympic officials involved in the Salt Lake City bid process were being investigated on bribery charges, John Hancock Financial Services, a major Olympic sponsor, decided to significantly scale back advertising for the Sydney Olympics (Bell, 1999) and a major donor withdrew a $10 million donation (Blevins, 2003).

SUMMARY

- Morality and ethics in the workplace should be key components of all industries, including the sport industry.
- Sport managers routinely face ethical situations, and the decisions they make impact a variety of stakeholders such as athletes, coaches, staff, corporate sponsors, and fans.
- Sport managers will be better equipped to deal with the daily dose of dilemmas if they have a sound grasp of their personal values, a commitment to professional ethics, a basic understanding of ethical theories, and the ability to apply moral reasoning and ethical decision-making to resolve problems.
- It is important for sport managers to develop and enforce codes of ethics to ensure appropriate actions of constituents.
- Social responsibility should be strongly encouraged by our sport leaders at both the organizational and individual levels.
- Reflection upon the ethical choices currently being made in the world of sports coupled with the knowledge and appreciation of ethical principles and moral behavior can help guide future sport managers toward making the "right" decisions.

Discussion Activities

1. Do sport organizations have a responsibility to their communities? Is the level of responsibility different for professional teams? College teams? Youth teams?

2. Do athletes have a higher standard for behavior than non-athletes? Should more be expected of professional athletes? Should college athletes be expected to behave better than other college students?

3. Your minor-league baseball team has regularly sold out each game, and you expect to sell out again this season. Despite the sellouts, your organization is experiencing a budget crunch and you are under pressure to deliver as much revenue as possible. You feel you could sell all of your seats, but the local Drug Abuse Resistance Education (D.A.R.E.) program has asked for you to set aside 250 tickets for each game to be used as rewards for school children who agree not to use drugs. Do you sell the tickets to the public or do you donate them to the D.A.R.E. program?

4. Your men's basketball coach, who has coached for 15 successful years, has been arrested for drunk driving and has admitted to the crime. You have to formulate some sort of disciplinary action. How severe should the penalty be for this type of offense? Should the coach be treated like any other university employee in a similar situation?

5. You have a football player who has been accused of a crime. The local police claim he signed for a package containing steroids and other illegal drugs. The athlete claims he did not know what was in the package. Should the athlete be able to continue to play? Will you support the player or take disciplinary action? What type of disciplinary action would be appropriate?

6. You are operating a youth baseball league. Throughout the season, the parents have gotten more vocal in criticizing coaches, umpires, and league officials. It has gotten to the point that the kids are becoming distracted on the field. What policies can you put into place to avoid this type of behavior? What could happen if this behavior is not controlled?

7. The day before the championship game you find out your star player may be ineligible due to a minor paperwork error. It appears that the player lives one block outside the district and should be playing for another team. The player has been on your team all season and you have received no complaints. The league office is not aware of the oversight, and it is possible that no one may ever notice. Should you report this to the league office? What is the right thing to do?

8. As a high school coach, what would you do if you found photos posted on Facebook of your players consuming alcohol at a party? Would it matter if they were starters vs. second team players?

9. Your star quarterback has a sprained knee, but he assures you he feels fine and wants to play. However, the team doctor has warned you that further damage to his knee might jeopardize the player's career. It is a playoff game and this quarterback has been the team leader all season. Would you let him play?

References

The Arizona Sports Summit Accord (1999). *Pursuing victory with honor*. Retrieved from http://www .charactercounts.org/sports/accord.htm

Babiak, K., & Wolfe, R. (2006). More than just a game? Corporate social responsibility and Super Bowl XL. *Sport Marketing Quarterly, 15*, 214–222.

Barnhouse, W. (2004). Brand says ethics tops the NCAA's agenda. *Fort Worth Star-Telegram*, p. D1.

Bauchamp, T. L. (1988). Ethical theory and its application to business. In T. L. Beauchamp & N. E. Bowie (Eds.), *Ethical theory and business* (3rd ed; pp. 1–55). Englewood Cliffs, NJ: Prentice-Hall.

Bell, A. (1999). John Hancock fights to clean up Olympics. *National Underwriter, 103*(23), 3.

Besser, T. L. (1999). Community involvement and the perception of success among small business operators in small towns. *Journal of Small Business Management, 37*, 16–29.

Billington, R. (1988). *Living philosophy: An introduction to moral thought*. London: Routledge.

Blevins, J. (2003, January 23). Major sponsors stand by U.S. Olympics despite ethical scandal. *Knight Ridder Tribune Business News*, p. 1.

Branvold, S. (2001). Ethics. In B. L. Parkhouse (Ed.), *The management of sport: Its foundation and application* (3rd ed.; pp. 162–176). New York: McGraw-Hill.

Broussard, C. (2003, September 26). NBA rookies get lessons in life skills. *The New York Times*, p. D7.

Carroll, A. B. (1999). Corporate social responsibility: Evolution of a definitional construct. *Business and Society, 38*, 268–295.

Ciokajlo, M. (2002, October, 10). Chicago Cubs face ticket-fraud lawsuit. *Knight Ridder Tribune Business News*, p. 1.

Creyer, E. H. (1997). The influence of firm behavior on purchase intention: Do consumers really care about business ethics? *Journal of Consumer Marketing, 14*, 421–32.

Crosset, T. W., & Hums, M. A. (1998). Ethical principles applied to sport management. In L. P. Masteralexis, C. A. Barr, & M. A. Hums (Eds.), *Principles and practice of sport management* (pp. 117–136). Gaithersburg, MD: Aspen Publishers, Inc.

Crouse, K. (2006, February 14). Recognizing good fortune, Cheek shares gold medal. *New York Times*, p. D1.

DeSensi, J. T., & Rosenberg, D. (2010). *Ethics and morality in sport management* (3rd ed.). Morgantown, WV: Fitness Information Technology.

Florio, M. (2012, December 28). Minority coaches not getting opportunities to run offenses. *NBC Sports.com*. Retrieved from http://profootball talk.nbcsports.com/2012/12/28/minority-coaches -not-getting-opportunities-to-run-offenses/

Footer, A. (2007) Biggio receives Clemente award honor: Astros star exemplifies sportsmanship, community service. *MLB.com*. Retrieved from http://mlb.mlb.com/news/article.jsp?ymd=2007 1027&content_id=2284369&vkey=news_mlb& fext=.jsp&c_id=mlb

Greenwell, T. C., Geist, A. L., Mahony, D. F., Jordan, J. S., & Pastore, D. L. (2001). Characteristics of NCAA conference codes of ethics. *International Journal of Sport Management, 2*, 108–124.

Helin, S., & Sandstrom, J. (2007). An inquiry into the study of corporate codes of ethics. *Journal of Business Ethics, 75*, 253–271.

Hitt, W. D. (1990). *Ethics and Leadership: Putting theory into practice*. Columbus, OH: Battelle Press.

International Olympic Committee. (2004). *IOC Code of Ethics*. Lausanne, Switzerland: Author.

ISU adopts ethics code after Salt Lake scandal. (2003, August 12). *The Toronto Star*, p. E05.

Kaptein, M. (2011). Toward effective codes: Testing the relationship with unethical behavior. *Journal of Business Ethics, 99*, 233–251.

Kohlberg, L. (1987). *Child psychology and childhood education: A cognitive-developmental view*. New York: Longman.

Lere, J. C., & Guamnitz, B. R. (2004). The impact of codes of ethics on decision making: Some insights from information economics. *Journal of Business Ethics, 48*, 365–379.

Levinson, M., & Matuszewski, E. (2012, November 12). Marlins can't take heat as salary dump leads to anger in Florida. *Bloomberg.com*. Retrieved from http://www.bloomberg.com/news/2012-11 -14/marlins-can-t-take-heat-as-salary-dump-leads -to-anger-in-florida.html

Mahony, D. F., Geist, A. L., Jordan, J., Greenwell, T. C., & Pastore, D. (1999). Codes of ethics used by sport governing bodies: Problems in intercollegiate athletics. *Proceedings of the Congress of the European Association for Sport Management, 7*, 206–208.

McNamara, C. (1999). *Complete guide to ethics management: An ethics toolkit for managers*. http://www .mapnp.org/library/ethics/ethxgde.htm

Moran, M. (2003, October 16). Coaches, NCAA agree to chart new course. *USA Today*, p. 7C.

Muret, D. (2012, August 27). Major Southern California sports facilities team up to create new fan code of behavior. *Street and Smiths SportsBusiness Journal*, p. 4.

NCAA Division I Manual (2003–2004 ed.). (2003). Indianapolis, IN: National Collegiate Athletic Association.

Powers, J. (2007, September 15). Sports debate: When to cry foul; Edge-seeking becoming win-at-any-cost cheating. *The Boston Globe*, p. A1.

Rokeach, M. (1973). *The nature of human values*. New York: The Free Press.

Sen, S., & Bhattacharya, C. B. (2001). Does doing good always lead to doing better? Consumer reactions to corporate social responsibility. *Journal of Marketing Research*, *38*, 225–243.

Shields, D. L. L., & Bredemeier, B. J. L. (1995). *Character development and physical activity*. Champaign, IL: Human Kinetics.

Smith, M. (2011, December 5). Shelton works to repair Fiesta Bowl's image. *Street and Smiths SportsBusiness Journal*, p. 31.

Solomon, R. C. (1992). *Above the bottom line: An introduction to business ethics*. Fort Worth, TX: Harcourt Brace.

Smith, A. C. T., & Westerbeek, H. M. (2007, Spring). Sport as a vehicle for deploying corporate social responsibility. *Journal of Corporate Citizenship*, p. 43–54.

Snider, J., Hill, R. P., & Martin, D. (2003). Corporate social responsibility in the 21st century: A view from the world's most successful firms. *Journal of Business Ethics*, *48*, 175–187.

Stead, W. E., Worrell, D. L., & Stead, J. G. (1990). An integrative model for understanding and managing ethical behavior in business organizations. *Journal of Business Ethics*, *30*, 185–195.

Stevens, B. (2008). Corporate ethical codes: Effective instruments for influencing behavior. *Journal of Business Ethics*, *78*, 601–609.

Taylor, A. J. (2007, December 19). Warrick Dunn, Habitat join forces. *Tallahassee Democrat*.

USA Gymnastics. (1996). *USA Gymnastics Code of Ethics*. Indianapolis, IN: Author.

Weinberg, R. S., & Gould, D. (2003). *Foundations of sport & exercise psychology*. Champaign, IL: Human Kinetics.

Weiss, M. R. (1987). Teaching sportsmanship and values. In V. Seefeldt (Ed.). *Handbook for youth sports coaches* (pp. 137–151). Reston, VA: AAHPERD.

Wood, G., & Rimmer, M. (2003). Codes of ethics: What are they really and what should they be? *International Journal of Value-Based Management*, *16*(2), 181–195.

Veeck, B., & Linn, E. (1962). *Veeck as in wreck*. New York: Putnam.

Zinn, L. M. (1993). Do the right thing: Ethical decision making in professional and business practice. *Adult learning*, *5*, 7–8; 27.

14

Global Sport Industry

Artemisia Apostolopoulou and Dimitra Papadimitriou

"SPORT IS PART OF EVERY MAN AND WOMAN'S HERITAGE AND ITS
ABSENCE CAN NEVER BE COMPENSATED FOR."

—Pierre de Coubertin

INTRODUCTION

During the 2003–2004 National Basketball Association (NBA) season, American Express
aired an advertisement tag-lined *Global Village*. The ad featured Don Nelson, then
coach of the Dallas Mavericks, shopping for international dictionaries and using his
newly-acquired vocabulary to communicate during practice with his international players: Tariq Abdul-Wahad from France, Dirk Nowitzki from Germany, Eduardo Najera
from Mexico, and Steve Nash from Canada. It was clear that American Express was
attempting to capitalize on the changing makeup and diversification of NBA rosters
that at the time included 67 international players from 33 countries around the world
(NBA, 2004). And that was just the beginning as participation of international athletes
in North American professional leagues has become even more widespread in the past
10 years. On the eve of the 2012–2013 season the NBA included 84 international players representing 37 countries and territories, with 29 out of the league's 30 teams having at least one international player on their roster (NBA, 2012). Leading the pack was
the San Antonio Spurs with players from Argentina, Australia, Brazil, Canada, France,
and the U.S. Virgin Islands. An examination of Major League Baseball (MLB) and the
National Hockey League (NHL) rosters around that time reveals similar trends with

---

Learning Objectives

After reading this chapter the student should have gained an understanding of
- Globalization trends occurring in the sport industry;
- Challenges facing organizations considering international expansion;
- The Olympic Movement, its member associations and main functions;
- Efforts of U.S. professional sport leagues to expand internationally;
- The structure of the European sport industry; and
- Opportunities for a career in international sport management and required skills.

28% of all players starting the 2013 MLB season born outside the US (Dominican Republic, Venezuela) and over 33% of NHL players born outside North America (Czech Republic, Russia, Sweden).

The influx of international players in North American professional sport leagues is not the only indication that sport is increasingly becoming a global product. To further fuel international interest and capitalize on growing markets, the NBA is conducting basketball clinics in Africa and holding *NBA Cares* events in India, while MLB is broadcasting games in 17 different languages and the National Football League (NFL) is playing regular season games across the Atlantic with tremendous success. Other indicators that point to this trend are the estimated 3.2 billion viewers, or 46.4% of the world's population, who tuned in to live coverage of the 2010 FIFA World Cup South Africa matches ("FIFA Reveals," 2011); the estimated 29.4 million tourists who traveled to the UK for the London 2012 Summer Olympic Games; the more than 2,000 staff members working for Nike Greater China in Shanghai; and IMG's 130-plus offices in more than 25 countries around the world. It is obvious that sport products and services are now being consumed by a greater number of nations than ever before via traditional and new media. Welcome to the era of globalization in sport!

Globalization has been defined as the "process by which the experience of everyday life, marked by the diffusion of commodities and ideas, is becoming standardized around the world" (Merriam-Webster, 2013). In their discussion focusing on sport within a global environment, Westerbeek and Smith (2003) identified seven driving forces of globalization: (1) economy, (2) technology, (3) social science, resources, and natural environment, (4) demography, (5) governance, (6) conflict and war, and (7) religion and cultural identity. The authors pointed to the release of trade barriers and the increase of trade agreements between nations, the high-speed flow of information through new and improved communication vehicles

(e.g., the Internet), and privatization as conditions that have facilitated the globalization of sport (Westerbeek & Smith, 2003).

Given these developments, it is imperative for sport managers to understand the **international environment** in which they will be called to operate. Sport professionals must be aware of the opportunities that are available on a global scale, as well as the challenges that arise from conducting business in this new global market. For sport managers focused on selling their North American product globally, as well as those looking to capitalize on international imports, an understanding of the global sport industry is paramount. Equally as important is for sport managers to be aware of potentially negative consequences of globalization in sport. Thibault (2009) raised concerns about four "inconvenient truths" that exist in a global sport market including sport manufacturers' labor practices, the movement of athletes beyond national borders, the involvement of global media corporations in sport, and the impact of sport on the environment.

The purpose of this chapter is to provide insight into the global marketplace for students who are preparing for a career in the sport industry. The Olympic Games are considered the original international sport property and provide an excellent starting point for the examination of the international sport environment. An overview of the Olympic Movement, including its member organizations and main revenue sources, will provide valuable insight into the international sport industry. We will also examine the impact of sport globalization in the United States (US) and describe initiatives undertaken by the four major North American sport leagues to grow their reach internationally. The next section of this chapter addresses the European sport industry, particularly aspects of the football (soccer, for American readers) sector. The chapter concludes with a discussion on career opportunities for sport managers as well as those skills necessary to become a successful international sport manager.

So grab your passport (maybe your visa, too), dictionary, and travel pack and get ready to embark on a tour of the global sport marketplace!

THE OLYMPIC MOVEMENT

There is little doubt that the modern **Olympic Games**, revived in 1896 by Pierre de Coubertin, represent one of the strongest examples of globalization in sport. Every four years the Games bring together a great number of nations to showcase a variety of athletic competitions and cultural events as well as

Photo by Lucretious, courtsey © of stock.xchng iv

their participants. Over time the world's most prestigious sporting event has grown to the point of incomparable international exposure, worldwide audience appeal, and multicultural activities that draw the attention of virtually every demographic. The **Olym-**

pic Movement is a global phenomenon that transcends the boundaries of sport and culture and extends to education, politics, economy, and technology. Its goal is to create a peaceful and better world by using sport to educate youth. This is clearly manifested through the International Olympic Committee's (IOC) global promotional campaigns: in 2004, the campaign *Celebrate Humanity* highlighted the Olympic values of hope, dreams and inspirations, friendship, and fair play while in 2008 the IOC campaigned with the message *The Best of Us* to promote excellence, friendship, and respect. In hopes of not only promoting Olympic ideals but also engaging young people, IOC's campaign gearing up for the 2012 Olympics was titled *Show Your Best*.

The Olympic Movement consists of the International Olympic Committee, National Olympic Committees, Organizing Committees of the Olympic Games, International Federations, National Governing Bodies, and athletes. These parties work closely to promote the fundamental principles of **Olympism** and to effectively operate business functions vital to the continuity of the Movement. The Olympic Charter, which guides the functions and operations of the Olympic Movement, defines Olympism as "a philosophy of life, exalting and combining in a balanced whole the qualities of body, will and mind. Blending sport with culture and education, Olympism seeks to create a way of life based on the joy of effort, the educational value of good example, social responsibility and respect for universal fundamental ethical principles" (IOC, 2011, p. 10). These principles of Olympism are brought to life by the IOC through six areas of action, including Sport for All ("sport belongs to everyone"), sport and environment ("preserving precious resources"), education through sport ("developing body, will and mind"), women and sport ("promoting women's participation"), development through sport ("putting human beings first"), and peace through sport ("forging friendships among athletes") (International Olympic Committee, 2012e).

Heading the Olympic Movement is the **International Olympic Committee**, which was created in 1894 and serves as the supreme and exclusive authority of the Olympic Movement (IOC, 2012h). The IOC is an international non-governmental, non-profit organization with offices in Lausanne, Switzerland. Its main responsibilities are to protect and grow the Olympic Movement globally, to select host cities, and to oversee the celebration of the Olympic Games every four years to support the development of sport at different levels and to promote ethics, gender equality, education, and the well-being of athletes, and to ensure a positive legacy from the Games to the host cities and countries (IOC, 2012h). The IOC, which is governed by the **Olympic Charter**, exclusively owns the Olympic Games and marketing rights to all Olympic properties, namely the Olympic symbol, flag, motto, anthem, identifications, designations, emblems, flame and torches. It is also responsible for reviewing the program of all Summer and Winter Olympic competitions following each Olympiad and deciding on the core and additional sports that will be included in the program of upcoming Games.

The IOC is represented in individual countries by **National Olympic Committees** (NOCs) that are tasked with developing and promoting the Olympic Movement and the values of Olympism in their countries. In doing so, each NOC is responsible for creating opportunities for participation in sport in their country at all levels, training athletes and educating sport administrators, selecting a city that may submit a bid to host the Olympic Games, and preparing and sending delegations to the Olympic and Paralympic Games ("National Olympic Committees," 2012). Currently, there are 204 NOCs over five continents recognized by the IOC. The NOC for the US is the **United States Olympic Committee** (USOC), located in Colorado Springs, Colorado. **International Federations** (IFs) are international non-governmental organizations recognized by the IOC that are in charge of developing one or several sports worldwide. Their responsibilities include establishing eligibility criteria for their sport(s), consulting with the IOC on technical and other matters involving the Olympic Games, developing athletes, and organizing competitions such as world championships ("International Sports Federations," 2012). The IOC currently recognizes 32 IFs. Some of the most prominent IFs include FIFA (football), FIBA (basketball), IAAF (athletics), and FIG (gymnastics). IFs also work with **National Governing Bodies** (NGBs) that are in charge of developing and promoting a sport on a national level. Examples of NGBs in the US are USA Basketball, USA Football, and USA Track and Field.

The **Organizing Committee of the Olympic Games** (OCOG) is formed once a city is awarded the honor and responsibility of hosting the Olympic and Paralympic Games and is disbanded about two years following the completion of the Games. The OCOG along with the NOC of the host country enter into a written agreement with the IOC ("Host City Contract") whereby they commit to handling all operational aspects and the execution of the Olympic and Paralympic Games. This daunting task includes, but is not limited to, the construction of venues, fulfillment of transportation and accommodation needs, media authorizations, medical provisions, ticketing, solicitation of national sponsorships, and security provisions (IOC, 2012f). In 2013 there were four OCOGs in operation servicing the London 2012 Summer Games (LOCOG), the Sochi 2014 Winter Games (SOOC), the Rio 2016 Summer Games (ROCOG), and the PyeongChang 2018 Winter Games (POCOG).

The promotion of Olympic ideals is further supported by a number of **IOC commissions** (e.g., Athletes' Commission, Ethics Commission, Olympic Solidarity Commission, Medical Commission) and other properties affiliated with the Olympic Movement, such as the Court of Arbitration for Sport (CAS), the International Olympic Academy (IOA), the **International Paralympic Committee** (IPC), Special Olympics Inc. (SOI), the World Anti-Doping Agency (WADA), and the Youth Olympic Games (YOG). The IPC is the international governing body of the **Paralympic Movement** serving athletes with a physical impairment. It is a non-profit organization established in 1989 and located in Bonn, Germany. Similar to the IOC, the main responsibilities of the IPC are to preserve and promote the Paralympic values of courage, determination, inspiration and equality and to ensure the celebration of the Summer and Winter **Paralympic Games** (International Paralympic Committee, 2013).

As worldwide interest in the Olympic Games has grown, so has the desire of broadcasting agencies and multinational corporations to share in the Olympic glory. The IOC has capitalized on that interest by designing and implementing the **Olympic Marketing Program** that involves their broadcasting and sponsorship agreements, ticketing, and licensing. Through this program the IOC is able to ensure financial stability and independence for the Olympic Movement family as 90% of the revenues is distributed to the NOCs, IFs, and OCOGs and only 10% is used for the operation of the IOC (IOC, 2012b). Total IOC marketing revenues have experienced tremendous growth from $2.630 billion in 1993–1996 to $5.450 billion in 2005–2008. The single greatest revenue source for the IOC over the past three decades has been broadcasting agreements that, for the 2009–2012 quadrennium, produced an impressive $3.914 billion (from $2.570 four years earlier) (IOC, 2012c). For the United States, NBC spent $2.3 billion for the right to broadcast the 2004, 2006, and 2008 Olympic Games, and another $2.001 billion for the 2010 and 2012 Games ("The Authoritative," 2003). In 2001 the IOC created the **Olympic Broadcasting Services** (OBS) to ensure greater control over the quality and distribution of Olympic Games coverage. The OBS, which serves as the Olympic Broadcast Organization or Host Broadcaster for all Olympic Games, is responsible for providing content from the Olympics to all official IOC broadcast partners. London 2012 became for the IOC a breakthrough opportunity in traditional and new media with a record number of broadcast hours, coverage in over 200 countries and territories around the world, and reach over a global audience of 4.8 billion. Additionally, London 2012 offered the first ever live 3D coverage of any Olympics, live broadcast from IOC's own YouTube channel, and partnerships with various social media platforms calling the event "the first social media Olympics" (IOC, 2012a).

Olympic sponsorship agreements at the highest level are handled through **The Olympic Partner (TOP) Programme**, which was created in 1985 following the successful 1984 Los Angeles Summer Olympics. (OCOGs have the opportunity to sell sponsorships at a national/domestic level provided those sponsorships don't conflict with the IOC's already established partnerships.) The TOP program gives a limited number of companies *exclusive worldwide marketing rights* to associate with the Summer and Winter Olympic Games and with the Olympic brand properties over a period of at least four years. Recognizing the tremendous effect that Olympic sponsorship can have on building a global brand, companies pay a lofty fee for the chance to be associated with the world's premiere sporting event and the potential to reach a broad global audience. The total sponsorship revenue generated through these Worldwide Olympic Partners has increased exponentially since the inception of the program: TOP I (1985– 1988) delivered $96 million, a mere fraction of TOP VII's (2009–2012) whopping $957 million. Current TOP sponsors include Acer, Atos Origin, Coca-Cola, Dow, GE, McDonald's, Omega, Panasonic, Procter & Gamble, Samsung, and VISA (IOC, 2012d). As part of becoming Olympic sponsors, companies also invest heavily in activating their partnerships through a variety of promotional and communications initiatives. Two notable examples of Olympic sponsorship activation from the 2012 London Games were Coca-Cola's *Move to the Beat* campaign, an appeal to youth through music, and McDonald's *Champions of Play* program that engaged children worldwide while focusing on the values of healthy eating and fun play.

The Olympic Games are idiosyncratic in that they are as much a global phenomenon with worldwide reach as they are a local project. This contradictory reality demands that those involved in bidding or hosting the Olympic Games address strategic issues that extend to many sectors in the society including politics, economy, technology, transportation, sporting infrastructure, communication and media, culture and national representation, tourism, etc. Greece, a comparably small European country that hosted the 2004 Olympic Games, faced that challenge.

From London's 2012 Legacy to Rio's 2016 Agony

For most cities, countries, and governments, worldwide exposure and financial gains are the two most significant motives behind their decision to bid for the Olympic Games. However, as Athens, Greece was gearing up for 2004, it seemed to be fueled by slightly different motives. Being the birthplace of the Olympics gave the country of Greece a special attachment to the Olympic Movement that became a driving force behind the country's efforts to *Welcome Home* the world. But even through the widespread enthusiasm and celebrations there was no shortage of concern that the gigantic endeavor of hosting the Olympic Games seemed like perfect suicide for a small nation the size of Greece, at least in terms of finances and social policy. Threats of national bankruptcy, bailout plans, and repeated austerity measures imposed on the citizens of Greece amidst a global economic recession seem to suggest that critics of the 2004 Olympic Games might have been right.

London, on the other hand, has enjoyed more positive attention after hosting successful Olympic Games in the summer of 2012. And even though it is hard to outline the Games' legacy in a few lines, it is worth pointing to the government and lottery funding of £1 billion that Sport England, the UK grant-giving agency, has to invest on sport development in 2013–2017, the significant urban transformation benefits achieved, and the global attention garnered by the host city and country. Despite its principal objective to *Inspire a Generation* to get more involved in sport (which served as the key pledge of London's bid) and the £9.3 billion investment in hosting the Games, there is much more that needs to be done in post-Olympics England to make life in highly-populated British cities less sedentary. As the euphoria from London 2012 is drying out, voices join to remind that the struggle against limited opportunities for sport is still present as cuts in social services, poverty, and inequality are keeping people away from sport.

On the other side of the world, the city of Rio de Janeiro, Brazil is preparing for the 2016 Summer Olympic Games, the first ever to be held in a South American country. Brazil is an emerging market and one of the top ten economies in the world. In addition to hosting the Olympics, which is undoubtedly a gigantic undertaking, Brazil will also serve as host to the 2014 FIFA World Cup, the second largest mega-event in the world. The preparation for these mega-events is already underway and will involve huge investments of private and public resources. The potential for these events to stimulate further growth and prosperity in the country seems very promising, even if it is too early to delineate the actual economic and social impacts. On time completion of infrastructure projects has emerged as a major issue in the preparation for the Olympic Games, along with security and financing, and the agony for Rio is high both among local organizers and international sport stakeholders.

Challenges in the Olympic Movement

The Olympic Movement faces numerous challenges, not the least of which is doping control issues and over-commercialization. **Drug testing** at the Olympic Games has become a sophisticated and quite successful process, especially since the establishment of WADA in 1999. However, there will always be incidents of cheating that go undetected that threaten the ideal of "clean" and fair competitions. One of the biggest doping scandals in sport involving highly accomplished cyclist and Olympian Lance Armstrong resulted in the IOC condemning Armstrong's actions and reinforcing the organization's commitment to forcefully fight doping in sport. It is imperative that the IOC, in cooperation with its member nations, maintains upgraded techniques and technologies (e.g., blood passports), rigorous control of athletes in and out of competition, and strict measures across the board in order to protect the integrity and spirit of the Games.

The second issue, **over-commercialization**, is potentially as harmful for the IOC. Marketing studies have repeatedly documented the positive outcomes that multinational brands receive by associating with the Olympic ideals, but scarcely acknowledge the backlash that could result for the Olympic Movement. In hopes of containing commercialization and keeping the focus on the sport, the IOC has instituted the *Clean Field of Play* policy that prevents advertising or other branding displays on the field of play as well as in areas surrounding the Olympic venues. More needs to be done, though, to balance sponsors' commercial interests with the Olympic image. Interestingly, the IOC has been aggressive in protecting Olympic properties from unauthorized use as well as guarding the investment of sponsors from **ambush marketing**. In preparation for the London Games, the local government passed legislation to regulate immediate areas around the Olympic venues (up to 200 meters) and prevent the display of flyers, billboards, or other types of advertising including the clothing of spectators that might compete with official Olympic sponsors. In addition, LOCOG developed educational programs to inform businesses and the public about the proper use of Olympic symbols. Programs were also put in place to prevent the sale of counterfeit London 2012 merchandise, as well as unauthorized broadcasting of the Olympic Games (i.e., Infringement Monitoring Program and Internet Monitoring Program) (IOC, 2012g).

Another major issue that future Organizing Committees of the Olympic Games will face is **gigantism**. Over the years the Olympic Games have expanded significantly. The large number of participants (athletes, delegation members, media, and visitors) and the number of competitions create immense pressure for host cities, especially in the areas of security and infrastructure. Ineffectiveness in security is a huge liability and can prove most damaging for the IOC and the host country. The criticism of the security measures implemented by Sochi 2014 (e.g., spectator's pass) suggests that keeping a balance between ensuring safe Games and protecting personal privacy as well as preserving the Olympic experience might be a challenging balancing act. Furthermore, environmental concerns stemming from the magnitude of the event and the number of people involved cannot be ignored. The IOC has been increasingly engaged in **sustainability** initiatives both with Olympic host cities (e.g., waste management program in London) as well as organizations like the United Nations to identify ways in which to preserve natural resources and minimize the impact of the Games on the environment.

The responsibility of the IOC to raise awareness about social, political, and environmental issues facing the world and the ability of the Olympic Games to become a platform for discussion and change is certainly an interesting topic of debate. **Gender testing**, for example, is an issue that resurfaced in the Olympics with the success of South African middle-distance runner Caster Semenya and the debate of whether or not she was a female. The IOC is confronted with addressing inefficiencies in gender testing methods while ensuring the rights of athletes as well as fair play. Furthermore, the broader issue of **gender equity** in Olympic competition and sport in general is a cause the IOC is championing. Although the Olympic Movement has not yet fulfilled one of its most historical aims, to end war, it has experienced dramatic growth and attracted huge economic and political support from both the private and public sectors. To safeguard its future and further development, the IOC will have to be proactive and dynamic in addressing looming social and economic challenges.

INTERNATIONAL EXPANSION OF US SPORT

As the U.S. sport industry continues to mature, professional sport leagues are investigating growth possibilities through expansion into foreign markets and the development of new fans. International markets have become the source of not only talent, but also substantial revenue for the leagues through the signing of broadcasting deals, the sale of licensed merchandise, and partnerships with foreign-based sponsors. The recent technological and communications advances allow US-based sport organizations to reach new consumers almost anywhere in the world. Even though their choices for global expansion might vary, one thing is constant: U.S. professional sport leagues consider international expansion the cornerstone for their future growth. Evidence of this is their investment in international divisions and international offices to handle leagues' business ventures outside U.S. borders.

The following sections provide specific examples of initiatives that each of the four major leagues has undertaken to expand their reach in other countries and to grow their profits. Sport management students interested in pursuing a career in the international sport setting must realize that U.S. leagues' efforts worldwide provide avenues for employment, as these properties depend on qualified professionals with an understanding of the sport industry as well as the global market to design global strategies and successfully execute international programs.

Major League Baseball (MLB)

For baseball fans in the United States and in many countries around the world, October means one thing: the World Series. But are these games between the two best MLB teams a true *World* Series? After all, the competition involves teams from North America only. Nevertheless, the games could be considered a *World* Series if one takes into account the number of international players on MLB team rosters. At the start of the 2013 season, 241 of the 856 MLB players, or about 28%, were born outside the United

States ("Opening Day," 2013). Another indication that North American baseball is becoming a global product is the widespread interest in and delivery of the game. In 2013 MLB games were broadcasted in 233 countries and territories in 17 different languages ("MLB International," 2013).

Major League Baseball has had an international presence for at least a century, mainly with exhibition games and tours as well as spring training, preseason games, and regular season games held outside North America. The league has held games in Japan, Mexico, Puerto Rico, and even Cuba; in March 2008 the Dodgers and Padres played the league's first ever exhibition games in China. Furthermore, the MLB has held the Major League Baseball Japan All-Star Series in Japan since 1986, and with baseball stars like Yu Darvish, Hiroki Kuroda, and Ichiro Suzuki having successful baseball careers in the US, the popularity of MLB in Japan has increased immensely. MLB held the fourth Japan Opening Series with the Mariners and Athletics playing the first two games of their 2012 season in Japan.

MLB established Major League Baseball International (MLBI) in 1989 and operates offices in Beijing, London, New York, Sydney, and Tokyo that work to grow the game of baseball and MLB's business globally. In addition to competitions, the league sponsors grassroots development and promotional programs all around the world. Examples include the *Envoy Program* (1991) that sends baseball coaches to non-traditional baseball countries around the globe in order to teach the game to native players, coaches, and umpires; the *Elite Camps* (1999); and the *Baseball Festival* (1995), which tours the world and promotes the game of baseball in a fun atmosphere ("Development Initiatives," 2008).

Scheduling conflicts and differences in drug-testing policies had kept MLB players from competing in the Olympic Games. However, the benefits of an international competition were not lost by baseball officials, especially following the IOC's decision in 2005 to remove baseball from the Olympic program beginning with the 2012 Summer Games. In 2005 plans were announced for a **Baseball World Cup Tournament**, a tournament that would be sanctioned by the International Baseball Federation and created jointly by baseball leagues and players' associations around the globe. The first **World Baseball Classic** (WBC) came to life in March of 2006 and included 16 teams: Australia, Canada, China, Chinese Taipei, Cuba, the Dominican Republic, Italy, Japan, Korea, Mexico, the Netherlands, Panama, Puerto Rico, South Africa, US, and Venezuela. Games were hosted in seven different venues in Japan, Puerto Rico, and the US and delivered an impressive 737,112 sold tickets (Bloom, 2008). At the end of the competition, Japan defeated Cuba 10-6 in a game played in Petco Park in San Diego to become baseball's first true *World* Champion. Since then there have been two more WBC tournaments in 2009 and 2013, with plans to hold future tournaments on a four-year cycle. The success of the WBC tournaments in terms of fan attendance and TV ratings serves as evidence that bringing high-caliber players from all over the world together in one global competition is an attractive proposition and a significant vehicle for the worldwide expansion of the sport of baseball.

National Basketball Association (NBA)

Basketball is an Olympic sport that is played worldwide in structured leagues and prestigious tournaments (e.g., Euroleague Basketball). In the 1992 Summer Olympic Games held in Barcelona, Spain, millions of basketball fans around the world were mesmerized by the stars of the first ever "Dream Team." Seen by many as a landmark in the league's international expansion, the participation of professional players in the Olympics provided the NBA with a vehicle to showcase to the world the talent available in the basketball Mecca. Some things have changed since then. Sub-par performances and game results have "embarrassed" NBA superstars and have showcased the strength of other countries in the sport. However, one thing has remained constant: the NBA's focus on developing and exploiting new markets and its unparalleled strength in creating new, loyal fans. Currently the league operates international offices in 15 markets worldwide that handle local TV and sponsorship deals and promote the NBA brand in their respective markets. All international efforts are overseen by the NBA Global division.

The NBA is the frontrunner among U.S. professional sport leagues in terms of their success in building a global brand. Since 1988 the league has held numerous exhibition, preseason, and regular season games in Europe, the Middle East, Latin America, and Asia. In 2006 the NBA launched its **NBA Europe Live Tour**, with four teams holding training camps abroad and competing against each other and against European basketball clubs in multiple European cities and countries (NBA, 2008). The NBA is taking full advantage of the fact that the last few years its team rosters have boasted some 70 to 80 international players, many of them superstars, who are seen as heroes in their native countries and whose careers in the US are followed closely by their countrymen. Conveniently, the selection of teams and locations of the league's international competitions reflects an effort to match the international players on the teams' rosters with their native countries, bringing Tony Parker (San Antonio Spurs) back to France, Pau Gasol (while a player of the Memphis Grizzlies) back to Spain, and Nene (Washington Wizards) back to Brazil. For the 2013–2014 preseason the league has made plans for eight NBA teams to play eight games in six countries, including first-ever preseason games in Brazil and the Philippines (NBA, 2013). In addition to the games, the NBA invests in these global markets via community improvements led by its *NBA Cares* initiative and a variety of other programs, such as *Basketball Without Borders*, through which players interact with the fans and help develop the game of basketball.

So, where does the NBA stand today? Is the league's investment in global initiatives providing a return? The answer is *yes*. There are many indications that the league's international efforts are returning a profit: NBA games and shows are televised in 216 countries and territories around the globe in 46 languages, adding a notable portion to the league's broadcasting revenues. The league's official website, NBA.com, which is conveniently available in many different languages besides English, averages more than 35 million page views daily, with more than half of those from outside North America. The league and its teams and players have an impressive 240 million global followers on social media, making the NBA the leading professional sport league on social media. In addition, a significant percentage of the league's merchandise sales come from overseas as NBA merchandise is sold in 125,000 stores in 100 countries around the world (Euroleague Basketball, 2012).

One market that is rapidly developing for the NBA is China. In June of 2002, audiences witnessed what may be considered by many the single most important development for the further global expansion of the NBA: the first ever selection of an international player, Yao Ming of China, as the Number 1 draft pick of the NBA. Ming's move to the United States and his career with the Houston Rockets created a chain of positive outcomes both for his franchise and the league as a whole, including a lucrative naming rights deal for the Rockets' Toyota Center, thousands of Chinese Rockets' fans, and more national and regional television deals in the country that holds 1.36 billion people, over a seventh of the world's population. More recently, the NBA is working to expand its reach to the fast-growing market of India, which is Asia's third largest economy (behind China and Japan) and home to 1.27 billion people. An NBA office in Mumbai, regular broadcast of NBA games, community events, and a visit from Commissioner David Stern are examples of the league's initiatives in one of the world's most promising markets (Lombardo, 2013).

Many are looking to see what the NBA will do next. There has been an ongoing discussion regarding expansion of the NBA to countries outside North America by placing an NBA team or an NBA division in Europe. However, the league has refrained from acting on these discussions. The lack of adequate facility infrastructure in Europe, competition from established European leagues and franchises, and other financial considerations such as tax rates could pose significant challenges should the NBA decide to introduce a European division. But even if an international division might not be in the league's near-future, be on the lookout for NBA teams holding more regular season games abroad, an NBA All-Star team touring overseas, and more NBA stores and restaurants opening in European and Asian cities.

National Football League (NFL)

Images of tailgating, Thanksgiving Day games, and Super Bowl Sunday are enough to get any American sport fan excited. However, these words have limited meaning outside U.S. borders. Being an American sport, and not an Olympic sport, with more than 95% of its players born in the US (Wertheim, 2004), the NFL is presented with a greater challenge when considering international expansion. And even though the 2013 NFL draft included three international first-round picks, there is still much work to be done. There is little doubt that any effort to create a global market for the NFL across seas would have to start with the education of audiences and the engagement of local stakeholders.

Nevertheless, that has not stopped the league from spreading the word about the sport that captivates an entire nation from August to January every year. The NFL has held exhibition, preseason, and regular season games in a number of countries around the world (e.g., Canada, England, Germany, Japan, Mexico) since 1986, when the first **American Bowl** was played in London, England (NFL, 2008a). In 2005 the Arizona Cardinals met the San Francisco 49ers in Mexico City for what was the first ever regular season game to be played outside of the US. The 2007 season marked the first time that a regular season NFL game was played outside of North America, with the New York Giants defeating the Miami Dolphins 13-10 in London's Wembley Stadium in front of a sellout crowd of 81,176. Since 2007 the NFL has played a game in London every season as part of its *International Series*, with plans to return to Wembley Stadium for two regular season games in 2013.

The most aggressive international move to date made by the NFL came in 1991 when the league launched the **World League of American Football** (WLAF) that marked the first time a U.S.-based professional sport league expanded to Europe. According to former NFL Commissioner Paul Tagliabue, that extension league provided a platform for the NFL to showcase the game of American Football to those outside the US (Madkour & Kaplan, 2003). In addition, the international league was seen as grounds to develop talent amongst players, officials, and management. In its original structure, the WLAF consisted of 10 teams from North America and Europe, and involved weekly intercontinental play from March through May. The extension league ceased operations after two seasons, and was reintroduced in 1995 in European cities only. In 1998 the league changed its name to **NFL Europe**, and in 2006 the league's name was modified to **NFL Europa**. In its latest form, NFL Europa consisted of six teams, five in Germany and one in the Netherlands. However, in June 2007, under the leadership of new Commissioner Roger Goodell, the NFL decided to disband its European league that was reportedly losing $30 million per year in favor of a different international strategy, one focused on playing regular season games abroad (potentially adding a seventeenth game to the regular season NFL schedule) and utilizing new technology to develop and reach fans worldwide ("NFL Folds," 2007).

Rising interest in the NFL in the form of increasing television viewership and amateur sport participation have made the UK an attractive expansion site for the NFL (Murphy, 2012). Beyond the UK, the NFL reaches markets worldwide through broadcasting of its games. For the 2005 season, for example, NFL programming was received in 234 countries and territories worldwide in 31 languages (NFL, 2008b). In addition, Super Bowl match-ups have attracted a growing international audience of over 100 million on average, with the majority of international viewers from Canada and Mexico ("The Super Bowl," 2013). Perhaps it will be a while before the NFL decides to place a team outside the US or host the Super Bowl in a foreign city. But there is no doubt that investment in international grassroots efforts assisted by digital media and improvements in travel and technology will continue to make foreign markets a source of profit for the league.

National Hockey League (NHL)

Ice hockey is played all over the world, with established and internationally recognized championships held in the Czech Republic, Finland, Russia, and Sweden, among other countries. Although it has been an Olympic sport since 1924, it wasn't until the mid-1990s that the NHL and the International Ice Hockey Federation (IIHF) agreed to allow NHL players to participate in the 1998 Nagano Winter Olympic Games in hopes of increasing the sport's profile and worldwide interest (Lapointe, 1997). Hockey fans around the world will tune in again for the upcoming 2014 Sochi Winter Olympic Games to enjoy performances by NHL stars, despite existing league concerns regarding player travel and insurance as well as media coverage (Brigidi, 2013).

Of the four U.S. major professional sport leagues, the NHL has the highest percentage of players born outside North America, with about 33% of its players originating from countries other than the US (NHL, 2012). To reflect the increasing number of foreign-born players on team rosters, in 1998 the NHL changed its traditional All-Star Game format and introduced a North America *vs.* The World All-Stars competition—until 2003 when the league went back to its classic East *vs.* West format. The international flavor of its rosters has provided a unique opportunity for the NHL to promote its product worldwide, especially in the native countries of its stars. NHL television programming is distributed in more than 160 countries around the world while international sales of NHL licensed merchandise exceed $1 billion (NHL, 2012).

As early as 1938, NHL teams played exhibition games in Europe. Building on ice hockey's global appeal, in 1989 the Calgary Flames and Washington Capitals held part of their training camps in (then) Czechoslovakia and Sweden, followed by preseason games in the (former) Soviet Union, while the league has also held exhibition and preseason games in Austria, England, Finland, and Germany, and a number of other European destinations (Pelletier, 2007). In 1997 the NHL opened its regular season in Tokyo, Japan (Pelletier, 2007). It was London's turn in 2007 to host the Los Angeles Kings and Anaheim Ducks as they competed in the first NHL regular season game to be held in Europe (Burnside, 2007). As part of the NHL Challenge Series, the Boston Bruins faced the Belfast Giants in Northern Ireland in 2010.

In 2004, four European cities and three North American cities held the **World Cup of Hockey**, an international tournament including eight of the world's ice hockey powerhouses. This tournament, which was a joint effort of the NHL and NHLPA, was only the second of its kind (the first World Cup of Hockey was held in 1996) (Bernstein, 2004). Besides the Olympics and IIHF-sanctioned world championships, other international ice hockey competitions over the years have included the Summit Series (1972), the Challenge Cup (1979), Rendez-Vous (1987), and Canada Cup (1976, 1981, 1984, 1987, and 1991) ("World Cup," 2003).

The examples described in this section indicate that the potential for growth in foreign markets is immense. However, this growth does not come without risks. In his overview of the global sport industry, Schaaf (2004) points to five considerations that sport organizations need to keep in mind when looking to become global brands:

(1) geography, (2) competition from existing events, (3) perception, (4) patience, and (5) talent. Schaaf (2004) suggests that international expansion could be hindered by geographical and time constraints, as well as the challenge of creating meaningful competitions for fans that are already loyal to existing events. He also stresses the importance of having business relationships that will give the perception of legitimacy to a new international initiative, patience from owners and/or other investors, and, finally, the cooperation from the actual players in securing a successful venture.

Challenges in the International Expansion of U.S. Sport

Even though international expansion is a promising avenue for future growth, there are some inherent challenges for U.S. sport organizations to consider when planning their international initiatives, not the smallest of which is **competition** from existing leagues and events in the markets where they are expanding. This becomes especially relevant when the leagues are considering the creation of international divisions. Along with this come **financial considerations**. Given its financial losses, it is questionable whether the WLAF/NFL Europe/NFL Europa would have been in business for that long without the backing of the National Football League. The challenge lies in balancing the need for growth with the financial stability of the leagues' operations. The example of Disney-owned ESPN's challenge to maintain a presence in the UK market after losing the rights to significant sport properties is a cautionary tale of the financial risk involved in those types of expansion ventures (Plunkett & Sweney, 2013). Finally, another major concern for the global expansion of U.S. sport that should not be overlooked is the possible **resistance** from foreign nations. The tragedy of September 11, 2001 and the events that followed were a clear indication that sentiments about the "American way" can vary greatly throughout the world. As LaFeber (1999) points out, US-driven efforts for global expansion might be viewed not as a form of globalization but rather as Americanization. Being sensitive to local cultures and taking into account national idiosyncrasies could make for a more successful international expansion.

THE EUROPEAN SPORT INDUSTRY

The organization of sport in Europe is based on a broad network of European sport governing bodies [e.g., Union of European Football Associations (UEFA), FIBA Europe] and umbrella sport organizations [e.g., European Olympic Committees (EOC), European University Sports Association (EUSA)] that aim to promote sports across the continent. These organizations are right holders of a huge number of major sporting events held regularly in European countries, including European championships in all recognized sports and various categories (e.g., Euroleague Basketball). In addition, National Governing Bodies of the various sports (e.g., Hellenic Basketball Federation) operate in each country and, along with the National Olympic Committees and state or non-governmental umbrella organizations, make up the sporting structure at a state level. Historically, however, it has been the sport clubs (e.g., Manchester United, Real Madrid) that have formed the backbone of the European sport system. Most often these are voluntary associations working to satisfy the needs and interests of their members (Rubingh & Broeke, 1998).

The current decade has brought a number of major sporting events to Europe, the most notable of those being the 2012 Winter Youth Olympic Games in Innsbruck, Austria; the 2012 Summer Olympic Games in London, UK; the UEFA 2012 EURO in Poland and Ukraine; and the 2013 Summer University Games in Kazan, Russia. A 2010 study commissioned by the European Commission on the contribution of sport to the growth of the **European Union-27** (EU-27) economy and to employment estimated the direct effect of the sport sector at 1.76% of the total EU Gross Value Added (or €173.86 billion). Moreover, the total direct and induced effects of the sport sector amounted to 2.98% of the EU Gross Value Added (or €294.36 billion). The same study reported that the European sport industry was responsible for 3.51% of EU employment, which translates to 7.378.671 jobs (direct and indirect effects) (European Commission, 2012).

The growth evident throughout the continent has given the European sport industry a distinctive position within the international sport industry. The EU included sport as a key element in its formulated 2004 Constitution and, based on the Lisbon Treaty, is in the process of formulating concrete sport policy on three subjects mainly: (1) the societal role of sport, (2) the economic dimension of sport, and (3) the governance of sport (European Commission, 2013a). In 2011, the need for developing a European dimension in sport was well established by the European Commission, which adopted an active role in supporting and supplementing its members' sport policy measures. By building on the 2007 White Paper on Sport, the Commission currently works on formulating concrete action in relation to a number of key issues including the fight

Photo courtesy © Andy Gillentine

against doping, health enhancement through sport, financial sustainability in sport, sport development and employability, good governance, and sport competition integrity (European Commission, 2013b).

The European Union with the 27 countries-members has provided a platform for the exchange of goods, players, and capital in relation to sport. The 1995 **Bosman ruling** by the European Court of Justice, which established free agency for out-of-contract players, has been considered a landmark decision with significant impact on the structure, development, and economics of professional football (soccer) clubs throughout Europe (Dobson & Gerrard, 1999). The freedom of contract significantly enhanced the transfer opportunities of professional football players in Europe and created millionaires who have more control than ever over their sporting career (Szymanski & Kuypers, 1999). As the EU enters in a prolonged period of economic uncertainty, issues of financial sustainability, the interaction between business and sport, and the significance of sport as economic activity seem to call for more thoughtful and collaborative action. As more forces join to keep the EU together, the role of sport in cultural integration and state equality becomes more prevalent than ever before in European history. So far sport has proven that it can be a stabilizer in the unionization process of the EU. Hopefully it can continue to serve as the platform on which to pursue social objectives by encouraging European cultures to come close to each other in this joint European effort.

Football in Europe

Over the past fifteen years there have been dramatic developments in the European football industry. The 2011 Deloitte and Touche annual review estimated that the total European football market for 2009–2010 grew by 4% reaching the amount of €16.3 billion (approximately US$15.7 billion) despite the tough economic conditions on the continent. More recent figures for 2011–2012 demonstrate another strong year in terms of revenue generation for the so-called "big five" European leagues (i.e., Premier League, UK; Bundesliga, Germany; La Liga, Spain; Serie A, Italy; and Ligue 1, France) as revenues grew by 2% reaching €8.6 billion (Deloitte, 2012). Among those five properties, the English Premier League remains the highest revenue generating league with €2.5 billion (2010–2011), surpassing Germany's Bundesliga, Europe's second best revenue regenerating league, by €769 million (Deloitte, 2012). The top 20 earning football clubs contribute over 25% (or €4.8 billion) of the total European football market, with Real Madrid reporting a 7% increase in the club's 2011–2012 revenues of €513 million. Data indicate that most top clubs continue to generate significant revenues through TV rights fees, gate receipts, and regional and international commercial partnerships, such as Manchester United's world-record shirt sponsorship deal with Chevrolet/General Motors worth $559 million over seven years set to begin in 2014 (Deloitte, 2013). This provides strong evidence that European football is growing in commercial terms and, consistent with the U.S. model, clubs are becoming profit-maximizing corporations (Drewes, 2003).

Moreover, the UEFA European Football Championship, most commonly referred to as **EURO**, is another clear indicator of the growth of European football. This tournament is considered the third largest sporting event in the world based on viewership, following FIFA's World Cup and the Summer Olympic Games ("A Whole New," 2008). The **UEFA EURO 2012** tournament, hosted jointly by Poland and Ukraine, scored record TV audiences as the final game in Kiev between Spain and Italy attracted 299 million individuals. This is a significant increase in ratings from the 237 million viewers who had tuned in to watch the EURO 2008 final match between Spain and Germany held in Vienna, Austria.

Professional football clubs in Europe vary significantly in terms of their legal structure and ownership. For example, the typical German club is a nonprofit entity with a large number of supporters sharing part of its ownership; whereas a few Italian clubs are often controlled by major companies (e.g., Juventus, AC Milan) (Hoehn & Szymanski, 1999). In Spain, the professional clubs are private companies, often with a single owner who works together with local and regional authorities to overcome financial problems. This is because most clubs, like Barcelona and Real Madrid, are associations with political power resulting from the large number of their members who are also fans (Garcia & Rodriguez, 2003). In France, clubs can vary from associations to corporations, while in Greece clubs are treated as commercial corporations.

In spite of the complexity in the legal structure of European football, many clubs have increasingly looked to the financial markets to supply investment capital. For example, Manchester United, a club that stands as a striking case of a business-like operation, represents one of the most attractive stock market investments, generating significant profits. Another good example of a club with global appeal is Real Madrid. By acquiring some of the world's greatest players (Beckham, Zidane, Raul, Figo, and Ronaldo) over the years, Real Madrid achieved vast international exposure and created new fans around the globe.

The European football model differs significantly from the American model in that it is based on a league hierarchy and the relegation rule, which allows changes in the clubs that are eligible to compete at various levels (Drewes, 2003). The right to play in the **UEFA Champions League** and the **UEFA Cup** is linked to the clubs' sporting performance in their national competitions, which again involve a relegation system. However, the most contemporary challenge for the European football industry is to come closer to the American model of professional leagues. In one such effort, 14 power football clubs from seven European countries (e.g., Ajax, Manchester United, Milan, Real Madrid) came together in 2000 to form the **G-14**, an organization of clubs that served as a negotiating partner with FIFA and UEFA on behalf of the clubs and their players, and which also explored plans for the creation of a closed Super League. Although the G-14 was disbanded in 2008, it was replaced by the **European Club Association** (ECA), an organization representing the interests of over 100 European football clubs.

Challenges in the European Sport Industry

As the European Union expands in geographical and political terms, so do the challenges related to the continent's sport industry. As described earlier, the European sport industry has special characteristics in terms of how sport is structured, developed, and governed in different countries. This raises major concerns over *the role of the European Union* and its ability to intervene and promote pan-European rules and regulations in issues such as club licensing, broadcasting rights, professional players' transfer and salaries, anti-doping, youth sportsmanship, and others.

In November of 2007 the Commission of European Communities published a **"White Paper on Sport"** that explored the social, economic, and organizational dimensions of sport and offered suggestions on how sport can be used to address challenges that are present in European society. According to the document, "The Commission acknowledges the essential role of sport in European society, in particular when it needs to bring itself closer to citizens and to tackle issues that matter directly to them" (Commission of European Communities, 2007, p. 2). Some of the issues discussed in this White Paper include public health, doping, integration, racism, violence, movement of players, protection of young athletes from exploitation, and corruption. The Commission has also highlighted the need for sport organizations "to maintain and develop a sustainable financing model" that will ensure their long-term support (Commission of European Communities, 2007, p. 12).

Another challenge facing European football is the application of the UEFA **Financial Fair Play Regulations** (FFP Regulations) that were first approved in May 2010, updated in 2012, and are currently implemented for a period of three years in order to be assessed for the first time during 2013–2014. The main objectives of this newly developed concept are (1) to enforce rationality in European club football finances and to protect long-term club viability, (2) to decrease pressure on players' salaries and discourage clubs from overspending, and (3) to encourage long-term investments in infrastructure, training facilities, and community schemes. The UEFA FFP Regulations aim to ensure that clubs balance their books and avoid spending beyond their means in search for fast success; otherwise clubs will face tough sanctions. Given the global economic austerity and the accumulated debts of many European football clubs, UEFA stresses that both the FFP Regulations and the UEFA **Club Licensing System** are essential proactive steps for protecting the future health and viability of Europe's most popular and most loved sport.

Interestingly, UEFA's break-even rules, which came to application in the 2012 and 2013 financial seasons, have found a great supporter in England's Football League. The League took similar action in February 2013 by introducing the British version of FFP Regulations for the Championship League and the **Salary Cost Management Protocol** for Leagues 1 and 2. Although the break-even aspect is not yet present in this framework, the Football League sets its own rules for ensuring self-sustainability at a club level, including measures for acceptable losses and owners' guarantee needed, salary and transfer fee control restrictions, and incentives for sensible infrastructure investments. However, before these financial regulations are fully adopted by European football clubs, UEFA has to defend them against complaints that they are anti-competitive. According to Jean Louis Dupont, the lawyer who represented Jean-Marc Bosman in 1995, a case has been filed with the European Commission arguing that the new UEFA measures restrict the amount of investments a club owner can make to improve team performance.

CAREER OPPORTUNITIES IN
THE GLOBAL SPORT MARKETPLACE

The globalization trend is evident in today's sport world, particularly the increasing expansion of U.S. sport organizations internationally, providing numerous career opportunities for sport management professionals. Job titles such as Director of International Sport Marketing, Vice President of Global Sponsorships, Senior Vice President of International Division, Vice President of International Television and Media, and Director of Global Market Development are common among those involved in international sport.

However, some of these career lines might not be obvious choices. This section outlines some areas that students interested in a career in international sport should examine.

1. **The Olympic Movement.** Many opportunities for a career in the international sport setting are related to the Olympic Movement and its organizations. In the US, this means becoming involved with the National Olympic Committee, the USOC, or any one of the National Governing Bodies (e.g., USA Basketball, USA Gymnastics, USA Track & Field, etc.). Another avenue is to pursue an internship or job with the International Olympic Committee (IOC) or the International Paralympic Committee (IPC), an International Federation (e.g., FIFA), or even any of the Olympic Games Organizing Committees, nationally or internationally (e.g., VANOC, LOCOG). A majority of NGBs place their job announcements on **www.teamworkonline.com**.

2. **U.S. Professional Leagues.** Each of the four major professional sport leagues is very active in global initiatives and even has an international division to handle that part of their business. Whether it is in licensing, television, the Internet, events, or any one of their international offices, there are a number of opportunities through the leagues for someone interested in a career in international sport.

3. **U.S. Professional Teams.** With the increasing number of international players on the rosters of U.S. professional teams, franchises require people who can assist those international players (e.g., interpreters), or can help the organization capitalize on the opportunities that are presented. For example, the signing of Yao Ming in Houston in 2002 created a unique opportunity to reach out to the Asian population in the area, and also deal with Chinese organizations (e.g., sponsors, television stations) interested in forming business relationships with the franchise.

4. **Sport Management Agencies.** US-based sport marketing and management agencies have long conducted business on a global scale. Companies such as IMG and Octagon each have international divisions and offices worldwide. Becoming involved in one of those offices could be the avenue to an international career in sport.

5. **Athletic Apparel and Footwear Companies.** For those interested in entering the apparel and footwear side of the industry, there are opportunities for an international career. US-based companies Nike and Reebok do business worldwide, from production and distribution to product promotion and sponsoring of interna-

tional events. Furthermore, foreign-based companies like Adidas and Puma have offices in the US and actively promote their products in North America. Working for one of those companies can provide the opportunity to be stationed overseas and pursue a career internationally. Take, for example, Puma. On its website the company advertises positions available not only in the US but also in Belgium, Chile, Hong Kong, Spain, Sweden, and Vietnam.

6. **U.S. Companies with International Sponsorships.** In 2002, *SportsBusiness Journal* published a special report on international sport. In that issue, it was reported that at the time there were 30 U.S. companies with overseas sports sponsorships and 65 overseas companies with U.S. sports sponsorships ("Overseas Companies," 2002; "U.S. Companies," 2002). Companies such as Coca-Cola, MasterCard, McDonald's, and Xerox have sponsored international sport organizations and events (e.g., Olympic Games) for decades. Consequently, they require personnel to handle those relationships. Although not always an obvious choice, this could be a great way to become involved in international aspects of the sport industry.

So, how does one prepare for such a career? What are those skills that will make you an attractive candidate for such a position? Here are some of the qualifications that employers will be looking for when hiring for a position in the international sector of the sport marketplace:

- **Educational background in international sport management.** Even if the program in which the student is enrolled does not offer a course related to international sport management, the student could take general business administration and international studies courses covering international business affairs.

- **Practical experience in international sport.** Especially if one is in the beginning of their career, the most appropriate way to obtain some experience in international sport might be through internships with an international sport organization or a U.S. organization doing business in other countries (Masteralexis & McDonald, 1997).

- **Foreign language skills.** The knowledge of a second (and even third) language enhances the appeal of a candidate when being considered for a position that involves dealing with people who speak another language. Although one would be advised to avoid doing business in a foreign language unless they are fluent, a basic knowledge of a foreign language could help form a warm relationship with international business partners (Gillentine, Goldfine, & Orejan, 2004; Gillentine & Orejan, 2003; Masteralexis & McDonald, 1997).

- **Knowledge and proficiency in new media.** As sport becomes more global, advances in technology and communications like the Internet, satellite television, international cell phones, and social media become more commonplace. A student preparing for a career in international sport should be knowledgeable about such platforms and able to incorporate them into their communications and business practices.

- **Cultural sensitivity and the ability to adapt to other cultures.** An international sport manager should be able to effectively communicate and work with partners from different parts of the world and also adapt to various working environments. Openness and sensitivity to other cultures are essential skills. For example, calling the winning team of the NFL Super Bowl or the NBA Finals a "World Champion" is not only inaccurate but potentially offensive, especially to non-Americans, and could be interpreted as shortsightedness or even arrogance. Without a doubt, a great way to develop cultural sensitivity would be to live in another country. But since that is not always possible, participating in a study abroad experience or a student exchange program could provide one with an understanding of cultural nuances and with a tolerance for differences in cultures. Other ways to obtain cultural training would be through university courses (e.g., history, geography, and world politics) or through regular interaction with people from other cultures.
- **Willingness to travel and/or relocate to another country.** Flexibility is important when working in the sport industry. It becomes even more important when one is involved in the international sector because spending a great deal of time overseas might be a large component of one's job description.

SUMMARY

- Over the past two decades we have witnessed significant movement and expansion in our industry; sport is becoming a global business. This globalization is facilitated by technological advances as well as administrative, political, and social developments worldwide.
- The Olympic Movement consists of the International Olympic Committee (IOC), National Olympic Committees (NOCs), Organizing Committees of the Olympic Games (OCOGs), International Federations (IFs), National Governing Bodies (NGBs), and the athletes and is responsible for the promotion of Olympic values and the regular celebration of the Summer and Winter Olympic Games. The Olympic Movement has experienced tremendous growth not only in participation and attendance figures, but also in broadcasting and sponsorship revenue.
- U.S. professional sport leagues (MLB, NBA, NFL, and NHL) are reaching consumers in new markets by holding games, tours, and clinics internationally. In addition, the increasing number of foreign players participating in US-based leagues has created inroads for expansion in those players' native countries through lucrative broadcasting, sponsorship, and licensing agreements.
- The structure of European sport is based on European sport governing bodies (e.g., UEFA) and umbrella organizations that promote the growth of sport throughout the continent. European sport differs from the league-based organization of U.S. sport; sport clubs (e.g., Manchester United) operate within a league hierarchy and relegation rules.
- Opportunities for a career in international sport exist with the Olympic Movement properties (e.g., IOC, USOC), with U.S. professional leagues and teams,

sport management agencies (e.g., IMG), athletic apparel and footwear companies, and with corporations involved in international sponsorships.

- For those considering a career in the global sport industry, an educational foundation in international business, practical experience internationally, foreign language skills, proficiency in new media, cultural sensitivity, an ability to adapt to other cultures, and a willingness to travel or relocate to another country are some of the skills needed to be successful.

Suggested Reading

Fairley, S., & Lizandra, M. (2012). International sport. In L.P. Masteralexis, C.A. Barr, & M.A. Hums (Eds.), *Principles and practice of sport management* (4th ed.; pp. 187–220). Sudbury, MA: Jones and Bartlett Publishers.

Fay, T., Velez, L., & Parks, J.B. (2011). A North American perspective on international sport. In P.M. Pedersen, J.B. Parks, J. Quarterman, & L.Thibault (Eds.), *Contemporary sport management* (4th ed.; pp. 392–413). Champaign, IL: Human Kinetics.

Foer, F. (2010). *How soccer explains the world: An unlikely theory of globalization.* New York, NY: HarperCollins Publishers.

Giulianotti, R., & Robertson, R. (2007). *Globalization and sport.* Oxford, UK: Blackwell Publishing.

Hums, M.A., & MacLean, J. C. (2004). *Governance and policy in sport organizations.* Scottsdale, AZ: Holcomb Hathaway, Publishers, Inc.

LaFeber, W. (1999). *Michael Jordan and the new global capitalism.* New York, NY: W. W. Norton & Company, Inc.

Li, M., MacIntosh, E., & Bravo, G. (2012). *International sport management.* Champaign, IL: Human Kinetics.

Maguire, J. (1999). *Global sport: Identities, societies, civilizations.* Cambridge, UK: Polity Press.

Riordan, J., & Krüger, A. (1999). *The international politics of sport in the 20th century.* New York, NY: Routledge.

Rubingh, B., & Broeke, A. (1998). The European sports club system. In L.P. Masteralexis, C. A. Barr, & M. A. Hums (Eds.), *Principles and practices of sport management* (pp. 195–207). Gaithersburg, MD: Aspen Publishers, Inc.

Schaaf, P. (2004). *Sports, Inc.: 100 years of sports business.* Amherst, NY: Prometheus Books.

Senn, A. E. (1999). *Power, politics, and the Olympic Games.* Champaign, IL: Human Kinetics.

Thoma, J. E., & Chalip, L. (1996). *Sport governance in the global community.* Morgantown, WV: Fitness Information Technology.

Westerbeek, H., & Smith, A. (2003). *Sport business in the global marketplace.* New York, NY: Palgrave Macmillan.

References

A whole new ball game: The corporate winners and losers in the quest for footballing glory. (2008). *CNBC European Business.* Retrieved from http://www.cnbc.com/id/19794221

Bernstein, A. (2004). NHL, union team up to fill World Cup roster. *Street & Smith's SportsBusiness Journal, 6*(39), 4.

Bloom, B.M. (2008, March 23). Inaugural Classic was . . . a classic. *The Official Site of Major League Baseball: News.* Retrieved from http://mlb.mlb.com/news/article.jsp?ymd=20080323&content_id=2453253&fext=.jsp&c_id=mlb

Brigidi, M. (2013). Sochi Olympics 2014: NHL "proceeding under the assumption" players will play, says Bill Daly. *Sbnation.com.* Retrieved from http://www.sbnation.com/nhl/2013/5/10/4318312/sochi-olympics-2014-nhl-player-participation

Burnside, S. (2007). By traveling to London, Ducks, Kings taking one for the team. *Sports.espn.go.com.* Retrieved from http://sports.espn.go.com/nhl/preview2007/columns/story?columnist=burnside_scott&id=3036914

Commission of European Communities. (2007). *White Paper on Sport.* Brussels, Belgium: Author.

Deloitte & Touche. (2012). *The annual review of football finance 2011: New rules, narrow margins.* United Kingdom: Sport Business Group, Deloitte & Touche LLP.

Deloitte & Touche. (2013). *Captains of industry football money league.* United Kingdom: Sport Business Group, Deloitte & Touche LLP.

Development initiatives. (2008). *The Official Site of Major League Baseball: International: Feature.* Retrieved from http://mlb.com/mlb/international/index.jsp?feature=development.

Dobson, S., & Gerrard, B. (1999). The determination of player transfer fees in English professional soccer. *Journal of Sport Management, 13,* 259–279.

Drewes, M. (2003). Competition and efficiency in professional sports leagues. *European Sport Management Quarterly, 3,* 240–252.

Euroleague Basketball. (2012). NBA Europe Live 2012 presented by BBVA to showcase Boston Celtics, Dallas Mavericks, and top Euroleague teams. *Euroleague.net.* Retrieved from http://www.euroleague.net/news/i/98392/180/nba-europe-live-2012-presented-by-bbva-to-showcase-boston-celtics-dallas-mavericks-and-top-euroleague-teams

European Commission. (2012). Study on the contribution of sport to economic growth and employment in the EU. Retrieved from http://ec.europa.eu/index_en.htm

European Commission. (2013a). Communication on sport adopted. Retrieved from http://ec.europa.eu/index_en.htm

European Commission. (2013b). Communication on sport: Developing the European dimension in sport. Retrieved from http://ec.europa.eu/index_en.htm

FIFA reveals 2010 viewing figures. (2011). Retrieved from http://theworldgame.sbs.com.au/news/1064369/fifa-reveals-2010-viewing-figures

Garcia, J., & Rodriguez, P. (2003). From sports clubs to stock companies: The financial structure of football in Spain, 1992–2001. *European Sport Management Quarterly, 3,* 253–268.

Gillentine, A., Goldfine, B., & Orejan, J. (2004). *An examination of the need for international education and second language acquisition in the sport industry.* Paper presented at North American Society for Sport Management Conference, Atlanta, GA.

Gillentine, A., & Orejan, J. (2003). Proceedings of *North American Society of Sport Management: An examination of second language requirements and international sport education at selected sport administration/management academic programs.* Ithaca, NY: Authors.

Hoehn, T., & Szymanski, S. (1999). The Americanization of European football. *Economic Policy,* 203–204.

International Olympic Committee. (2011). Fundamental principles of Olympism. *Olympic Charter.* Retrieved from http://www.olympic.org/Documents/olympic_charter_en.pdf

International Olympic Committee. (2012a). Olympic broadcasting and digital media. *IOC Marketing: Media Guide—London 2012.* Retrieved from http://www.olympic.org/Documents/IOC_Marketing/London_2012/IOC_Marketing_Media_Guide_2012.pdf

International Olympic Committee. (2012b). Olympic marketing revenue distribution. *Olympic Marketing Fact File.* Retrieved from http://www.olympic.org/Documents/IOC_Marketing/OLYMPIC-MARKETING-FACT-FILE-2012.pdf

International Olympic Committee. (2012c). Olympic marketing revenue generation. *Olympic Marketing Fact File.* Retrieved from http://www.olympic.org/Documents/IOC_Marketing/OLYMPIC-MARKETING-FACT-FILE-2012.pdf

International Olympic Committee. (2012d). Olympic sponsorship. *IOC Marketing: Media Guide—London 2012.* Retrieved from http://www.olym

pic.org/Documents/IOC_Marketing/London _2012/IOC_Marketing_Media_Guide_2012.pdf

International Olympic Committee. (2012e). Olympism in action. *Olympic.org*. Retrieved from http:// www.olympic.org/olympism-in-action

International Olympic Committee. (2012f). Organising Committees for the Olympic Games. Retrieved from http://www.olympic.org/ioc-gov ernance-organising-committees?tab=main-tasks

International Olympic Committee. (2012g). Protecting the Olympic brand. *IOC Marketing: Media Guide—London 2012*. Retrieved from http:// www.olympic.org/Documents/IOC_Marketing /London_2012/IOC_Marketing_Media_Guide _2012.pdf

International Olympic Committee. (2012h). The Organisation. *Mission*. Retrieved from http://www .olympic.org/about-ioc-institution

International Paralympic Committee. (2013). About us. *Paralympic.org*. Retrieved from http://www .paralympic.org/TheIPC/HWA/AboutUs

International Sports Federations. (2012). *International Sports Federations (IFs)*. Retrieved from http://www.olympic.org/content/The-IOC/Gov ernance/International-Federations/

LaFeber, W. (1999). *Michael Jordan and the new global capitalism*. New York, NY: W. W. Norton & Company, Inc.

Lapointe, J. (1997). Hockey: The N.H.L.'s Olympic gamble; Stars' participation in Nagano could raise sport's profile. Retrieved from http://query .nytimes.com/gst/fullpage.html?res=9901EFD91 438F935A2575AC0A961958260

Lombardo, J. (2013). In India, Stern sees opportunity—and cricket. *Street & Smith's SportsBusiness Journal, 16*(2), 6.

Madkour, A., & Kaplan, D. (2003). Tagliabue keeps his focus on the future. *Street & Smith's SportsBusiness Journal, 6*(19), 26–27.

Masteralexis, L.P., & McDonald, M.A. (1997). Enhancing sport management education with international dimensions including language and cultural training. *Journal of Sport Management, 11*, 97–110.

Merriam-Webster. (2013). Globalization. *Merriam-Webster Dictionary*. Retrieved from http://www .merriam-webster.com/dictionary/globalization

MLB International. (2013). MLB International. *MLB.com: International*. Retrieved from http:// mlb.mlb.com/mlb/international/mlbi_index.jsp

Murphy, C. (2012). Global touchdown: Why the NFL loves London. Retrieved from http://edi tion.cnn.com/2012/10/26/sport/nfl-london-fran chise-patriots

National Basketball Association. (2004). International players in the NBA. Retrieved from http:// stats.nba.com/players.html#players?ls=iref:nba :gnav

National Basketball Association. (2008). History of games played by NBA teams in Europe: 2006. *NBA.com*. Retrieved from http://www.nba.com /europelive2007/history

National Basketball Association. (2012). Record-tying 84 international players on opening-night rosters. Retrieved from http://www.nba.com /2012/news/10/30/international-players-on-open ing-night-rosters/index.html

National Basketball Association. (2013). NBA announces comprehensive global games schedule for 2013–14 preseason. *NBA.com*. Retrieved from http://www.nba.com/2013/news/03/05/2013-14 -global-preseason-release/index.html

National Football League. (2008a). History: 1981– 1990. *NFL History by Decade*. Retrieved from http://www.nfl.com/history/chronology/1981- 1990#1986

National Football League. (2008b). International programming. Retrieved from http://www.nfl.com /global/programming

National Hockey League. (2012). Quick facts about the NHL's international profile. *NHL International*. Retrieved from http://www.nhl.com/ice /page.htm?id=26372

National Olympic Committees. (2012). Mission. *Olympic.org*. Retrieved from http://www.olympic .org/ioc governance-national-olympic-committees

NFL folds Europe league, to focus on regular-season games abroad. (2007). *ESPN.com*. Retrieved from http://sports.espn.go.com/nfl/news/story?id=292 0738

Opening day: Over 28 percent of MLB players are foreign-born. (2013). *Fox News Latino*. Retrieved from http://latino.foxnews.com/latino/sports /2013/04/03/over-28-percent-players-were-foreign -born-in-mlb-opening-day/

Overseas companies and their U.S. sports sponsorships. (2002, April 22–28). *Street & Smith's SportsBusiness Journal, 4*(53), 23–24.

Pelletier, J. (2007, September 14). NHL overseas history [Blog post]. Retrieved from http://www .greatesthockeylegends.com/2007/09/nhl-overseas -history.html

Plunkett, J., & Sweney, M. (2013). Disney considers ESPN exit from British TV sports coverage. Retrieved from http://www.guardian.co.uk/me dia/2013/feb/06/disney-considers-espn-exit-uk -sports

Rubingh, B., & Broeke, A. (1998). The European

sports club system. In L.P. Masteralexis, C.A. Barr, & M.A. Hums (Eds.), *Principles and practices of sport management* (pp. 195–207). Gaithersburg, MD: Aspen Publishers, Inc.

Schaaf, P. (2004). *Sports, Inc.: 100 years of sports business*. Amherst, NY: Prometheus Books.

Szymanski, S., & Kuypers, T. (1999). *Winners and losers*. Harmondsworth: Viking.

The Authoritative Annual Research Guide & Fact Book. (2003). Broadcast rights to major sports properties. *SportsBusiness Journal, 6*(36), 82.

The Super Bowl tackles audiences abroad. (2013). Retrieved from http://www.alsintl.com/blog/super-bowl-international-audience/

Thibault, L. (2009). Globalization of sport: An inconvenient truth. *Journal of Sport Management, 23*, 1–20.

U.S. companies and their overseas sports sponsorships. (2002, April 22–28). *Street & Smith's SportsBusiness Journal, 4*(53), 22.

Wertheim, L.J. (2004). The whole world is watching. *Sports Illustrated*, 70–86.

Westerbeek, H., & Smith, A. (2003). *Sport business in the global marketplace*. New York, NY: Palgrave Macmillan.

World Cup of Hockey 2004 to feature eight national teams. (2003). *Hockey Canada*. Retrieved from http://www.hockeycanada.ca/en-ca/news/2003-gn-007-en

15

Sport Management Internships

John Miller

INTRODUCTION

Consider fictional student Shirley Knot, a sport management student at a regional university. The sport management program curriculum at her school does not require an internship experience and does not have an organized list of internships. Further, she finds that approximately 65% of the students in her program enroll and complete internships, and 35% do not. Undaunted, Shirley investigates potential internship placement suggestions from the career development office. She discusses the idea of doing an internship with a sport management professor, who encourages her to find an internship for 6 credit hours. She needs to find a paid internship so she can pay for her tuition as well as take two more classes to graduate. Location is a consideration for her because an internship, especially an unpaid one, will need to be within reasonable driving distance of her apartment. However, she finds out that the internships are unpaid or

---

Learning Objectives

After reading this chapter, the student should be able to identify and explain the following considerations:
- Why an internship experience can increase the likelihood of a student attaining employment at an increased salary;
- How an intern may network to find gainful employment in the sport industry after an internship;
- The capabilities or abilities a competent sport management professional should exhibit as well as why and how an intern may better develop them;
- The policy areas that an intern should be familiar with prior to applying for an internship;
- Different ways an intern can investigate a potential organization and why this is important in providing a successful experience;
- Legal concerns that an intern should address while investigating a potential organization; and
- How each of the evaluation processes can assist the intern in making the experience a truly academic learning experience.

**"We had no room under the salary cap,
so we signed an unpaid intern."**

too far away. Of the paid internships available, they are either not in the area of sport management in which she is interested or seem too good to be true. After several unsuccessful efforts in applying for paid internships or those close to her home in the sport industry, she lets her plans for taking such an experience go unfulfilled. As a result, when Shirley graduated she possessed no real sport management-related experiences other than her job at a retail store in the mall.

Many graduating sport management students may find themselves in similar situations. The question then becomes: Why are sport management-related internships important? This chapter will discuss the significant benefits and concerns that you will encounter in pursuing an internship in the professional sport industry.

In light of the continued expansion of the sport industry, one might surmise that jobs are available. However, there is tremendous competition to attain positions in the professional sport industry. Internships can assist you as a future sport manager in obtaining professional employment faster, at higher starting salaries, and with higher levels of job satisfaction than those that did not participate (Gault, Redington, & Schlager, 2000). The Graduate Admission Management Council (2012) also reported that individuals who did an internship had a higher success rate (70%) of receiving an offer for a job than those who attended job fairs (34%), applied directly to the company (32%), used a headhunter (26%), or applied through online job search sites (15%). Furthermore, recent survey results revealed that 2012 graduates who received a job offer through an internship received a salary increase from pre-degree earnings (84%) that exceeded the increase received by others who had a job offer (70%) (Graduate Admission Management Council, 2012).

In the fast-paced world of the professional sport industry, a person needs to be book smart as well as street savvy. As a future sport manager, you will need to hit the ground running and understand the intricacies of your chosen career path. John Dewey (1938) stated that hands-on learning in a particular field offers the best training for people new to a career. The internship experience has traditionally been identified as the most critical element for the professional preparation of future sport managers (Cuneen & Sidwell, 1994; Miller, 2010; Stier, 2002; Sutton, 1989). Selecting a career path is amongst the most important decisions you will make in your life. As a future sport management professional, you can "stack" the odds in your favor or empower yourself for future jobs by obtaining a specific internship in sport management. A prime reason why internships are so important for you is that they may improve your chances of getting a job in the professional sport industry.

To be prepared for the professional industry, little else compares to observing, learning, and interacting with experienced professionals who are willing to share their unique individual skills. Interaction at positive internship sites can offer you opportunities that cannot be found by staying in the classroom, like our fictional student. Primary among these opportunities is having the ability to network with others, supervisors as well as co-workers, in the internship. More about internship networking will be discussed next.

NETWORKING IN INTERNSHIPS

A potential advantage to an internship is that it may provide you with an "in" to a full-time position with the company at the completion of your internship. Pianko (1996) reported that some organizations hired as many as 70% of their new full-time college individuals who had participated in their company's internship program. More recently, a national survey reported that more than 55% of college students that graduated in 2012 took part in an internship experience (National Association of Colleges and Employers, 2012b). The survey also revealed that employers converted almost 59% of the class of 2011 interns into full-time hires. This percentage reflected an all-time high since the National Association of Colleges and Employers (NACE) began reporting conversion rates in the early 2000s. Even if you do not get a position in the company at which you interned, you should take advantage of opportunities to network and meet many contacts, which are worth their weight in gold in the business world. Since internships are relatively short and sometimes unpredictable, you should make the most out of the experience. Gaining pertinent experience in your selected field of sport management and making connections with professionals can make the whole experience worthwhile, even if it was not flawless. In this way, you can take charge of your education and your future!

Internship experiences are effective ways to "test the waters" before taking a permanent position; they have proven to be valuable devices in helping to recruit candidates, direct career paths, and increase the number of individuals that maintain their career path (Leach, 1998). Some studies have suggested that organizations tend to hire students who have obtained experience within their organization through an internship program (Altschuler, 2002; Goetz, 1995; Pianko; 1996; Yates Borger, 2000). A previous report indicated that the cost of hiring an intern as a permanent employee of the organization was approximately one-third the cost of recruiting and training a person with no previous familiarity with the workings of the organization (Croan, 1996). One of the reasons that students obtain positions may be their ability to network within the cooperating organization. While the cooperating agency may not hire the intern, the potential for developing significant professional relationships exists. These relationships can then provide an intern with important networking opportunities that may positively impact his/her future.

ESTABLISHING NETWORK TIES

Some estimates indicate that approximately 50% of professional industry hiring, in the United States, is accomplished through **network-based referrals** (Tomaskovic-Devey & Stainback, 2007). Using social networks to recognize and hire an employee has been reported to be favored by a number of organizations because of its efficiency, low cost, and ability to provide information unavailable through formal sources (Granovetter & Tilly, 1988; Marsden, 1994; Resnick & McBrier, 2000). According to the **social network theory** (Granovetter, 1983), while network-based referrals can come from close friends or relatives (otherwise referred to as strong ties), the majority of such referrals come from professional acquaintances or "weak ties" in which there is relatively infrequent contact. Granovetter (1974) reported that weak ties exhibited an important role in an individual's prospect for job attainment since there is a

> . . . structural tendency for those to whom one is only weakly tied to have better access to job information one does not already have. Acquaintances, as compared to close friends, are more prone to move in different circles than oneself. Those to whom one is closest are likely to have the greatest overlap in contact with those one already knows, so that the information to which they are privy is likely to be much the same as that which one already has. (pp. 52–53)

In other words, information about a new position may have a higher probability to be ascertained through weak ties rather than strong ones. Thus, it is important for you to identify significant individuals who may be considered "weak ties."

It is essential to remember that the use of weak ties in finding jobs is best done when it connects you with someone who is in a position of authority within the occupational structure of the organization or may have influence on similar authority outside of the organization. For example, a student who interned with the San Antonio Spurs may have worked indirectly under the director of marketing but directly under the assistant director of marketing for the Spurs. During the internship experience the student also became familiar with the director and assistant director of event management for the San Antonio organization.

In this scenario, it is the intent of the intern to remain with the San Antonio Spurs on a professional level in the area of marketing. While the intern may have done a good job, no marketing positions were open. However, a desired position was available in another NBA team. Because of the intern's positive relationship with "weak ties" such as the director and assistant directors of marketing and event management, the likelihood of obtaining the position with the other NBA team is greatly enhanced.

PERSONAL CONTACTS

Generally, job searches may be categorized into informal or formal methods. Formal methods of locating a position include employment agencies, placement offices, newspapers, and recruiters. Informal methods include finding a job through organizational networking (Drentea, 1998). Granovetter (1995) conducted an investigation to determine how people locate their job. He reported that the majority of respondents used informal methods such as the use of personal contacts of any kind. Within the context of this study, personal contacts were defined as

> . . . some individual known personally to the respondent, with whom he originally became acquainted in some context unrelated to a search for job information, from whom he has found out about his new job, or who recommended him to someone who then contacted him. (Granovetter, 1995, p. 11)

IDENTIFYING PERSONAL NETWORK TIES

To fully take advantage of networking within a sport organization, you need to keep in mind who the personal contacts may be. As a guide, it is suggested that you develop a list of individuals identifying weak ties as well as personal contacts as defined by Granovetter (1973; 1995; see Table 15.1). As can be seen, the individuals identified in the table are those with whom you have infrequent interaction, even to the extent that a person uses friends in other sport organizations.

Table 15.1. Personal Network Ties

•	People in Authority in Sport Organizations Where Internship Took Place
•	People in Authority in Other Sport Organizations
•	Acquaintances in the Sport Organization Where the Internship Took Place
•	Friends in Other Sport Organizations
•	Sport Management Professors or Internship Coordinator
•	Would This Person Give Me a Positive Recommendation?

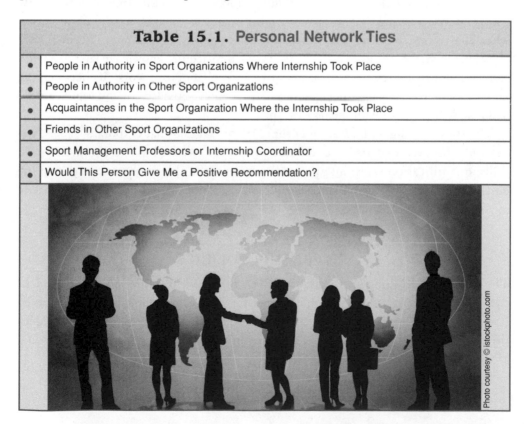

Photo courtesy © istockphoto.com

Linking Theory to Practice

According to Stark and Lowther (1988), a competent professional should exhibit conceptual, technical, and integrative capabilities. Thus, competent professionals are often depicted as possessing the ability to link theoretical knowledge with suitable values and attitudes when making multifaceted judgments within vague parameters (DeSensi, Kelley, Blanton, & Beitel, 1990; Stark & Lowther, 1988). However, Useem (1995) reported that while employers were satisfied with graduates' professional attitudes and their technical abilities, they were not content with the interns' skills or their ability to apply conceptual theories to real-world situations. Skills that you should understand as particularly important in a management-oriented setting are: 1) leadership; 2) problem-solving skills; 3) written communication; 4) ability to work in a team; 5) analytical/quantitative; 6) strong work ethic (National Association of Colleges and Employers, 2012c).

Levine (2005) stated that college graduates often have difficulty "processing language or communicating verbally (both speaking and writing), an inability to focus attention or reason quantitatively, and a serious lack of problem-solving skills" (para. 12). Employers are looking for graduates who have work and life skills and are especially wanting graduates who have, amongst others, well developed communication, team-work, and problem-solving skills (ACNeilsen, 2000). A previous study reported that employers thought college graduates often did not possess the ability to solve complex, ill-structured problems (Jones, 1997). According to Jones (1997) the employees frequently tried to develop a single "right" answer while infrequently suggesting alternatives, even when they were requested to develop more than one strategy. In fact, Useem (1995) questioned whether students will ". . . be prepared to acquire knowledge later in a work environment that stresses personal initiative and collaborative work" if they "acquire knowledge by passively listening to authoritative figures at the lectern and experience no dialogue with them or with themselves" (p. 23).

The Business Higher Education Forum (1995) revealed that corporate leaders, nationwide, believed that graduates did not possess ". . . leadership and communication skills; quantification skills; interpersonal relations; the ability to work in teams; the understanding to work with a diverse work force at home and abroad; and the capacity to adapt to rapid change" (p. 3).

EXAMINATION OF SPORT MANAGEMENT INTERNSHIP POLICIES

The standards requiring universities to offer an internship in the sport management curriculum provides little support of any specific, consistent standards and/or practices (Commission on Sport Management Accreditation, 2012). As a result you should identify the **internship policies** required by your university or department. The following are some potential policy areas that you should investigate:

1. Credit requirements—General requirements may include being a sport management major, successfully completing at least 50% of the total credit hours required at the institution, and possessing an overall grade point average of 3.0.

2. Grade point average—Many sport management departments may specify that students must hold a cumulative 3.0 GPA to qualify for internships. Possessing an overall GPA makes sense since an individual who has shown to be better educationally prepared may attain better internship opportunities (Beard 1997). Since in classes that teach skills, grades are often utilized as a measure in forecasting success, the 3.0 average provides a rational cutoff (Maynard, 1999).

3. Deadlines for application—Often students who desire to apply for an internship may be required to submit an application (along with a résumé) by a deadline. The deadline should be during the term prior to the term that the internship is to take place so that there is sufficient time to help the student find appropriate placement (Verner, 2004).

4. Identification of organizations—Sport management departments sometimes have a list of organizations in which a previous student(s) had a successful experience. You should strongly consider asking if there are any existing policies regarding internship sites. These policies may outline the responsibility of the organization to willingly to provide students with appropriate supervision and with an opportunity to perform professional quality work. These policies can also identify the characteristics of the person who is knowledgeable about the professional quality work that the student is supposed to perform. For example, if a facility management supervisor fails to communicate or delegate job responsibilities, this may very well result in a "non-learning" experience for you.

5. Number of hours required for completing the internship—While COSMA does not specify standard hours that an intern must complete, internships may be full-time 40 hours per week. You should inquire whether the internship must be completed in one semester or if it can be taken over continuous semesters. This is especially critical if you are initiating an internship during the university's summer session or plan on taking additional classes when serving in an internship.

6. Evaluation of Internship—Henry, Razzouk, and Hoverland (1988) indicated that the internship experience should be graded as a pass/fail system for evaluating your performance; however, the evaluation process is totally at the discretion of the university. Additional concerns regarding evaluation and assessment of the internship experience will be addressed later in this chapter.

You may also investigate policies that address: a) professional attitude, dress, and appearance requirements of the student during the internship; b) potential of unethical or illegal requests; c) need for confidentiality; and/or d) what to do if an organization where a student is interning goes out of business or relocates (Somerick, 2001). Addressing these issues may help you to identify and select a good internship site; this will be discussed in the next section.

Screening and Selecting the Sport Management Site

As mentioned at the start of this chapter, one of the items that you should research is the location and reputation of the potential organization. Once you have adequately addressed policies that impact the internship, consideration should be given to **screening** for potential internship site selection. This should be done to ensure that the essence of an internship program satisfies both the industry reality and student expectation. Hite and Bellizzi (1986) indicated that if the internship site is not carefully considered the intern may have an unsatisfactory experience due to three key points: a) unclear standards; b) misinterpretation or misrepresentation by students regarding the expectancies of the position, and c) misrepresentation by the firm concerning the required responsibilities. To prevent any of these from occurring the student intern must identify, screen, and monitor potential sport management sites well in advance of the commencement of the internship. Suggested ways for you to gain this knowledge are to review literature related to their specific strengths and desires in sport management, visit the websites of the potential internship sites, attend professional conferences/conventions, and/or volunteer for activities within your field(s) of interest.

You should be very wary about any agency that may place interns with mentors who use them as clerical staff. A general rule of thumb for the potential intern to consider regarding whether the experience will be meaningful is: **if the assignment may be carried out by the intern's on-site supervisor or someone of equal status, the internship has potential to be a meaningful experience** (Verner, 2004). By investigating the strengths and weaknesses of internships offered by an organization, you can ensure the experience is successful. These assessments can provide you with an opportunity to construct meaning and apply your theoretical and technical competencies to further develop your skills.

Photo courtesy © Andy Gillentine

An additional consideration when screening for appropriate sport management internship sites concerns the recognition and competency of the organization as it applies to your area of interest. What would appear to be a career "fit" that looks good on paper may be addressed through the internship experience. Therefore, you should not look at the experience as important simply to obtain any professional position but also to help in identifying your specific sport management career path. Sometimes students searching for an internship site apply to organizations that may have an availability that is close to, but not specifically within, the area in sport management the students desire to work. For example, should you wish to learn about facility management, it would not be beneficial for you to apply for an internship in sport marketing. While these areas are within the confines of sport management, the integration of principles for each of these sub-areas is totally different, potentially depriving you of an appropriate learning opportunity. While you may successfully pass the internship class in the immediate future, the actual impact may prevent you from being adequately prepared for a professional sport management position.

The potential organization should also provide you with opportunities to **observe and participate** in management related issues. To make certain these items occur, you, in conjunction with the on-site supervisor and faculty advisor, should compose a written list of responsibilities expected of you. At the start of the semester in which your internship will be conducted, it is generally a good idea for you to meet with their on-site mentors to talk about how you will be evaluated. You and your mentor then sign an internship evaluation agreement that outlines specific evaluation criteria. Although the evaluations may vary slightly due to differences in tasks across the organizational areas, normal criteria to be evaluated include quality of task performance, attendance and punctuality, attitude and enthusiasm, communication skills, creativity, honesty, and initiative.

As stated earlier in this chapter, you need to have a **clear picture of all the duties and responsibilities** that are expected of a sport manager. Questions that you may ask when screening organizations may include the following:

1. Will the organization allow the interns to be actively involved and receive ongoing feedback?
2. Will the interns be put into positions that will allow them to apply theoretical knowledge to long-standing and new real-world open-ended issues and problems?
3. Will the interns be put into positions that will allow them to integrate discipline-based knowledge with their process skills, including problem solving, information literacy, critical thinking, analysis, communications, and teamwork?
4. Will the interns be put into positions that will allow them to become increasingly more advanced in their abilities and skills?
5. Will they be provided time for continuous evaluation and reflection?

It is important for you to understand "how" to have a successful internship experience. Internships, when designed and implemented effectively, can help you learn to navigate the sport business world as well as offer an opportunity to gain insights from mistakes that would likely be damaging under other conditions (Smith, 2010). However, not all internships are reputable or challenging. Some positions that might look like internships may be just part-time temp jobs that anyone could fill. Or in the worst case be simple, boring busywork that the employer would rather not assign to full-time employees. Although such internship opportunities may be attractive to you, especially if they are paid, chances are slim you'll be provided a résumé-building experience that will enhance your prospects of obtaining your "dream job" without careful consideration. While you may rely on your internship academic advisor to determine the reputability of an organization, the following are some tips in identifying questionable internship sites:

1. It guarantees that you will be able to earn a great deal of money (even though it is an internship).
2. You cannot locate the organization in the Yellow Pages or on the Internet.
3. You can find the organization on the Internet but there is no information about internships.
4. You find that the organization mainly promotes its "internships" on flyers all over campus.
5. The employer doesn't inquire about your experience, academic preparation, background, or career interests to see if you're a good fit for the position.
6. You do not get straight answers about your responsibilities in the position.
7. The organization's offices are in a questionable location, such as a warehouse area or dilapidated strip mall.
8. The employer doesn't require you to complete a job application prior to offering you the internship.
9. Remember two things as you pursue internships. First, if it sounds too good to be true—it is. Second, if your instincts are telling you to get out as fast as you can, do so!

You should consider these points prior to taking part in an internship. Failure to do so may result in you not only finding yourself in a fraudulent environment that will not help you gain employment in the professional industry. Additionally, you should investigate issues such as **paid internships, unpaid internships, workmen's compensation, and general liability issues** when screening a potential organization (Brown-Foster & Moorman, 2001; Miller, Anderson, & Ayres, 2002; Miller & Wendt, 2010; Swift & Russell, 1999). The following will describe specific areas that the student should take into consideration when searching for an internship site.

Paid Internships

Potential employers can attract capable students to internships by offering a salary or monthly stipend. According to Michael True, a college internship center director, if a student sees two internships that are basically the same, yet one is paid and one is not, it's no secret that they'll go after the paid one. Students are committed to that project, paid or not. But if they're paid, they have an accountability to that job (Loretto, 2012).

Gillentine and Miller (2010) reported that generally the types of organizations that are most likely to pay the intern are professional teams, clubs, retail establishments, and facility/event management. However, intercollegiate athletic departments and the media-related sport organizations are much less likely to pay a salary (Gillentine & Miller, 2010). According to Cook, Parker, and Pettijohn (2004) payment was not found to be a primary issue regarding a student's involvement with the internship program. Under the Fair Labor Standard Acts of 1938 (FLSA), **employers are not required to pay interns who qualify as trainees**. However, FLSA provides little guidance for distinguishing between trainees and employees (*Reich v. Parker Fire Protection District*, 1993). The FLSA regulates the minimum wage and overtime compensation issues in the United States as they pertain to companies engaged in interstate commerce with a minimum of two employees and exhibit $500,000 in yearly sales. The FLSA also compels an organization to pay eligible employees the federally prescribed minimum wage. To that end it has been reported that most student interns are entitled to a minimum wage (McDonald, 1996). According to Gregory (1998):

> If an intern does the work of a regular employee, and displaces an employee, that is not lawfully countenanced, because the intern is providing free labor. The professed willingness of an individual intern to work for free is probably irrelevant. Interns willing to work for free, or for academic credit in lieu of paid compensation, may nevertheless be employees subject to the FLSA, although in the latter case, the academic credit granted usually militates in favor of finding the intern is not a statutory employee. These concerns have led to "intern contracts," whereby some businesses . . . have even started requiring interns to sign contracts specifying that they will accept a small stipend or college credit in lieu of the minimum wage. (p. 245)

If the internship is paid the organization can limit the hours of the intern, thus preventing him or her from becoming eligible for benefits. This allows the organization to categorize the intern as a temporary employee (Sturges, 1993). Should this situation arise, you should still expect the organization to pay at least minimum wage or comparable to the wages earned by others in the organization doing similar work.

Results of a national survey reported that about 60% of 2012 college graduates who took part in paid internships received at least one job offer (National Association of Colleges and Employers, 2012a). The same study revealed that 37% of unpaid interns received job offers while 36% of graduates with no internship experience received job offers. Thus, unpaid interns managed to achieve a 1% better chance of receiving job offers than graduates who had not taken part in an internship. Interestingly, the study also indicated that overall almost 47% of the internships in 2012 were unpaid, including nearly 33% of internships in the for-profit sector.

Unpaid Internships

A myth exists that unpaid internships cannot be included in a résumé. However, many, if not most, student interns work for free. In fact it has been estimated that at least 50%

of all internships are unpaid (Barry, 2001; Gilbertson, 1997). As such, every experience related to a particular internship should be included on your résumé. As a student, you should include applicable coursework; co-curricular activities; community service; volunteer experience; and previous internships on your résumé. It is important to remember that it is the applicable skills and experiences you possess that future employers are looking for when evaluating job applicants.

To be held not liable from the FLSA, the organization must illustrate that it did not achieve any direct advantage from the work of the interns. If the organization can prove such evidence, the interns would be considered non-employees and not under FLSA. As a result, under FLSA, organizations are not obligated to pay interns who qualify as student learners. According to Kaplan (1994) six conditions are needed for student learner status to exist. First, the student intern cannot take the place of a regular employee. Second, the student is not absolutely assured of a job when the internship is over. Third, the intern and the organization agree that the student is not entitled to wages during the internship experience. Fourth, the student intern receives training from the organization. Fifth, the training should be comparable to the training by the school. Finally, the training must provide some benefit to the student intern.

The United States Department of Labor has made clear that ". . . the only acceptable activities for unpaid interns are those that are purely for teaching purposes and do not help with [a host organization's] day-to-day tasks" (Coker, 2009, p. 37). Furthermore, the Department of Labor has stated that ". . . internships in the 'for-profit' private sector will most often be viewed as employment, unless the [six-part] test is met" (Wage and Hour Division, 2010, para. 2). Should the organization you are interning at receive a direct advantage or benefit from your work, you should be classified as an employee (Schneider & Stier, 2006). Additionally, in a review of significant internship sites, Edwards and Hertel-Fernandez (2010) found that many unpaid internships had no explicit academic or training component. However, should your most significant benefit be receiving academic credit, then the host organization does not have to pay you.

Receiving Credit Instead of Pay

Misusing sport management student interns may violate the federal Fair Labor Standards Act (FLSA). According to the Wage and Hour Division (2010) of the FLSA,

> In general, the more an internship program is structured around a classroom or academic experience as opposed to the employer's actual operations, the more likely the internship will be viewed as an extension of the individual's educational experience (this often occurs where a college or university exercises oversight over the internship program and provides educational credit). (para. 5)

I have found, as an internship supervisor, that potential employers often require students to receive college credit. To some internship agencies, the experience you will receive in an internship provides a greater likelihood of obtaining a job, in which the benefit exists. Thus, a double edge sword is presented as you may be required to take an internship to satisfy your graduation requirements but you may not be to pay for room, board, or college credit if you are not paid for the internship.

To combat the pay versus no pay issue you may consider following items. First, try locating applicable internships in areas that family members reside. Doing so will minimize paying for rent and/or food. Second, since many programs require an internship to be six credits, see if you can split your internship over successive semesters, especially if the intern site is near the university you are attending. In this way, you will be able to pay for the internship class, as you would for any other class, and still be able to live in relatively normal circumstances. Third, see if your university offers transcript notations for internships. Transcript notations are used at a number of universities for approved experiential learning opportunities such as internships. Transcript notations often apply only to those experiences that are associated with students' academic coursework. According to Loretto (2012) transcript notations can be employed when an internship does not qualify for credit or if students elect not to do the internship for credit due to academic requirements or additional tuition costs required by the college. A fourth suggestion is to determine if your university has a program that provides funding for students doing unpaid internships, especially if they are summer internships. Schools such as Princeton, Duke, and Connecticut College as well as many others offer such programs (Lee, 2006).

Workmen's Compensation

Even though an organization may not provide an intern with enough hours to be considered an employee and therefore not eligible for certain benefits such as **workmen's compensation**, the organization is held liable for medical benefits and wages if the intern is injured on the job (Kaplan, 1994). There are several reasons for this. First, many state workmen's compensation laws do not distinguish between employees and trainees (Swift & Kent, 1999). Secondly, workmen's compensation boards may determine that interns contribute enough to a company to qualify as employees and receive this benefit (*Evanson v. Univ. of Hawaii*, 1971). Thirdly, some courts have held that even though a student is not paid for an internship, he or she gains important training and valuable experience that is equivalent to wages. For example, in *Hallal v. RDV Sports, Inc.* (1996) the plaintiff was enrolled in a sports internship class that was required within the university's curriculum. Although he was only involved in the program for academic reasons, the court held that he was still considered an employee. Therefore, it would be wise for the student intern and faculty advisor to investigate whether the potential organization possesses an effective **risk-management program** to cover interns under workmen's compensation even though it is not required to do so.

You as well as your faculty advisor must also note that the workmen's compensation statute may hold that an internship employer in a university-sponsored internship program is considered to be an employer of a student intern, unless that internship is not paid. If the internship is an unpaid experience the responsibility for coverage reverts back to the university (Henry, et al., 1988; *Kinder v. Industrial Claim Appeals Office*, 1998).

Sexual Harassment

You should be aware that as an intern you will not be provided protections against discrimination stipulated by Title VII of the Civil Rights Act of 1964 because of your unpaid status (Edwards & Hertel-Fernandez, 2010). Sexual harassment is more about power than it is about sex. You as an unpaid intern may find yourself in positions of great vulnerability with a relative lack of power in comparison to the supervisors or experienced co-workers (Clement, Miller, & McGlone, 2010). This type of situation occurred in *O'Connor v. Davis* (1997). During her internship, O'Connor was subjected to repeated sexual harassment by her supervisor (*O'Connor v. Davis*, 1997). As a result of the harassment, she filed a claim under Title VII. However, the district court dismissed her complaint because she was not an employee (only an unpaid intern) and therefore not entitled to Title VII protections. This dismissal was later affirmed by the U.S. Court of Appeals. In another harassment case involving an intern (*Lowery v. Klemm*, 2006), the appellate court initially extended protection to unpaid interns; however, it was overturned by the state Supreme Judicial Court of Massachusetts, thereby maintaining the precedent that unpaid interns do not qualify for the same discrimination and harassment protections afforded traditional employees. These two court cases reflect a very important message in that the legislation or State Supreme Court rulings vary in each state.

While researching a specific organization, you should consider whether the organization provides any **orientation** to company policies concerning sexual harassment. This is an especially critical step since interns may be more vulnerable to sexual harassment than students or full-time employees (Bowen & Laurion, 1994). Therefore, sexual harassment may be a chief consideration when the institution is sending students to an organization as interns. However, you must understand that it is the responsibility of the organization to protect all employees from harassment; thus, you should be encouraged to follow the same avenues of reporting incidents of harassment as the regular, full-time employees (Kaplan, 1994).

General Liability

There is a potential that during the internship experience the student may be injured or may injure someone else. While workmen's compensation can protect the intern as well as the sponsoring organization, the organization may be liable for the negligent act of a regular employee resulting in an injury to another. It is imperative for interns to understand whether they will be categorized as a" **"regular"** or **"non-regular"** employee.

Miller et al. (2002) reported that factors that may sway the intern's description as an employee include number of hours worked, wages earned, indirect benefits received, discretionary decision making power, and genuine benefit to the ongoing operations of the organization. Thus, it is recommended that individuals entering an internship experience review the internship agreement with the on-site and faculty supervisors to gain a better understanding of their position or designation within the organization. The agreement must include provisions that assign legal responsibility for potential injuries that may take place during the internship (Miller et al., 2002).

EVALUATING THE STUDENT INTERN

The National Society for Experiential Education has identified **two key stratagems** that you and your faculty supervisor may consider to create a strong academically related internship. First, it is suggested that you work closely with faculty member(s) and an on-site mentor to recognize and express acceptable educational objectives relating to what you intend to learn and do in the internship (Gillentine & Miller, 2010). Gillentine and Miller (2010) proposed this step is critical so that you and your supervisors understand how the skills and knowledge can be demonstrated as end products of the experience as well as the conditions that are likely to help promote these types of skills. Secondly, while many internships concentrate on the attainment of specific skills techniques and skills related to appropriate professional practices, the internship can also aid in your intellectual development (Smith, 2010). An internship can help you learn how to reflect in action, develop new methods of reasoning, construct and test new categories of understanding, experiment with different action strategies, and try new ways of framing problems (Barnes, 2010; Schön, 1987).

Despite the major differences between college and work environments, there are ways that you can involve yourself in the learning experiences to more effectively prepare you for the transition to the workplace. The primary objective of when you are engaged in an academic internship is your ability to **integrate** classroom teaching with field-based application opportunities to develop your potential management skills. Clear objectives, regarding the proposed learning outcomes, provide the basis for internship evaluations. Therefore, the learning assessments of your internship should provide a precise and comprehensible description of learning as well as the methods and reporting strategies used should enhance learning (Guskey, 1994). A series of goals in communications, listening, writing, problem solving, critical thinking, and critical reading can be useful to helping you identify priorities (Jones, 1997). Each objective may be based on a comprehensive review of the literature and outline a comprehensive framework for each major skill and then define in greater specificity key dimensions associated with strong mastery. Thus, while true learning is multifaceted, appropriate evaluation should be also considered (DeSensi, Kelley, Blanton, & Beitel, 1990). With that in mind, you should understand the importance of the following strategies that you may be required to complete.

Weekly Journals

Miller and Gillentine (2010) suggested that journal essays are one of the best ways available for you to develop **reflective learning**. Research has found that interns that have incorporated weekly journal reports as an integrative activity demonstrated the ability to transfer classroom knowledge to the "real world" (Eyler, 1994). The journal essays may be beneficially used for you to think critically about the aptitudes required for a particular sport management position (Young & Baker, 2004). You then can reflect on your particular strengths and weaknesses for the position and indicate how you plan to improve the future quality of your work. The internship journal can also provide you with the opportunity to identify specific situations that may be encountered in the organization and critically think about how you might handle the situation if you were in a decision-making position. Additionally, not only will these weekly reports allow you the time to reflect upon your internship experience but they help maintain regular contact between you and the instructor when class meetings are not possible. In some cases, the faculty supervisor cannot make regular visits. However, through reading the weekly essays, the faculty advisor can keep track of your progress and the quality of your experiences while recognizing potential problems.

On-site Supervisor Evaluations

The on-site supervisor may be asked to provide a mid-term and a final grade for their interns based upon the interns' performance in the organization. At the start of the semester, you may meet with your faculty and on-site supervisor to discuss how you will be assessed. You as well as the faculty and on-site supervisor all sign an internship grade agreement that outlines detailed evaluation criteria. Items that you may view included within the internship grade agreement are: a) quality of task performance; b) dependability; c) self-reliance; d) communication skills; e) creativity, honesty, and initiative; f) interpersonal relationships; and g) professionalism. On pre-destined mid-term and final due dates, your on-site supervisor may submit a grade as well as a detailed written evaluation of you to the faculty supervisor.

Internship Projects

Often the most significantly weighted item when grading you is the **quality or professionalism of task performances**. For example, after a careful mentoring and observation phase, the on-site supervisor may ask you to evaluate a marketing plan to increase the number of season ticket-holders. This would involve integrating your academic knowledge with information you have acquired through your organizational experiences. Other projects you may be assigned in an internship may include the renovation of a sport facility, designing media guides, developing fundraising plans, or creating policy manuals (Cuneen & Sidwell, 1994). Therefore, you should be given, or even better you should ask for projects that allow you to integrate your conceptual competencies with the technical skills to develop novel solutions to a problem.

Mid-Semester Internship Evaluation

During the middle of the respective semester you may be required to meet with the faculty supervisor to present verbal reports, to indicate any problems you are having, to help provide solutions to other interns who might be having problems, or to obtain information on policies, performance appraisal strategies, and portfolio preparation. If you cannot meet directly with your faculty supervisor other options such as phone conversations can be supplemented by faxes, e-mail, or regular mail. You should also meet with the on-site supervisor on a formal basis to receive an assessment during the middle and end of the semester. This assessment should **recognize your strengths and weaknesses** as well as provide suggestions concerning how you may improve on your responsibilities. The mid-semester evaluation conference is significant as it provides you an opportunity for well thought out feedback, from the faculty as well as the on-site supervisor, regarding your performance up to that time. Additionally, it gives you and your respective supervisors a chance to reevaluate goals for the remainder of the internship. At no time should you become defensive when given appropriately constructive feedback by supervisors during the mid-semester evaluation.

Final Evaluation Report Portfolio

You may be required to complete **final portfolio reports** to indicate your overall sport management experience as well as critique your own performance. Portfolios can also be used to measure your **development and progress**. Items that you may be required to include in a portfolio are a collection of materials such as proposals, brochures, reports, workshop outlines, memos, or letters that you have produced. Additionally, written evaluations written by colleagues or the supervisor may be included.

To best critique the internship experience, you should be provided the opportunity to reflect on your learning outcomes and how you were able to reach those outcomes. Additionally, you should be able to reflect on areas of the internship that could be improved upon, what behaviors you engaged in most often, which courses best equipped you for the internship experiences, and whether these experiences had an effect on career interests.

Becoming an Effective Intern

Now that you have learned about the need to properly select and prepare yourself for an intern experience, what should you do to make sure that the experience is a good one? The following information will detail what you should and should not do to make your internship experience successful. First, are the dynamic dozen positive things you can do:

1. **Always Be on Time**
   It sounds simple, but punctuality speaks volumes about your professionalism. Chronic lateness or absence can doom an internship, especially if you don't provide notice. If you are going to be late, call your supervisor as e-mails may get lost in junk mail or otherwise go unnoticed until it is too late.

2. **Be Modest**
   Don't always inform your bosses every time you do something right. Your superiors should be aware of what you are doing, so there's no need for you to point out your every accomplishment.

3. **Be Careful What You Say**
   Stay on the safe side with your new colleagues. Avoid discussing religion, politics, bosses, or any other private matters. You're new on the scene, and can't afford to get caught up in the crossfire of what you inadvertently say.

4. **Act Like a Professional**
   Do not think like a temporary employee. That includes knowing what to wear. If

you look the part, it'll be easier for management to picture you fitting in full time. If you want to get hired full-time, act like you're in it for the long haul.

5. Don't Complain

Don't complain—about the organization, your assignments, your supervisor— even to other interns who may be your "best" friend forever. Do not say "that's not in my job description," even if it isn't, 'cause it is. A positive outlook could make or break you in management's eyes.

6. Know What is Happening

Show an interest in the company and learn as much as you can about it and its place in the industry. Also pay attention during meetings. Doodling or daydreaming during meetings will attract negative attention right off the bat.

7. Ask Questions . . . to the Right People

You might have a 4.0 grade point average, but you still don't know it all. This is a good thing because you often are not expected to. Do not guess what you should do if you don't understand how to go about an assignment. Ask your supervisor for clarification and what resources are available to you. Just be smart about whom you seek answers from and when.

8. Build Social Connections

Everyone has rubbed elbows with the annoying person who spends more time trying to schmooze the higher-ups than doing work. Although getting the job done is of paramount importance, don't underestimate the importance of building a social connection with co-workers. Just do it with integrity.

9. Build Professional Connections

Developing relationships and cultivating strong senior supporters who can fight for you to get hired is key. Networking with mentors, including those outside your functional area, can assist you in learning about the people and their roles throughout the organization.

10. Speak Up

If you would like to continue working in the organization professionally, let it be known in subtle fashion. Although actions speak louder than words, mentioning your future desire to continue working in the organization to your supervisor can go a long way in your getting the position.

11. Keep the Line Open

Even if you had a positive experience but don't receive a job offer, maintain your relationship with the organization in some fashion. Send articles that might be of interest to your organizational supervisor.

12. References are Important

There's another reason to stay in touch with your organizational supervisor: Even if she didn't offer you a job from the organization where you achieved positive results, staying fresh in her mind will most likely provide you with a good reference when you start interviewing elsewhere.

CONCLUSION

Significant differences exist between the cultures of college and work (Holton, 1998). Usually, university students get regular feedback about their performance through grades and comments from faculty and peers. Feedback in the workplace is infrequent and less precise (Holton, 1998). As a student, you are usually provided a great deal of direction in your classes. Conversely, those who work in the professional industry usually work in highly unstructured environments and engage in tasks that have few directions and they experience less personal support than in college and also encounter frequent and unexpected changes.

How can you productively make the transition to becoming a competently skilled professional as previously identified? Internships can provide you provide opportunities to learn about life in the "real world" without the commitment of a full-time position. Internships can present you with an opportunity to evolve from learning career-related skills in the classroom to the application of these skills in a management-oriented environment. This can help you not only "get a leg up" on the competition but also obtain a position at a higher salary.

To better prepare yourself for the internship experience and, ultimately, the workplace, you should consider following recommendations. First, you should concentrate investigating and selecting sport related organizations that will allow you to integrate your conceptual and technical competencies to further develop such skills as leadership, teamwork, problem solving, time management, communication, and analytical thinking within the classroom setting. Secondly, you should focus on developing personal traits such as ethics, adaptability, self-management, global consciousness, and a passion for life-long learning. Finally, you should take any opportunity to apply theoretical concepts of sport management to "real" learning experiences such as volunteer or summer work prior to the internship experience.

Discussion Activities

1. Discuss the importance of an internship. Why are these experiences even more important in the sport industry?
2. Discuss how the student can "get ahead in the networking game." Identify people and their positions in the sport industry that may assist you in obtaining a professional position in the sport industry.
3. Conduct a search for possible internships in the sport industry that interest you. What are the job requirements for the positions? Are the internships paid? Will you need to relocate? How do you apply for this position?
4. As a form of self-evaluation, make a list of all of your strengths and weaknesses. Once completed, discuss ways to maximize your strengths and develop your weaknesses. Do you have the strengths needed for the internships you identified in question 2?

References

ACNielsen Research Services. (2000). *Employer satisfaction with graduate skills. Research report*. Evaluations and investigations programme higher education division, DETYA.

Altschuler, G. C. (2002, April 14). A tryout for the real world: Interning is good for the résumé. Better yet, it may get you hired, *New York Times*, p. 4A.

Barnes, J. (2010). The importance of internships in sport management academic programs. In J. Miller & T. Seidler (Eds.), *A practical guide to sport management internships* (pp. 3–13). Durham, NC: Carolina Academic Press.

Barry, G. (2000, February 11). Interns get head start at careers, *St. Petersburg Times*, p. 9B.

Beard, F. K. (August, 1997). *Inside the advertising and public relations internship*. Paper presented to the Internships and Careers Interest Group of the Association for Education in Journalism and Mass Communication, Chicago, IL.

Bowen, M., & Laurion, S. (August, 1994). *Incidence rates of sexual harassment in mass communications internship programs: An initial study comparing intern, student, and professional rates*. (Report No. CS508696). Syracuse, NY: ERIC Clearinghouse on Information & Technology (ERIC Document Reproduction Service No. ED 374485).

Brown-Foster, S., & Moorman, A. M. (2001). *Gross v. Family Services Agency, Inc.*: The internship as a special relationship in creating negligence liability. *Journal of Legal Aspects of Sport, 11,* 245–267.

Business-Higher Education Forum. (1995). *Higher education and work readiness: The view from the corporation*. Washington, DC: Business-Higher Education Forum and the American Council on Education.

Clement, A., Miller, J., & McGlone, C. (2010). Sexual harassment issues in sport management internships. In J. Miller & T. Seidler (Eds.), *A practical guide to sport management internships* (pp. 193–203). Durham, NC: Carolina Academic Press.

Coco, M. (2000). A try before you buy arrangement. *Advanced Management Journal, 65*(2), 41–43.

Coker, L. (2009). Legal implications of unpaid internships. *Employee Relations Law Journal, 35*(3), 35–39.

Commission on Sport Management Accreditation. (2012). FAQs. Retrieved from http://cosmaweb.org/FAQs

Cook, S. J., Parker, R. S., & Pettijohn, C. (January/February, 2004). The perceptions of interns: A longitudinal case study. *Journal of Education for Business, 79*(3), 179–185.

Croan, M., (August 12, 1996). They aren't paid, but interns' experience will pay off, *Roanoke Times & World News (Va.)*, p. C1.

Cuneen, J., & Sidwell, M.J. (1994). *Sport management field experiences*. Morgantown, WV: Fitness Information Technology.

DeSensi, J. T., Kelley, D. R., Blanton, M. D., & Beitel, P. A. (1990). Sport management curricular evaluation and needs assessment: A multifaceted approach. *Journal of Sport Management, 4*(1), 31–58.

Dewey, J. (1938). *Experience and education*. New York, NY: Macmillan.

Drentea, P. (1998). Consequences of women's formal and informal job search methods for employment in female-dominated jobs. *Gender and Society, 12,* 321–338.

Edwards, K. A., & Hertel-Fernandez, A. (2010). Policy memorandum: Not-so-equal protection: Reforming the regulation of student internships. *Economic Policy Institute*. Retrieved from http://www.epi.org/publica tion/pm160/

Evanson v. University of Hawaii, 483 P.2d 187, 190 (Haw. 1971).

Eyler, J. (1994). Comparing the impact of two internship experiences on student learning. *Journal of Cooperative Education, 29,* 41–52.

Fair Labor Standards Act of 1938, 29 U.S.C. §§ 201–219 (2010).

Gault, J., Redington, J., & Schlager, T. (2000). Undergraduate business internships and career success: Are they related? *Journal of Marketing Education, 22*(1), 45–53.

Gilbertson, D. (1997, October, 19). Glamorous internships with a catch: There's no pay, *New York Times*, p. C16.

Gillentine, A., & Miller, J. (2010). Steps in preparing for the internship experience. In J. Miller & T. Seidler (Eds.), *A practical guide to sport management internships* (pp. 41–48). Durham, NC: Carolina Academic Press.

Goetz, T. (January 17, 1995). To serve them all my days: Are internships education or exploitation?, *Village Voice*, p. A6.

Graduate Management Admission Council. (2012). *2012 Global management education graduate survey*. Retrieved from http://www.gmac.com/~/me dia/Files/gmac/Research/curriculum-insight/2012 -gmegs-survey-report-early-release.pdf

Granovetter, M. (1973). The strength of weak ties. *American Journal of Sociology, 78,* 1360–1380.

Granovetter, M. (1983). The strength of weak ties: A network theory revisited. *Sociological Theory, 1,* 201–233.

Granovetter, M. (1995). *Getting a job: A study of contacts and careers*. Chicago, IL: The University of Chicago Press.

Granovetter, M., & Tilly, C. (1988). Inequality and labor process. In N. J .Smelser (Ed.), *Handbook of Sociology* (pp. 175–221). Newbury Park, CA: Sage.

Gregory, D. L. (1998). The problematic employment dynamics of student internships. *Notre Dame Journal of Law Ethics and Public Policy, 12,* 228–264.

Guskey, T. (1994). Making the grade: What benefits students? *Educational Leadership, 52*(2), 14–20.

Hallal v. RDV Sports, Inc., 682 So. 2d 1235 (Fla. Dist. Ct. App. 1996).

Henry, L. G., Razzouk, N. Y., & Hoverland, H. (1988). Accounting internships: A practical framework. *Journal of Education for Business, 64*(1), 28–31.

Hite, R., & Bellizzi, J. (1986). Student expectations regarding collegiate internship programs in marketing. *Journal of Marketing Education, 8*(3), 41–49.

Holton, E. F., III. (1998). Preparing students for life beyond the classroom. In J. N. Gardner and G. Van der Veer (Eds.), *The senior year experience: Facilitating integration, reflection, closure, and transition* (pp. 95–115). San Francisco, CA: Jossey-Bass.

Jones, E. A. (1997). *Goals inventories: Writing, critical thinking, problem-solving, speech communications, listening, and critical reading*. University Park, PA: National Center on Postsecondary Teaching, Learning, and Assessment.

Kaplan, R. K. (1994). The legal side of internship programs. *CPC Journal, 19*(5), 47–49.

Kinder v. Industrial Claim Appeals Office, 976 P.2d 295 (Colo. Ct. App. 1998).

Leach, T. (May, 1998). College internship: An aid to recruitment. *Law and Order,* 57–59.

Lee, J. (2006). Colleges make way for internships. *The New York Times*. Retrieved from http://www.nytimes.com/2006/07/19/nyregion/19interns.html?_r=0

Levine, M. L. (2005, February). College graduates aren't ready for the real world. Retrieved from http://www.surveyu.com/images/pdf/gradsnotready_02-18-2005.pdf

Loretto, P. (2012). The golden age of internships: An opportunity for employers to get talented, skilled employees. Retrieved from http://internships.about.com/od/typesofinternships/a/paidintenships.htm

Lowery v. Klemm, 825 N.E. 2d 1065 (Mass. App. Ct. 2005).

Marsden, P .V. (1994). The hiring process: Recruitment methods. *American Behavioral Scientist, 37,* 979–991.

Maynard, M.L. (Winter, 1999). Challenging the 3.0 GPA eligibility standard for public relations internships. *Public Relations Review, 25,* 495–507.

McCormick, D. W. (1993). Critical thinking, experiential learning and internships. *Journal of Management Education, 17,* 260–262.

McDonald Jr., J. J. (1996, September 1). Shop talk: Education versus exploitation, *Los Angeles Times,* p. D1.

Miller, G., & Gillentine, A. (2010). Sport management internship assessment and evaluation. In J. Miller & T. Seidler (Eds.), *A practical guide to sport management internships* (pp. 90–99). Durham, NC: Carolina Academic Press.

Miller, J. (2010). Choosing an internship area: The major specialties. In J. Miller & T. Seidler (Eds.), *A practical guide to sport management internships* (pp. 25–39). Durham, NC: Carolina Academic Press.

Miller, J., & Wendt, J. (2010). Safety and negligence sport management internship issues. In J. Miller & T. Seidler (Eds.), *A practical guide to sport management internships* (pp. 123–132). Durham, NC: Carolina Academic Press.

Miller, L. K, Anderson, P. M, & Ayres, T. D. (2002). The internship agreement: Recommendations and realities. *Journal of Legal Aspects of Sport, 12*(1), 37–60.

National Association of Colleges and Employers. (2012a). *60 percent of paid interns got job offers.* Retrieved from http://www.naceweb.org/Press/Releases/60_Percent_of_Paid_Interns_Got_Job_Offers.aspx?referal=pressroom&menuid=278

National Association of Colleges and Employers. (2012b). *Employers report record intern-conversion rate*. Retrieved from http://www.naceweb.org/s04252012/intern-conversionrate/?referal=knowledgecenter&menuid=112

National Association of Colleges and Employers. (2012c). *What employers want to see on a résumé*. Retrieved from http://www.naceweb.org/press/releases/what-employers-want-to-see-on-a-resume.aspx?referal=pressroom&menuid=273

O'Connor v. Davis, 126 F.3d 112 (2d Cir. 1997).

Pianko, D. (1996). Power internships. *Management Review, 85*(12), 31–33.

Reich v. Parker Fire Protection Dist., 992 F.2d. 1023, 1025 (10th Cir. 1993).

Schneider, R. C., & Stier, W. F., Jr. (2006). Sport management field experiences as experiential learning: Ensuring beneficial outcomes and preventing exploitation. *Sport Management and Re-*

lated Topics (SMART) Journal, 2(2), 36–43. Retrieved from http://www.thesmartjournal.com/volume2.html

Schön, D. A. (1987). *Educating the reflective practitioner: Toward a new design for teaching and learning in the professions.* San Francisco: Jossey-Bass.

Smith, S. (2010). Designing sport management internships. In J. Miller & T. Seidler (Eds.), *A practical guide to sport management internships.* Durham, NC: Carolina Academic Press.

Somerick, N. M. (Spring, 2001). Strategies for managing an intern's performance. *Public Relations Quarterly, 46*(1), 23–25.

Stark, J. S., & Lowther, M. A. (1988). *Strengthening the ties that bind: Integrating liberal and professional study.* Report of the Professional Preparation Network. Ann Arbor: University of Michigan.

Stier, W. F. (2002). Sport management internships: From theory to practice. *Strategies, 15*(4), 7–9.

Sturges, J. S. (1993, October). When is an employee truly an employee? *HR Magazine, 38*(10), 56–58.

Sutton, W. A. (1989). The role of internships in sport management curricula: A model for development. *Journal of Physical Education, Recreation, and Dance, 60*(7), 20–24.

Swift, C. O., & Russell, K. (1999). Business school internships: Legal concerns. *Journal of Education for Business, 75*(1), 23–26.

Tomaskovic-Devey, D., & Stainback, K. (2007). Private sector workplaces since the Civil Rights Act discrimination and desegregation: Equal opportunity progress in U.S. *American Academy of Political & Social Science, 609*(1), 49–84.

Useem, M. (1995). Corporate restructuring and liberal learning. *Liberal Education, 81*(1), 18–23.

Verner, M. E. (2004). Internship search, selection, and solidification strategies. *Journal of Physical Education, Recreation, and Dance, 75*(1), 25–27.

Wage and Hour Division. (2010). Fact sheet #71: Internship programs under the Fair Labor Standards Act. *United States Department of Labor.* Retrieved from http://www.dol.gov/whd/regs/compliance/whdfs71.htm

Yates Borger, J. (July 2, 2000). Summer internships offer students an edge: Employers get help while workers learn. *Star-Ledger (Newark, N.J.).* Available at 2000 WL 23586820.

Young, D. S., & Baker, R. E. (2004). Linking classroom theory to professional practice: Internship as a practical learning experience worthy of academic credit. *Journal of Physical Education, Recreation, and Dance, 75*(1), 22–24.

Epilogue

In 1983, Miller Lite conducted a national survey on "American Attitudes on Sports" and discovered that 98% of Americans are affected by sport on a daily basis (Mullen, Hardy, & Sutton, 2000). In the two-plus decades since the distribution of that report, the sport industry has continued to undergo dramatic change. The size and scope of the industry today has evolved in a much broader and deeper spectrum than the initial design put forward by Walter O'Malley and Dr. James Mason to train future "sport managers" for Major League Baseball teams. It is hard to imagine, considering the broad reach of to-

"I have full-ride offers from major preschools, but I might jump right into kindergarten."

day's sport industry, that even 2% of the U.S. population would not be impacted in some manner by the sport industry.

Nearly every Fortune 500 Company, as well as smaller regional and national businesses, has some vested interest in the sport industry. Companies become involved by supporting local universities or colleges, buying signage at Minor- or Major-League Baseball parks, arranging stadium and arena naming rights deals, promotional sponsorships, and developing regional television contracts with conferences and regional broadcasting rights holders (Pace & Branch, 2005). A wide range of organizations are involved in the industry, including ticket printers, credit-card verification software providers, computerized ticketing companies (Paciolan, Ticketmaster, Stub Hub), sport marketing consulting firms (Muhleman Marketing, Turnkey Sports, GameDay Consulting), and sport executive search firms (TeamWork Consulting & WomenSportsJobs.com). It becomes readily apparent the sport industry is more extensive than just collegiate and professional sport franchises.

The challenge for today's sport management students as they prepare to enter the workforce will be to identify "what they are bringing to the table." Newcomers will only be "invited" into the sport industry if they can contribute something *of substance* and be able to demonstrate that their contribution is *substantially different* from everyone else's. Ask your parents or grandparents what life, in general, and sport, specifically, was like 45 years ago. The simplicity and lack of technology will amaze you. Now consider for a moment that if you begin your career in 2020 at the age of 22, you will likely retire near 2063 at the age of 65. How much will things have changed during that time? Aspiring sport managers need to invest the time and effort to develop some idea of what the future may hold. It will be your responsibility to identify and project what consumers (present and future) want, and develop ways to provide it.

In the 2nd edition of *Foundations of Sport Management*, Goss, Jubenville, and Crow (2009) encouraged readers to examine trends and ideas that will affect both the short- and long-term operations of sport industry. The authors also suggested that aspiring sport industry professionals consider the following areas to help make them unique when entering the workforce:

- Developing an appreciation for research
- Identifying new areas of future growth and entrepreneurship
- Developing your own professional philosophy

DEVELOPING AN APPRECIATION FOR RESEARCH

Sport managers have access to timely, credible, and relevant information to make business decisions and must be able to evaluate that information before using it, specifically regarding how knowledge is developed, produced, consumed, and utilized (Thomas, 1996). Therefore, developing an understanding of and appreciation for research has become a critical professional component for students and practitioners alike. To that end, if sport is to fulfill its role as a prominent social institution and social product, its managers must begin to fully and completely acknowledge and embrace research as the foundation upon which to build sound business models, formulate ethical imperatives, and generate long-term goals that are good for society (Lumpkin, Stoll, & Beller, 1999).

Research that is both grounded in academic theory and driven by the needs of practitioners can be shifted toward a more precise study of distinct phenomena, ideas, and events (Goss & Jubenville, 2007a). Scientifically known as phenomenology, such a perspective on research in both short-term and long-

> ### The Scholarly Sport Practitioner
>
> An employee who understands how to unite sport organizations through management practices and utilizes the power of knowledge to build a culture of continuous learning for successful organizational and stakeholder management. This critical thinker and learner will embrace research and understand how to apply the information it yields as part of day-to-day and strategic approaches to management (Goss & Jubenville, 2007b).

term decision-making and problem solving is anything but new. This phenomenological approach to research in the sport industry is important because it will allow for the development of a new prototype of sport manager and leader. We call this new prototype the Scholarly Sport Practitioner (Goss & Jubenville, 2007b).

IDENTIFYING AREAS OF FUTURE GROWTH
AND ENTREPRENEURSHIP

The expansion of the sport industry has been accelerated by the rapid changes both in consumer consumption habits and in technology. Initiatives and innovations developed due to these areas of focus will upend current notions of management, production, and consumption of sport, asking managers to look at their organizations as systems. This reconceptualization is necessary if change is to be truly innovative (Goss & Jubenville, 2007c). Currently three growing areas of emphasis that are *ripe* for future growth and entrepreneurial activities are: 1) the event environment, 2) the digital connectivity available to consumers, and 3) the safety and security of events and facilities (Gillentine, 2014).

The Event Environment

Today's consumer has different expectations than consumers from decades past. Modern consumers expect the experience to begin *prior* to arriving at the event or venue and to continue to engage them during and after the event (Gillentine, 2014). "The capacity of sport organizations (venues) to facilitate and moderate engagement from various audiences" will in essence dictate the level of success experienced by the event or facility (Ayers, 2014). Sport managers will need to become innovative and engage a variety of technological advances in order to keep up with this increasing consumer demand. It will be important for sport managers to incorporate all of the technological advances available to best meet the increasing demands of the event environment.

Connectivity

The dramatic increase in mobile usage and smart phone and tablet apps available has profoundly impacted sport consumption. While discussing sport media consumption patterns with the *SportsBusiness Journal* in 2005, ESPN and ABC Sports head George W. Bodenheimer commented that, "It's a three-screen world now. TV is your first screen.

The computer is your second screen. And your digital device is going to be your third screen" (King, 2005, ¶25). In today's environment, the third screen may well be the primary option event for those consumers attending the event (Gillentine, 2014). In order to meet the consumption, engagement, and connectivity demands of modern consumers, sport managers must place the highest emphasis on ensuring connectivity availability at events and facilities are the best available.

Entrepreneurship

The changing expectations from consumers in terms of the environment and technology offer sport mangers (existing and aspiring) a great opportunity to exercise creative ideas and concepts. The development of mobile apps and the infusion of

The sport industry has some big shoes that need to be filled. Are you ready to fill them?

those into the sport experience is a growing market. This advance accompanied with the continued development of niche sports and experiences may offer newcomers to the sport industry an outstanding entry point (as well as offering current sport industry professionals a vehicle for advancement). The challenge for the future will be to see if one or more can develop a business model that will catapult the sport beyond its current status.

DEVELOPING YOUR OWN PROFESSIONAL PHILOSOPHY

So now the ball is in your court (or field, or pool, or rink, or pitch). Embarking on your career in the sport industry, you will be challenged to develop a professional philosophy, to include your values, morals, ethical code, and work habits, that will ultimately determine your success. You will need to be your own strongest advocate but also give others (internship supervisors, bosses, colleagues) many reasons to support and mentor you along the way. While the level you reach is ultimately your responsibility, the network of support you develop along the way will form the foundation upon which you grow.

Finally, as you progress in your career—give back. Help students at your alma mater get internships and entry-level positions. Make a donation to your alma mater to support sport management scholarships and/or student organizations. Participate in the department's golf tournament and/or other activities to demonstrate your support of the program and students. The sport industry can provide a challenging, dynamic, rewarding, and impactful career . . . so don't forget to enjoy the ride.

> "DON'T LET THOSE THAT WON'T EVEN TAKE THE FIRST STEP, TALK YOU OUT OF GOING THE EXTRA MILE!"
>
> —*Stephen C. Hogan*

Discussion Activities

1. What are you prepared to do better than anyone else? What can you positively and unquestionably prove you are able to do better than anyone else?
2. Dr. Dimitris Gargalianos, a sport management professor at Democritos University of Thrace, Greece said, "It is better to know than to have, but it is better to understand than to know." Explain this statement and relate it to your future in the sport industry.
3. What is your dream job? What are the actual skills required of this position? Do you have those skills? What is your plan to acquire the skills you may not currently possess?
4. Prepare or update your personal résumé. Have someone else review it for you and gather their comments. Compare those comments against the qualifications of your dream job.

References

Gillentine, A. (2014). The Impact of Digital Technology on the Sport & Entertainment Industry. Sports Venues Management Training Conference. Beijing, China.

Gillentine, A. (2014). The Evolution of Sport and Entertainment Consumption. International Conference of Sport, Leisure and Hospitality Management. Taipei, Taiwan.

Gillentine, A. (2012). Moving Mountains: The Need for Shifting Paradigms in Sport Management. In Gillentine, A., Baker, B., & Cuneen, J. (Eds). *Critical Essays in Sport Management: Exploring and Achieving a Paradigm Shift.* Phoenix: Holcomb Hathaway Publishing.

Goss, B. D., & Jubenville, C. B. (2007a). Phenomenology. Retrieved February 12, 2008, from: http://www.jsasonline.org/vision.htm

Goss, B. D., & Jubenville, C. B. (2007b). Scholarly Sport Practitioner. Retrieved February 12, 2008, from: http://www.jsasonline.org/level2/scholar.htm

Goss, B. D., & Jubenville, C. B. (2007c). Social Responsibility. Retrieved February 12, 2008, from: http://www.jsasonline.org/level2/social.htm

Goss, B., Jubenville, C., & Crow, C. (2009). Your future in the sport industry. In A. Gillentine and R. B. Crow (Eds.), *Foundations of Sport Management.* (2nd Ed. pp. 281–296). Morgantown: FiT Publishing.

King, B. (2005, March 14). Reaching today's fans. *SportsBusiness Journal*, 17–21.

Lumpkin, A., Stoll, S. K., & Beller, J. M. (1999).

Sport ethics: applications for fair play. Boston: Edward E. Bartell.

Mohanty, J. N., & McKenna, W. (1989). *Husserl's phenomenology: a textbook.* Washington, DC: University Press of America.

Mullin, B.J., Hardy, S., & Sutton, W.A. (2000). *Sport marketing.* Champaign, IL: Human Kinetics.

Pace, D., & Branch, D. (2005). Your future in the sport industry. In A. Gillentine & R. B. Crow (Eds.), *Foundations of Sport Management* (1st Ed. pp. 197–206). Morgantown: FiT Publishing.

Roy, D.P., & Goss, B.D. (2007). A conceptual framework of influences on fantasy sports consumption. *Marketing Management Journal, 17*(2), 96–108.

Smith, C. (1962). *Phenomenology of perception.* New York: Humanities Press.

Thomas, J. R. (1996). *Research methods in physical activity.* Champaign, IL: Human Kinetics.

Thurston, P., Clift, R., & Schacht, M. (1993). Preparing leaders for change-oriented schools. *Phi Delta Kappan, 75*(3), 259–265.

U.S. Census Bureau. (n.d.). *Hispanics in the United States.* Retrieved February 19, 2008, from http://www.census.gov/population/www/socdemo/hispanic/files/Internet_Hispanic_in_US_2006.pdf

Wheatley, M. J. (1993). *Leadership and the new science: learning about organization from an orderly universe.* San Francisco: Berrett-Koehler Publishers, Inc.

Glossary

80/20 principle: a marketing principle suggesting that a focus be made on moving consumers up the consumer escalator while keeping the existing heavy user segment content, as heavy users are known to be responsible for up to 80% of all purchases, though they may represent as few as 20% of all consumers.

action sports: athletic endeavors considered to have a higher level of inherent danger than others, involving speed, height, extreme physical exertion, highly specialized gear, or spectacular stunts; also called adventure sports or extreme sports.

ad valorem taxes: a tax, duty, or fee that varies based on the value of the products, services, or property on which it is levied.

administrative rules and regulations: directives enforced by administrative agencies that generally carry the force of law as if they were passed by Congress or the state legislature, and violators of the rules and regulations are subject to the penalties provided in them.

The Age Discrimination in Employment Act (ADEA) of 1967: U.S. law initially passed to protect workers age 40 and older from age discrimination. The ADEA was amended by the Older Workers Benefit Protection Act of 1990 (OWBPA) to include a focus on age discrimination and loss of workplace benefits.

agencies: businesses or services authorized to act for others.

AIDA: advertising concept that stands for awareness, interest, desire, and action, which is designed to move consumers along in the progression toward actual product purchase.

alternative dispute resolution (ADR): resolving a dispute through any means other than litigation or negotiation.

ambush marketing: a direct competing brand in the same product category staging a presence to create confusion in the mind of the consumer regarding who is the official sponsor.

American Bowl: NFL exhibition, in which preseason and regular season games are played in a number of countries around the world.

Americans with Disabilities Act (ADA) of 1990: U.S. law that protects individuals with disabilities from being discriminated against in the workplace.

appeal: the transfer of a case from a lower to a higher court for a new hearing.

arbitration: the submission of a dispute to a neutral third party (arbitrator) who listens to all parties, considers the legal position of each, then renders a decision to resolve the dispute.

arbitrator: neutral third party who acts much like a judge and listens to all parties in an arbitration, considers the legal position of each, then renders a decision to resolve the dispute.

Arizona Sports Summit Accord: edict issued in May of 1999 by a gathering of nearly 50 influential sport leaders that encourages greater emphasis on the ethical and character-building aspects of athletic competition. The goal of formulating this document was to establish a framework of principles and values that would be adopted and practiced widely by those involved with sport organizations.

assumed risk: the inherent danger within an activity.

athlete agent statutes: laws that seek to protect prospective professional athletes and regulate athlete agents.

balance sheet: a snapshot of a business's financial condition at a specific moment in time, usually at the close of an accounting period, which comprises assets, liabilities, and owners' or stockholders' equity.

barriers to effective communication: variables that impede productive interaction and correspondence, the three most notable being linguistic, psychological, and environmental.

Baseball World Cup Tournament: plan announced in 2004 by Bud Selig, the Commissioner of MLB, which called for a 16-team tournament to be held during spring training in warm-weather cities across the U.S.

behavioral approach: in conceptualizing leadership, this approach emphasized what leaders and managers actually did on the job, as opposed to their personal characteristics; theorists focused not only on what leaders would do, but also on how often and at what intensity they would do certain things to distinguish themselves as leaders.

benefits: the distinct advantages gained from an investment.

Bill of Rights: the first ten amendments to the U.S. Constitution, added in 1791 to protect the essential rights and liberties of all citizens.

blog: short for "weblog," a type of website that presents regular entries of an individual's commentary and descriptions of events, usually in reverse chronological order, and that gives readers the opportunity to comment.

booking: the act of engaging and contracting an event or attraction.

Bosman ruling: 1995 ruling by the European Court of Justice, which established free agency for out-of-contract players; it has been considered a landmark decision with significant impact on the structure, development, and economics of professional football (soccer) clubs throughout Europe.

brand equity: all of the distinguishing qualities of a commercial brand that result in personal commitment to and demand for the brand.

brand insistence: behavior in which the consumer wants or is willing to buy or purchase a specific product only.

brand loyalty: a more intense form of brand insistence in which the consumer develops a passion about or loyalty to a specific product.

brand preference: the extent to which a customer prefers to use a certain product or service.

brand recognition: the extent to which a brand is recognized for its advertised attributes or communications.

breach of warranty: a breach by a seller of the terms of a warranty.

business (personal) financial management: directing and controlling the use of cash flow and monetary operations and funds.

buy in: the incentive for companies or potential sponsors to invest in a program, event, team, etc.

case law: law based on judicial decision and precedent rather than on statutes.

case study method: a curriculum that presents students with the opportunity to read previous cases in order to learn how courts make legal decisions by applying relevant law to the facts of the case.

cash budget: a forecast of estimated cash receipts and disbursements for a specified period of time.

cash flow: money entering and exiting an organization; cash inflows and outflows in your personal life and in various business enterprises.

casuals: types of visitors who were not drawn in by the event being studied.

Certificates of Participation (COPs): public financing instruments that involve the governmental entity creating a corporation to buy/build a public assembly facility, such as an arena or convention and visitors' center; financing is obtained by buying a share of the lease revenues of an agreement made by a municipal or governmental entity, rather than the bond being secured by those revenues.

charitable immunity: immunity from civil liability, especially for negligent torts, that is granted to a charitable or nonprofit organization.

charitable organizations: institutions or organizations established to help the needy or for humanitarian or philanthropic purposes beneficial to the public.

circuit: the area or district under the jurisdiction of a judge in which periodic court sessions are held.

civil law: the body of laws dealing with the rights of private citizens; includes everything that is not criminal law.

civil rights: the rights belonging to an individual by virtue of citizenship, especially the fundamental freedoms and privileges guaranteed by the 13th and 14th Amendments to the U.S. Constitution and by subsequent acts of Congress, including civil liberties, due process, equal protection of the laws, and freedom from discrimination.

Clayton Antitrust Act: law passed by the U.S. Congress in 1914 as an amendment to clarify and supplement the Sherman Antitrust Act of 1890, which prohibited exclusive sales contracts, local price cutting to freeze out competitors, rebates, interlocking directorates in corporations capitalized at $1 million or more in the same field of business, and intercorporate stock holdings.

Club Licensing System: essential proactive steps for protecting the future health and viability of European football.

clutter: the result of too many sponsors being associated with a sport entity in which no single brand image stands out as the sponsor.

code of ethics: a system of principles governing morality and acceptable conduct.

collective bargaining agreement (CBA): a negotiation contract outlining the collective bargaining terms drawn up by the owners and union representatives, who are acting on the behalf of workers and employees.

Commission on Sport Management Accreditation (COSMA): an independent accrediting body that promotes and recognizes excellence in sport management education through specialized accreditation.

commitment: in sport, the frequency, duration, and intensity of involvement, or the willingness to expend money, time, and energy in a pattern of sport involvement.

common law: the system of laws originated and developed in England and based on court decisions, on the doctrines implicit in those decisions, and on customs and usages rather than on codified written laws.

competition: a contest for some prize, honor, or advantage; rivalry for supremacy.

competitive balance: when conditions exist within competition that cause parity, or equality, in amount, status, or value.

competitive imbalance: when conditions exist within competition that cause a disparity in amount, status, or value.

complex information: information in a piece of communication that is potentially confusing to the receiver, which must be carefully presented.

compliance: observance of official requirements.

compound interest: interest that is calculated not only on the initial principal but also the accumulated interest of prior periods.

conceptual skills: in sport management terms, these skills involve the ability to conceptualize how all the different parts of the organization fit together so that established goals and objectives can be achieved.

conduct: the way a person acts, especially from the standpoint of morality and ethics.

consideration: the payment of money by one party to the other, who in turn provides something of value.

consumer escalator: a marketing model in which the goal is to move consumers from non-aware/non-consumers onto a consumption "escalator" and ultimately up each level from light to medium to heavy users.

contemporary theories: leadership theories, developed in the past two decades, that presented a broader perspective of the leader-follower relationship as they examined the changes in the followers that came as a result of leader influence, and characterized the leader as charismatic, inspirational, visionary, and/or transformational.

content: the subject matter or essential meaning of something.

contingency approaches: see definition for **situational approaches**.

contract: an agreement, or exchange of promises, that creates legally enforceable duties and obligations for all parties to the contract.

conventional: the second of Kohlberg's three stages of moral reasoning, which is based on a person's conformance to society's rules and is the level of most adolescents and adults in societies.

Copyright Act of 1976: law that extended the length of protection for individual authors to the author's entire life plus fifty years and did the same for works for hire with seventy-five years.

core: the basic or most important part.

corporate social responsibility: obligation of a corporate business to fulfill a role within the surrounding community, assuming economic, legal, ethical, and philanthropic responsibilities.

corporation: a company formed by an agreement between the state and the persons forming the company, with the state requiring legal documentation of the agreement.

counteroffer: an offer made in return by one who rejects an unsatisfactory offer.

Courts of Appeals: a court to which appeals are made on points of law resulting from the judgment of a lower court.

credibility: the quality of being believable or trustworthy.

crime: an act committed or omitted in violation of a law forbidding or commanding it and for which punishment is imposed upon conviction.

criminal law: law that deals with unlawful acts committed against the public as a whole, in which a defendant is accused of violating a statute defining a criminal act, thereby committing a crime.

crowd management: organizational tool used to assist venue directors and/or event coordinators in providing a safe and enjoyable environment for patrons.

culture: the socially transmitted behavior patterns, arts, beliefs, institutions, and all other products of human work and thought.

damages: money ordered to be paid as compensation for injury or loss.

decision making: choosing a course of action based on the evaluation of necessary information.

Declaration of Independence: the declaration of the Congress of the Thirteen United States of America, on the 4th of July, 1776, by which they formally declared that these colonies were free and independent States, not subject to the government of Great Britain.

defection: to abandon a position or association; in sport sponsorships, to cause a company or sponsor not to renew.

demographics: the characteristics of human populations and population segments that are used to identify consumer markets, and those that describe their state of being, such as income level, education level, zip code, marital status, age, race, religious affiliation, occupation type, number of children in the home, and gender.

deontology: ethical theory concerned with duties and rights, based on the idea of absolute rules of moral behavior.

Department of Education: the United States federal department, created in 1979, that administers all federal programs dealing with education, including federal aid to educational institutions and students.

depreciation: the allocation of the cost of an asset over a period of time for accounting and tax purposes.

direct spending: dollars spent explicitly for a specific program or purpose.

director of finance: assistant to the head of the management team who is responsible for fiscal accountability, budgeting, cost control, contract negotiations, and financing.

director of marketing: assistant to the head of the management team who is responsible for market planning, advertising, and sales (i.e., sponsorships, merchandise, and tickets).

director of operations: the primary assistant to the head of the management team who has a wide variety of departmental responsibilities, including event coordination; engineering; security, safety, and medical services; and maintenance and housekeeping.

discretionary expense: a recurring or non-recurring expense for goods and services that are either non-essential or more expensive than necessary; examples include entertainment expenses, wellness programs, and speakers; also referred to as step cost.

discrimination: treatment or consideration based on class or category rather than individual merit; partiality or prejudice.

disseminator: an informational role filled by the sport manager in which he or she screens information and passes it along to employees who otherwise would probably not have access to it.

disturbance handler: a decisional role filled by a sport manager in which the individual is responsible for reacting to changes affecting the organization that are unexpected and beyond his or her immediate control.

diversity: a range or variety; having difference among the assembled or included parts of a group.

diversity of citizenship: a condition in which the parties to an action are of diverse state or national citizenship.

division of labor: a directive that shows the separation of departments by function or specialization.

downward flow of communication: when information is transmitted from upper levels of management to the middle and lower levels of the organization.

drug testing: testing administered to detect the presence of drugs, especially from a blood or urine sample and especially for illegal substances.

economic benefit: a measure of the economic gain in the local economy.

economic impact: the total economic gain or loss after accounting for an event's costs.

economic responsibilities: implicit requirement of organizations to produce goods and services and sell them at a profit, because that is how a capitalist society operates.

eduselling: a process by which sport professionals approach new users of the products or services more as "teachers" than as salespeople.

effective planning: a process in which the sport manager determines the most efficient method(s) to utilize when constructing communication to peers, employees, and the public.

emotional content: the emotions or feelings inherent in a communication that often offer information other than that of the intended message.

equilibrium price: the point where the supply curve and the demand curve overlap.

English Premiership: the Division I Football (Soccer) League in England.

entrepreneur: a decisional role filled by a sport manager in which he or she looks for ways to improve his or her work group, adapt to internal and external changes, and direct the organization toward opportunities that initiate growth.

entrepreneurship: the process whereby an individual or group of individuals uses organized efforts to create value and grow by fulfilling wants and needs through innovation and uniqueness.

environment: the totality of circumstances or conditions surrounding an individual or group of individuals.

epistemology: the branch of philosophy that studies the origin and nature of human knowledge, its presuppositions, and its validity.

Equal Access Act: act that prohibits any school receiving federal funds from denying equal access to, or discriminating against, any student desiring to conduct a meeting on school premises, when the meeting deals with religious, political, or philosophical subjects.

equilibrium price: the point at which the supply curve and the demand curve overlap, where the amount of product demanded equals the amount of product supplied.

equitable treatment: handling or dealing with equally.

Establishment Clause: a clause in the U.S. Constitution forbidding Congress from establishing a state religion.

ethical challenge: moral conflict; an ethical situation that requires a choice between options that are or seem equally unfavorable or mutually exclusive; also called an ethical dilemma.

ethical dilemma: see **ethical challenge**.

ethical responsibilities: requirement of organizations to operate by established norms defining suitable behavior.

ethics: a set of principles or values that are used to determine right and wrong.

Euro 2004: 2004 European soccer tournament that saw record TV audiences, topping those from the 2000 tournament by more than 15%; it was estimated that 2.5 billion individuals, or about 80 million per match, watched.

European Union: an economic and political union established in 1993 after the ratification of the Maastricht Treaty by members of the European Community, which forms its core. In establishing the European Union, the treaty expanded the political scope of the European Community, especially in the area of foreign and security policy, and provided for the creation of a central European bank and the adoption of a common currency by the end of the 20th century.

European Club Association (ECA): organization representing the interests of over 100 European football clubs; replaced the G-14 in 2008.

evaluation: the process of examining a system to determine whether or not certain criteria were met.

exclusivity: having the exclusive right or privilege.

expense: any cost of doing business resulting from revenue-generating activities.

expense budget: a calculation of projected future expenses analyzed in relationship to cash available, which is used to make planning and management decisions.

explicit expenditures: the cost of overtly making one choice over another.

fad: a fashion that is taken up with great enthusiasm for a brief period of time; a craze.

fantasy sports: sports competitions with imaginary teams that the participants own, manage, and coach, with the games based on statistics generated by actual professional sports players and teams.

federal court system: court system established by the federal government and having jurisdiction over questions of federal law.

federal question: a question that falls under the jurisdiction of a federal court because it requires a resolution of the construction or application of federal law.

The Federal Trademark Act of 1946: statute that authorizes owners of trademarks to register them with the U.S. government, and provides protection against others who seek to use the trademark without permission; also known as the Lanham Act.

federal trial courts: courts that operate essentially the same as state trial courts, providing a trial of the case before a judge and jury; also called U.S. District Courts, followed by a geographical description of the location of the court (e.g., United States District Court for the Western District of Pennsylvania), of which there are 94 throughout the U.S., with at least one located in every state.

feedback: information gathered from within the organization and its customers and given to upper management, preventing them from being out-of-touch.

figurehead: the first of three interpersonal roles a sport manager must fulfill, which involves fulfilling certain ceremonial functions as the result of being in charge of a certain department or the organization as a whole.

final portfolio reports: formal assessments written at the conclusion of an internship by interns in order to assess their overall experience as well as critique their performance.

financial considerations: concerns about cost or funding.

Financial Fair Play (FFP) Regulations: aim to ensure that clubs balance their books and avoid spending beyond their means in search for fast success; otherwise clubs will face tough sanctions.

fit: in sport marketing, the compatibility of the sport property's image with the desired image of the brand, as well as how well needs are matched between the target market of the sport entity and the target market of the brand.

fixed cost: a cost that does not vary depending on production or sales levels, such as rent, property, insurance, or interest expense; also referred to as non-variable cost.

flow of communication: the direction information travels among stakeholders: downward, upward, and laterally.

foundations: institutions founded and supported by an endowment.

future value: the value at some point in the future of a present amount of money.

G-14: a proposal, also referred to as Super League, offered by the European football (soccer) industry to come closer to the American model, which would include football giants like Ajax Amsterdam, Manchester United, AC Milan, and Real Madrid.

gender discrimination: discrimination based on sex.

gender equity: a cause championed by the IOC, which supports equal treatment of men and women in their respective competitions at the Olympic Games.

gender testing: the issue of verifying the eligibility of an athlete to compete in a sporting event that is limited to a single sex.

general liability: liability for bodily injury, death, or damage to property owned by others to which an employer may be subject either directly or by reason of liability arising out of an act, error, or omission of its employee, agent, or officer in the course and scope of employment.

general obligation bonds: bonds typically used to finance traditional capital projects such as highways, roads, and sewers that will be paid back through the taxing power of the issuing authority. General obligation bonds are issued against the general full faith and credit of state and local governments.

generally accepted accounting principles (GAAP): a combination of authoritative standards, set by policy boards made up of the American Institute of Certified Public Accountants (AICPA) and Financial Accounting Standards Board (FASB), in addition to the Security Exchange Commission (SEC), an agency of the federal government, that establish the accepted ways of doing accounting.

gigantism: excessive growth of a body or any of its parts.

globalization: the process by which the experience of everyday life, marked by the diffusion of commodities and ideas, is becoming standardized around the world.

goals: in regard to a mission statement, the achievable statements provided by management, ideally developed through consultation with all stakeholders in the venue, usually based on the mission statement and used to justify the fiscal resources requested in a budget document.

grassroots programs: programs that focus on people or society at a local level rather than at the center of major political activity.

gross negligence: acting in such a reckless manner that the court will consider that the defendant exhibited a conscious indifference toward the safety of the plaintiff, even though the defendant did not intend to injure the plaintiff.

hazing: to persecute or harass with meaningless, difficult, or humiliating tasks.

human skills: in sport management terms, these skills involve aspects of leading, communicating, motivating, and, in general, dealing with all aspects of employee relations on a daily basis.

idealized influence: the position of role model that the transformational leader assumes in the eyes of his or her followers.

image: a distinctive but intangible quality that surrounds a product that is to make it appealing to the consumer.

image enhancement: the positive effects done to the image of a company or sponsor as part of being associated with a certain event, team, or fundraiser.

implicit expenditures: the intangible benefits lost by making one choice over another.

income statement: a business financial statement that lists revenues, expenses, and net income throughout a given period.

indirect spending: dollars spent as a secondary result of direct spending.

individualized consideration: the role of coach or mentor that the transformational leader assumes in the eyes of followers in an organization.

induced spending: dollars spent by wage earners as a result of increased money flow caused by direct and indirect spending.

induction: the act or process of inducing or bringing about.

infringement: encroachment of a right or privilege.

inspirational motivation: the idea that transformational leaders will inspire and motivate those around them, encouraging others to find challenge and personal meaning in their work, and will thereby foster enthusiasm throughout the organization.

instrumental values: in ethical theory, the means that one will use to achieve the ends.

intellectual stimulation: the component of transformational leadership theory that resides in the leader's ability to challenge followers to be more creative and innovative, and to be supportive of follower efforts even when in error.

intentional torts: civil wrongs that occur when the party acting wrongfully, called the tortfeasor, intends to cause the harm by committing the act that causes the injury.

intermediate appeals court: a court whose jurisdiction is to review decisions of lower courts or agencies.

International Association of Assembly Managers (IAAM): a group composed of leaders who represent a diverse industry—entertainment, sports, conventions, trade, hospitality, and tourism—and manage, or provide products and services to, public assembly facilities like arenas, amphitheaters, auditoriums, convention centers/exhibit halls, performing arts venues, stadiums, and university complexes.

international environment: cultural or social conditions extending across or transcending national boundaries.

international federations (IFs): federations that are responsible for developing their sport(s) worldwide and for staging world championships.

International Olympic Committee (IOC): an international, non-governmental, nonprofit organization whose main responsibility is to organize the Olympic Games, but that also owns the rights to the Olympic properties, including the Olympic symbol, flag, motto, emblem, anthem, flame, and torch.

International Paralympic Committee (IPC) is an international non-profit organization and the global governing body for the Paralympic Movement.

internship policies: the rules, guidelines, and specifications given by the department that is offering the internship.

interview: a formal meeting in person in which questioning is used to gather data and opinions.

involvement: to occupy or engage the interest of; when referring to sport consumers, can be behavioral (the actual doing of a sport activity), cognitive (seeking out information and knowledge about a sport), and affective (the feelings and emotions a sport consumer has for a particular activity or team).

IOC commissions: groups whose duty is the promotion of Olympic ideals (e.g., marketing, medical, ethics, nominations, press, TV and Internet rights, Olympic solidarity).

job description: a summary of all the roles and responsibilities of a particular job.

judgment: a determination of a court of law; a judicial decision.

justice: the upholding of what is just, especially fair treatment and due reward in accordance with honor, standards, or law.

kinesics: the appearance and physical mannerisms of a speaker.

Lanham Act: statute that authorizes owners of trademarks to register them with the U.S. government, and provides protection against others who seek to use the trademark without permission; also known as the Federal Trademark Act of 1946.

lateral flow of communication: when information travels between the various individuals or groups at the same or equivalent levels of management.

law: a body of enforceable rules, established by the lawmaking authorities of a society, governing the relationships among individuals, and between individuals and their government.

law of demand: the law that states that when the price of an item declines, the demand for that item increases.

leader: the second interpersonal role a sport manager must fulfill, which involves directing subordinates toward the achievement of assigned tasks and may require the manager to hire, train, supervise, motivate, and evaluate employees in the workplace.

legal capacity: a person's capability and power under law to engage in a particular undertaking or transaction or to maintain a particular status or relationship with another.

legal responsibilities: requirements for organizations to reach goals within legal constraints.

legality: adherence to or observance of the law.

legislature: an officially elected or otherwise selected body of people vested with the responsibility and power to make laws for a political unit, such as a state or nation.

levels of branding: the levels used to assess consumer enthusiasm or intensity toward a specific brand, starting with brand recognition and brand preference, on through to brand insistence and brand loyalty.

leveraging: developing an integrated plan that specifies the role promotional tools will play and the extent to which each will be used.

liaison: the third interpersonal role a sport manager must fulfill, which involves developing and cultivating relationships with individuals and groups in other departments or from different organizations.

lifestyle marketing: type of marketing technique in which the company attempts to cut through all the other selling messages by appealing to consumers who have or desire the lifestyle depicted in the sport sponsorship relationship.

limited duty: the limited responsibility of management to protect those involved in an event who are at risk for injury, such as the obligation of baseball franchises to protect their fans from foul balls.

limited liability company (LLC): a business entity formed upon filing articles of organization with the proper state authorities and paying all fees; LLCs provide the limited liability to their members and are taxed like a partnership, preventing double taxation.

linguistics: the study of the nature, structure, and variation of language, including phonetics, phonology, morphology, syntax, semantics, sociolinguistics, and pragmatics.

litigation: the process of filing a lawsuit so that a court can resolve the disagreement.

marginal cost: how much more an individual has to spend to get more of what he or she wants, without worrying about what already has been spent.

marketing objectives: the reasons or goals behind a particular promotion or marketing campaign that clearly identify the desired results.

mediation: the submission of a dispute to a disinterested third person who intervenes between the parties in an attempt to settle their dispute without going to court.

mediator: the third party in a mediation who communicates with all parties to the dispute, presents proposals from each party to the other, and facilitates resolution of the dispute, if possible.

message credibility: believability or trustworthiness associated specifically with the source and content of a message.

minors: in legal terms, persons under the age of 18.

mission statement: guidelines that outline the parameters for operating a venue and provide the basis for the development of goals and objectives for the venue.

monitor: an informational role filled by the sport manager in which he or she must search the internal and external environment for information that could affect the organization.

monopoly: a company or group having exclusive control over a commercial activity.

moral behavior: the execution of an act deemed right or wrong.

moral development: a process of growth in which a person's capacity to reason morally is developed through cognitive maturation and experiences.

moral reasoning: the decision process in which an individual determines whether a course of action is right or wrong.

morals: the fundamental baseline values that dictate appropriate behavior within a culture or society.

municipal bonds, or **munis**: bonds in the capital market issued by state and local governments to finance their capital spending programs for building arenas, stadiums, parking lots, and infrastructure upgrades, including roads, water/sewer, utility right of way, and other utility needs. The bonds are issued by municipalities, subdivisions of states; they are tax exempt because the interest investors receive is exempt from federal taxation.

myopia: in sport marketing, the result of sport personnel focusing solely on the sport product and not considering the needs and wants of consumers.

myth: a popular belief or story that has become associated with a person, institution, or occurrence, especially one considered to illustrate a cultural ideal, which may often seem like fact but is not always the case.

National Governing Bodies (NGBs): respective organizations that develop sport on a national level; e.g., USA Track and Field.

National Olympic Committees (NOCs): individual countries representing the IOC that are responsible for promoting the Olympic Movement nationally, developing athletes, and sending delegations to the Games.

natural rights: rights that are not derived from any government, but are God-given and inherent to all people.

NBA Europe Live Tour: with four U.S. teams hold training camps abroad and compete against each other and against European basketball clubs in multiple European cities and countries.

negligence: the failure to exercise ordinary care, or the degree of care that the law requires, by acting differently than a person of ordinary care would have acted under the same or similar circumstances.

negotiation: a process involving formal or informal discussions in order to reach an agreement.

negotiator: a decisional role filled by the sport manager in which he or she is responsible for conferring with employees and work groups located within the organization, as well as those that are on the outside.

NFL Europa: extension league created after the World League of American Football (WLAF) disbanded after two seasons, which was reintroduced in 1995 in European cities only; currently consists of six teams in the Netherlands, Germany, and Scotland.

niche events: events specially suited to a person's interests, abilities, or nature; appealing to a distinct segment of a market.

noise: the collective dissonance caused by radio, television, the Internet, billboards, print advertisements, etc. that helps desensitize the consumer to all messages.

non-price promotions: publicity other than price promotions that are designed to make the activity or event more attractive and enjoyable to consumers, such as giveaways, fireworks, autograph-signing sessions, and concerts.

non-variable cost: a cost that does not vary depending on production or sales levels, such as rent, property, insurance, or interest expense; also referred to as fixed cost.

objectives: the activities to be implemented to reach the overall goal, sometimes called action strategies.

observational studies: a data-gathering procedure used primarily in the psychology and sociology fields in which information is obtained by observing and recording subjects' behavior without their knowledge.

offer and acceptance: a process that involves the involved parties making a series of proposals to the other until the negotiations culminate with an agreement.

Office of Civil Rights (OCR): the division of the Department of Education has been charged with enforcing Title IX, which is the law that prohibits sex discrimination in education agencies that receive federal funding.

Older Workers Benefit Protection Act of 1990 (OWBPA): amendment to the Americans with Disabilities Act of 1990 meant to include a focus on age discrimination and loss of workplace benefits. The OWBPA also provided for older worker protection in the area of protocol establishment that must be followed when employers are asked to waive their rights when filing settlement claims regarding age discrimination.

Olympic Broadcasting Services (OBS): created by the IOC to ensure greater control over the quality and distribution of Olympic Games coverage.

Olympic Charter: governing body of the International Olympic Committee.

Olympic Games: a group of modern international athletic contests, revived in 1896 by Pierre de Coubertin, held as separate winter and summer competitions every four years in a different city.

Olympic Marketing Programme: the driving force for the financial stability of the Olympic Movement, which produces revenues through broadcasting rights, sponsorship, ticketing, licensing, and other means.

The Olympic Movement: the term used to refer to the incomparable growth of international exposure, worldwide audience appeal, and multicultural activities that draw the attention of virtually every demographic of the Olympic Games.

The Olympic Partner (TOP) Programme: introduced for the first time in the 1984 Los Angeles Olympic Games, this program, operated by the IOC, handles Olympic sponsorship agreements and gives sponsors exclusive rights to associate with the Olympic Games and use all Olympic properties.

operating expense: expense arising in the normal course of running a business, such as an office electricity bill.

opportunity cost: what one gives up in turn for obtaining what one wants.

Organizing Committee of the Olympic Games (OCOG): formed after a city has been awarded the honor and responsibility of hosting the Olympic and Paralympic Games, its role is to handle all operational aspects of the Games and to ultimately put on the events.

over-commercialization: the overwhelming presence of commercial business, marketing, etc. that may be so saturated as to deter consumers.

paid internship: a paid appointment in which the individual undergoes supervised practical training for future employment.

Paralympic Games: major international multi-sport event, involving athletes with a range of physical disabilities.

Paralympic Movement: see **International Paralympic Committee**.

participant-oriented organizations: organizations often managed by individuals with very specialized skill sets, such as municipal parks, YMCAs, recreation departments, collegiate recreation settings, and special events.

partnership: a company owned by two or more individuals who have entered into an agreement.

perception: recognition and interpretation of sensory stimuli based chiefly on memory.

personal credibility: believability or trustworthiness associated specifically with a person or organization's character or past actions.

phenomenology: the study of distinct phenomena, ideas, and events; a description, history, or explanation of phenomena.

philanthropic responsibilities: requirement for organizations to give back to their communities.

planning: formulating a scheme or program for the accomplishment or attainment of a specific goal.

podcast: a digital media file distributed over the Internet using syndication feeds for playback on portable media players and computers.

postconventional: the third of Kohlberg's three stages of moral reasoning, in which the individual's values are formed independently of social norms.

pouring rights: the exclusive ability to sell soft drinks, bottled water, and beer in a facility.

precedent: a judicial decision that may be used as a standard in subsequent similar cases.

preconventional: the first of Kohlberg's three stages of moral reasoning, which is characterized by a separation between conventions and the individual.

The Pregnancy Discrimination Act: an amendment to Title VII of the Civil Rights Act of 1964, which provides protection for pregnancy-based discrimination including pregnancy, childbirth, and pregnancy-related medical conditions.

present value: the value of what a cash flow to be received in the future is worth in today's dollars.

price promotions: type of publicity in which the actual cost of consuming an event is manipulated or lowered to encourage people to attend.

primary skills: in sport management terms, these are the skills necessary to direct employees toward the achievement of established goals and objectives, without which a sport manager would be ineffective.

private law: law that governs the relationship among private citizens.

private seat licenses (PSLs): an amenity offered at certain venues in which the purchaser obtains exclusive use of his or her own private seat(s).

pro forma statements: statements based on hypothetical figures used as a means of assessing how assets might be managed under differing future scenarios.

procedural law: the method of enforcing rights and obligations given to citizens by substantive law.

product adoption process: an extension of the AIDA concept that awareness builds interest and knowledge of a brand's associated benefits, which in effect, creates an image in the mind of the consumer.

product purchase intentions: a key sales objective that is most often measured to assess consumers' tendencies and perceptions when buying certain products.

products liability: liability imposed on a manufacturer or seller for a defective and unreasonably dangerous product.

proxemics: the study of how individuals communicate through their use of space.

psychographics: the use of demographics to study and measure attitudes, values, lifestyles, and opinions, as for marketing purposes; often refer to consumers' state-of-mind, exploring the likes and dislikes of consumers and using the similarities to create the segments.

psychological: of, relating to, or arising from the mind or emotions.

public assembly facilities: assembly halls, conference centers, stadiums, arenas, etc. that are available to fulfill the needs of public meetings, conventions, and conferences, as well as host a number of different events such as athletic contests, concerts, conventions, and trade shows.

public good: the well-being of the general public.

public law: law that governs the relationship between citizens and their government.

public relations: a program designed to influence the opinions of people within a target market through responsible and acceptable performance, based on mutually satisfactory two-way communication.

racism: discrimination or prejudice based on race.

reasonably prudent person standard: standard applied by the court that will determine if the defendant acted as a reasonably prudent person would have acted under the same or similar circumstances.

recall: the ability of a spectator to remember and correctly identify a sponsor's brand without input or prompting.

recognition: the ability of a spectator to correctly identify the brand of a sponsor from a list.

Recreational Use statutes: legislation that provides liability protection to owners and operators of recreational facilities by placing responsibility for injury on the participant who voluntarily assumed the risk; the statutes cover activities such as equestrian activities, snow skiing, roller skating, whitewater rafting, snowmobiling, amusement rides, and, in a few cases, provides protection for "any sport or recreational opportunity."

reflective learning: an educational philosophy meant to engage one's knowledge about the world and others critically and analytically, including self-assessment of teaching goals, responsibilities, and effectiveness.

regional multiplier: the value multiplied by direct spending to estimate total spending, or economic benefit, which is used to measure how many times money changes hands in the community before it leaves or leaks out of the region.

relational: of or arising from kinship; indicating or constituting relation.

renewal: the act of restoring or resuming a contract.

request for proposal (RFP): an invitation for providers of a product or service to bid on the right to supply that product or service to the individual or entity that issued the RFP.

resistance: the act or power of resisting, opposing, or withstanding.

resource allocator: a decisional role filled by a sport manager in which he or she distributes organizational resources to different employees or work groups.

return on investment: the income that an investment provides in a year.

revenue bond: bond issued by a municipality to finance a specific public works project and supported by the revenues of that project.

revenue budget: a calculation of projected future revenue used to make planning and management decisions.

risk management: the process to reduce or limit risk exposure in a venue.

risk management plan: a document defining how reducing or limiting risk exposure will be implemented in the context of a particular project.

Robert's Rules of Order: procedures that assure legislative fairness, maximum participation, and an orderly process by participants, while protecting individuals from domination by certain vocal sub-groups.

S corporation: a C corporation—also known as a standard business corporation—that files IRS form 2553 to elect a special tax status with the IRS.

Salary Cost Management Protocol: the Football League sets its own rules for ensuring self-sustainability at a club level, including measures for acceptable losses and owners' guarantee needed, salary and transfer fee control restrictions, and incentives for sensible infrastructure investments.

Scalar Principle: principle referring to the chain of command that denotes a clear line of authority from the top to the bottom of the organization.

scheduling: the reservation process and coordination of all events to the venue's available time.

scholarly sport practitioner (SSP): the next-generation evolution in the sport industry's work force, which understands how to unite sports organizations through management practices and utilizes the power of knowledge to build a culture of continuous learning for successful organizational and stakeholder management.

screening: to examine (a job applicant, for example) systematically in order to determine suitability.

segmentation: the process of dividing large, unlike groups of consumers into smaller, more defined groups of people who share similar characteristics.

semantics: the meaning or interpretation of a word and/or sentence.

semi-variable cost: a cost that has a fixed cost component and a variable expense component.

sexism: discrimination based on gender.

sexual harassment: employment discrimination consisting of unwelcome verbal or physical conduct directed at an employee because of his or her sex.

Sherman Antitrust Act: an 1890 federal antitrust law intended to control or prohibit monopolies by forbidding certain practices that restrain competition.

simple interest: the interest calculated on a principal sum, not compounded on earned interest.

situational approach: in the study of leadership (also referred to as "contingency theories"), this approach resulted in an understanding that the traits and behaviors identified previously would be successful only to the degree to which any particular situation allowed; intervening, or moderating, factors were considered in this approach.

social institution: any place where there is a set of rules for behavior; examples include churches, colleges, and places of business.

sociodemographic: of or relating to characteristics of a particular group or demographic, such as certain age groups, people of the same income levels, gender, etc.

sociolinguistics: the impact that differing social and/or cultural groups have on the meaning and interpretation of language.

sociological analysis: thorough examination of a social institution or societal segment as a self-contained entity or in relation to society as a whole.

sole proprietorship: a company owned by one person.

sovereign immunity: an exemption that precludes bringing a suit against the sovereign state without the state's consent; often known by the maxim "the king can do no wrong."

Span of Management: principle that refers to the number of employees reporting to a specific manager.

spokesperson: an informational role filled by the sport manager in which he or she communicates information to groups that are outside the organization.

sponsorship: the provision of resources (e.g., money, people, equipment) by an organization (the sponsor) directly to an individual, authority, or body (the sponsee), to enable the latter to pursue some activity in return for benefits contemplated in terms of the sponsor's promotion strategy, and which can be expressed in terms of corporate, marketing, or media objectives.

sponsorship activation: the idea that for every dollar spent on a sponsorship fee, an equivalent dollar is typically spent in the promotion of the sponsorship.

sport sociologist: one who studies human social behavior in sport, including the analysis of sport as an industry, the political and cultural implications of sport, sport and globalization, the relationship between gender, class, and economics, deviance in sport, and the social organization of sport.

sport sociology: the method of analyzing sport from a cultural perspective that concerns itself mainly with how humans relate to each other in the sport context, how values affect these relationships, and how humans organize sport activities.

sportsmanship: conduct and attitude considered as befitting participants in sports, especially fair play, courtesy, striving spirit, and grace in losing.

standard: a requirement of moral conduct.

state action: an action in which the federal or state government is responsible for the specific conduct about which the plaintiff complains.

state court systems: court systems that generally hear matters that occur within the boundaries of the state, and involve disputes that involve state law.

statement of cash flow: a financial statement that shows the sources and uses of cash for a business over a certain period of time.

statutes: particular laws passed by the U.S. Congress or a state legislature that declare, command, or prohibit some conduct, or require citizens to act in a certain manner.

step cost: a recurring or non-recurring expense for goods and services that are either non-essential or more expensive than necessary; examples include entertainment expenses, wellness programs, and speakers; also referred to as discretionary expense.

strict liability: liability that is imposed without a finding of fault.

substantive law: the law that defines, describes, or creates legal rights and obligations.

Super League: a proposal, also referred to as G-14, offered by the European football (soccer) industry to come closer to the American model, which would include football giants like Ajax Amsterdam, Manchester United, AC Milan, and Real Madrid.

supply: the quantity of a product that an owner is willing to offer or make available at a given price.

Supreme Court: the highest federal court in the United States, consisting of nine justices and having jurisdiction over all other courts in the nation.

surveys: paper forms used to gather a sample of data or opinions considered to be representative of a whole group, sometimes referred to as questionnaires.

sustainability: creates and maintains the conditions under which humans and nature can exist in productive harmony, that permit fulfilling the social, economic, and other requirements of present and future generations.

symbiotic: a relationship of mutual benefit or dependence.

target market: the group of people at which all marketing efforts are aimed.

technical skills: in sport management terms, these skills involve a knowledge of operations, activities, and processes necessary to accomplish organizational goals and objectives.

teleology: a doctrine explaining phenomena by their ends or purposes; a focus on the consequences of an action.

terminal values: in ethical theory, the ends toward which one is striving.

time-switchers: people who plan to attend an event, but cancel or change time in order to attend to something else.

timetable: a chart used to provide the schedule of tasks and when they need to be completed; can be seen as a countdown to an event.

time value of money: the idea that a dollar now is worth more than a dollar in the future, even after adjusting for inflation, because a dollar now can earn interest or other appreciation until the time the dollar in the future would be received.

Title VII: law passed in 1964 that protects employees and prospective employees from discrimination by making it unlawful for an employer to discriminate against a person in employment activities (i.e., hiring, firing, compensation, promotion, classification) based on race, color, religion, sex, or national origin; formally referred to as Title VII of the Civil Rights Act of 1964.

Title IX: law passed in 1972 as part of the Educational Amendments Act that prohibits sex discrimination in education agencies that receive federal funding; formally referred to as Title IX of the Education Amendments of 1972.

TOP sponsors: companies that have been granted a four-year contract deal with The Olympic Partner Programme that includes both the Summer and Winter Games; they are granted the right to Olympic affiliation in every participating country with worldwide exclusivity in their product category.

tort: a civil wrong—other than a breach of contract—for which an injured party can recover damages.

tort claims acts: statutes in which the state has agreed to accept liability for certain tort claims.

tortfeasor: a person who commits a tort.

trademark: word, phrase, logo, or other graphic symbol used by a manufacturer to distinguish its product from those of others.

trait theories: some of the earliest systematic attempts to conceptualize leadership, these approaches focused on the characteristics, or attributes, that distinguished leaders from nonleaders; traits under investigation included physical characteristics (e.g., height, appearance), personality traits (e.g., arrogance, self-esteem), and general ability traits (e.g., intelligence, insight, energy).

trial court: the court before which issues of fact and law are tried and first determined as distinguished from an appellate court.

UEFA Champions League: the Union of European Football Associations' football (soccer) league that is open to each national association's domestic champions, as well as clubs who finish just behind them in the domestic championship table.

UEFA Cup: championship title of the UEFA Champions League.

Uniform Athlete Agents Act: act that provides for the uniform registration, certification, and background check of sports agents seeking to represent student athletes who are or may be eligible to participate in intercollegiate sports; also imposes specified contract terms on these agreements to the benefit of student athletes, and provides education institutions with a right to notice along with a civil cause of action for damages resulting from a breach of specified duties.

Unity of Command: principle that states that an employee should only have one boss to which he or she reports.

upward flow of communication: when information is transmitted to upper levels of management from the middle and lower levels of the organization.

U.S. Congress: the national legislative body of the United States, consisting of the Senate and the House of Representatives.

U.S. Constitution: the fundamental law of the United States, framed in 1787, ratified in 1789, and variously amended since then, which prescribes the nature, functions, and limits of the government.

U.S. District Courts: courts that operate essentially the same as state trial courts, providing a trial of the case before a judge and jury; also called federal trial courts. There are 94 throughout the U.S., with at least one located in every state.

utilitarianism: an ethical theory whereby morality is assessed by whether or not the action creates the greatest good for the greatest number of people.

value: worth in usefulness or importance to the possessor.

variable expenses: unavoidable periodic cost that does not have a constant value, such as electric, gas, and water bills.

verdict: the finding of a jury in a trial.

vertical integration: the degree to which a firm owns its upstream suppliers and its downstream buyers.

Volunteer Protection Act: act that provides protection to volunteers, employees, and the volunteer organization itself, so long as the organization has insurance in the amount required by the statute to cover losses sustained by injured participants.

waived: given up; relinquished.

warranty: a promise or guarantee that products will comply with a certain standard.

welfare: health, happiness, and good fortune; well-being.

White Paper on Sport: published by the Commission of European Communities in November 2007, which explored social, economic, and organizational dimensions of sport and offered suggestions on how sport can be used to address challenges that are present in European society.

word of mouth: advertising through personal recommendations among consumers.

workers' compensation: compensation for death or injury suffered by a worker in the course of his or her employment.

World Baseball Classic (WBC): competition including teams from 16 counties to determine a world champion in baseball.

World Cup of Hockey: an international ice hockey tournament, introduced in 2004 in four European cities and three North American cities, which included eight of the world's ice hockey powerhouses.

World League of American Football (WLAF): extension league introduced in 1991 that provided a platform for the NFL to showcase the game of American Football to those outside the U.S., especially in Europe.

Writ of Certiorari: a common law writ issued by a superior court to one of inferior jurisdiction demanding the record of a particular case.

Index

About the Editors

 **Andy Gillentine**, PhD, has recently been appointed as professor and chair of the sport and entertainment program at the University of South Carolina. Prior to this appointment, he held positions as the associate dean, associate professor, and director of the sport administration programs at the University of Miami (2002–2010) and as graduate program director at Mississippi State University (1995–2002). In April of 2009, he received the Sport Management Outstanding Achievement Award from the National Association of Sport and Physical Education. Additionally, he served as athletic director and coach for over 15 years and is nationally recognized for his expertise in sport management curriculum and program development.

He was appointed as one of the founding Commissioners of the Council of Sport Management Accreditation (COSMA). Prior to the COSMA appointment, Gillentine served as chair of a joint task force of NASPE/NASSM charged with formalizing the curricular standards required for accreditation. In 2007, he was appointed to serve as a board member of the Miami Dade Sports Commission, which is charged with developing and expanding the presence of the sport industry in Miami Dade County and South Florida. Previously he served on the Sport Management Program Review Council Executive Board and as chair of the National Sport Management Council.

His research interests are sport marketing, professional development, and management issues in sport. Dr. Gillentine is also recognized as one of the leading experts in the study of the legal, managerial and marketing aspects of tailgating at sport and entertainment events. Dr. Gillentine has conducted research projects for numerous sport organizations that have resulted in over 50 publications and over 100 national and international presentations. In 2007 he was appointed as a Research Fellow of the Research Consortium of the AAHPERD, the largest professional organization of sport and physical educators in the US. His textbook, *Foundations of Sport Management*, co-edited with Brian Crow, is widely used in Sport Management Programs throughout the country and is currently in its second edition.

 **R. Brian Crow**, EdD is a professor in the Department of Sport Management at Slippery Rock University, where he teaches courses related to sport marketing, budgeting, and global sport management. Crow earned a doctor of education degree in Higher Education Administration (1994) and a master of business administration degree (1991) from West Virginia University, as well as a bachelor of science degree in marketing from West Liberty State College (1988).

Dr. Crow was recently the president of the North American Society for Sport Management (NASSM). Prior to this election, Crow was NASSM's Business Office Manager for two years and a member-at-large on the executive council. Crow recently ended his three-year tenure as editor-in-chief of the *Sport Marketing Quarterly*, a publication he presently serves as a member or the editorial review board. He was a founding board member of the Sport Marketing Association.

As a consultant, Crow founded GameDay Consulting, LLC, in 2004 and has developed guest service training workshops for thousands of front-line employees. He conducted mystery shops for the Buffalo Bills, Pittsburgh Steelers, Baltimore Ravens, Houston Texans, West Virginia University, University of Pittsburgh, University of Kentucky, University of Oregon, and Bowling Green State University in recent years. He writes about guest services in the sport industry at www.gamedaycertified.com.

About the Authors

Artemisia Apostolopoulou, PhD is a professor of sport management in the School of Business at Robert Morris University. She teaches courses in sport marketing and promotion. Her research interests include branding and brand extension strategies, sport sponsorship, and sport licensing. She has presented work in numerous national and international conferences and her publications have appeared in *Sport Marketing Quarterly, European Sport Management Quarterly*, the Journal of Product & Brand Management, and the *Journal of Promotion Management*. Dr. Apostolopoulou is originally from Greece.

Paul J. Batista, attorney at law, associate professor, Sport Texas A&M University; BS, Trinity University, 1973; JD, Baylor University Law School, 1976. Professor Batista is admitted to practice before the United States Supreme Court, is licensed to appear in all of the courts in Texas, is a former county judge of Burleson County, Texas, and is a certified mediator and arbitrator. He is a tenured professor, has taught sport law at Texas A&M since 1991, has received the Texas A&M Association of Former Students Distinguished Achievement Award in Teaching, the Student Led Award for Teaching Excellence, and has been named a Montague Center for Teaching Excellence Scholar. Professor Batista was a NCAA scholarship athlete (baseball) and was a certified contract advisor with the National Football League Players Association (NFLPA) from 1986 to 1998. His primary research interest is sports related liability issues in school settings, with particular emphasis on First Amendment religion and free speech issues. He has delivered research presentations at numerous conferences throughout the United States, as well as in Canada, China, Germany, Slovenia, and South Korea.

Matthew Bernthal, PhD, is an associate professor in the Department of Sport and Entertainment Management at the University of South Carolina. His research interests lie primarily in sport marketing and consumer behavior in sport and entertainment.

Matthew T. Brown, PhD, is chair of the Department of Sport and Entertainment Management at the University of South Carolina. He researches and teaches in the area of sport finance. In addition to his academic background, Dr. Brown has been treasurer and business manager for several baseball organizations. Prior to joining the faculty at South Carolina, Dr. Brown was a member of sport administration faculty at Ohio University.

John Clark, PhD, is an associate professor of sport management and the director of the MBA program at the Robert Morris University School of Business. He has conducted and published research in the areas of sport marketing such as sport sponsorship, customer loyalty, sport sales, and cause-related sport marketing programs.

Galen Clavio, PhD is an assistant professor in the sport management program at Indiana University. He has published extensively on the subjects of sport communication, video games in sports, and social media communication and marketing functions in the sport enterprise. Clavio has also served as an industry consultant on the usage of Facebook, Twitter, and other social media as a primary means of leagues, teams, and athletes communicating directly with fans.

Greg Greenhalgh's, PhD, primary research interest focuses on the marketing of sport organizations, specifically investigating what attracts fans and sponsors to niche, or non-mainstream, sports and how these sports can position themselves to be more sustainable in the future. His other research interests include the use of new social media, such as Twitter and Facebook, and their effects on the dissemination of sports information, as well as sport and the natural environment.

T. Christopher Greenwell, PhD, is an associate professor at the University of Louisville. He received his doctorate in sport management from The Ohio State University, his MS in sport management from Georgia Southern University, and his BBA from McKendree College. He teaches in the areas of sport marketing, sport publicity, and event management. He has had recent articles published in the *Sport Marketing Quarterly, The International Journal of Sport Management*, and *Contemporary Athletics*.

Bernard Goldfine, PhD, is a professor of sport management at Kennesaw State University. He has taught a variety of undergraduate and graduate courses, including sport facility and event management, for over 20 years. His research interests include sport facilities, sport policy, leadership, and physical activity. He has completed numerous presentations and articles for publication at the state, national, and international levels, as well as contributed to textbooks on facility design projects. Dr. Goldfine received his bachelor of arts from the University of California, Santa Barbara, and his master of arts and PhD from the University of Southern California.

Josh Harris, MA, is the Director of Ticketing at Talladega Superspeedway, a NASCAR motorsports facility owned and operated by International Speedway Corporation. Harris received his master's degree in sport administration from the University of Miami in 2006, where he was chosen by faculty as the Outstanding Graduate Student, and his bachelors of business administration from Mississippi State University in 2004. He previously held positions at IMG as Ticket & Business Development Manager for IMG Tickets, the University of New Hampshire Athletic Department, and the University of Miami Athletic Department. Harris currently resides in Anniston, AL.

Catriona Higgs, PhD, is a professor and chairperson of the Sport Management Department at Slippery Rock University in Pennsylvania. Her research interests include diversity issues in sport management, program assessment, and teaching/learning processes. She has presented/published extensively in these areas both at the state and national levels.

Jeremy S. Jordan, PhD is an associate professor in the sports and recreation management program at Temple University. His research focuses on organizational behavior and human resource management issues within sport organizations, specifically, examination of the influence of organizational justice on employee attitudes and behaviors demonstrated in the workplace. He teaches courses in management, organizational behavior, and legal issues in sport. Published manuscripts have appeared in the *International Journal of Sport Management, International Sports Journal, Physical Educator*, and the *Journal of Applied Research in Coaching and Athletics*.

Aubrey Kent, PhD, is chair and associate professor in the sport management program at Temple University. Over his career, Dr. Kent has focused his sport industry research in the area of industrial/organizational psychology, and more recently in the area of corporate social responsibility. He teaches courses in management and the current issues facing the sport industry. His published work includes articles in the *Journal of Sport Management, The European Journal of Sport Management, Sport Marketing Quarterly, The Journal of Park and Recreation Administration*, the *International Sports Journal*, and the *Journal of Applied Sport Psychology*.

Heather Lawrence, PhD, is an associate professor of sports administration at Ohio University. She has published and presented extensively in the areas of sport event and facility management, premium seating in sport, intercollegiate athletics, and gender equity. Dr. Lawrence is also the co-editor of the textbook *Event Management Blueprint: Creating and managing successful sports events*.

Nancy L. Lough, PhD, is a professor in UNLV's College of Education, where she also serves as director of marketing. Her areas of expertise include leadership development, gender equity, sport marketing and sponsorship. Dr. Lough served as editor of *Sport Marketing Quarterly* from 2010 to 2012, director of the Center for Sport Education Leadership and president of the Sport Marketing Association. She has been quoted extensively via media outlets such as the *LA Times, Canada's Globe & Mail*, and *Street & Smith's SportsBusiness Journal*.

John Miller, PhD, received his doctorate at the University of New Mexico in sport administration. After completing a 16 year career as a distinguished intercollegiate swimming coach, he spent 10 years at Texas Tech University in the Department of Health, Exercise, and Sport Sciences where he was the director of the sport management graduate program as well as associate chair and professor. He is currently the associate dean and professor of the College of Health and Human Services at Troy University in Troy, Alabama. He has written more than 60 publications in sport management in peer-reviewed academic journals, edited a book on sport management internships, and conducted more than 120 presentations at national and international conferences. Dr. Miller serves as the editor of the *Journal of Legal Aspects of Sport* as well as on six editorial review boards of nationally recognized academic sport management journals.

Dimitra Papadimitriou, PhD, is an assistant professor in the Department of Business Management at the University of Patras, Greece. Her research interests include organizational performance of national sport governing bodies and local sports clubs, as well as nonprofit board effectiveness. In addition, she is involved in multi-disciplinary research in the areas of volunteer management, brand management, and Olympic sponsorship. She has published her research in *Sport Management Review*, *European Sport Management Quarterly*, *Sport Marketing Quarterly*, the *International Journal of Sports Marketing & Sponsorship*, and *Managing Leisure*, and has presented work in numerous national and international conferences.

Dennis Phillips, PhD, has been a college professor and administrator for 40 years, the past 22 at the University of Southern Mississippi. He has taught undergraduate and graduate courses including Sport Law, Policy & Governance of Sport, Sport Psychology, Organizational Leadership, Facility Management, Sport Marketing, Policy and Governance in Sport, Sport Finance and Economics, Sport Ethics, and Coaching, in the Sport Coaching Education, and Sport Management teaching program at USM. He has held administrative positions as assistant director of the School of Human Performance and Recreation, and program coordinator for sport management. Dr. Phillips has been a college assistant athletic director at Springfield College, assistant director of marketing and special events for the Volleyball Hall of Fame, and is the current Faculty Athletics Representative (FAR) for Southern Miss to Conference USA and the NCAA.

Tom Regan is an associate professor of the Department of Sport and Entertainment Management at the University of South Carolina. Dr. Regan served as department chair from 1987 to November 2007. His research focuses on the economic impact of sport and entertainment events on regional economies and the financing and feasibility of live entertainment events. He has completed numerous studies on professional, collegiate, and touring sports. Publications have highlighted his work on the Denver Broncos Football Club, the University of South Carolina athletic department, NASCAR, golf in South Carolina, USTA and WTA professional tennis, and other studies involving live entertainment. He was invited to the Brookings Institute to discuss the impact of professional sport facilities on regional economies. He has consulted with many professional organizations concerning financing venues and determining the economic benefit of facilities, events, and teams. Dr. Regan's education experience includes bachelor and master of accounting degrees from the University of Wyoming and a doctorate degree in sports administration at the University of Northern Colorado.

Tom Sawyer, EdD, is a NAS Fellow and professor of physical education and recreation and sport management at Indiana State University. Dr. Sawyer has over 40 years' experience in higher education. He began as an instructor of health and physical education, has been a director of recreational sports, department head, department chair, associate athletic director, director of articulation and transfer, director of the college prison education programs, executive director of regional education centers, and an interim dean of continuing education. He has written over 175 peer-reviewed articles for notable professional journals, made over 250 state, regional, national, and international presentations, and written 12 professional books and over 45 chapters. Dr. Sawyer has been selected to receive Indiana State University's three most distinguished awards given to faculty—the Caleb Mills Distinguished Teaching Award (1995), Distinguished Service

Award (1997), and the Theodore Dreiser Distinguished Research and Creativity Award (2010).

Lynn L. Ridinger is chair and associate professor of sport management at Old Dominion University in Norfolk, Virginia. Her research focuses on issues related to sport consumer behavior and involvement with women's sports. Her published work includes articles in *Sport Marketing Quarterly, Sport Management Review, International Journal of Sport Management, Journal of Sport Behavior*, and *Leisure Sciences*. She teaches courses in sport marketing, event planning, sport ethics, sport psychology, and research methods. Dr. Ridinger holds a PhD from The Ohio State University, an MA from Kent State University, and a BS from Central Michigan University. Prior to earning her doctorate, she worked as a high school athletic director and coach.

Matt Walker is an associate professor and division chair in sport management at Texas A&M University. His primary research interest lies generally in the area of organizational theory, but more specifically in the areas of corporate social responsibility (CSR) and philanthropic practices of organizations within the sport industry. Dr. Walker has presented his research at numerous academic conferences and his published manuscripts have appeared in the *Journal of Sport Management, Management Decision, Journal of Business Ethics, International Journal of Sport Management, International Journal of Sport Finance*, and *Business Research Yearbook*.